In memory of Linda Brandon
(St Hilda's College, 1978–81)
who continued to share thoughts
on Charlotte Brontë.

'I wanted to speak, to rise – it was impossible . . .'

Charlotte Brontë, 'Roe Head Journal'
(14 October 1836)

CONTENTS

PICTURE ACKNOWLEDGEMENTS

FOREWORD

A recent book of nineteenth-century photos shows a cramped and gloomy terrace house in Manchester. This is where Charlotte Brontë, aged thirty, lodged in August 1846 when her father had an eye operation (without anaesthetic). 'Utter privation of light', the surgeon ordered. In this unromantic setting, as she sat with Mr Brontë in a darkened room, she thought up *Jane Eyre*.

Crucial to Charlotte's life was her power to write out of darkness – the dark of an unseen self. During her years as an unwilling schoolmistress, she sometimes wrote with eyes closed against the scrutiny of her pupils. Later, she told her editor of a wish 'to walk invisible'. To uncover the woman who became the writer meant a break with Brontë legend.

The romantic image of doomed genius in a wild moorland far from civilisation was promoted by Mrs Gaskell in her *Life of Charlotte Brontë*, published in 1857. It captivated the Victorians and persisted through the twentieth century in books, plays and films. To question Brontë myth was risky in the early 1990s when I was writing this book; since then it's become de rigueur, thanks largely to Lucasta Miller's groundbreaking history of *The Brontë Myth* (2001). But this biography started out with a different, though related purpose: to explore the extreme disjunction between Charlotte's mousy behaviour in public (the decorous figure relayed by Mrs Gaskell) and what Charlotte termed her 'home character'.

Initially, this was part of a wider plan. Long ago, I planned a book to be called 'Lives for Women', beginning with Charlotte

Brontë and taking in Emily Dickinson, Olive Schreiner, and two advanced women, Minny Temple and Constance Fenimore Woolson, who were models for the woman who 'affronts her destiny' in Henry James. I had a notion that unknown modes of being – clues to unseen elements in women's nature – lurked in an uncharted region of muted, ill or interrupted lives. Each of these women was distanced from norms in some way or another, and each developed a distinctive character, unlike other women of their time. The plan at the outset was to explore this home face of emancipation, as a venture parallel to the public aspect of the Woman Question from 1840–1920. The book was to end with Virginia Woolf's attraction to the Brontës, and the bias of her novel *Night and Day* (1919), in which votes for women served as background to the less obvious and more difficult issue of private feeling. Jane Eyre's refusal to capitulate to a series of social plots on offer, in essence a refusal to violate her nature, was to pose this larger question. For advancing nineteenth-century women there's a gap between public and private that became explosive. This gap lent itself to overblown legends of pathos and doom rather than what the writings reveal: the strength to turn loss to gain and the impact of an invisible voice.

Although, at first, I'd meant to write no more than a chapter on Charlotte Brontë, once I came upon the manuscript fragments that comprise her Roe Head Journal, and picked up the explosiveness of her voice as a young woman, it framed a question that drove a full-length biography: what was the story of that voice rising in private outbursts in the late 1830s? In 1847 the voice burst upon the public with a passion and vehemence that people could hardly believe came from a woman, and if it were indeed a woman, she was one who would not be acceptable to her sex. So Charlotte went masked in public, even with her friendly fellow-writer Mrs Gaskell, allowing the more conventional Mrs Gaskell to hear only her sorrow, not her sarcasm and laughter. Deliberately, Mrs Gaskell separated this 'poor creature' from her work, playing to a Victorian audience for whom acceptable women were quiet and modest. Yet all the while, a voice that could not sound in public spoke intimately – irresistibly – to 'Reader'. This voice and its story veered away from pathos, declaring 'it would take a good deal to crush me'.

The archival work which began at the same time on Emily Dickinson, Minny Temple, and the woman James called Fenimore, had the same effect as Charlotte's letters and fragments. A shift away from an established image led to further research, and in each case, evidence of an unseen story prompted an unfolding narrative. What was to be one book turned into three. All the same, though each of these lives took its own direction, the question of women's nature continued to rise.

In approaching a biographic subject, it often happens that a certain phrase will resonate: 'I wanted to speak, to rise – it was impossible,' Charlotte confessed at the age of twenty. Seventeen years on, the most autobiographical of her heroines, Lucy Snowe, is asked who she is: what is the source of her increasingly visible gifts as a person and teacher? Her answer: 'I am a rising character'.

To rise in these terms is an imaginative act. This is the single most important fact in Charlotte's life, and to bring it out, the inclusive biographical tome would be inappropriate, for it requires the biographer to take the reader through acres of juvenilia, extending into the juvenilia of Charlotte's brother Branwell. Their shared fantasies of high life were a dead end, as Charlotte – rather belatedly – came to recognise. It's in fashion to upgrade Branwell, but a new multi-volume edition of his writings confirms how persistently unreadable he is, including as it does a so-called 'novel' of 1845 – no more than thirty rambling pages. Amongst Charlotte's early writings are gleams of future promise, and to see her story in a meaningful way – to see up close the transformations of genius in the making – biography can select for these and bring them together. I wanted to follow her rising character, especially the struggle to kill off adolescent dreams without killing the passionate nature that fuelled them.

She had to translate passion into something realistic, into a character commensurate with the mentor she called 'Monsieur' – one who could know her as she felt herself to be – and this speaks to all who sense a desire that goes beyond the appeal of modish men and women. Charlotte Brontë confides what it's like to succumb to that allure, and the terrific drama open to a writer who turns from it with truth-seeking resolve. When Lucy says, 'in dead trance I studiously held the quick of my nature', she's at one with a storm, its disruptiveness, which she calls 'nature's language'. Her similar identification with a buried nun, who spoke out of turn in accord with a nature other than what custom decreed, was to have a counterpart in Woolf's great white monster of the lower waters who'd explode if brought to the surface.

A being without form is a subject that draws me. It can't be defined, any more than genius can be defined, but I'm drawn to those who see it, like sighting a fin in the waste of waters in *The Waves*: an unseen form of life one must pursue. In 1929, the year she published *A Room of One's Own*, Woolf sighted it in Mary Wollstonecraft, who 'cut to the quick of life'. Like Charlotte Brontë, Woolf lit on that 'quick', the quick of life that a novelist or biographer can't ignore. At that time, she spoke of 'the great problem of the true nature of woman' as a mystery she could not solve. Facing this mystery so much earlier, Charlotte Brontë had the intelligence to look beyond immediate economic and political goals towards enduring issues of education, emotion and emergence in the largest sense of what women at full strength will contribute to civilisation.

At the time I did this book, many letters and essays were scattered, and vital material (like the Roe Head Journal and telling letters to publisher, George Smith) existed only in manuscript. Since then there have been two indispensable publications: the three-volume edition of *The Letters of Charlotte Brontë* and *The Brussels Essays*. Their availability has necessitated updating the notes for the convenience of readers, but wherever space allows I have retained the manuscript source as my actual source. Several new studies and handbooks, prompting adjustments to the text, are listed in a revised bibliography. The directness of the Brontë voice can cross barriers of time and place, to find a new audience. The Brontë Society has translated its guidebook into Urdu, to serve a growing Pakistani interest in the Brontës, since women in that community are said to be in a similar position to those sisters. This biography seeks what's hidden in women's lives, not only then but now. What is passion for a woman? How might she emerge from silence, raise her voice, reach out to others? Charlotte Brontë had the courage to enter this region, to meet the shades who lived there, and find words for their experience.

Lyndall Gordon, 2008

THE UNSEEN SPACE

'A private governess has no existence', wrote Charlotte Brontë to her sister, Emily, in the summer of 1839. Her employer, Mrs Sidgwick, kept her sewing all evening alone in the schoolroom before she retired to her bedroom on the servants' floor. When the eyes of ladies and gentlemen fell on a governess, 'it seemed as if they looked on vacancy', said their youngest sister, Anne, who was dismissed in the same year by the Inghams of Blake Hall. This apparent vacancy was the space they made their own; here, protected by its very obscurity, the rising character of Charlotte Brontë took shape.

Once, she spoke of a 'secret' life. She denied the 'externals' of three nineteenth-century sisters who taught the children of their social superiors, and lived out the rest of their short, unobtrusive lives in a Yorkshire parsonage. For beneath that 'unpretending outside' lay a secret fire that 'kindled the veins' of writers. From 1846 to 1853 the Brontë sisters published their combined *Poems*, *Agnes Grey*, *Jane Eyre*, *Wuthering Heights*, *The Tenant of Wildfell Hall*, *Shirley*, and *Villette*. Yet to strangers they seemed 'nothing'; and 'less than nothing' as employees in country houses.

Charlotte nursed a dream of social emergence all through her youth. In February–March 1839, at the age of nearly twenty-three, two months before she took up her first post as governess, she wrote a story about a teacher who has no looks or means, but does have spirit. Elizabeth Hastings, as she is called, arrives in an imaginary metropolis from a remote moorland, not unlike Charlotte's home in the village of Haworth on the moors of West Yorkshire. The new teacher at once wins recognition for her 'superior talent'. Dressing 'plainer if possible than ever' but still with 'fastidious care & taste', her public restraint is an admired counterpoise to private gifts. Soon she gains a large circle of friends and constant invitations.

This dream was shattered in May 1839 when Charlotte began as governess at Stonegappe, a large house on the brow of a hill four miles from Skipton in Yorkshire. Her employer soon put her in her place.

'I said in my last letter that Mrs Sidgwick did not know me', Charlotte wrote to Emily on 8 June. 'I now begin to find that she does not intend to know me . . . I *used* to think I should like to be in the stir of grand folks' society but I have had enough of it – it is dreary work to look on and listen.'

Indifference was harder to bear than sewing dolls' clothes which Mrs Sidgwick pressed on her evening hours. However Charlotte tried to please – however Anne tried at Blake Hall – neither won the slightest recognition. Their gifts of mind were invisible; their employers could not see what did not reflect themselves. Later, in Charlotte's most famous novel, *Jane Eyre*, two sisters, Diana and Mary Rivers, must leave their home, Moor-House, to serve as governesses in families 'by whose wealthy and haughty members they were regarded only as humble dependants, and who neither knew nor sought one of their innate excellences, and appreciated only their acquired accomplishments as they appreciated the skill of their cook, or the taste of their waiting woman.' Anne Brontë noted the deadening effect of six years in the solid homes of merchant and gentry: 'Never a new idea or stirring thought came to me from without; and such as rose within me were, for the most part, miserably crushed at once, or doomed to sicken and fade away, because they could not see the light . . . The gross vapours of earth were gathering around me, and closing in upon my inward heaven.'

Were the sisters to surrender the 'inward heaven' to the obliterating gaze of employers or could they devise strategies for its survival? Effaced by the current model of womanhood (which *Jane Eyre* parades in the airs of Lady Ingram and her daughter – named, perhaps, after the Inghams who scorned Anne), there remained the shadow in which Charlotte lived: the dark dress of the governess; the shade of her closed eyelids as she wrote; the cover of 'Currer Bell', the indeterminate name on her books. In this shadow there lurked the shape of an unknown character as it came into being: the source of a new voice of truth that was to burst on Victorian society in the late 1840s.

The silent cover may have been something of a challenge as well as protection: it was never penetrated by the mannered wives who gave their orders to Charlotte and whose blandness she was required to imitate in lowly form. Certain of her contemporaries, Thackeray and Matthew Arnold, who perceived the passion, were made uneasy: their response was to nail her as plain spinster in need of a man. Only a few recognised her for what she was: the independent schoolfriend, Mary Taylor; the lifelong confidante, Ellen Nussey; the demanding teacher, Constantin Heger; the fellow-novelist, Mrs Gaskell; intermittently, the young publisher, George Smith; and steadily – and rather surprisingly – the local curate Charlotte was at length to marry, Arthur Bell Nicholls.

Even with these, she could not presume on more than limited understanding. Her sisters alone saw her unshaded self. She had glossy mid-brown hair and expressive grey eyes, intent as she listened, kindling when she was roused to speak. Speech did rise easily to her lips amongst familiars. Others saw a diffident, rather childlike figure, carrying herself a little awkwardly like one with early hip trouble. The set of her mouth was marred by uneven front teeth which she wished to order under the new ether, but never did. She became resigned to the fact that her features 'never yet submitted to any line of regularity – but have manifested such a spirit of independence, unedifying to behold –'. Her brow was too wide for beauty, her nose not dainty, and mouth and eyes drawn together, as though strong features had concentrated at the centre of her face. To have so strong a facial character, to look in any way odd, was not fashionable for Victorian women, who managed to look as uniform as eggs, smooth and oval. So Charlotte grew to be ashamed of her face, and devised a manner to counter it. In public she presented a frail, modest figure, the epitome of sobriety.

The usual view of Charlotte Brontë has been a figure of pathos in the shadow of tombstones. But if her inward and creative life is seen to coexist with externals, the picture shifts. We see a stranger creature: a survivor who mocked her brother's graveyard postures of doomed genius; a determinedly professional writer who was impatient, sarcastic, strong in spirit, with an unquenchable fire. This 'home' character, at odds with her public image, drove her life in a volcanic way beneath the still, grey crust. 'Shadow' recurs in her writings, not as feebleness but as a potency that goes unseen.

There is no final truth about a life, and each age will distil its view. The mid-nineteenth-century novelist, Mrs Gaskell, Charlotte's friend and first biographer, spoke to Victorians about loss and grief, and this has remained the usual perspective. But the time has come to bring out the strength that turned loss to gain. It is well known that Charlotte endured a life of extraordinary suffering, but what made her different from many who face death, loneliness, and unrequited love were acts of creation, almost never mentioned in her slave-to-duty letters. Brontë facts are so voluminous that it is tempting to stitch together an apparently seamless story which elides the gaps in the life where facts vanished. I intend to open up these gaps with the help of Charlotte Brontë's autobiographical fictions which speak to specific men in a direct manner denied to Victorian women who meant to be ladies. At the same time, they speak to her readers across the centuries, revealing a hidden life, as well as abundant creative energy. This, then, is a writer's life which will trace the rising spark, secret 'books', and bold words which did not fear to speak about the experience of those alone and silent, unregarded and socially obscure: a new voice of passionate communion.

Where does immortality begin? What conditions converged to promote her gifts? Charlotte Brontë had far more than a fair share of the uncontrollable obstacles in a writer's way – a formidable father whose needs came first, depressions, bars to women's writing – and yet writing continued almost to the end. What drove her on was a renewed capacity for passion, truth, utterance. To say that she sorrowed, trembled, shrank is to say that she was like other women of the 1840s. But she was not like them. She shrank, sometimes, but was also articulate, daring, and full of purpose.

To elicit the exact nature of that purpose, there looms before me the mirage of a record that will distil from her life its form and meaning. Whether it is to be a mirage or reality turns on the problem that vital parts of her life are obscured by decisions made after her death. Many of her letters, as well as large batches from her closest correspondents, disappeared: whatever conflicted with the growth of the Brontë legend. What remains unknown about Charlotte Brontë lies *between* the facts. To complement the well-researched detail of Winifred Gérin, followed admirably by Rebecca Fraser, we need to enter that unseen space in which gifted women of Charlotte's time were forced to live.

When Charlotte was four, Emily nearly two, and Anne four months old, the Brontë family arrived in the Pennine village of Haworth, in the north of England, in April 1820. Seven laden carts bumped up the steep, cobbled high street towards the Parsonage, above the Church of St Michael and All Angels, crowning the village. It was a square Georgian parsonage, built of grey stone. The Revd Patrick Brontë, his wife, Maria, who was ailing since the last birth, and their six children came (in the words of Mr Brontë) as strangers in a strange land. Patrick himself came from Ireland; Maria from the far south-west tip of England, Penzance, in Cornwall; and in moving to this parish on the edge of harsh moorland, they had left behind them the more sociable parish of Thornton, near to the Yorkshire city of Bradford, where they had lived happily from 1815 to 1820 and where their last four children were born. At the start, in Haworth, the Brontë family seems to have been on its own, perhaps because Mrs Brontë remained too weak to be active in the parish, perhaps because old families, the Heatons and Greenwoods, yeomen by origin but long risen to wealth and superiority, did not take up Mr Brontë with anything like the attentions of pious Miss Firth in Thornton. For the rest of their lives, the younger Brontë children would retain some sense of themselves as strangers, in a way that made it difficult for them to leave the family group.

This strangeness was not, in origin, at all romantic, for it had to do with their father's swift change of class, and a determination, which was to become pronounced in Charlotte, to prove her standing as the daughter of a gentleman. Her grandfather, Hugh Brunty, was a farm labourer, virtually illiterate but something of a story-teller, who had migrated from the south to the north of Ireland. Her grandmother, Eleanor (or Eilís) McClory, was born a Catholic. Patrick, born on St Patrick's Day, 1777, was the eldest of ten Brunty children. The family lived on a diet of buttermilk and bread made from a mixture of potatoes and oatmeal which, Patrick believed, induced the dyspepsia that troubled him all his life. Tall, with red hair and pale blue eyes, he read avidly by the light of a flickering rush – one possible cause of failing eyesight as he grew older. A love of *Pilgrim's Progress*, *Paradise Lost*, Homer and other Greek and Latin classics transformed his life, moving him from a peasant's position, apprenticed to a blacksmith at the age of twelve, to village schoolmaster at the age of sixteen, where five years later his religious intelligence caught the attention of the Revd Mr Tighe, a Methodist and friend of Wesley. Mr Tighe was a Fellow of St John's College, Cambridge, and sent Patrick there in 1802 to read theology and classics. So there, at St John's, was the Irish peasant in the company of the young Lord Palmerston who was to become Prime Minister: both practised firearms as part of a volunteer civilian corps in case of Napoleonic invasion from across the Channel. There, too, aided by a £10 annuity, with the backing of the reformer, William Wilberforce, Patrick moved into the inner circle of the Evangelicals (the revolutionary party dedicated to renewing the established church from within), which led finally to a gentleman's position in the Church of England. Two letters of 1804, by a celebrated preacher, Henry Martyn, backed Patrick at this transforming time:

> An Irishman of the name of Bronte entered St John's a year & a half ago as a sizar [servant to more affluent students] . . . For the character of the man I can safely vouch as I know him to be studious, clever, & pious . . . There is reason to hope that he will be an instrument of good to the church, as a desire of usefulness in the ministry seems to have influenced him in no small degree.

He returned only once, after ordination in 1806, to the Brunty family in County Down, though he did send his mother money for the rest of her life. It was during his years at Cambridge that he changed his name, choosing 'Brontë' possibly because the Greek word signified the voice of thunder but most likely because he identified with fearless fighters. In 1799, Nelson had been made Duke of Bronti (in Sicily), and this was the source of the name for Charlotte who, in *Shirley*, spelt out the proud title, 'Admiral Horatio, Viscount Nelson, and Duke of Bronti', whom she describes as small, pale and suffering, 'yet potent as a giant and brave as a lion'.

After curacies in Essex and Shropshire, the Revd Patrick Brontë settled in Yorkshire, first as curate to the hymn-writer, John Buckworth, at Dewsbury from 1809 to 1810, then a few miles away as curate at Hartshead, a parish that was at the centre of industrial unrest, where he fought against the Luddites when they broke new machinery which threatened their jobs in the factories. This coincided with a Continental trade embargo during the Napoleonic wars which hit Yorkshire's woollen industry. For a while Yorkshire seemed on the brink of revolution. Mr Brontë stood by factory-owners and Tory gentlemen, in particular a predecessor in the church, the martial Revd Roberson of Liversedge, who was fierce against the rioters. Mr Brontë remained on cordial terms with Mr Roberson who was known as 'Duke Ecclesiastic' because he was 'a very Wellington in the Church'.

While at Hartshead, thirty-five-year-old Mr Brontë, who still spoke with an Irish accent, met ladylike Maria Branwell. She was of a merchant's family with Methodist leanings, and came north to be a companion to a Methodist cousin, Jane Fennell, in West Yorkshire. Maria was then twenty-nine, recently orphaned, with an annuity of £50, and was accustomed to mix in good society. Her portrait in profile shows a slight woman with a strong nose and underlip, in a dainty, white, short-waisted dress. After a warm, playful correspondence on Maria's part, she and Patrick were married on 29 December 1812 at Guiseley, just north of Leeds. At first they lived in Hightown where Maria was born in 1814 and a second daughter, Elizabeth, in 1815. After they moved to congenial Thornton, Maria continued to have a baby every year: Charlotte was born in 1816; an only son, Patrick Branwell, in 1817; a fourth daughter, Emily Jane, in 1818; and their last child, Anne, early in 1820.

It was at this moment that Mr Brontë was offered a Perpetual Curacy in Haworth, a parish known for its great eighteenth-century preacher, William Grimshaw, who conducted an Evangelical revival in Yorkshire. Haworth was also at the centre of a wool-producing area, with sheep grazing on the moors, and no one was very poor, though children still, before the Factory Act of 1833, worked long hours. There were two drawbacks to Haworth, apart from its steep position: there was a strong body of Dissenters in the parish, and – more serious – the village was excessively unhealthy, even by the unsanitary standards of the day, with no sewers and polluted water. The average age of death in Haworth was twenty-five.

On arrival at the Parsonage, all the children, except for the baby, Anne, were packed into a narrow room, no bigger than a passage, above the front door. There they remained, unnaturally good and quiet as Mrs Brontë died slowly on the other side of the wall. From January 1821, stomach cancer struck cruelly and her death was expected almost every day. She died in September 1821 with the words, 'Oh God, my poor children!' She must have known that their father was not partial to little ones. While she was ill, Mr Brontë made it clear to them that he, too, must not be disturbed. Outside, a narrow gravel path led from the yard (where the coach stopped) round the corner of the house into a small plot of grass, with a thorn tree and a few stunted shrubs, enclosed within a low stone wall which separated the Parsonage from the close-packed graves of the churchyard. But the children found release on the moors.

These long low moors, with poor fringes of stunted copse, are neither grand nor romantic, 'scarcely striking', as Charlotte said. They were not the backdrop to endless licence but an alternative to restriction, establishing in earliest childhood a contrast between restriction and freedom that was to be central to their work. In this sense, the moor may have been the visible counterpart of their searching minds: space as counterpoise to strict training, quiet considerateness, and constant proximity to the facts of pain and death. Jane Eyre has a notion that, in the last extremity, she will cast herself on the breast of nature as on the body of a mother. The Brontë children would lie on a bank of heath, with the bees humming overhead on a hot July day. On

dimmer days, the moor was soggy, rough, and bleak, stretching
to the waves and shadows of the horizon; in winter there were
dramatic storms and wide blankets of snow. As they grew older
and ventured farther, each ridge rose against the sky, with its
invitation to discovery. They would pause to examine a bit of
moss, a heath-bell, or a fungus which had spread its bright
orange amongst the brown leaves. They found the 'fairy cave'
under Peniston Crag and, far off, a beck that fell over a granite
crag into the 'bottom'. A favourite place was the distant 'Meeting
of the Waters' in Sladen Valley, an oasis of green turf, broken by
small clear springs.

As the children explored what Charlotte called 'our Land of
Silence', reports reached them of wilder and more challenging
spaces: Mungo Park's explorations of the source of the Niger in
1805–6; Major Denham's ventures between 1822 and 1825 into the
north and centre of Africa; and the pull-out maps in the Revd J.
Goldsmith's *Grammar of General Geography* (1823) revealed many
kingdoms on the Gold Coast. The arctic expeditions of Ross and
Parry in the 1820s caught the fancy of Emily and Anne, and
formed a basis of their Gondal saga. Charlotte, too, was drawn to
'the vast sweep of the Arctic Zone', the bleak, uninhabited shores
of Lapland, Greenland and Siberia, in a much-read book at the
Parsonage, Thomas Bewick's *History of British Birds*. The earliest
drawing she kept was a copy of a Bewick woodcut of a cor-
morant on a stormy shore. Bewick opened her eyes to 'pictured
thoughts that breathe and speak and burn'.

The extreme contrast between subdued children packed into
a tiny room and exposure to unlimited space when they
emerged, was reflected in the setting of Haworth itself with its
narrow, close-packed street that led upward towards the moor.
The high street was so sheer that horses' hooves had to catch at
stones placed edgeways, as though they clambered up boulders.
The street curved past tight-packed houses, past drinkers in the
Black Bull, past apathetic faces on Sundays, heavy in their pews,
some resting after long trudges, some sleeping – to be 'knobbed'

by the sexton with his long staff, some roused during Mr Brontë's sermon to a gleam of a question or a glint of objection; then on past the church, the graveyard, and the Parsonage at the top of the village, toward the open sky. The sisters seldom turned down into Haworth. Mr Brontë did not wish his family to mix with factory hands. Poised at the interface of two distinct worlds, they turned their backs on the village to climb above it, to cross and recross the moor, pushing further as they grew older and stronger, leaping the streams, resting on rocks, as they forged their way towards the secret place where the waters met in a burst of springs.

The moor offered a suggestive landscape for Charlotte Brontë's mature writing. She remade *Pilgrim's Progress* (another favourite at the Parsonage) as the trials and ventures of people who refuse to relinquish their souls to the solicitations of circumstance. Fixed in her earliest consciousness was this act of forging a path of one's own through uncharted land, a basis for later explorations of states of mind: impulse, anger, passion, the suppressed urge for larger activity, the secret freedoms of mind and spirit – at active play within the moral net. Keats once said that a man's life of any value is an allegory; Charlotte was to reinvigorate allegory in her own terms, testing the legitimacy of vehemence, ambition, and outrage in a woman's life that never questioned the moral absolutes of care and faith.

Charlotte's keen sense of right and wrong came in formal terms from her father's sermons and from the strict pieties of Aunt Elizabeth Branwell, her mother's older sister, who at the age of forty-five (a year older than Mr Brontë) had come from Cornwall to nurse Maria in the last stages of her illness, and then stayed until some alternative might be found. 'Aunt', though a devout Wesleyan, was a person of sober rectitude, not inspiration – the high imaginative challenges of the moral life came to the Brontë children from their eldest sister, Maria. Where Aunt, reproving and joyless in her black silk dress, ran the household, it was Maria who took the place of mother to the younger children. Maria would have been seven when her mother died in 1821 – a precocious seven: conversant with her father's conservative politics, keeping pace with *Blackwood's Magazine*, and able to hold her own in discussions with him. Her extraordinary intelligence made her something of a companion to her father between the ages of seven and ten when she was sent away to school.

Apart from Maria, Mr Brontë remained withdrawn from his children – their 'prattle' distressed him – and concerned himself only in his son's development. In this, he was no different from other fathers of the day. His daughters (except, briefly, Anne) did not share in the classical training that their brother, Branwell, received in his father's study. Branwell had wild red hair and a racing volubility in the glow of his father's encouragement and pride. He had the confidence of a boy expected to distinguish himself and lead the family. Emily, in contrast, kept her eyes averted and did not often talk. She had beautiful eyes, at times dark grey, at times dark blue. Like Charlotte, she was pale, with straight brown hair (which they frizzed in their teens in disfiguring attempts at fashion). Anne's hair was curly; she was the best looking of the sisters, with a clear, almost transparent skin and fine eyebrows. All the sisters learnt sewing and household tasks with Aunt Branwell, a small figure in gigantic, old-fashioned caps, who was displeased with her move from Cornwall to Yorkshire, but doing her duty. The reserved habits of Papa and Aunt may explain the report of Charlotte's behaviour as a child who was prone to say 'very little about herself and averse from making any display of what she knew'.

By shutting himself in his study, year by year, and absenting himself from meals, Mr Brontë managed to know little of his daughters' potentialities and nothing of their writing. Decades later, when Charlotte revealed her authorship of the phenomenally successful *Jane Eyre*, she did not presume on his interest. She knew better than to mention her writing more than once a month. Pictures of Mr Brontë show his alert, hard stare above his prominent cheekbones. He looks proud and self-sufficient, the sort with ready opinions, who seems to engage with ease yet guards himself against the encroachments of emotion. He was an assiduous priest who thought visiting and cottage lectures the most important part of a minister's duty, and believed in extempore, colloquial preaching accessible to the most illiterate members of his congregation, without departing from 'the dignified simplicity of the scriptures'. He also concerned himself with child labour in the mills and resisted the New Poor Law (which introduced the dreaded poorhouse). Later, he was unafraid of offending the rich who resisted the cost of improving sewerage and a polluted water supply. All the same, Mr Brontë, a Tory, fought against the democratic tendencies of the age – fought physically in 1811–12 against the Luddite Rising. Proud of his training in the use of firearms, he still put a loaded pistol in his pocket every morning, and a loaded gun hung on the wall of his study with his books (on two small hanging shelves between the windows). There he sat with his two pipes and his spittoon, making copious notes on purgatives which 'give tone to the bowels' in the margins of *Modern Domestic Medicine*, writing unremarkable didactic verse (laced with hellfire and endless woe), and preserving his domestic oblivion with solemn appeals to God in the strong Scotch accent of the north of Ireland.

After Mrs Brontë died, Mr Brontë made three attempts to remarry. First, he approached hospitable Miss Elizabeth Firth of Kipping House, Thornton, an orphan in command of her own fortune who was twenty years younger than himself. Miss Firth declined the offer, but remained gracious to Mr Brontë after her marriage in 1824 to the Revd Mr Franks (Vicar of Huddersfield). Mr Brontë was again ambitious when he approached Isabelle Dury, the Rector of Keighley's sister. Miss Dury said that she would never be so 'very silly' as to marry a man with no future and encumbered with six children. Then, in 1823–4, Mr Brontë wrote to an old flame, Mary Burder, with renewed attentions after an absence of fourteen years. During Mr Brontë's first curacy in Wethersfield, Essex, he had courted Miss Burder and written to her between 1808 and 1810, and she had accepted his proposal; but something happened to give her an impression of 'duplicity'. It is not surprising that Miss Burder still preferred to remain single, for Mr Brontë's letters do not reflect her: they are pious, self-justifying, elaborately courteous, and show only a perfunctory concern for her feelings. In his strongly marked hand, with dashing strokes through his 't's, these are the rhetorical letters of a suddenly determined man, who would settle his domestic affairs. Mr Brontë was not one to draw out a woman. He was too absorbed in his own needs — strict routine, quiet and privacy, and the demands of his dyspepsia — to notice much.

So, no new mother appeared on the scene, and when clergymen visited the Parsonage, they rarely brought their wives. While Mr Brontë taught Branwell in his study, Aunt retreated from unaccustomed northern chill to the fire in her room, taking meals on a tray. What did the five girls do and say when they were alone during the three years at home which followed their mother's death?

The life of Charlotte Brontë presents an experiment in which a woman, isolated with her sisters from society, used her isolation to explore hidden aspects of character. There is a curious precursor to this experiment in one which Mr Brontë devised in 1824 to elicit the characters and talents of his children. To test a notion that his children might reveal more of themselves if they were unseen, he called them to him, one by one, and, placing a mask over each face in turn, he invited answers to his questions.

When he asked seven-year-old Charlotte what was the best book, she answered: 'The Bible.'

And what was the next best book?

'The Book of Nature.'

The mask upon the children's faces was meant to free their speech, but their words were smoothly obedient. Though Mr Brontë was satisfied by what seemed to him apt answers, the experiment failed, for it revealed nothing that did not reflect adult opinion in the Parsonage. Already, the Brontë children were trained and impenetrable, and since no writing survives from early childhood, it is impossible to know what they truly felt and thought. Anne, aged four, said that what a tot required was 'Age and experience' – bleating Aunt Branwell whose room she shared. Her answer gave no indication of the stoicism to come, nor of the acute watcher behind her silence, nor of the defiant resourcefulness of the future heroine of *Wildfell Hall* who supports herself and her son rather than stay with her dissolute husband. Emily, aged five, said that the way to handle a naughty boy like Branwell, was to 'Reason with him, and when he won't listen to reason, whip him'. Tall like her father, and most like him in temperament, her answer did forecast her fierceness, projected into Heathcliff, the hero of her only known novel, *Wuthering Heights*. But Emily's words showed no sign of the unorthodox imagination that could call the divine spirit her 'slave' as well as her 'king'. Branwell, aged six, repeated the standard view that the difference between the minds of men and women might be judged from their bodies. Charlotte did give an accurate and clever answer with 'The Book of Nature', but she was certain of her father's approval, for her answer reflected his love for long, lonely walks, going back to rambles as a young man in the foothills of the Mountains of Mourne in his native County Down. Elizabeth, aged nine, asked how to educate a woman, said it was to rule her household well. By the time she left for school later that year, she was designed for a future as housekeeper by her father's decision to educate her at a lower standard than the others. She remains the least known of the Brontë children, possibly less clever than the rest, or perceived as such, and perhaps with something of Anne's silent stoicism. The most pious response to Papa's questions came from ten-year-old Maria.

'What is the best mode of spending time?' asked Mr Brontë.

'By laying it out in preparation for a happy eternity', was the prompt reply of this prodigy of self-denial who was soon to prove the point by braving to the borders of death the freezing and starving which marked the start, in 1824–5, of The Clergy Daughters' School at Cowan Bridge.

During the first half of 1824, the need to educate his daughters was much on Mr Brontë's mind. How was he to afford it? His income was under £200. This had been supplemented by his wife's annuity, but it was a life-annuity and returned to the Branwells at her death. Maria's family offered no help for her children, which may have caused some coolness between Mr Brontë and them. The Branwells never invited any Brontë to Cornwall; there seems to have been little further communication between the two families. Then, Mr Brontë's failures to secure another wife with private means, ending with Miss Burder's outraged silence at the beginning of 1824, had practical consequences for his five daughters. They would be portionless, and therefore unlikely to find husbands. It was now essential to prepare them to earn their livings. The most common position for impoverished ladies was that of governess, so Mr Brontë had to find a school which would provide the necessary education. A plan to send the girls to boarding school may have been, also, an inducement to Miss Branwell to stay on at the Parsonage.

A charity school for the daughters of poor clergymen had recently opened at Cowan Bridge, near Kirkby Lonsdale, in Lancashire. The assisted fees were £14 a year, with an extra £3 for 'accomplishments': French, music, or drawing. For the four girls of school-going age, this added up to well over a quarter of Mr Brontë's annual income, but he resolved to send them, and they went fully aware of the financial burden and of the absence of any alternative.

Maria and Elizabeth entered The Clergy Daughters' School in July 1824, after a family bout of whooping cough. Charlotte and Emily, who entered the school later in the year, had longer to recover. The future for each girl as 'governess' (except for Elizabeth) was written in the school's register, beside her name and comments on her skills – or lack of them: their poor sewing (despite Aunt's efforts in her main area of expertise) and scrappy knowledge. Nor were they numerate. But Maria and Elizabeth, aged ten and nine, could write well, Charlotte, at eight, was 'altogether clever of her age', and Emily, at six, could read 'very prettily'.

The school was situated below fells in a picturesque but damp place. Its unhealthiness was compounded by poor sanitation and a meagre, sometimes inedible diet, largely composed of dry bread, burnt porridge, and bakes of dingy odds and ends from a dirty kitchen. Hungry as they were, the girls often could not bring themselves to swallow such food, and were soon semi-starved.

The school's founder, William Carus Wilson, the Vicar of Tunstall, had devised a harsh regime with the idea of instilling Christian resignation, reinforced by his constant reminders to the girls that they were objects of charity. In Charlotte's later view, low morale, semi-starvation, and physical neglect predisposed most of the pupils to infection. Maria and Elizabeth, perhaps weakened also by the after-effects of whooping cough, either fell prey to tuberculosis or the latent disease took hold. Many other pupils caught typhus and, in the spring of 1825, an uncontrollable epidemic swept the school.

On 10 August 1824, when Mr Brontë took Charlotte to join her older sisters, he appears to have noticed nothing wrong with their school; nor did he notice the decline of his eldest daughters when Emily joined the school in November. This oblivion seems so peculiar that it suggested a misleading idea that Mr Brontë did not take Emily himself on a fifty-mile journey along the coach road from Leeds to the Lakes. But it is conceivable that he would have been satisfied with Maria's elevated spirit and Elizabeth's brave face while himself performing the orotund courtesies that had marked his astonishing rise from a two-room hovel with a mud floor, from Patrick Brunty – descendant of peasants called some variant of Prunty – to the Revd Brontë, a gentleman of the West Riding of Yorkshire.

From the time of her arrival at the school, Charlotte was forced to watch Maria's repeated humiliation at the hands of a schoolmistress called Miss Andrews, the Miss Scatcherd of *Jane Eyre*. Many years later, Charlotte told Mrs Gaskell that Lowood School in *Jane Eyre* was an accurate record of conditions at Cowan Bridge. Miss Scatcherd, who is described as small, dark, smartly dressed, with a rather morose look, persecutes the uncomplaining Helen Burns, an exact portrait of Maria Brontë. She dislikes her 'cast of character', the elder girl tells the younger, with calm insight. Maria's was a mind of rare grace; she was strikingly mature in her reading and thinking, but this was disregarded because she was always in trouble for untidiness. In Charlotte's version of what happened, Maria became her teacher's prime victim. Sent in disgrace to stand in the middle of the classroom, she appeared detached:

> 'She looks as if she were thinking of something beyond her punishment – beyond her situation: of something not round her nor before her. I have heard of day-dreams – is she in a day-dream now? Her eyes are fixed on the floor, but I am sure they do not see it – her sight seems turned in, gone down into her heart.'

However Maria excelled at lessons, Miss Andrews would attack her for dirty nails even though frozen water had made washing impossible. Rebellious but helpless, Maria's younger sisters saw her fetch a bunch of twigs, unloosen her pinafore, and receive several strokes on the neck. Charlotte quivered in 'impotent anger', but Maria preached a creed of endurance. The purpose of life, as Maria had said behind the mask, was to look beyond life. Charlotte recalled her words: '. . . God waits only the separation of spirit from flesh to crown us with a full reward. Why, then, should we ever sink overwhelmed with distress, when life is so soon over, and death is so certain an entrance to happiness: to glory?'

This is the language of Evangelicalism, not inconsistent with the Calvinism of William Carus Wilson. As well as vicar, he was a local landowner whose seat was Casterton Hall. Ostensibly, Carus Wilson was a public benefactor who had collected funds and contributed generously towards a school which would educate the daughters of poor clergymen at reduced cost; in practice, Carus Wilson was a manipulative, rather sinister man who saw girls as weak and sinful and whose school would attempt to save them by trying to stamp out their nature: by cutting off their hair, by chilling their bodies, by depressing their appetites with inedible food, and birching them into submission. This sanctimonious man was hand-in-glove with the sadistic God of his books for children, a God who took care to destroy children's bodies for the good of their souls ('in love to her poor little soul [the Lord] caused the candle to set fire to her clothes' is one item from his catalogue of holy injuries). Maria's belief in the taint of nature made her accept Miss Andrews' punishments even as her body flagged.

To deny nature was to be an ideal product of The Clergy Daughters' School. In *Jane Eyre*, when the school's founder visits Lowood, he objects to a girl's curls. The hair curls naturally, says the superintendent, Miss Temple. 'Naturally!' exclaims Mr Brocklehurst. 'Yes but we are not to conform to nature: I wish these girls to be the children of Grace'. He commands the teachers 'to mortify in these girls the lusts of the flesh; to teach them to clothe themselves with shamefacedness and sobriety'.

Charlotte's sense told her it was not the divine will that the bodies of her schoolmates be subdued; it was a class ideology, epitomised in Carus Wilson, a member of the gentry whose own womenfolk were not expected to surrender any of their vanities of dress and coiffure. The punitive element was backed by current middle-class dogma that poverty was largely deserved. This dogma, in fact, had the support of Mrs Brontë in an undated manuscript treatise she wrote on 'The Advantages of Poverty in Religious Concerns':

But O, what words can express the great misery of those who suffer all the evils of poverty here, and that, too, by their own bad conduct, and have no hope of happiness hereafter, but rather have cause to fear that the end of this miserable life will be the beginning of another, infinitely more miserable, never, never to have an end!

If the children of the poor were famished and cold, Mrs Brontë advised them to turn the mind to the world to come. When she considered 'them' from her superior standing, she cannot have conceived that her own daughters might suffer, as they now did, 'the evils of poverty'. It is startling to turn from her engaging letters to such pieties as would have been acceptable to Carus Wilson who, in the figure of the Revd Mr Brocklehurst, chides the superintendent at Lowood when she gives girls the nourishment their bodies crave: 'Oh, madam, when you put bread and cheese, instead of burnt porridge into these children's mouths, you may indeed feed their vile bodies, but you little think how you starve their immortal souls!' Later, Charlotte told Mrs Gaskell that 'the pain she suffered from hunger was not to be told'.

As winter came on, with the deep snows of January and February, the Brontë daughters and the others had to walk two miles, each Sunday, to the church at Tunstall where Carus Wilson officiated. The church was too far for the girls to return to the school for lunch; instead, they were given minute portions of cold meat and bread to sustain them through the afternoon service. After that, their route back to school lay along an exposed hill road, as an icy wind flayed their faces. Though they longed for a fire on their return, the big girls formed a tight ring which blocked most of the warmth. Behind them the Brontës crouched, wrapping their arms in their pinafores.

In February 1825, eight months after her arrival at the school, the uncomplaining Maria was sent home with neglected consumption. As she sank into illness, she remained alert to her mother's pieties derived from the Methodism of the Branwells. Denying life, the girl humbled her spirit with eyes turned on heaven – doing so more unflinchingly than her mother who, naturally, found it hard to accept prolonged pain, as Patrick Brontë had put it to the Revd John Buckworth (his Vicar in Dewsbury) in November 1821: 'During many years she had walked with God, but the great enemy, envying her life of holiness, often disturbed her mind in the last conflict.' Maria, the daughter, was absolute for death, and, as such, a formidable model against whom Charlotte was to shape her alternative, and to whom Emily and Anne submitted in different ways: Emily with her denial of the world and neglect of the body, starving it, granting it no mercy in the weeks before her death in December 1848; Anne struggling in her 'Last Lines' for submission to her own premature death in 1849. Branwell, like Anne, would have been at home with Maria as she faded between February and May. His poem 'Misery' is haunted by the image of Maria who embodied a perfection he could never attain:

> . . . And wildly did I cling to thee.
> I could not, would not, dared not part
> Lest hell again should seize my heart . . .
> But we are sundered – thee, thy grave,
> And me, this dreary wild will have.

Lines on a sister's death which Branwell read at this time in *Blackwood's Magazine* seemed so apt that he could quote them ten years later: 'That hour so far more dreadful than any hour that can darken us on earth, when she . . . descended slowly, slowly into the horrid clay, and we were born deathlike and wishing to die out of the churchyard'.

Maria died at the age of eleven in May 1825, and it is likely that her sublime fortitude left a stronger impression on her brother and sisters than the death of their mother. Later that May, Elizabeth was sent home in the terminal stage of tuberculosis,

and died swiftly in June. She was ten. The successive deaths were
formative for the remaining four. Maria was buried while
Charlotte and Emily were still at school, but Mr Brontë, taking
fright at last, removed them on 1 June, and they would have
attended Elizabeth's funeral. Amongst the fragments of
Charlotte's writings is a scrap of fiction in which a girl called
Jane Moore thinks of her sister's funeral day and 'the rigid &
lengthened corpse' laid in her coffin, of people pressing round to
gaze at her for the last time, 'of the kiss that she herself was
bidden to give the corpse, of the feeling which then first gushed
into her childish & volatile heart that Harriet had left them for
ever.'

Charlotte spoke of Maria incessantly in the years that followed. When she made new friends at the age of fifteen, she
described Maria 'as a little mother among the rest, superhuman
in goodness and cleverness', Ellen remembered. 'But most
touching of all were the revelations of her sufferings, – how she
suffered with the sensibility of a grown-up person, and endured
with a patience and fortitude that were Christ-like.' All her life,
Charlotte recalled scenes of cruelty, branded on her memory
during her ten months at the school, which she held back from
Jane Eyre, thinking readers would not believe them. One morning, after a blister had been applied to Maria's side, she was too
weak to get up with the bell at six. When Miss Andrews came by,
she jerked Maria from the bed and whirled her to the middle of
the floor, reviling her for dirty habits. Quieting murmurs of
indignation from her fellow-pupils, the sick girl, with slow
movements, began to draw her stockings over her wasted legs,
and then was punished for being late. Ellen said that seven years
later Charlotte was still reliving the decline of her eldest sister.
'She talked of Elizabeth also, but never with the anguish of
expression which accompanied her recollections of Maria.'

Charlotte told Mary Taylor, another new friend, about a
dream in which Maria and Elizabeth returned to life. She was
called to meet them in a drawing-room, and they had become

fashionable and trivial. At fifteen, the dream came to Charlotte as a momentary challenge to the model of spiritual elevation she could never forget. The child who put the Bible before Nature; the schoolgirl who clung to that memory of Christ-like fortitude; the grown woman who wrote of life ahead as a path to be followed for which one prayed for aid: for all Charlotte's subsequent defiance of convention, her thinking was shaped by her sister. The novelty of Charlotte's emergence must be seen in relation to the alternative model Maria presented, all the more potent for the fact that her perfection was sealed by a death that appeared to Charlotte in the light of martyrdom. She believed Maria, like Elizabeth after her, was destroyed by the school, and that she herself was marked ever after in mind and body by what happened there. In *Jane Eyre*, the questioning employer, Mr Rochester, remarks to Jane, the governess, that anyone who survived Lowood 'must be tenacious of life'. Such a school was bound to have 'done up any constitution! No wonder you have rather the look of another world.'

Against her sisters' unresisting deaths, Charlotte shaped herself as survivor, and so, too, her survivors in fiction. All live by the Christian ideal of humility, but refuse to surrender control of their destinies to fallible figures of authority: a founder of a charity school, a compelling lover, a guardian uncle, a dogmatic missionary. Charlotte was as strenuous, in her way, as the school – she, too, saw life as moral struggle – but she did not deny women their initiative: her novels showed them a difficult but stimulating pilgrimage that would be determined by clear judgement of the idols about them. Her venture, often mistaken by her contemporaries for irreligious licence, was to revise the map of the soul for the charity schoolchild, the dependent girl, the overlooked governess, the lowly teacher – those trained to present a humble façade. Maria Brontë was a model of self-discipline and transcendence, but she was not, in her sister's view, a model to follow.

When Ellen asked Charlotte how a young child could have

judged Maria, Charlotte replied that she had begun to analyse
character at the age of five. At eight, she watched her sister grant
the sanction of her religious intelligence to what Charlotte perceived to be sadism. The charity school was designed to humble
girls whose lack of funds would necessitate a future of servitude
and self-abnegation. With Charlotte, it had the reverse effect.
Instead of turning heavenwards, an independent self rose into
being. A new strong voice questioned the application of religious
rhetoric to abuse of schoolgirls, in Jane's replies to Rochester:

'You have lived the life of a nun: no doubt you are well drilled
in religious forms; – Brocklehurst, who I understand directs
Lowood, is a parson, is he not?'

'Yes, sir.'

'And you girls probably worshipped him, as a convent full of
religieuses would worship their director.'

'Oh no.'

'You are very cool! No! What! a novice not worship her
priest? That sounds blasphemous.'

'I disliked Mr Brocklehurst; and I was not alone in the feeling. He is a harsh man; at once pompous and meddling: he cut
off our hair; and, for economy's sake, bought us bad needles
and thread, with which we could hardly sew.'

. . . 'And was that the head and front of his offending?'
demanded Mr Rochester.

'He starved us when he had the sole superintendence of the
provision department, before the committee was appointed;
and he bored us with long lectures once a week, and with
evening readings from books of his own inditing, about sudden
deaths and judgments, which made us afraid to go to bed.'

It is fair to say that hair-cutting was common enough at girls'
schools, based on the notion it was women's nature to be vain. In
The Tenant of Wildfell Hall, Anne Brontë would protest against a
double standard in the education of boys and girls which

assumed that boys, made of sterner stuff, were to be strength-
ened by exposure to worldly temptation while girls had to be
shut away, protected from their very selves as embodiments of
that temptation. Charlotte would make the same protest in a
letter to a retired headmistress, Miss Wooler, in 1846. Where boys
were formed for leadership, girls were formed for self-denial.
What Charlotte inveighed against was not altruism and discipline – these she endorsed – but the attempt to break the spirit.
The pioneer of women's education, Dorothea Beale, who taught
at The Clergy Daughters' School in 1857, more than thirty years
after Charlotte left, gave a sombre account of the lingering effect
of Calvinistic harshness: 'its direct results on the education of the
young were disastrous indeed. Hearts . . . were turned to stone,
or depressed into hopeless terror; worst of all, religious forms,
phraseology, even emotions were assumed by those who were
prone to self-deception, or over-anxious to please.'

In the early 1850s, Charlotte expressed wonder that she
should have outlived the rest, but her determination to struggle and live, and her need to acknowledge the existence of
natural feelings, owed something, ironically, to Carus Wilson,
whose subjection of nature provoked instinctive resistance – a
salutary rage, *Jane Eyre* implies. There was a burning energy in
her that refused to be subdued. And when this energy manifested in a girl, the Victorians found it suspect. They sniffed
rebellion, coarseness – that is, if Currer Bell turned out to be a
woman. When Mrs Gaskell published her friend's biography in
1857, she herself deplored an occasional 'coarseness' in the
novels, and begged the public 'to consider her life' as explanation. She presents 'a life of desolation' alongside a crowd of
tombstones which look over the wall of the Parsonage: the
pathos of overwhelming grief will excuse excess of passion. I
am not suggesting that Mrs Gaskell did not present a great
truth of Charlotte Brontë's life. She defended her friend with
sense, eloquence, and courage in terms that spoke to their age.
Mrs Gaskell was writing with conviction about a woman she

knew, and this Charlotte — as she appeared to a solicitous contemporary — is always with us. But reading the documents a
hundred and fifty years later, writing for another age, I begin to
see that the darkness of grief (so compelling to Victorians) has
obscured a deeper, more portentous darkness in which a new
form of life evolved. Mrs Gaskell saw (with sincerest pity) her
friend's isolation, her single state, and above all, her grieving
over those ever-present stones that marked the early deaths of
Brontë after Brontë. Her Charlotte is not a fiery survivor but a
poor relic of a doomed family. Mrs Gaskell was an accomplished
story-teller, always alive, but it's long been recognised that she
could not resist her tendency to dramatise her particular view
and was therefore not always accurate in reports of others.
Dickens was vastly entertained by her false report that he had
bought a dinner service of *gold* plate, and teased her that everything in his household was encrusted with gold, even the
clothes of his daughters. Mrs Gaskell insisted that the George
Eliot who had written *Scenes of Clerical Life* and *Adam Bede* was a
certain Joseph Liggins of Nuneaton, because she was reluctant
to believe that books she admired had been written by the
Marian Evans who lived openly with George Henry Lewes.
Earlier on, she circulated a rumour that Charlotte Brontë was
doomed by mortal illness, an inference from the deaths of
Charlotte's sisters which proved damaging to Charlotte who
denied it in vain. She notes how refined Charlotte was in her
person, how exquisitely neat, how modest and delicate, how
dutiful to her father. All this is true — but only part of the truth.
Mrs Gaskell, aware of the Victorian taboo against the woman
who resists self-denial, does not bring out the subversive side of
this life. For Charlotte's challenge is to link the moral fervour of
the nun — for whom she had much affinity — with a refusal to
deny nature.

　　Given the restrictiveness of home and village, and the repression of the charity school, how did Charlotte Brontë expand her
imaginative space? This was a lifelong pursuit, but two aspects of

her childhood – the expanse of the moors behind her home and her rage at school – opened up an interior landscape which remained peculiarly her own. This converged with the burning aims of Maria (in *Jane Eyre* she is called by her surname, 'Burns', at school). Recent scholarship has shown that though Mr Brontë repudiated Calvinism, his ministry was more given to awareness of hell than salvation. In September 1824, he saw an upheaval of a bog on the moors as a warning against sin. A horror of sin was the bias, too, of Aunt Branwell, despite family ties with milder Wesleyan Methodism rather than the more Calvinistic Methodism of Whitefield. She taught her nieces – especially her favourite, Anne – to distrust natural impulse as the prompting of the devil and to regard independence of judgement as a sin of pride. Maria might be seen as a product of this form of piety, as of The Clergy Daughters' School, yet in Charlotte's fictionalised view, she transcended it. In her longest, loftiest speech, 'Burns' expounds a creed of her own, the invention of a purer spirit than that of the punitive ethos that pervades the school. She has a vision of a spirit that passes on to some being higher than man, which will never, she believes, be allowed to degenerate from man to fiend: 'No; I cannot believe that: I hold another creed; which no one ever taught me, and which I seldom mention; but in which I delight, and to which I cling; for it extends hope to all . . .'

In July 1826, a year after Maria's death, Papa gave Charlotte her mother's copy of *The Imitation of Christ*, abridged by John Wesley in 1803. There is no knowing how closely, if at all, Charlotte read this book, but it might have helped her to assimilate the tragedy she had witnessed in terms of 'the pattern' of a life that requires trial and discipline: 'There is no other way to life and true inner peace than the way . . . of daily self-denial: our merit and spiritual progress do not consist in great delight and consolation, but rather in the bearing of great burdens and troubles'.

In childhood Charlotte formed a dual allegiance to the Bible and Nature, to the burdened pilgrimage on the one hand and the free-ranging moors on the other. In this way, she recast Maria's model as a creed of her own: her sister's martyred yet independent spirit sanctioned her need to transcend the conditions of her life.

FALSE IDOLS, TRUE FRIENDS

'What is now called the nature of women is an eminently artificial thing —'. In 1861, John Stuart Mill was contemplating the impediments in the way of a woman brought up to custom's rule, who 'attempts to express in books anything drawn from the depths of her own nature.'

Forty years earlier, the Brontës' hilltop location, which placed them in the closest relation to nature, did detach them to some extent from custom. The death of their mother in 1821 left her daughters without a domestic model. Aunt Branwell, who had no fondness for children, did not figure as such. She was respected and obeyed, no more. Like Mr Brontë, she kept to her room for reasons of health: she feared the northern climate and the cold passages of the Parsonage, carpetless because of Mr Brontë's fear of fire (he kept buckets of water, in readiness, on the landing of the staircase). Aunt's fear was catching cold: she took to pattens (protective clogs), clicking along the passage and up the stairs. The three remaining girls, Charlotte, Emily, and Anne, were compelled to sew their samplers during long afternoons in her overheated room. Charlotte completed her sampler during her tenth year, 1825–6. Aunt made them also sew charity clothing, on the barren principle that it was not for the good of the needy so much as for the good of the sewers. Jane Eyre, gazing out at the horizon and longing for the stir of activity, argues that women suffer, just as men would, from confinement and 'stagnation'. Though Aunt had the intelligence to hold her own in political exchanges with Papa, her room and domestic education held no appeal. And so long as the sisters remained at the Parsonage, outside models did not impinge: there was no other educated family in the village, and they were too poor to mix much with the gentry.

Had Mr Brontë remarried, it is possible his daughters might have taken the imprint of conventional women, but as it turned out, there was only Aunt with her false front of light auburn curls, her reproval when a girl said 'spit', and her mannered way of offering snuff to visitors with a little laugh as though she expected and enjoyed their surprise. And there were the cowed pupils of Cowan Bridge, none of whom invited emulation. It is curious that no schoolgirl of that time remembered the Brontës, despite the constant proximity of boarders. Mrs Gaskell suggests that the Brontës were masked at school as completely as when Mr Brontë had placed an actual mask upon their faces.

The authentic women were servants: first, their fond young nurses, Nancy and Sarah Garrs, who had moved with the children from Thornton and disliked Aunt as 'so cross-like' and 'so close [stingy]'; and then, when Aunt, with righteous economy, dismissed them (in 1824 when the four older girls were sent to school), they were followed by fifty-three-year-old Tabby — Tabitha Aykroyd — who made the kitchen a warm centre and gave the children her brusque affection. She fed them well and baked them cakes, dealing out her downright views on whom she liked or not. Home for Charlotte was an image of Tabby blowing the fire in order to boil the potatoes to a sort of vegetable glue, while Emily secured the best piece of the leg of mutton for her dog. Emily, in particular, was attached to the kitchen: as an adult, she preferred baking bread (with a German grammar propped against the bowl) to genteel exile in other houses; later, a kitchen, with its fire and Yorkshire accents, was to be a dramatic centre in *Wuthering Heights*. Its eerie scenes as well as its strong rural character may have drawn on Tabby's stores of local tales and legends which gripped the children around the fire. So, in the unbroken years at the Parsonage from the summer of 1825 to the start of 1831, the girls moved between the physical hearth of the kitchen and the upstairs life of the tiny bedroom where, in 1826, when Charlotte was ten, their imaginative expansion began.

In the same summer that Mr Brontë gave his daughter *The Imitation of Christ*, he gave his son a box of twelve soldiers. Where *The Imitation* looked to the stillness of prayer that awaits death, the soldiers provoked amoral 'plays' of power and exploration. The title of the first play, 'Young Men' (June 1826), bears out the girls' entrance into a world of action. The soldiers, led by the son of the Duke of Wellington, and by sons of Ross and Parry, set off for West Africa where they established themselves in a number of 'lands', one belonging to each of the children: Wellington's land belonged to Charlotte, Parry's land to Emily, Ross's to Anne, and Sneaky's to Branwell – this last being the land of an unreliable character associated with the enemy, Napoleon. (Branwell's familiarity with England's old enemy came from Scott's *Life of the Emperor Napoleon*.) He drew exquisitely detailed maps of these lands, with coloured outlines as in Goldsmith's *Geography*. In 'Our Fellows', a play established in July 1827, the children took their characters from the titles of the 1825 edition of Aesop's *Fables*: Charlotte was Hay Man, Emily was Clown, Anne was Hunter, and Branwell was Boaster. In another play called 'Tales of the Islanders' (1829), Branwell appears as 'Little King', an imperious, spoilt boy, given to unpredictable acts of violence. The play did not include a single woman; all actors were famous doctors, politicians, and writers of the time, as Charlotte described them at the age of thirteen:

We then chose who should live in our islands. The chief of Branwell's were John Bull, Astley Cooper, and Leigh Hunt etc; Emily's Walter Scott, Mr Lockhart, Johnny Lockhart etc; Anne's Michael Sadler, Lord Bentinck, Henry Halford etc; and

I chose Duke of Wellington and son, North and Co. . . . The
next day we added many others to our list of men, till we got
almost all the chief men of the kingdom.

Papa's hero, the Duke of Wellington – Irish, dominant, mili-
tary – emerged quickly at the centre of these plays, together
with his two sons, the active Arthur Wellesley (otherwise called
the Duke of Zamorna after a town in Spain associated with the
Peninsular Wars) and the more passive Charles Wellesley who
took on the role of inquisitive onlooker and cynical, small-
minded writer under the name of Charles Townshend. The
opposition to the Wellesley family was a rebellious character,
Alexander Percy, first called Alexander Rogue, then called the
Earl of Northangerland, and finally, Alexander Ashworth.
Percy/Ashworth had the glamour of evil, and was inexplicably
cruel to his two sons, Edward and William, whom he abandoned,
but he nurtured his daughter, Mary Percy. Versions of these
characters were to figure repeatedly in Charlotte Brontë's writings.

While she joined Branwell in the anarchic war games of what
became the Glass Town Confederacy and, later, Verdopolis or
Angria*, she also began a different sort of 'bed play' with Emily
on 1 December 1827 and March 1828. Charlotte was then eleven,
Emily nine. 'Bed plays mean secret plays', Charlotte wrote in
March 1829, 'they are very nice ones.' These night 'plays', too
secret to be written down, represent the first inventive bond
between sisters which excluded their brother and became, eventually, a way of life.

When Charlotte left for school in 1831, Emily began further
plays alone with Anne: this was the start of their Gondal saga,
the prose of which has disappeared – only poems remain, and a

* Named, possibly, after Kanhoji Angria who founded a pirate kingdom on the
coast of India which resisted submission in the late seventeenth and early eighteenth centuries until the British, under Clive, took it in 1756.

few cryptic remarks. Emily and Anne had been dissatisfied with the minor roles assigned to their heroes by a dominant brother and sister, and they were bored with Charlotte's languishing heroines and Branwell's battles. Gondal's chief actors were head-strong women; it was ruled by the ruthless Augusta Geraldine Almeda who ruins men. War in Gondal, unlike Branwell's pomp and parade, was stark. Unlike the warm 'infernal' Africa of Angria, Gondal was an island in the north Pacific, with a setting and climate rather like Yorkshire: moors, mists, and frozen gloom. Its people were hardy. Freedom was their blessing; prison their hell. Emily's Gondal poems of freedom and prison devel-oped directly into the great poetry and fiction of her maturity. For Charlotte, it was different: Angria had for her an opiate effect, as though for years she were caught in a dream from which she emerged only by enormous efforts of will. Her part in the Angrian saga was to develop love interest and to try to make sense of Branwell's wars by granting character to the actors. The heroes of Branwell's tales, like Alexander Rogue, were ambi-tious, unscrupulous men who precipitated civil war. As 'chief genius', Charlotte restored soldiers to life so that the game could go on (for Branwell was always raining destruction upon his creations – he was that sort of god).

Branwell, as the only son and the only one to have a classical education, was the destined leader; his sisters prepared them-selves to live through him: the family's hope of brilliant promise. As a boy, Branwell set the pace for his sisters, tossing off works with speed and abandon. Following his lead, his sisters tried out different genres within the expanding plot of the plays: letters, portraits, reviews, journals, poems, and satires. Christine Alexander has noted that nowhere in the juvenilia did Charlotte adopt the voice of a woman: she identified with the power of men, and their privilege of public expression. Unequal to Branwell in nineteenth-century society, she assumed equality through the male voice of her narrator, 'Charles Thunder' or 'Charles Townshend', precursors to the famous 'Currer Bell' who published *Jane Eyre*: Charlotte always referred to 'Currer Bell' as 'he'.

Sharing closely then, and sometimes competitively, in her brother's dreams and writings, Charlotte participated in his ambitions: they modelled their writings on those of Sir Walter Scott (1771–1832) and Lord Byron (1788–1824), both on their father's shelves, alongside Shakespeare, Milton, Bunyan, Dr Johnson, and Wordsworth. Mr Brontë's time for his daughters' education was limited to whatever was left over from parish duties: he set them passages from the Bible, Mangnall's *Historical Questions*, Linley's *Grammar*, and Goldsmith's *Geography*, but his main contribution to their education was the encouragement he gave to reading, and the freedom he allowed them in their choice of books. When Charlotte opened Byron, she read *Cain*, written in 1821 ('a magnificent poem'), and the licentious *Don Juan* (1819–20), neither at the time approved reading for young girls, as well as Byron's acceptable *Hebrew Melodies* (1815) and fashion's choice, *Childe Harold's Pilgrimage* (1812, 1816, 1817). She thought all novels after Scott seemed 'worthless'. Aunt gave the children Scott's *The Tales of a Grandfather* for Christmas in 1828, and in 1832 Mr Brontë bought Moore's recently published *Letters and Journals of Lord Byron, with notices of his life*. Branwell took on the Byronic role of the 'wandering outlaw of his dark mind' who pierces 'the depths of life'; for Charlotte, the outlaw was a shade less compelling, but she shared with Branwell the Byronic drama of dark genius – the idea of living more intensely through creative acts:

> What am I? Nothing: but not so art thou,
> Soul of my thought! with whom I traverse earth,
> Invisible but gazing, as I glow
> Mixed with thy spirit . . .

The great verbal power that was to emerge in Charlotte Brontë ten years later came from an extraordinary liberty to transgress the frontiers of feeling which is commonly silenced –

to a degree that words for such feeling hardly exist – and it is obvious that this liberty was the fruit of the Romantic movement. But where the speakers for Romanticism were almost invariably men, her books claimed this range for women, and in a way that, eventually, proved far from imitative. She had the courage to speak what she called 'Truth' on the basis of her own solitary experience, and this is what made her novels exceptionally dependent on the events of her life. Between novels, she spoke of having to 'accumulate', in other words, to live through the matter of the next novel. As an adolescent, before she had much experience to speak of, the feelings she expressed *were* imitative, in fact banal extravaganzas of romantic longing. Yet drawn out as the Angrian dream was, it did habituate her to a vital freedom of expression through the licence of an alternative fictional world. This eloquence would combine, later, with a hidden range of passions in new models of womanhood, which explains why the mass of readers hailed her books, while some reviewers savaged her for sins against the social code. Crudely, they slotted her with the political rebel, the ungodly, the kind of woman who could not be called a 'lady'.

At the same time as she shared her brother's ambitions and his imaginative world, she knocked against him almost from the start of their partnership, rebelling, in turn, against his Byronic postures as rebel and outcast. Now and then her satiric voice – often obscured by her own voluminous gush – asserts itself to laugh at the absurdity of Branwell's artistic pretensions. In 'Corner Dishes: A Day Abroad' and in 'My Angria and the Angrians' (both dated 1834), she draws a portrait of seventeen-year-old Patrick Branwell Brontë as Patrick Benjamin Wiggins: a low, slight person with a hat at the back of his head, from which projects a prominent Roman nose (propping spectacles) and, projecting even further as seen from the side, two great bushes of 'carroty hair', almost like two spread hands: 'His form was that of a lad of sixteen, his face that of a man of twenty-five; . . . his features not bad, for he had a . . . small mouth and well-turned chin. His figure, too, though diminutive was perfectly symmetrical, and of this he seemed not unconscious, from the frequent and complacent looks he cast down on his nether man.' Every now and then, he touched his chest with the tip of his forefinger and pushed it out to make it appear broader.

The boastful Wiggins is said to be planning a tombstone with the inscription that as a poet he surpassed Byron and as a rebel he surpassed Alexander Rogue. He declares himself a native of 'Howard', a great city with twenty grand hotels, but the narrator, Charles Wellesley, at once scuppers these lies: 'I knew well enough Howard is only a miserable little village, buried in dreary moors . . .'

When asked about his relatives, Wiggins concedes 'some people who call themselves akin to me in the shape of three girls. They are honoured by possessing me as a brother but I deny that they're my sisters.'

Wellesley asks if Charlotte Wiggins, [Emily] Jane Wiggins, and Anne Wiggins are as odd as Benjamin himself, who replies with extreme loftiness:

Oh, they are miserable silly creatures not worth talking about. Charlotte's eighteen years old, a broad dumpy thing, whose head does not come higher than my elbow. Emily's sixteen, lean and scant, with a face about the size of a penny, and Anne is nothing, absolutely nothing.

Charlotte wrote this at the time Branwell did his famous portrait of his three sisters, and it may be her satiric comment on his version of their appearance. Charlotte looks ruddy, square-faced, and determined; Emily taller than her sisters, her round face closed off; Anne smaller (she was only fourteen), and to one side; the centre of the portrait was to have been Branwell himself, positioned between Emily and Charlotte, but for some reason he painted himself out – the shadow of Branwell behind the paint looks disproportionally large. This would fit the playful conclusion of Charlotte's narrator that nothing short of the splendid palace of Cock Hill will do for such as Wiggins.

This satire does not suggest a shy or meek nature; Charlotte held her own against her brother, scoring her points with verve as she mocks Branwell's tastes for brass bands and boxing (influenced by the landlord of the Black Bull, Thomas Sugden). She invented cool literary characters, Charles Townshend and Captain Tree, who show up Branwell's wildly poetic personae as Young Soult* and Henry Rhymer. Charlotte's closeness to her brother in the character of the Genii**, Tallii (Charlotte) and Brannii (Branwell), did not preclude very early ridicule of Branwell's poetic pretensions with two astute satires in the second half of 1830. In 'Visit to Young Soult', the attitudinising poet excuses his excesses on the modish grounds of 'enthusiasm'. As Young Soult admits, 'my feelings do sometimes carry me utterly beyond the control of reason and politeness.' In 'The Poetaster: A Drama', Henry Rhymer is a similar self-admiring versifier, given to ecstasies over 'the whining wind', the moon and the nightingale, and other standard Romantic props. In this her only play, Charlotte spoofs the delusions of literary ambition as well as the absurd posturings of doomed genius. Rhymer, like Branwell, fancies the Graveyard School, and relishes the melancholy surrounding the decline and death of neglected greatness: '. . . From the grave of genius shall arise a fixed star ascending to the heaven of literature . . . in the midst of poets which are its fellows, to all eternity. This delicate frame was not formed to bide all blasts. Soon must the feeble texture be rent under the proud swellings of that keen and sensitive spirit which it enwraps.' He forces his effusions on the respected writer, Captain Tree, who kicks Rhymer out. When Rhymer's chagrin leads to violence and a near-miss with the gallows, it is generally agreed that what

---

* The name was derived from Napoleon's Marshal Soult who was Wellington's opponent in the Peninsular Wars and at the Battle of Waterloo.
** Under the influence of *Tales of the Genii* (1764).

he really needs is 'some useful employment'. Tree muses how mistaken it is to believe that literature is the spontaneous over-flow of powerful feelings. True art depends on the patience to eliminate the repeated word and round the sentence.

So, at fourteen, Charlotte already knew the difference between abandon and professional discipline. Yet it has to be owned that most of her juvenilia is boring, and no less boring for being so voluminous. It is customary to say that the Angrian saga looks forward to Charlotte Brontë's mature work, and mark the resemblance between the masterful Zamorna and the later Rochester, master of Jane Eyre. But what dulls Zamorna is the monotony of power and the spinelessness of his string of women. So long as Charlotte was in thrall to the world she shared with Branwell, she had no conception of her sex except as a series of palpitating hearts, on offer when heroes turn from their central concern with control and violence.

Angrian women were drawn after portraits of society pets in annuals and other illustrated magazines (like Aunt's copies of the *Ladies Magazine*) which directed the readers of the 1820s and 1830s to the fashion for 'silver-fork' fiction – stories of aristocracy. Charlotte did elaborate drawings of the lovelies of Aunt's gener-ation, transforming them into large-eyed Angrian heroines, dripping with jewels. Her illustration of Zamorna's first love, Marian Hume, was a copy of W. H. Finden's engraving of the Countess of Jersey after a painting by E. T. Parris which Charlotte would have seen in Moore's *Life of Byron*. She darkened the eyes and gave more prominence to a rope of pearls looped beneath a swelling breast.

Her illustrated stories reflect the magazine premiss that pas-sion was reserved for beauties. Charlotte decided at the age of twelve that she would never marry. Instead, she would be a writer: her ambition is patent in the high position of authors in Glass Town, in the constant address to the reader, in her dating and signing most manuscripts, and above all in her care to pre-serve her writing in handsewn 'books' which imitate professional layout with their title page, contents, and meticulous print – the first of these was written for her sister, Anne, when Charlotte was ten. This game of publication was a secret. The print and booklets are minute – difficult to read – and the writers take the further cover of pseudonyms. She was reading widely – Virgil's *Eclogues* and Ovid (keeping up with Branwell), more Scott and Byron, Edward Young (*The Complaint, or Night Thoughts on Life, Death, and Immortality*), and Cowper (all the Brontës refer to 'The Castaway'), as well as habitual reading of the Bible – but, at this early stage, none of the great women writers came her way. Her father's bookshelves contained no Fanny Burney, no Mary Wollstonecraft, no Mary Shelley, no Jane Austen; nor did she borrow them from the nearest lending library, in Keighley, to which the Brontës were accustomed to walk four miles each way.

In the profusion of stories which Charlotte made into miniature books, every man is plotting, every woman is waiting – adorned with feathers and properly equipped with ivory fans. In a typical poem, 'Long My Anxious Ear Hath Listened', written when Charlotte was fourteen, a woman waits with 'tearful eye' and 'burning heart'. Nature grieves with her: winds, fitful, sigh; birds of ill omen wildly cry. Here, to heavy, hymn-like strains, is the usual image of the lovelorn maiden whom Charlotte would later infuse with a real agony of mind and spirit:

> All my days were days of weeping;
> Thoughts of grim despair were stirred;
> Time in leaden feet seemed creeping;
> Long heart sickness, hope deferred,
> Cankered my heart.

Such women have their glimpse of passion, and then have nothing at all to do but pine: the deserted young innocent, Marian Hume, who turns into a 'blighted lily'; her successor, Mary Percy, who calls herself a 'creeping plant' when she forgives Zamorna his neglect; and his slavish mistress, Mina Laury. A clever, erect army daughter and helpmeet in Zamorna's plots, Mina seems less passive than his weeping wives, but she outdoes them in self-abasement: '. . . I've nothing else to exist for, I've no other interest in life'. Zamorna's pleasure is all she asks.

Obviously, what kept this world going for Charlotte was the erotic charge: the suspense of the women, Zamorna's inflammatory words, and their dazed surrender to him – or to some other overbearing and careless cad. The advantage for Charlotte was that, as each of Zamorna's loves faded, she could call up the next and enjoy, as her heroines on the whole could not, repeat thrills of seduction. The limitations of mixed society in Haworth made her all the more susceptible to magazine codes of sexual behaviour, in particular the 'patient Grizzles': 'I recollect when I was a child getting hold of some antiquated odd volumes and reading them by stealth with the most exquisite pleasure.' One 'black day', when Mr Brontë found her wallowing in 'foolish love-stories', he burnt them – but too late. Charlotte had taken the imprint of this design. Her mistake, understandable in the absence of any domestic model, was to link desire with warped and, for women, futile codes of expression.

Charlotte's gains, then, did not lie in Angria, except for the habit of writing and its professional aspirations. To read through the juvenilia is to marvel less at literary connections than at the amazing leap from these banal romances of the 1830s to the bracing realism of her first mature novel in 1846, narrated in a cool, steady voice far removed from the inflated tones of Angria. When Charlotte left home for school in 1831, her fantasy life was bound to Branwell. Their bond was intense and reciprocal. What changed her, and when did it happen?

One answer is the real passion and pain of Charlotte's encounter with a Brussels teacher, M. Heger, beginning in 1842. A letter to Branwell from Brussels in 1843 shows that even then, at the age of twenty-seven, she still clutched at Angria. But all the while that she lived in Angria, she was struggling against it. This struggle was going on almost from the start of her bond with Branwell. Angria was the wrong world: its sexuality was 'infernal' but irresistible. From thirteen until well into her twenties, she worshipped false idols: women who fawned on men and existed solely as their diversion. Charlotte's more secret plays with Emily and her satires on poetic pretension were the first signs of a time to come when she would leave Branwell in his flaming sunset while she pressed on towards a region of her own.

The sustained self-command to curb banal dreams began, at fourteen and a half, with Charlotte's strenuous efforts at a new school, Roe Head, first as pupil, then as teacher. In place of Zamorna's amours, the long stints at school restored meaning to a pilgrim's progress. Self-command was hard-won, but crucial to the pattern laid down in Charlotte's youth. In these years she veered between the 'burning clime' of her world with Branwell and the model of Maria as she faded in the freezing dormitory, between the drug of dreams and the renewed discipline of school.

Of the four Brontës, it could be said that Anne was the watchful critic, Emily the seeker after divine communion, Branwell the failed leader, and Charlotte the secular pilgrim shaping an exemplary character through knowledge and self-discipline. While the younger two held to their given selves with an uncompromising integrity that excluded the rest of the world, Branwell and Charlotte set up patterns that would propel them into adulthood: Branwell's unfortunate alternation of daring and collapse, Charlotte's of swooning and duty. The discipline of Cowan Bridge, designed to nip a child 'in the bud' (to use Carus Wilson's words) had been destructive – of physical lives, though not the invincible Brontë spirit. At Roe Head, under the benign regime of Miss Wooler, Charlotte began to flourish in a new way. The loss of imaginative space that would be intolerable for her sisters was compensated for Charlotte by a thirst for knowledge.

Roe Head School, at Mirfield, twenty miles south-east of

Haworth, was a spacious oak-panelled house with bay windows and deep window seats. Built before 1740, it stood on high ground in open country not far from the industrial towns of Huddersfield (whose smoke could be seen in the distance), Bradford, and Leeds. Tall, cylindrical chimneys, like round towers, advanced through brown woods. It was a landscape from which trade and machinery had banished seclusion but to Charlotte, at a distance, it looked active and cheerful enough. Most of the pupils at Roe Head came from the immediate region which interested Charlotte as the scene of her father's first Yorkshire ministry and his fights with rioting workers – eventually her setting for *Shirley*. This was an area of mill-owners who had come up in the world and who tended to keep their wealth within the family by intermarriage, as the Nusseys and the Taylors had done in a previous generation, in their small world of Birstall, Gomersal, and Hunsworth. Roe Head School gave Charlotte entrée. At fourteen, she came upon a closed-in society and way of life entirely new to her: a tight network of 'visiting' families, like the Nusseys, with their deeply rooted sense of place. Her schoolmates would have changed their dress three or four times a day in the course of their social rounds. They ridiculed Charlotte, at first, for her odd appearance: her rusty-green dress and crimped hair which set off a thin 'dried in' face. She looked (girls said) like a little old woman when she arrived at school in a covered cart.

The school was run by four Misses Wooler who came from a family of landowning farmers; 'Sister Margaret' was in command. Unlike the plain purposefulness of advanced women in the second half of the nineteenth century, Miss Margaret Wooler, at nearly forty, wore embroidered white dresses – like an abbess, her pupils thought – with hair plaited in a coronet above long ringlets to her shoulders. She was known to give half her income to charity. Her educational emphasis was on health, conduct, and the elevated tone of her favoured *belles lettres*. Later, Charlotte may have drawn on Miss Wooler for portraits of

Frances Henri and Miss Temple as calm heads of orderly unambitious girls' schools. Ambition, space, a future room of one's own, so to speak, was not much talked of in the 1830s. If such a wish existed at all in girls' minds, it lurked in shadow, fearing the stigma of selfishness. For Miss Wooler and her like ran schools for 'ladies', a full generation before Miss Buss and Miss Beale established the first schools in England to open the way for able girls. All Charlotte had at Roe Head was a year and a half to cram all she could of grammar, politeness, French, and geography, underpinned by Mrs Chapone's *Letters on the Improvement of the Mind* (1773) – which, in the 1830s, had to suffice. The very fact that in this brief time she could mop up all the school had to offer, suggests the limitations of Roe Head.

When she arrived at the school in January 1831, she was prodigiously well read but behind in formal subjects like grammar and geography; by the time she left, at the age of sixteen, in June 1832, she was the school's top pupil. Ellen Nussey, there at the time, recalled a Charlotte far from Mrs Gaskell's pathetic image of 'a victim to secret terrors and superstitious fancies': a laughing girl who showed no timidity in the presence of other girls, who was bold, clever, and outspoken. She displayed an exceptional familiarity with Holy Writ, and took particular delight in sublime passages in *Isaiah*. Another fellow-pupil, Mary Taylor, remembered her knowing 'things that were out of our range altogether.'

Her eagerness for learning went cloaked in Miss Wooler's irreproachable maxim to 'bend inclination to your duty'. It was her duty, Charlotte declared, to cover subjects in minimum time because she was an expense to her godmother, Mrs Atkinson, who paid her fees. Rich Mrs Atkinson (née Frances Walker of Lascelles Hall) had offered to send Charlotte to Roe Head where her niece, Amelia Walker, went to school. Mrs Atkinson was the wife of the Vicar of Hartshead whom Mr Brontë had known from the time of his curacy there, and the pair lived only a mile from the school at the Green House, approached by a stone-pillared gate and sweeping drive – the miserable scene, for

Charlotte, of grateful visits. The charitable offer had been made in response to Mr Brontë's severe illness in 1830 when his friends were alerted to the precariousness of his children's position. Charlotte, acutely aware of her responsibilities as the eldest child, told Miss Wooler's pupils that she must use every moment to fit herself to earn her living. But she wanted more than the stock of accomplishments necessary to a future governess. When she was given a book, her shortsighted eyes dived towards it; when she was told to hold up her head, up came the book, close to her nose. Girls like Mary Taylor could not help laughing. Mary remembered that 'she always appeared to be seeking something, and moving her head from side to side to catch sight of it.' At outdoor games, Charlotte could not see the ball; she stood on the sidelines with a book. As evening fell, when the eight or ten boarders chatted around the fire, Charlotte crouched at the window, still working. They asked her if she could see in the dark. 'Her idea of self-improvement ruled her even at school', Mary recalled. 'It was to cultivate her tastes. She always said that there was enough of hard practicality . . . forced on us by necessity, and that the thing most needed was to soften and refine our minds. She picked up every scrap of information concerning painting, sculpture, poetry, music, etc., as if it were gold.'

For a while in the early 1830s, drawing became Charlotte's chief interest as she caught Branwell's new ambition to be an artist. Mr Brontë paid a generous £2 a lesson to the Leeds artist, William Robinson, who taught the Brontës at home. Charlotte would draw for nine hours at a stretch, and if she did not succeed in her own eyes she would burn the result. During the vacation, she asked Ellen Nussey to correspond with her in French – there was one stilted exchange. She redoubled her efforts to enter this language: in 1836 she confessed that if it were not for her reserve, 'I should long ago have been set down by all who knew me as a Frenchified fool.' Overtly, she deprecates her latent, unEnglish expressiveness, but it was one of her first triumphs of deviant character.

When Jane Eyre is allowed to start French, she is charmed to learn the first two tenses of the verb, *Etre*. To be, she learns, is not to suffer in helpless fury, but to direct one's existence. Education counters the maddened imagination of the child-Jane in the fearful Red Room, just as Charlotte's years at Roe Head countered the anarchic world she shared with Branwell. While the favoured Branwell remained at home, blithely unkempt with his wild red hair and racing volubility, Charlotte was earning Miss Wooler's silver badge for correctness of speech and manners. It may have been at this stage that she gave up the 'strong Irish accent' the girls noticed on her arrival at school. Neither in fiction nor in life does the schoolgirl give up the spiritedness of the child, but she gains the means to direct it. Helen Burns' example of the higher courage of restraint is not lost on the wondering Jane who must incorporate her self-command. Jane also learns the graces of order from calm Miss Temple: 'I had imbibed from her something of her nature and much of her habits: more harmonious thoughts, what seemed better regulated feelings had become the inmates of my mind. I had given in allegiance to duty and order'. Our identification with cowed girls at Lowood should not disguise the fact that Charlotte herself took a severe view of the necessity of discipline. When she came to be a governess, she loathed spoilt children. At the end of *The Professor*, Frances Henri decides to send her sensitive son away to school, in full awareness that he will suffer, because she believes that lack of discipline will unfit him for adult life. Charlotte was obviously thinking of Branwell's wildness.

Separated from Branwell, at the age of fourteen, and detached further after 1837–8 when he took to drink and opium, she had to face the loss of her dream-partner. Anne and Emily sufficed to themselves, and neither shared her thirst for learning. She was handicapped, at first, by intense homesickness as a stranger amongst girls whose families were accustomed to wealth and position, and interconnected by a myriad ties of locale and marriage. It is easy to enlarge on the weakness that has won the

hearts of generations of Brontë devotees, but she seized the possibilities within the circumscribed life on offer. She had to push
beyond the paltry limits of girls' education in the 1830s, and studied French not as polite accomplishment, but to extend the
bounds of English. Her strangeness at school, parted for the first
time from all her family, made her weep, but it also introduced
her to other girls of her age, Ellen Nussey and Mary Taylor, who
were to play vital parts in her life.

When Ellen arrived at Roe Head, after 'the half' had started,
she was left downstairs in the schoolroom while the others had
games. Awed by the array of books and the long crimson-
covered table down the centre of the room, Ellen slowly became
aware that she was not alone. In the bay window stood a dark
figure, shrinking to hide her tears. Ellen asked what was the
matter and the girl said she was 'homesick'. When Ellen owned
that she herself might soon be in need of comfort, a faint smile lit
Charlotte's face as the two girls touched hands. Charlotte saw a
pretty girl, a year younger than herself, with brown eyes and
dark soft curls. These fell from a centre parting and clustered
about her eyes and neck, baring her forehead. Ellen remembered that 'Charlotte's appearance did not strike me at first as it
did others. I saw her grief not herself particularly.'

In after years, Charlotte spoke of Ellen as a conventional well-
bred girl. Ellen was the youngest of twelve children and came
from a family which had been for centuries landowners and
Justices of the Peace in the district. They had 'old money' in contrast to the new wealth of Yorkshire manufacturers. The Nusseys
were a respected 'county' family, Conservative in their politics.
When Charlotte was invited to visit the Nusseys at The Rydings,
some ten miles from the school, she saw a castellated hall with a
brook (now obscured by a neon-lit petrol station and almost
swallowed by industrial sprawl). With its large rookery and fine
chestnut trees, one split by storms, The Rydings was to be a
source for Thornfield in *Jane Eyre*: the seat of a well-to-do country gentleman. Branwell, who walked forty miles to visit

Charlotte there, thought his sister had entered into 'paradise'. In fact, the Nusseys were less grand than may have appeared. Ellen's mother was the daughter of a cornmiller; her late father, a cloth manufacturer. Their hold on The Rydings was insecure – they had to leave it in 1837 – and there was not much money. Like Charlotte, Ellen could not expect a marriage portion, or very little.

According to Charlotte, Ellen became her friend because they 'suited', but this underplays Ellen's capacity to share Charlotte's intense life. Charlotte cast her as a 'comforter', calm and steady, but she was more than that. She was 'true' in the Old English sense of the unfeigned, as well as 'true' in a sense which became current in 1839 of remaining constant to type, and she gave Charlotte's unfeigned vehemence an unconditional assent which freed her friend to say what she thought and felt. Ellen's attentive affection always brought Charlotte relief and new life so that, in time, Ellen came to leave 'an uneasy vacuum behind her', as Charlotte put it. 'When you are a little depressed it does you good to look at Ellen and know she loves you. I am not acquainted with anyone whose influence is at once so tranquil and so genial as hers.'

Charlotte's letters to Ellen were no less free than those to her sisters, and more frequent since she and Ellen cultivated the notion they sufficed for each other in a 'nonentity' that defied 'outsiders'. One result of Charlotte's bonding with Branwell, followed by her departure for school, was that she lost Emily – the secret Emily of the 'bed plays' (and it is possible that several of Charlotte's future schemes – her teaching arrangement in 1835 designed to take Emily with her to Roe Head, her venture abroad with Emily in 1842, her determination in 1845 to publish Emily's poems together with her own – were all attempts to recover a lost closeness). Her union with Ellen was, in part, a match for that of Emily and Anne who would stand with arms interlaced, 'like twins' said Ellen, inseparable companions in the very closest sympathy which never had any interruption.

From the time of Ellen's first visit to Haworth, in the summer of 1833, Emily (aged fifteen) and Anne (aged thirteen) were unusually at ease with her which, given their mutual reserve, Emily's indifference whether she pleased or not, and Anne's shyness, suggests again that Ellen was not entirely conventional. She saw that though Emily's reserve seemed impenetrable, she was 'intensely lovable' as she looked and smiled simultaneously, a curiously intent gaze: '. . . One of her rare expressive looks was something to remember through life, there was such a *depth* of soul and feeling, and yet shyness of revealing herself, a strength of self-containment seen in no other.' She seemed to Ellen to invite confidence in moral power. This coexisted with the mischievous child out on the moors. Tall, long-armed, more fully grown than her elder sister, Emily would lead the short-sighted Charlotte, who was afraid of animals, close to one, and break out laughing at her terror. By the age of fifteen Emily was free of Aunt's room, while Anne was subject, still, to the sewing regime.

Ellen had the readiness, social ease, and sense of character to look past superficial eccentricities, and the sisters did not hesitate to include her in their nightly confidences. Ellen and Charlotte introduced the two younger girls to Miss Wooler's habit of strolling up and down, arm-in-arm with her pupils, after her day's work. The four would pace around the dining-room table, in two pairs, Emily and Anne, Charlotte and Ellen, with arms about each other's waists. Though not creative, Ellen did not jar their private world, and if we recall how very easily the Brontës were jarred by other contacts, this in itself was no mean achievement.

Later, Ellen was convinced that Emily's characters in *Wuthering Heights* derived from weird stories which Mr Brontë used to tell with gusto of some of the old inhabitants in out-of-the-way places over the moors: '– I used to shudder at his recitals, & I can see his eyes now as they gleamed at my . . . blanched look for I was frightened in my innocence & ignorance of such beings as he described – these stories were always given in *early* days as we sat round the breakfast or tea-table in his study when Miss Branwell presided . . .' Unlike Ellen, the Brontës heard these stories with grim humour.

Mary Taylor (sometimes called Pag or Polly) had nothing of Ellen's considerate empathy: she was forthright and tactless. At Roe Head she told Charlotte she was very ugly. Later, when Mary apologised, Charlotte said, 'Polly, you did me good.' It took Mary's bluntness to shake the dreams of lovelorn Beauty. When Charlotte told Mary how she used to stand on a stone in the burn at Cowan Bridge, watching the water as it flowed, Mary said, 'you should have fished!' When Charlotte confessed to 'making out', and described the miniature booklets she and the others wrote for themselves alone, Mary retorted, 'it's like growing potatoes in the cellar!' They astonished each other with every exchange.

Mary had no time for impractical maundering; her no-nonsense manner came from her Dissenting family. Though Mary was connected with Ellen through marriage, the Taylors (with heads in books) kept more to themselves than the Nusseys, and the two families could not have been further apart politically. Mary, like her father, was alert to social injustice. The Taylors lived three and a half miles from the Nusseys, in the Red House at Gomersal, built in 1660 by one William Taylor. Later, Charlotte immortalised the house as Briarmains in *Shirley*. It was built of red brick and, downstairs, in the hall and drawing-room, statues from Italy stood in alcoves. Mr Taylor, whose business took him to the Continent, spoke fluent Italian and French, and when Charlotte was older, he lent her the novels of George Sand. She was intrigued by Mr Taylor's unusual combination of Yorkshire bluntness and European culture which, later, she recreated in the ambiguous figure of Mr Hunsden in *The Professor*. A manufacturer of army cloth and also a banker, Mr Taylor gave up banking when he lost money, and set his mind on paying all his creditors, which he continued to do until his death in 1841. According to his will, his sons were to complete this task, and two of them did so. Charlotte would describe the Taylors (with fidelity, said Mary) as the Yorkes in *Shirley*: 'Yorkshire has such families here and there amongst her hills and wolds – peculiar, racy, vigorous; of good blood and strong brain; turbulent some-what in the pride of their strength, and intractable in the force of their native powers; wanting polish, wanting consideration, wanting docility, but sound, spirited, and true-bred as the eagle on the cliff or the steed in the steppe.'

Mary's independence, her bracing honesty, and her deter-mination to survive without concession to artifice were traits derived from her father, a man of sagacity who could bear no control. In this, Charlotte thought him 'thoroughly English' with no sign of Norman ancestry. Mary was shrewd and obser-vant, a girl who knew more of the world and who could gratify her friend's curiosity. She liked to inform, Charlotte to analyse and question: they were, in this way, complementary. Mary's retorts were provocative, not hurtful. Girls in their teens often damage one another with an insidious meanness designed to subdue the more original of their sex to the norms of the small-est minds. Mary's words had the opposite effect: they were a spur to thought. Though her Radicalism, like her practicality, struck sparks, she invited energy, not submission. And whatever challenges she might have thrown, she was drawn to the creative spark of the Brontës, not least the dramatic Branwell. Her frank-ness about this provoked Branwell's contempt, and Charlotte concluded that a woman could not afford to confess her feelings. Like Charlotte, Mary did not expect to marry and had the back-ing of her father who urged her never to marry for security or position.

Mary was not talkative. When she appeared at the school in her reddish dress with short sleeves and a scoop neck in the style worn by girls at the time, Miss Wooler thought her 'too pretty to live', but soon found she was up against a stubborn character who was impervious to rebuke. When Charlotte and Mary com-pleted the school's limited curriculum, Miss Wooler set them to learn Blair's *Belles Lettres* by heart. Charlotte persevered, but Mary refused this barren exercise. She was prepared to accept the punishment of going to bed without supper every night for a month rather than capitulate, and she did this imperturbably, as Ellen recalled: 'When it was moonlight, we always found her engaged in drawing on the chest of drawers, which stood in the bay window, quite happy and cheerful. Her rebellion was never outspoken.' Neither did she seem to mind that she and her sister, Martha, were not dressed as well as other girls. Their dark blue coats were too short and their black beaver bonnets were plain, but they wore them contentedly. What really concerned Mary was how to break out of the constriction of women's lives. Later, Charlotte recalled her in Rose Yorke, aged twelve, sitting on the floor beside a bookcase, her mouth moving as she reads *The Italian* (1797) by Ann Radcliffe, a book which makes her long to travel: 'First this hemisphere where we live; then the other. I am resolved that my life shall be a life: not a black trance like the toad's . . .' She sees women buried in houses like windowed graves. She is a girl who feels 'monotony and death to be almost the same.' It seems to her preferable to try all things and find them empty, than to try nothing and leave life a blank.

A sequel to Charlotte's fictional portrait of the defiant Rose Yorke is Mary's fictional portrait of Dora in her polemical novel, *Miss Miles, or A Tale of Yorkshire Life Sixty Years Ago* (1890). Dora's servile position in the shadow of her oblivious stepfather consigns her to a dependent death-in-life until she begins to earn her living as a public speaker with a covert feminist message. The following private exchange between Dora and a friend, Maria Bell, who earns her living as a teacher, suggests the subversive tie that developed between Mary and Charlotte:

'Maria,' said the girl [Dora], 'if people knew that the women in the churchyards were alive – those in the coffins I mean – and were waiting for us to dig them up, do you think anyone would do it?'

'Dora do be quiet!'

'Answer!'

'Well, of course they would.'

'No, they would not! They would say ladies did not want to
get up – that they had all they wanted, and that men did not
like them to get out of their graves.'

Mary first mentioned this novel in a letter to her friend after
the publication of *Shirley*, Charlotte's most feminist novel. What
did Charlotte write in her many letters to Mary, nearly all of
which Mary destroyed as dangers to Charlotte's reputation? Did
she meet Mary's daring with a strong voice of her own, as, in a
sense, their feminist novels still speak to each other?

Mary was 'nearly as mad as myself', Charlotte said in 1836.
When she drew Mary as Rose Yorke, she saw her 'thick sown
with the germs of ideas her mother never knew. It is agony to
her often to have these ideas trampled on and repressed' by a
mother who would make her a woman of dreary duties. Sparks
of intelligence flashed from her glance, and gleamed in her language. Where her younger sister, Martha, had the piquancy and
prattle that appealed to men, Mary had 'a fine, generous soul, a
noble intellect profoundly cultivated, a heart as true as steel.'
Though she was better-looking than her sister, she did not have
the manner to attract, and this was part of her honesty.

Mary's 'madness' and her withdrawal from the ploys of charm
fitted the honesty of the Brontës – particularly the more intransigent younger sisters. Ellen said that Charlotte's sense of
difference did not derive from shyness or vanity, but from the
fact that she could not hope to be understood. Even her appearance was against this: she looked small and young for her years.
Once, when she returned to school from a visit to her father's
friend, Mrs Franks (née Miss Firth), she complained that she had
been babied: 'one tall lady *would* nurse me.' Another time, at a
Sunday-school party at the Parsonage, Ellen witnessed the sisters'
attempt to play games suggested by other young women. The

Brontë faces were puzzled and submissive, but studious to please their guests. Ellen was struck by the contrast between the sisters' constraint with strangers and their 'entire unconventionality' on their own.

Mary's independence and Ellen's insight shaped Charlotte from the age of fifteen, an alternative group to sisters and a channel for social and economic attitudes beyond the scope of the Parsonage. Ellen was Charlotte's prime confidante, as well as her adviser in matters of taste. Later, when Charlotte became a celebrated author and succumbed eventually to invitations to visit London, it was Ellen to whom she wrote for advice on appearance. Could Ellen procure a plait of brown hair to shape a fashionable coronet? Alas, it did not quite match her own hair, and a brown silk ribbon had to do for evening parties. (In the event some London ladies sneered at the contrivance.) The three friends were separated for stretches of their lives, but they always wrote to one another, letters which sift character and debate possibilities open to women of their time. Though Charlotte and Mary corresponded about politics (the Reform Bill, say, on which they took opposite sides), they were not bent on usual forms of political action. Where Mary concerned herself with rights for women to work in other than menial positions, Charlotte concerned herself with states of mind – the images of womanhood which were, in their way, more deeply enslaving than absent rights. Her art was based on her own character and those of her sisters and friends: familiar women in their retiring habits and mutual support, but all the same a new breed, crawling out from under the stone of history and coming together in the early 1830s, just before the start of the suffrage agitation that would bring women to the surface of public life.

3

EGYPT AND THE PROMISED LAND

'At 19 I should have been thankful for an allowance of a 1d a week. I asked my father, but he said what did a woman want with money?'

Between the age of nineteen and twenty-five, Charlotte Brontë set out to earn her living as teacher and governess. She shared with Mary a covert wish for economic independence, unusual in their generation, which she presented in terms of the obligatory mode of selfless obedience: 'I am sad, very sad at the thought of leaving home but Duty – Necessity – these are stern mistresses who will not be disobeyed.'

In July 1835 Charlotte was preparing to return to Roe Head as a teacher. For three happy years, from the summer of 1832 to 1835, she had taught her sisters at home, with particular success in her favourite subject, French, for later, Emily's French was good enough to benefit from advanced study abroad. Mr Brontë bought a piano for his daughters: Anne learnt songs, while Emily took the lead with precision and brilliancy. Now, with the expense ahead of Branwell's training as an artist, Charlotte resolved to do what she could for Emily who was turning seventeen. Teaching would cover the cost of Emily's education; at the same time, Emily, prised loose from Anne, would bond with her at Roe Head.

So, on 29 July, two sisters emerged again from the Parsonage into what Mr Brontë called 'this delusive and ensnaring world'.

No one in 'this land of probation', he warned as they left, 'could lie beyond the reach of temptation.'

These were rather odd fears for two young women going to Miss Wooler's safe school where Charlotte taught grammar to 'dolts', and Emily, waking each morning to thoughts of home and moor, forced herself through another day of wretched longing. Mr Brontë's pious warning showed no awareness of the real dangers to his daughters, deathly homesickness for Emily, dispiriting grind for Charlotte, but his distrust of 'the world' did fit their aversion as they nerved themselves to enter it. Mrs Gaskell contrasts 'that happy home circle in which alone their natures expanded; amongst all other people they shrivelled up more or less.' Emily lasted three months. Silent, tall, and one of the oldest girls in the school, she had little or nothing of Charlotte's hunger for knowledge, nor Charlotte's gift for friendship. At Roe Head she starved to a point when Charlotte became afraid she would die. By mid-October a pale, wasted Emily was back at Haworth.

'Liberty', Charlotte explained, 'was the breath of Emily's nostrils. Without it, she perished. The change from her own home to a school, and from her own very noiseless, very secluded but unrestrained and inartificial mode of life, to one of disciplined routine (though under the kindest auspices) was what she failed in enduring. Her nature proved here too strong for her fortitude.'

Anne, at nearly sixteen, dispatched in place of Emily, managed to hold on for two years, from the end of 1835 till the end of 1837, before she, too, collapsed. Where Charlotte had an explanation for Emily's collapse, she had none for Anne, and the most obvious reason is that Charlotte had less sympathy for her youngest sister. They competed for Emily; and Anne, who was a much stronger character than she appeared, did not make way for Charlotte. In return, Charlotte ignored Anne during her two years at Roe Head; she would not allow the presence of this quietly ambitious, observant, and deep sister to alleviate her scorn for the mental shallowness of everyone else. Scorn warped her to the point of hatred, too obsessed with her own emotions to think of her sister who would have been separated in any case by the distance of teacher from pupil. The pairings of Charlotte and Branwell, Anne and Emily, seem inflexible at this stage. Charlotte's letters and scraps of writing between 1835 and 1837 show that she never invited Anne to join in the Angrian dream; nor did she ever, for a moment, consider their opportunity to shape a drama of their own. When Anne eventually fell ill in the autumn of 1837, Miss Wooler thought it no more than a cold; Charlotte, waking suddenly to danger, blazed at Miss Wooler in protective fury. She could not forget Maria and Elizabeth. In a sense, those deaths set up a resistance to the outside world in all the sisters, and a recurrent pattern of venture and collapse. Miss Wooler, shocked by Charlotte's accusations, wrote at once to Mr Brontë, and Anne, too, went home.

All this time, Charlotte was confronting a different problem: acute constriction of mental space. Forty years later, she might have had access to higher education, but in the 1830s colleges and universities had not yet opened their doors to women. With the advantage of hindsight, George Eliot, writing in 1871–2, places her intellectual heroine, Dorothea, in precisely this period – the early 1830s – a period with as yet no public awareness of the intellectual needs of women, particularly women in provincial backwaters, whose aspirations came into conflict with obstructive custom and meanness of opportunity. It is easy to groan over women's lives; Charlotte herself groaned incessantly – and can we blame her? Yet, unlike Dorothea, unlike Maggie Tulliver, unlike all those duty-bound Victorian women, Charlotte Brontë did not fail to develop her gifts. Constricted as she was in her early twenties, depressed, sometimes 'mad', it was in fact during this unpromising time, between 1835 and 1841, that she invented the central character and exercised the voice of the novels to come.

It was not a thought-out enterprise; it happened in the way it so often happened for women: inadvertently, in the corners of life, under cover of night, on scraps of paper, in the course of a letter. She craved guidance, but was rebuffed by celebrities to whom she wrote. Still in thrall to society fiction, she did not at once direct her spurts of daring. They scattered here and there, amidst the salons of Angria and soggy, self-pitying poems. But to sift the treasure from the dross is to see the extraordinary promise hidden in the shadow of her prison.

Enlightened, for her time, as Miss Wooler may have been about the needs of pupils, she did not consider those of a young teacher who was expected to be on duty at all times, including weekends. During her first 'half', Charlotte once forgot herself, 'quite gone' as she dreamt of Zamorna dismounting from his black horse, with the African sky above him 'quivering and shaking with stars' and blotting out the dull day of the Roe Head classroom.

'Miss Brontë, what are you thinking about?' said a voice, and Miss Lister thrust her little rough head into her teacher's face.

Her only freedom from pupils was a short spell in the early evening while they did their homework. As darkness fell, Charlotte would lie on her bed in the empty dormitory and release her imagination – as she describes in a journal fragment of February 1836. She notes the time: 7 pm.

> I now assume my own thoughts; my mind relaxes from the stretch on which it has been for the last twelve hours, and falls back onto the rest which nobody in this house knows but myself. I now, after a day of weary wandering, return to the ark which for me floats alone on the billows of this world's desolate and boundless deluge.

It often happened that she had wandered too far to recover the ark, and at such times she would subside into gloom – a mood that deepened, slowly, into depression. To Ellen and Mary, alone, Charlotte confided her frustration; and she expressed it with abandon in her 'Roe Head Journal': 'Must I from day to day sit chained to this chair prisoned within these four bare walls, while these glorious summer suns are burning . . .' It was in these autobiographical fragments that we first hear the vehement voice of Jane Eyre when she says: '. . . I shall be called discontented. I could not help it: the restlessness was in my nature; it agitated me to pain sometimes.' Only when Jane is alone can she open her inward ear to a tale that never ends – a tale her imagination creates – 'quickened with all of incident, life, fire, feeling, that I desired and had not in my actual existence.' The source of Jane's outburst lies in a few disconnected scraps – rather different from the formal 'booklets'. But without the bursts of fury and determination kept alive in her 'Journal', imagination might have atrophied and spirit frozen. Collectively, the 'Journal' is a series of explosive ventures to repossess the unseen space.

The Brontës had in common their commitment to what was natural and roaming in their childhood selves: in so far as the duties of adulthood forced them to relinquish those selves, to mask them with proprieties, to waste their energies in teaching (for which none of them had the slightest vocation), and in Branwell's case to advance manly fashion into the great world, they shrivelled – with the exception, in adulthood, of Anne whose ambition was cooler than Charlotte's and more contained. Of the four Brontës, she was the only one who, in time, could bear long periods, without complaint, in uncongenial society. Her judgements, severe and caustic though they were, did not shake her mind. She shared Emily's detachment, but was able to disguise it, and better, make use of it for social observation.

Though Charlotte held out longer than Anne at Roe Head, she was in a bad way nearly all the time, despite Miss Wooler's affection for her and her friends' concern. From the start, she allowed her complaints to sap her energy and erode her morale. So long as Charlotte had been a pupil, her prime concern had been to feed her mind. Now, as teacher, she came up against the vacuousness of the feminine mould. In none of her pupils could she see any promise. It is unlikely that the school was totally devoid of interest – Anne, if no one else, was there for two out of three years. More likely, Charlotte's scorn for her pupils came from not doing as she wished. Yet not to do as you wished, to put others before yourself, was the essence of Christian morality. To prefer to write would have appeared to her a selfish whim.

Occasionally, she visited the Red House at Gomersal. Mary demanded to know, in her blunt way, why Charlotte went on teaching when she was paid so little that all she could do was clothe herself and Anne. Charlotte said there was nothing else to do.

Mary was becoming aware that there was no chance of work in England in which a woman would not be subordinate and underpaid. Amongst the opportunities for women to work in mines, as factory hands, milliners, domestics, or teachers, it struck Mary that it would be healthiest to be a washerwoman but, for that, pay was below subsistence. Her observations revived the revolutionary protest of Mary Wollstonecraft who said in 1787: 'few are the modes of earning a subsistence and those very humiliating.' Later, Mary went on to challenge the economic position of women in a series of articles written for the *Victoria Magazine* in 1865–70 (and collected in 1870 as *The First Duty of Women*). Their first duty was to provide for themselves, even though they were told that their main business was to influence others. 'How do they make a business of it?' Mary demanded. 'What time does it begin in the morning? And how do they fill, say a few hours every day in the doing of it?' In the same scornful tone, she attacked feminine helplessness, so charming in young girls, as a trait that wore badly with the passage of years, and mocked the current definition of woman as 'a creature who likes self-sacrifice'. Again, her novel argued the futility of women in her own generation. Since her correspondence with Charlotte was destroyed, we must have recourse to Mary's books for the economic concerns she would have shared with Charlotte as two women determined to earn their livings at a time when it was still rare for middle-class women to do so. Survival through work – work which did not kill the spirit – was a central issue in their lives, as it was not for Ellen who was close to Charlotte in a different way through her understanding of mood and character. Of this, there is ample evidence, but what did Mary and Charlotte say to each other when they were alone?

Mary deliberately curtailed what she told Mrs Gaskell after Charlotte's death, aware that there were things that could not be said in the 1850s, things that would damage, further, her friend's reputation as unladylike rebel, things that would counter the model of duty. In her novel she was free to demonstrate the case of Dora who, as despised dependant of her stepfather, becomes a non-person, sinking for a while out of sight. Then there is the case of Amelia Turner whose family will not allow her to work when her mill-owning father fails. To work would be to 'insult' her father. So Amelia becomes a grey-faced invalid. '. . . I am in prison,' she owns, 'I can do nothing.' Even for the independent teacher, Maria Bell, there is not always work to be had. The industrial system has highs and lows: in hard times, Maria's school dwindles. As a working woman who cannot afford fashion, she is shunned by women of her own middle class, and her life is solitary. The happiest lot falls to Sarah Miles, the woman most like Mary Taylor, whose Dissenting background gives her strength and voice. She looks 'longingly at the horizon' wondering 'whether there was another kind of people over there, and if she could become a denizen among them.' This is surely what Charlotte shared with Mary: her women, too, gaze at the horizon, longing to break out of an enclosed existence.

When Charlotte confessed the failure of even a benign headmistress to give her a reasonable income, Mary diagnosed the danger of self-sacrifice. She recognised in self-sacrifice a warping substitute for useful action when she said that Charlotte 'seemed to have no interest or pleasure beyond the feeling of duty.'

Certainly, she had rectitude. Aunt and Papa had counselled her to avoid the temptations of free will. This led to a double life, conscious as she was of the tug between duty and dreaming, conscious of the dwindling space in which to exercise her imagination, conscious too of her secret difference from the propriety a teacher was expected to exemplify, and of an uncrossable gap between this secret self and the twaddle of mindless girls.

'If you knew my thoughts', she confessed to Ellen, 'the dreams that absorb me; and the fiery imagination that at times eats me up and makes me feel Society as it is, wretchedly insipid, you would pity and I dare say despise me.'

Throughout the three years at Roe Head, a divide remained between teaching and the craving to write. In the fastness of her mind, and in the privacy of letters and journal, she flayed her pupils as the enemy. 'Dolts' intrude on her thoughts. Their stolid incomprehension saps her spirit. The journal explodes over girls who stare at her with dropped jaws as she writes with eyes closed. Her eyes were shut to close off blank faces and hold thoughts intact against impinging norms:

I am just going to write because I cannot help it. Wiggins [Branwell] might indeed talk of scriblomania if he were to see me just now encompassed by the bulls . . . all wondering why I write with my eyes shut – staring, gaping long their astonishment. E. Cook on one side of me E. Lister on the other and Miss W[oole]r in the background. Stupidity the atmosphere, school-books the employment, asses the society. What in all this is there to remind me of the divine, silent, unseen land of thought, dim now and indefinite as the dream of a dream, the shadow of a shade.

On the same fragment as the 'unseen land of thought', a poem examines the aims and dangers of mental exploration, using the dream of the lower waters in a way that prefigures Virginia Woolf:

> Look into thought & say what dost thou see
> Dive, be not fearful how dark the waves flow
> Sink through the surge & bring pearls up to me
> Deeper aye deeper, the fairest lie low
>
> I have dived I have sought them but none have I found
> In the gloom that closed over me no[ne] flowed by
> As I sunk through the void depths so black & profound
> How dim died the sun & how far hung the sky
>
> What had I given to hear the soft sweep
> Of a breeze bearing life through this vast realm of death
> Thoughts were untroubled & dreams were asleep
> The spirit lay dreadless & hopeless beneath.

Years later, in *Villette*, Charlotte would re-explore the strangeness of living between the surface deadness of a school and the dark sea of the interior world which could wreck the restless spirit. Here, the gloom induced by the deathly 'realm' (of Roe Head) seems to enclose the diver and preclude discovery.

There were times when it seemed to Charlotte that a 'voice' woke a dormant power that could 'smite torpidity I sometimes think dead'. As evening fell it came to her 'like a breeze with a voice in it', awakening sensations which often lay dormant beyond 'Haworth & home'. It seems as though a creative impulse would come like grace from on high, like a divine call to prophecy – but, as yet, she had nothing to say beyond the banalities of romantic dreams. Another fragment recounts the triumph of torpor:

> All this day I have been in a dream half-miserable & half ecstatic[,] miserable because I could not follow it out uninterruptedly, ecstatic because it showed almost in the vivid light of reality the ongoings of the infernal world [Angria]. I had been toiling for nearly an hour with Miss Lister, Miss

Marriott*, and Ellen Cook striving to teach them the distinction between an article and a substantive. The parsing lesson was completed, a dead silence had succeeded it in the schoolroom & I sat sinking from irritation & weariness into a kind of lethargy.

Her lethargy then deepened into heavy depression over a wilful pupil during French: a 'violent' irritation seized her which she tried to subdue, though her fingers trembled 'as if I had had twenty-four hours of tooth-ache & my spirit felt heavy to a desperate degree of despondency.' After tea that day, she had to take a long walk, and came back exhausted from the 'vulgar familiar trash' of Miss Lister and Miss Marriott. 'If those girls knew how I loathed their company they would not seek mine as they do.' She could not conceal her depression from Miss Wooler who tried to get her to talk, but she could not rouse herself.

Charlotte's 'infernal' dreams and Miss Wooler's mild concern had its comic side. One evening, when her pupils were in bed and Charlotte had the dining-room to herself, she began an erotic dream of a swarthy moor called Quashia, an African portent of Heathcliffian ferocity. There he was, asleep on a disordered couch, his athletic limbs stretched out, his brown chest heaving wildly through the more than half-unbuttoned waistcoat, his hair dishevelled on his forehead, his teeth glancing through parted lips, his breath snorting tempestuously from distended nostrils, when the door of the dining-room opened 'and Miss Wooler came in with a plate of butter in her hand.

"A very stormy night, my dear!" said she.

"It is, ma'am," said I.'

Kind Miss Wooler! She had not the remotest idea of the wild thrills of Africa.

---

* The Marriott family owned the land on which the school was built. The Misses Wooler were therefore tenants of the Marriotts.

Later, Charlotte spoke of her depression at Roe Head as 'a continual waking Nightmare', part of the horror of which was knowing what a burden she was to others.

'I could have been no better company for you than a stalking ghost', she apologised later to Miss Wooler.

While 'the ladies' (as the girls were called) went to the schoolroom to do homework, the ghost crept up to the dormitory to be alone for the first time that day. She lay on the bed, and drank in delicious solitude. 'The stream of thought checked all day came flowing free and calm along its channel. My ideas were too shattered to form any definite pictures as they would have done in such circumstances at home.'

One such time, as she lay in a trance on her bed, the ladies came to get their curlpapers. Jolted by voices talking of her, the weirdness of her ghostly transit between two worlds struck her with anguish. To which world did she belong? In the absence of Branwell and her sisters, the erotic dream life appeared 'infernal'. Yet the alternative, the curlpapers, was worthless artifice. Was she to belong nowhere? Her memory of this moment formed the basis for scenes in two future fictions in which a young woman in a girls' school is perceived, and perceives herself, to be apart and other: Miss Hall in 'Ashworth' (1839–41) and the heroine of Charlotte Brontë's last, unfinished work, 'Emma' (1853). Here is the autobiographical source, written when Charlotte was twenty, amongst the Roe Head fragments:

> . . . I wanted to speak, to rise – it was impossible – I felt that this was a frightful predicament – that it would not do. The weight pressed me as if some huge enemy had flung itself across me. A horrid apprehension quickened every pulse I had. I must get up I thought & I did so with a start. I have had enough of morbidly vivid realizations. Every advantage has its corresponding disadvantage . . . . Miss Wooler is impatient.

> October 14th 1836

The writing at the end of the fragrnent is misaligned as though Charlotte were scribbling in the dark.

Once, in the schoolroom, the spirit of all Angria crowded out the sight of girls. A creative moment rushed upon her, a sense that she might write better than she had ever done before. 'But just then a dolt came up with a lesson. I thought I could have vomited.'

The Roe Head fragments provide some access to the sources of her creativity. The less interesting fragments are those which record a degree of success when Angrian characters move towards Charlotte with ready ease – at such times the journal sweeps into the fictional routines she had practised at home. There is this backward yearning when she sits down, deliberately, to call up spirits from 'the vasty deep'* and hold half an hour's converse with them: 'Hush! there's a knock at the gates of thought and memory ushers in the visitors. The visitors! there's only one: a tall gentleman with a presence . . .' The figment sits down opposite and looks at her fixedly with blue menacing eyes. She starts to converse with him – he brings news that the Angrians are fighting still. And so she glides into Angria, a patrician society of 'darlings of fame' and 'monarchs of mind'. It is as though the figures move forward into her line of vision and then, as they come closer, she hears them speak: 'I hear them speak as well as [Lady Amelia] does. I see distinctly their figures – and[,] though alone[,] I experience all the feelings of one admitted for the first time into a grand circle of classic beings – recognizing by tone, gesture and aspect hundreds who I never saw before, but whom I have heard of and read of many a time . . . I know nothing of people of rank & distinction, yet there they are before me in throngs . . .' It is as banal as any adolescent dream.

The striking fragments are when struggle persists and becomes her subject: it is here the crucial voice breaks through,

* Shakespeare: 'I can call Spirits from the vastie Deepe' (*Henry IV*, Part I: III, i).

not the imitative sentiments of Angrian romance, but the restless fury that seems to take Charlotte to that psychic edge of the woman apart and alone, forcing the young writer to confront that condition which, later, her novels would explore with such boldness. In one fragment, probably composed in May 1837, the Angrian throng is eclipsed by the appearance of a new kind of woman. As she crosses the room, the writer has a glimpse of a woman free of artifice. Her grace is not calculated; it is 'unstudied, prompt & natural'. Her clear utterance is rapid and rather abrupt – different from the low, subdued melody of society ladies – and her manner seems to blend the standard image of Angrian beauty with the animation of a woman like Charlotte and the quiet calibre of Anne Brontë who was sitting before her in the schoolroom as she wrote:

> The quick glances of her eye indicating a warm & excitable temperament the mingled expression of good nature & pride, spirit & kind-heartedness predominating in every feature, all these are as clearly before me as Ann[e]'s quiet image, sitting at her lessons, on the opposite side of the table –

Recollection of her room at the Parsonage, with its narrow bed and bare, whitewashed walls, was another entrée to the dream, restoring a past in which dreams came with spontaneous ease: 'Remembrance yields up many a fragment of past twilight hours – spent in that little unfurnished room – There have I sat on the low bed-stead my eyes fixed on the window, through which appeared no other landscape than a monotonous stretch of moorland, a grey church tower, rising from the centre of a church-yard so filled with graves, that the rank-weed & coarse grass scarce had room to shoot up between the monuments. Over these hangs in the eye of memory a sky of such grey clouds as often veil the chill close of an October day . . .'

Often, this scene failed to induce the dreaming mood as she sat in the schoolroom or lay in the dormitory. The wind emphasised her exile when it deepened its tone as the night advanced, 'coming not in gusts, but with a rapid gathering stormy swell, that wind I know is heard at this moment far away on the moors at Haworth. Branwell & Emily hear it and as it sweeps over our house down the churchyard & round the old church, they think perhaps of me & Anne'.

The dismay of Charlotte and Anne may be imagined when they received an invitation from Mrs Franks (pious, hospitable Elizabeth Firth of Thornton to whom Mr Brontë had proposed soon after the death of his wife). She now lived with her husband in Huddersfield, three miles from Roe Head, and expected to have the sisters for a week of their precious vacation in June 1836. They concocted a polite reply to the effect that Papa could not possibly spare them for more than a weekend after their long absence from home. Then Papa let it be known to Mrs Franks that he would gladly spare them:

My Dear Madam,

My dear little Charlotte has informed me that you and Mr Franks have been so kind as to invite her and Anne to pay you a visit for a week, but that through impatience, as is very natural, they have curtailed this invitation to a few days. I have written to them to countermand this intention. I esteem it as a high privilege that they should be under your roof for a time, where, I am sure, they will see and hear nothing but what, under providence, must necessarily tend to their best interest in both the worlds . . .

On Mrs Franks' wedding tour in 1824 she had visited the ill-fed, sickening children at The Clergy Daughters' School, but had seen nothing to disturb her. It is unlikely that Charlotte would have forgotten this. The resistance of the sisters to her invitation in 1836 suggests that Mrs Franks was not a woman to pass through their barrier of shyness. She must have been one of numerous benevolent matrons who performed their acts of charity with a rectitude that was an end in itself.

When the sisters arrived on the five o'clock coach at Huddersfield Vicarage, they found Mrs Franks' grand relations from Lascelles Hall, including Amelia Walker. Amelia, once a schoolmate, now moved, as Victorians put it, in another sphere. Charlotte and Anne were granted this opportunity to mix with their betters.

'They were wondrously gracious', Charlotte relayed to Ellen. 'Amelia was almost enthusiastic in her professions of friendship; she is taller, thinner, paler, and more delicate-looking than she used to be, very pretty still; very lady-like and polished, but spoilt, utterly spoilt by the most hideous affectation.'

Her scorn was partly for her own dreams of high life. On the following Tuesday, the sisters visited Amelia at Lascelles Hall, an eighteenth-century stately home, two miles from Huddersfield. Charlotte reported further to Ellen: 'Miss Amelia changed her character every half-hour; now she assumed the sweet sentimentalist, now the reckless rattler. Sometimes the question was "Shall I look prettiest lofty?" and again "Would not tender familiarity suit me better?" At one moment she affected to enquire after her old school-acquaintances, the next she was detailing anecdotes of high life.' Amelia was to provide a source for the snobbish Amelia De Capell in 'Ashworth' (1839–41) and for the shallow artifice of Ginevra Fanshawe in *Villette* (1853).

Charlotte's scorn for the spoilt lady, her impulse to retch at the sight of a pupil and, above all, the unstilled craving to write, made her fear that she might appear mad. There were times when she could not sleep or even attend. She labelled her condition religious melancholy. As such, the agonised cry, the longing, the self-doubt, were communicable and, to Victorians, eminently acceptable. Protestantism (as Jane Eyre would assert to Rochester) licensed equality: souls were equal before God, and could make equal claims to the suffering that proclaims – even in the severe discourse of self-abnegation – a sense of identity. When Charlotte appeared to have a religious crisis in 1836, she had no other terms in which to express her unused life.

'I am a very coarse, commonplace wretch', she told Ellen. 'I have some qualities which make me very miserable, some feelings what you can have no participation in, that few, very few people in the world can at all understand. I don't pride myself on these peculiarities, I strive to conceal and suppress them as much as I can, but they burst out sometimes and then those who see the explosion despise me, and I hate myself for days afterwards.'

While in part she exulted in the creative impulse she called 'divine', she saw a certain kind of dreaming as her vice. These fantasies played out the emotional and sexual desperation of women who acknowledge desires which they cannot fulfil in their own way: a powerful man like Zamorna seems to inflame but not satisfy their needs by his abrupt, controlling embraces and indifference to the character and feeling that are part of his lovers' desires – abject, abandoned desires. Charlotte's awakening passions left her 'polluted' – she tried out this word on Ellen. 'I abhor myself – I despise myself – if the Doctrine of Calvin be true I am already an outcast – you cannot imagine how . . . intractable all my feelings are –'.

It helped to see Ellen as well-bred and conventional, for then, if Ellen accepted her, she was not so deviant as she feared. Ellen's responsiveness was her support. It was more than 'suiting' each other; Charlotte poured out her grateful love: 'I wish I could see you my darling, I have lavished the warmest affections of a very hot tenacious heart upon you – if you grow cold – it's over –'.

In December 1836, we glimpse the end of a 'half' at Roe Head: Charlotte mending Miss Lister's clothes before she packs them, the 'terrible fag' of Geographical Problems, and Miss Wooler's voice, interrupting Charlotte's letter to Ellen, calling something about a girl's nightcaps. For Charlotte to escape the minutiae of school into the reaches of her imagination was to be tempted by the 'infernal world' of passion – taboo for middle-class women who wished to be thought refined, and even more taboo for the clergyman's daughter who had been brought up to an awareness of the higher virtue of self-denial. Part of the shock of *Jane Eyre*,

when it burst on the Victorian scene in 1847, was the unmistakable pulse of passion. Could this be a *woman*'s voice, reviewers
wondered. They could hardly credit it.

If passion was 'infernal', it is not surprising that Charlotte
should have desired, or told herself that she desired, purity. She
talked of the 'Well of Life in all its cleanness'; she said: 'I know the
greatness of Jehovah . . . I adore the purity of the Christian faith'.
But she could not transcend the 'infernal world'. Her heart was
'corrupt', she cried to Ellen on 6 December 1836, 'cold to the spirit
and warm to the flesh'. She wept at the contrast of Maria's perfect
self-denial with her own uncertainty if she had ever felt true contrition. The seeker after grace, her father preached, would not be
satisfied with mere obedience, but experience full horror at sins
inwardly committed, knowing that those who sin in one way are
'guilty of all'. Only by such moral abasement, Mr Brontë advised,
would evil passions begin to lose their hold. Charlotte told herself
that she was 'longing for holiness which I shall *never, never* attain.'

Then, at Christmas, she swung into the alternative mode:
reunion with Branwell and Emily renewed her courage. Firing
each other's ambitions, Charlotte and Branwell took a mutual
decision to send samples of their work to established poets. On 29
December, Charlotte sent some of her poems to the Poet
Laureate, Robert Southey. They were accompanied by a letter
which has not survived, but the playback in Southey's famous
reply shows that Charlotte had confided to him that she lived in
a visionary world, assuming Southey did likewise and would
stoop to speak to her 'from a throne of light & glory'. She also
confided an explicit ambition 'to be forever known' as a poet.
This letter was evidently written in ardent excitement, not
unlike the letter that Branwell wrote to Wordsworth at the same
time. Where Wordsworth had welcomed the advances of Maria
Jane Jewsbury, who said her writing was intended as a 'public
tribute' to the poet whom she studied each day as his humble
'pupil', Branwell's assurance provoked Wordsworth to contemptuous silence.

It was a winter of hopes and plans. Once together, the Brontës recovered their fire and conviction. Anne resumed the habit of roaming the moor with Emily to get in the right 'humor' for writing. At nine, when Aunt retired, the sisters put away their sewing, blew out the candles, and began to pace the room, their forms glancing into the firelight and out into the shadow. Their walk was a march, free and rapid, which kept time with thoughts and feelings. Now and then, Charlotte, in sheer exuberance, broke rank and made a graceful pirouette (though she had not learnt to dance), then fell back in step with her sisters' march. Sometimes, on an impulse, she would dramatise her story, inviting bursts of merriment. Emily or Anne would silence her with a cautious 'Hark!' and warn, 'Papa will wonder what we are about if he hears us laughing so much.'

The secrecy of the evening ritual, and the 'treasure' it shared, gave rise to Charlotte's poem called 'Evening Solace':

> The human heart has hidden treasures
> In secret kept, in silence sealed –

For those whose days were constrained by household duty, night offered the only untrammelled time – to voice, touch, laugh, and whirl. For the sisters (as later for Emily Dickinson and, still later, for Virginia Woolf's heroine in *Night and Day*), night was for thinking. In the dormitory at Roe Head, Charlotte had thrilled listeners with ghost tales after lights out. A letter to Ellen recalled '"the singular property of seeing in the Night time" – which the ladies at Roe Head used to attribute to me.' When Ellen visited the Parsonage, she thought they blew out the candles for economy. But darkness was a liberating cover; invisibility, a form of freedom.

The vacation ended without word from the reigning poets. It was three months before Southey's reply came. He was replying to a 'flighty' girl in need of a 'dose of cooling admonition':

Keswick.
March 1837

Madam,

. . . Literature cannot be the business of a woman's life, and
it ought not to be. The more she is engaged in her proper
duties, the less leisure she will have for it, even as an accomplishment and a recreation. To those duties you have not yet
been called, and when you are you will be less eager for
celebrity . . .

Charlotte replied with apparent propriety which completely
reassured Southey, but her letter reverberates with veiled sarcasm. The brilliant verbal glide of her abjection to Southey was
her first public performance of a role she was to make her own:
hiding undaunted creative fire under the public mask of perfect
docility. She reassured Southey that her daily duties as a teacher
did not allow 'a moment's time for one dream of the imagination.' She went on:

In the evenings, I confess, I do think, but I never trouble any
one else with my thoughts. I carefully avoid any appearance of
preoccupation and eccentricity, which might lead those I live
amongst to suspect the nature of my pursuits . . . I have
endeavoured not only attentively to observe all the duties a
woman ought to fulfil, but to feel deeply interested in them. I
don't always succeed, for sometimes when I'm teaching or
sewing I would rather be reading or writing; but I try to deny
myself . . . Once more allow me to thank you with sincere
gratitude. I trust I shall nevermore feel ambitious to see my
name in print; if the wish should rise, I'll look at Southey's
letter, and suppress it.

Publicly, ever after, Charlotte gave out that Southey had done her
good in showing her that what she wished could not be. Even to
herself, at times, she played out the role of slave-to-duty, as in a

poem called 'Teacher's Monologue', written shortly after
Southey's letters, on 12 May 1837:

> In vain I try. I cannot sing
> All feels so cold & dead . . .

At twenty-one, youth 'departs'; its 'rejoicing ardour dies'. Life
stretches out as blank 'toil'.

It is easy to press for pity but more interesting to wonder to
what degree pathos was conceived as poetic – in the way
Branwell played out his pathos with Byronic confidence in the
power of gloom. Charlotte had, as her brother had not, a capacity to detach herself from the posture which makes her own
poems so wet and weak. At the same time as she dripped the
obligatory poetic tear, she was trying out a defiant voice in her
journal and letters, the forms through which her art grew.
Crushing as Southey was, she responds with humour and cool
control. There is no fret in her reply; instead, she appropriates
Southey's discourse and returns it to him in more polished form.
Nowhere is she more assured than in the evenness of the statement: 'In the evenings, I confess, I do think . . .' Present-day
audiences hear the sarcasm undetected by Southey, and never
fail to laugh. It could be said that in March 1837 Charlotte forged
a voice to carry beyond her age.

This second letter to Southey was a flawless performance
open to contradictory interpretation. Southey himself was mol-
lified by the veneer of womanly obedience: 'You have received
admonition as considerately . . . as it was given', he replied
promptly on 22 March. Yet, as Charlotte distilled the feminine
cant required by Southey, she was manifesting a conspicuous lit-
eracy which took command of the structures within which
women of her time must live. If she was not to communicate
through the high form of poetry (though Southey 'kindly
allows' her to write for her private amusement), she could still
communicate through the form of the letter. She deals her

words like blades, sculpting the caricature of feminine obedience as it takes shape under the injunctions of the Laureate who reserved creativity for men alone. She mimics the accents of subjection. She does not fail to observe her obedience to a righteous father: 'I try to deny myself; and my father's approbation amply rewarded me for the privation.' The first heady letter had implied her mental release from the constrictions of feminine duty. She had wished for an authoritative sanction of an alternative future. She had sought a literary father or guide. Then, at Southey's signal, she switched from 'I am a poet who desires to be forever known' to 'I am a dutiful daughter of a clergyman.' Sustaining these alternative selves – the romantic enthusiast and obedient girl who did not presume to think – she could slide from one to the other with practised, almost professional facility: a play of legitimate utterance versus secret script. Utterance is smooth, logical, and drives to a point of consensus; it mimics the given structures. But writing, as a serious activity from which women were barred, throbs with an energy that deviates from the contemporary image of a lady as delicate and passionless.

Charlotte did take seriously Southey's final warning to be calm. Like the young Florence Nightingale, she feared that dreaming would unfit her for life. Southey may, in fact, have advanced her withdrawal from Angria. She wrote on his letter: 'Southey's advice to be kept for ever. My twenty-first birthday. Roe Head, April 21, 1837'.

The struggle to break with dreams compounded with the shock of Anne's illness in the autumn of 1837 brought Charlotte close to breakdown. After her explosion to Miss Wooler, she decided to leave Roe Head.

Miss Wooler argued her continued affection for Charlotte. She did not wish to lose her, especially in view of the fact that Charlotte now carried the main burden of teaching. Miss Wooler pleaded two sleepless nights, crying over Charlotte's fury. This did not win Charlotte's respect.

'Am I to spend all the best part of my life in this wretched bondage', she asked herself, 'forcibly suppressing my rage at the idleness, the apathy and the hyperbolical and most asinine stupidity of these fat-headed oafs, and on compulsion assuming an air of kindness, patience & assiduity?'

She cooled down over the winter vacation. Branwell, now taking art lessons in Leeds, had first claim on family resources. Anne's health, though improved, was still in need of care. So Charlotte backed down and prepared to return to Roe Head. On 29 January 1838, she wrote 'Parting', an Emily-type poem in which the mind defies bondage:

> We can burst the bonds which chain us,
>> Which cold human hands have wrought,
> And where none shall dare restrain us
>> We can meet again, in thought.

It proved no more than a brave gesture. The school had moved to the less attractive Heald's House, Dewsbury Moor, close to Miss Wooler's ailing mother. Before the end of the first half of 1838, Charlotte collapsed and on 23 May went home. Miss Wooler, always kind, gave her a parting present of two poems by Sir Walter Scott, *The Vision of Don Roderick* (1811) and *Rokeby* (1813).

The return to Haworth, Charlotte told Ellen, at once 'roused and soothed me'. Mary and Martha Taylor came on a visit; their company, she said, was 'one of the most rousing pleasures I have ever known.' Mental peace returned for almost a year until she forced herself, once more, to earn her keep.

Back in Charlotte's 'Land of Silence', the three sisters were united once more. At their favourite 'Meeting of the Waters' on the moor above the Parsonage, Emily would lose her reserve, as her fingers stirred the tadpoles, moralising on the strong and the weak, the brave and the cowards – no coward's soul hers. She held to this scene as the strongest of earthly attachments, and spoke of 'those first feelings that were born with me' which obliterate all derivative schemes of existence:

> I'll walk where my own nature would be leading:
> It vexes me to choose another guide.

Emily began wasting, again, in her only teaching post in a large school at Law Hill near Halifax. She told Charlotte that her hours at Miss Patchett's were six in the morning until eleven at night. 'This is slavery', Charlotte declared to Ellen. 'I fear she will never stand it.' As she predicted, Emily declined further, and left, perhaps dismissed, in March 1839, after six months.

Later, in *Wuthering Heights*, Catherine Earnshaw speaks of 'exile' from a landscape that was more to her than home; it embodies her very self, 'half savage and hardy, and free . . .' Elizabeth Hastings, Charlotte's homesick teacher in a novella she wrote in 1839, has similar needs: 'So wild was her longing that when she looked out on the dusky sky . . . fancy seemed to trace on the horizon the blue outline of the moors.' This is not the longing of a romantic dreamland, it is the loss of freedom for women who have to submit to restriction: for Elizabeth, the schoolroom which was the middle-class woman's sole means of respectable support.

In the Brontës' childhood, a habit of release had established itself which found expression in dreams and writing, but which was so fundamental to their lives that to leave the moor was to be exiled from the self. For Emily to do so led to self-starvation and pining illness, and for Branwell, it led to failures, relieved by entertaining talk and yards of unreadable writing.

His sisters were more self-contained, living behind their wall of silence. Their lives and work might be seen as reciprocal tests which ask what unknown modes of being lie in the shadow of muted lives. What is passion for a woman? How might she emerge from silence, raise her voice, pick up her pen? Charlotte was not as shrinking as she appeared; she had the courage to enter uncharted regions of women's lives, to meet the shades who lived there, and find words for their experience.

To raise this voice in her time was to challenge contemporaries who condemned her work as rebellious and unChristian. 'Conventionality is not morality' was her defiant reply. If the moors played some part in prompting her impulse to exploration, what prompted the new model of womanhood which now emerged? How exactly did it detach itself from the orthodox pieties of an Evangelical faith, represented in ideal form by the memory of Maria?

The reckless honesty of the 'Journal' was modified, publicly, by her long training in decorum, and controlled further by the covert power she had found in the cool voice of her reply to Southey. Bringing these gains together in that quiet space at home, from mid-1838 to the spring of 1839, she gave shape to an apparently insignificant creature whose place in society was tenuous, but who was bent on survival.

Charlotte had moved from one heroine to another as each dulled in turn until, in 1837, a new kind of woman passed across the writer's line of vision, obliterating for a moment the fashionable throng. Then, in the latter half of 1838, when Charlotte realised that if she could not endure schools, she would have to be a governess, a fictional governess called Miss West appears in a prose fragment.

It was as though Charlotte were trying on the public facade she meant to present: a 'smile intelligent, but retiring'; a 'quiet aspect of serious reflection – which it seemed could never be broken or kindled by any feeling of undue warmth'; a 'look which seemed ever waiting to gratify the wishes of others & never sought sympathy for self' – an impenetrable decorum which revealed 'no quick acute sensations to be renounced'. There is unmistakable zest in the construct of this anti-self, prefiguring the teacher, Miss Snowe, in *Villette*: 'In herself she was nothing – a frozen automaton . . .' The inflexible correctness of this facade was designed to preserve her powers intact. Like Charlotte, Miss West has 'insignificant proportions – plain dress & thin irregular features'. In society she is a shadowy figure, gliding unobserved through crowded rooms in her dark dress, yet 'it is not in Society that the real character is revealed.'

Alone in her room, the 'shade of habitual studied reserve' lightens as Miss West thinks of one person who had seen her as she really is. She is susceptible to a man of 'acute sagacity' who infers her real disposition from 'those moments of awakened feeling, those sudden flashing fits of excitement which she could not always control'. Privately, Miss West has the same contempt for her pupils that Charlotte had felt at Roe Head; she has the same proud containment: 'She never by inadvertent breath or glance betrayed the scorn that often swelled at her heart. She listened to all sympathized with all & never for a moment required sympathy or attention in return'. She scorns in particular those of her charges (including one called Amelia, presumably after Amelia Walker) who talk vapidly of conquests without 'the force of passion or intense energy of enthusiasm'. A poem on the preceding page defines the character of a different sort of woman who burns with unseen passion and 'powers of bliss all self contained'. Obscure, little-seen, unheard, she appears voiceless, except, of course, in the poem itself:

> And if I hoped or feared or loved
> No voice was heard to speak.

If this voice does sound it emerges in the schooled tones of Lowood*, recessed from the public in 'deep shadowy solitude'. The speaker sits alone by her chamber candle 'doubly shaded' by

---

* The name, Lowood, for the strict school in *Jane Eyre*, the novel which Charlotte Brontë began in the second half of 1846, goes back to the Miss West poem of c.1838.

night and surrounding trees. She is 'born to be/A being all
unchained and free' but wonders how far she is an oddity:

> Have many lived as I have lived
> Existence but a reverie . . .

Miss West wears 'the constant mask which hid & smoothed
her natural features'. Questions prod the mask: '– How does she
look thus freed from disguise & restraint? . . . What kind of
thoughts are those contracting her marked forehead & burning
in her quick eyes? You see little of beauty to admire in those features – but surely they ever flow with meaning & a strange
meaning too . . .'

A mystery is circled: there is a face to be read; a nature to be
defined. A few months later, in February–March 1839, Charlotte
pursued this mystery further in the shape of Elizabeth Hastings
as she emerges from the shadow of a beloved brother who has
become an outlaw. In Henry Hastings, Charlotte appropriated
the prototype of a Cain-like wanderer, which Branwell had
adopted in 1837. The novella, 'Henry Hastings', coincides with
the start of Branwell's problems.

It was in 1839 that Branwell first took opium, and began to
admire the addicted Romantics, Coleridge (author of the celebrated opium-vision, 'Kubla Khan', 1797) and De Quincey (author
of *Confessions of an English Opium Eater*, 1821) above Wordsworth.
Branwell may have aspired to be a great poet who was drunk on
the milk of paradise, but instead he was gripped by nightmares
(Mr Brontë made copious notes, dated 1838, next to the entry
on 'Nightmare' in his copy of *Domestic Medicine*). In 1835, while
Charlotte was teaching at Roe Head, Branwell, who had talent
for drawing, hoped to study at the Royal Academy of Arts
in London. His portfolio was not as yet adequate for entry, but
his hopes remained high. In 1838–9 Branwell had a studio in
Fountain Street, Bradford (the nearest city to Haworth), but by
1839 he was mostly at home again. Branwell's scenario was pathos

on a grand scale. His proudest poem, outlined in his letter to Wordsworth, foretold his own path to ruin: '. . . I have striven to develop strong passions and weak principles struggling with a high imagination and acute feelings, till, as youth hardens towards age, evil deeds and short enjoyments end in mental misery and bodily ruin.' Spectacular self-destruction costs money, which meant, for Branwell's sisters, an urgent need to work. This need Charlotte built into her story of Elizabeth who still cares for her brother, in much the same way that Charlotte still cared for Branwell as the brother of brilliant gifts. Like Branwell, Henry retains his standing as a poet and 'Chronicler of the Angrian Wars'. Brother and sister are bonded, too, by natural affection: 'It was very odd but his sister did not think a pin the worse of him for all his Dishonour. It is private meanness, not public infamy, that degrade a man in the opinion of his relatives . . . he was the same brother to her he had always been . . .'

When they are reunited, he tries to explain his crimes, but his sister understands already – she knows that his passions are 'naturally strong, & his Imagination . . . warm to fever'.

Encouraged by her warmth, he builds 'Castles in the air' while his sister 'caught his spirit & answered in a quick excited voice' (suggesting the way Charlotte caught fire from Branwell). Elizabeth tries to conceal him from the law – in vain.

As her brother fades from the story, her initiative grows and, with it, her visibility. At first, she appears a nonentity. Townshend, the man-about-town, travelling with her by coach, observes a 'quiet aspect & plain demure dress' and great reserve. Here is the prototype of Jane Eyre and Lucy Snowe: a shadowy figure in the glare of society. In an opera box, she accompanies Jane Moore who has a profusion of silky ringlets, bright as gold. By the side of this 'superb animal' sits her unknown companion, as Townshend catches sight of her again, 'that pale undersized young woman dressed as plainly as a Quakeress in grey' and without a curl in sight. This companion is seen to be 'a dim dusk foil' to Jane Moore's 'diamond lustre – a little shade just at her elbow, hustled backwards and forwards by the men – Pagans that were crowding to the shrine of their idol.'

The ambition was immense. Charlotte was calling up the almost ghostly figure of a woman free from the trappings of the idol. The Angrian fantasy of West Africa has virtually disappeared; we are in the mannered drawing-rooms of early Victorian England set over against the distant moor – to Townshend, a 'rough, wild country' – from which Elizabeth emanates and to which she longs to return.

As men at the opera survey the idols, Townshend wonders at the 'mortal' who sits in the shade. His attempts to place her revive the question provoked by Miss West. What is the nature of the governess or companion who lives out her life in the shadow of the 'eminently artificial thing'? Seeing Elizabeth through the uncomprehending eyes of Townshend, the reader draws closer to this quiet but intransigent 'mortal'. This is her character from the moment we first glimpse her travelling the roads from her moorland origin to the centre of society.

At a dinner, as Townshend helps himself to vegetables, his eye falls 'on the little individual I had resolved not to see'. His view of her is a series of negations: 'She was eating nothing – listening to nothing – not a soul had addressed a word to her . . . I can't pretend to say what thoughts were in her mind'. Then he notices that Elizabeth is absorbed in a painting on the wall. For a moment, he has a glimpse of 'a neglected human being – turning from the hollow world, glittering with such congenial & selfish splendour before her – to the contemplation of . . . something that touched her spirit to the quick'. He observes further that she veils this with 'an indifferent expression'. On close inspection, Townshend finds that she is not ugly: her eyes (like Charlotte's, again) were 'very fine & seemed as if they could express anything . . . but her features were masked with an expression foreign to them – her movements were restrained & guarded . . .'

Elizabeth goes on to found a school of her own. 'She was

now . . . dependent on nobody – responsible to nobody –'. As she discovers her agency, the narrative abandons the onlooker's point of view and Charlotte blends with Elizabeth. Introspection reveals that independence is not enough. The teacher never meets anyone equal to herself in mind, '& therefore not one whom she could love'. She does need love. Charlotte's buried desire is blatant in this story: 'always burning for warmer, closer attachment – she couldn't live without it –'.

At this point, Sir William Percy, the apprehender of Henry, comes into focus. He notes her quick glances and gauges correctly 'what she imagined buried out of sight in her inmost heart'. He perceives her conflict between desire and retirement, her fear lest her remotest approach appear intrusive. A chill character, warmed only by his whims, Sir William toys with a freak of fancy for Miss Hastings. One day, when she cannot hide the fact that she is drawn to him, he invites her to become his mistress: 'yield to your nature & let me claim you this moment as my own –'.

Instinct is not denied. It is not to be minimised: 'Miss Hastings was silent – but she was not going to yield – only the hard conflict of passionate love . . . compelled her for a moment to silent agony.'

She tells him honestly: 'I am afraid of nothing but myself'.

Then she leaves him beside the tomb of one of Zamorna's rejects, Lady Rosamund Wellesley, whose stone is engraved with the word 'Resurgam', ['I shall rise']. As Elizabeth turns away, she embodies that rise in secular form.* No figment of superhuman purity or tainted weakness, Elizabeth proves the existence of

---

* This promise recurs at least six times in the course of CB's career: first, in the 'Roe Head Journal' where the difficulty of rising is used quite literally but resonates as an emblematic condition of CB's restricted existence at the school; in a letter of Dec. 1840, CB speaks of her 'rising talent'. In her fiction, the promise to rise appears in the image of Elizabeth Hastings as she turns from the grave of Lady Rosamund. In *Jane Eyre*, 'Resurgam' is engraved on the tombstone of Helen Burns. Finally, in *Villette*, the heroine describes herself as 'a rising character'. See below, chapters 5 and 8.

something stronger than instinct. At nearly twenty-three, Charlotte Brontë saw that fulfilment could not be passion alone; it had to be the creation of character.

Character was the basis for her refusal of her first proposal, in March 1839, at the time she wrote this novella. When the Revd Henry Nussey, Ellen's dull brother, proposed to the grave image that Charlotte had assumed in his presence, she felt obliged to reveal that this was not her real character: at home he would find her eccentric, romantic, satirical. It was her 'habit to study the characters of those amongst whom I chance to be thrown', she told him on 5 March, 'and I think I know yours and can imagine what description of woman would suit you for a wife. The character should not be too marked, ardent and original . . . As for me, you do not know me . . .' So Henry Nussey went on to number three on his list.* Character, again, was her excuse to Ellen, a few days later: in marriage, she could not hide her 'natural' home character. 'I could not sit all day making a grave face before my husband.' Though she believed no other offer would come her way, she did not hesitate to refuse a security which many in her position would have accepted. Two months later, Charlotte began a fresh attempt to earn her living. She went out twice as governess between May 1839 and the end of 1841. These exiles proved worse than school. Where Miss Wooler had seen Charlotte as a professional colleague, mothers saw her as a faceless functionary. This was her stint in 'the land of Egypt and the house of Bondage'.

Anne (aged nineteen) set the example, overruling family objections, and went off on her own, on 8 April, to Blake Hall,

---

* Henry Nussey's absurdly solemn diary notes, early in 1839, some 'favourable intelligence' passing between him and his sister, Ellen. On 1 March he reports the failure of his first choice: 'a decisive reply from MAL's papa. A loss, but I trust a providential one. Believe not her will, but her father's. All right. God knows best what is good for us, for his church, & for his own Glory . . . Wrote to a Yorkr Friend. C.B.' On Sat. 9 March he records her prompt refusal: '. . . Received an unfavourable report fm C.B. The will of the Lord be done.' His third choice accepted his proposal.

Mirfield, where she remained with the Inghams until Christmas. In May, Charlotte set off for her first post as governess, with the Sidgwicks near Skipton. Her gain, as Anne's, was inside knowledge of those above her in the class system. Class, she found, mattered more to wives who took care to reflect their husbands' standing. When Mr John Benson Sidgwick strolled with Mathilda (aged six and a half) and John Benson, Jr (aged four), Charlotte was ordered to follow a little behind. Except for the resonance of 'ordered', Charlotte notes this matter-of-factly compared with her surprise at his wife's refusal to know her. Her bedroom was on the third floor where servants slept, and in the evenings she was expected to watch over the children on the second floor – never invited to join the party downstairs in the drawing-room. This outraged Charlotte in view of some past acquaintance with Mrs Sidgwick who had been Sarah Hannah Greenwood of Keighley near Haworth. Before her marriage into the widely connected Sidgwick family, she had been known as the daughter of John Greenwood of Knowle House, a prominent Whig and wealthy cotton manufacturer. All her Greenwood relations would have been familiar to Charlotte, including her brother-in-law, the Rector of Keighley, one of Papa's few clerical friends. The fact that Charlotte, as a clergyman's daughter, would have mingled with the Greenwoods at local church events, had led her to believe that the Sidgwicks would treat her as one of the family. (Anne had similar expectations of the Inghams who were connected by marriage to Ellen Nussey and had ties with Miss Wooler. Mrs Ingham's sister, Miss Lister, had been at Roe Head – in fact she appears several times in Charlotte's journal as one of the pupils who bored her. Miss Lister would therefore have been at school with Anne.) It was the discovery that work placed a governess beneath notice which rankled more than relentless hours, 'oceans' of needlework, and vicious children. Aware that Miss Brontë had no standing, John Benson, Jr, threw a stone at her head. When she did not betray him, the boy made the famous remark, 'I love 'ou, Miss Brontë', whereupon Mrs Sidgwick exclaimed: 'Love the *governess*, my dear!'

At this period, clergy women were apt to be sensitive about their status. From the end of the eighteenth century, clergymen in the Church of England were acquiring new dignity and leadership in the community as they came less under patronage. There is some difference between the servile self-importance of Mr Collins, reflecting the grandeur of his patroness, Lady Catherine de Bourgh (in *Pride and Prejudice*, drafted in the 1790s), and the more independent (and presumptuous) self-importance of Mr Elton in *Emma* (1815). In the course of Mr Brontë's moves from Ireland to Yorkshire in the first two decades of the nineteenth century, he had acquired a high-bred manner and could, on occasion, mention his acquaintance with Lord Palmerston at Cambridge. As the Perpetual Curate of Haworth, he mixed at church parties with the best families and was listed alongside the gentry as one of the first gentlemen in the county. This, despite the fact that Mr Brontë never earned more than £200 a year. His daughters were raised with him above the status where birth and income would once have left them.

As part of the current attempt to move the Brontës out of legend, Tom Winnifrith has suggested that their social behaviour was not a matter of Romantic solitude, but had to do with the pervasive mundanities of class: a touchiness that had its source in Mr Brontë's peasant roots, disguised by his assumed name and mysterious hints of ancient ancestry. The families were conveniently distant in Ireland and Cornwall, and Mr Brontë seems never to have mentioned them. Though the Branwells' middle-class status had been superior to that of the Brunty family, it may not have been superior enough for Patrick Brontë. His politics aligned him with Tory gentlemen who distrusted the uneducated worker and opposed reformers who wished to extend the vote.

Once, Ellen suggested to the Brontës that factory girls in Haworth talked too familiarly of their masters, using Christian names. They should be taught better manners, Ellen said. Emily retorted in her quick way: 'Vain attempt!' In withholding herself from social commerce, in the proud purity of her self-reliance, she outdid her father. In Haworth, the Brontës could sometimes nurse a superiority that was, in social terms, somewhat precarious: a Perpetual Curate was not a humble position, but neither was it elevated, being slightly inferior to that of Vicar or Rector. Also, the presence of a large body of Dissenters around Haworth meant that there were fewer parishioners to owe Mr Brontë the respect due to their minister, and this fact would have weakened his position with the landowning classes. So, class was alive at the Parsonage, and Charlotte and Anne took it with them to Stonegappe and Blake Hall.

Stonegappe, twenty miles north of Haworth, had been built at the end of the eighteenth century by Mr Sidgwick's father who had made his fortune from cotton-spinning mills at Skipton. William Sidgwick had belonged to the class of rising industrialists who displaced old landowners by exploiting employees. He had worked between a hundred and a hundred and twenty children thirteen hours a day. When such conditions were queried in 1816, he said: 'I think the health of children employed much better than the health of children roaming at large.'

The Sidgwicks' house was almost as grand as Charlotte might have hoped in her Angrian dreams. It stands secluded at the end of a drive, guarded by great trees, in a commanding position overlooking Lothersdale and the steep hills beyond. The hills are green and lush, in contrast with the bleakness of the moors. Below, in the valley, runs the River Ayre, perhaps one source for the name of Jane Eyre. It is well-known that Stonegappe was the source for Gateshead in *Jane Eyre*, and it is likely that Jane's position as an interloper in an uppish family owed something to the position in which Charlotte found herself when she joined the Sidgwicks in May 1839. Certain scenes in *Jane Eyre* (where the spoilt son, John Reed, throws a book at Jane's head, and where Mrs Reed scolds Jane) draw on Charlotte's brief history at

Stonegappe – only Jane, aged ten, stands firm, while Charlotte, aged twenty-three, could not conceal angry tears.

Charlotte soon became as alert as Agnes Grey (the governess of Anne's first novel) to the tabooed position of a clergyman's daughter who must work for her living. Such women often had a better education, moral insight, and elegance of language, but these counted for nothing in social terms. As the accomplishments of a governess they were, of course, requisite, as today we expect polished functioning from domestic utilities. So, then, Charlotte's bitter sense of herself as a 'commodity'. So, too, her plaint to Emily that 'a private governess has no existence, is not considered as a living and rational being except as connected with the wearisome duties she has to fulfil.' Charlotte later told Mrs Gaskell that she lost her character in other people's houses, where she had to assume a tepid front foreign to her natural exuberance.

To Mrs Sidgwick, Charlotte appeared prickly. She was over-sensitive. If asked to join the family when they walked to church, she thought she was ordered about as a slave; if left alone, she felt excluded.

To Charlotte, Mrs Sidgwick's 'animal spirits' and 'bustling condescension' did not add up to 'refinement of feeling'. When she scolded Charlotte for depression, it was the first time in more than a month that she had spoken to her employee for five minutes. This was the occasion when Charlotte could not hold back her tears. She usually blamed herself for her 'wretched touchiness' which made her 'wince as if I had been touched with a hot iron: things that nobody else cares for enter into my mind and rankle like venom. I know these feelings are absurd and therefore I try to hide them but they only sting the deeper for concealment. I'm an idiot!' Self-blame jostled with hatred that festered in silence: '. . . I kept the padlock of silence on mental wealth in which [the industrialist] was no sharer.' These words in *The Professor* look back to Charlotte's own experience in the family of a Yorkshire industrialist. In the novel, the superior worker,

William Crimsworth, realises that his employer would have liked him better had he been less intelligent. Ignored and slighted, Crimsworth, like Charlotte, feels 'the rust and cramp' of imagination ('my Darling, my Cherished-in-secret, Imagination, the tender and the mighty'), like a plant growing 'in humid darkness out of the slimy walls of a well'. Through this character, Charlotte projects her fear that her gift might atrophy or worse. The darkness of night that freed imagination could end in a dungeon darkness of mental stress. Concealment was the warping part of living in dreams – what Mary Taylor had called, in her downright way, 'growing potatoes in the cellar'.

Charlotte was to draw more substantially on her experience as a governess in *Jane Eyre* and, once more, in *Shirley* where the ex-governess, Mrs Pryor, reveals the truth of that life to her daughter, Caroline. Here, an employer, called Mrs Hardman, speaks the exact words of a reviewer of *Jane Eyre* who set out the position of the governess in a way that confirmed Charlotte's experience with Mrs Sidgwick. The governess is 'a tabooed woman' and also 'a bore' because she continually crosses the path of gentlemen and ladies who should not notice her. Consequently, the governess must 'live alone' and never transgress the barrier between her and the class she serves. In Mrs Pryor's own words, this taboo began 'to produce mortal effects on my constitution, – I sickened.' Mrs Hardman then warns the governess (as Hannah Sidgwick warned Charlotte) that she is the victim of self-esteem. If she does not cultivate humility, she will die an inmate of a lunatic asylum.

During the second month at Stonegappe, in July 1839, Charlotte began to crack. When she did not conceal shortness of breath, Hannah Sidgwick accused her of affectation.

Charlotte's aversion for her employer was not lessened by her awareness that, without sympathy for children, no amount of accomplishment would make the post bearable. When her charges were unruly, she could wish herself a housemaid or a kitchen girl 'rather than a baited, trampled, desolate, distracted

governess.' Playtime was worse than school hours. It was humiliating to realise that an ignorant nursery-maid with a robust
manner often managed better with spoilt children, while
Charlotte remained ineffective. Later, she summed up the lot of
the governess: 'tyrannised over, finding her efforts to please and
teach utterly vain, chagrined, distressed, worried – so badgered,
so trodden on, that she ceased almost at last to know herself, and
wondered in what despicable, trembling frame her oppressed
mind was prisoned'.

Her trembling was not wholly pathetic. Her torrent of adjec-
tives suggests indignation if not rage. Nor was she entirely
'desolate': hospitality was offered by the local vicar, Edward
Carter, and his wife, sister to Miss Wooler. Mr Carter had, in fact,
prepared Charlotte for confirmation in 1832 when she had been a
pupil at Roe Head. Charlotte therefore knew him quite well,
but though she made do with the Carters, she complained privately that this was not the society she wanted.

Fortunately, the post was for less than two months, and from
the summer of 1839 until the start of 1841, Charlotte remained
thankfully at home. Anne, too, returned, dismissed by the
Inghams, in December 1839. (In later life, Mary Ingham remarked
that she 'had once employed a very unsuitable governess called
Miss Brontë'.) That winter, Tabby became lame and had to take
a rest. While she stayed with her sister in a house she had bought
with her savings, Charlotte, Emily, and Anne took up house-
keeping with alacrity. Emily was in charge of the kitchen and
baking; Charlotte chose to do the ironing, impervious to Aunt's
wrath when she burnt the clothes in her first effort. She was
happier doing servant's work at home – black-leading the stove,
making beds, sweeping floors – than living as a lady elsewhere. 'I
hate and *abhor* the very thoughts of governess-ship', she said that
December, aware that she had only a reprieve before she must
'force' herself to take another post.

In this mood of revolt, Charlotte prolonged her reprieve by
giving a possible employer, Mrs Edward Halliley, her 'coup de

grâce' early in 1840. A letter from Charlotte to Ellen on 29 May 1840 owns to relief that she had answered advertisements in vain. In any case, she was resolved to find employers with 'minds and hearts not dug out of a lead-mine, or cut from a marble quarry.' Her aversion to the Sidgwicks was part of a larger problem: though she craved a field for her efforts, the work open to her demeaned her talents. Jane Eyre, enclosed in her lot as teacher and governess, cries out for liberty. As a teacher at Lowood School, Jane's eyes lift to the far-off horizon which she longs to cross to the stir of cities and public event, but she is forced to seek, at best, 'a new servitude'. In Jane's next post as governess, at Thornfield, she stands on the roof, gazing once more at the horizon, and thinks how many lives 'are condemned to a stiller doom than mine'. The mood matches that of a drawing Anne did while a governess with the Inghams: it shows the back of a young woman gazing out to sea from a rocky promontory, a hand shading her eyes, as she scans a radiant horizon. Emily, too, was to present this mood in *Wuthering Heights* when Catherine Earnshaw rebels against a wife's domestic confinement and strains out of her bedroom window towards the limitless freedom of the moor.

When Charlotte made up her mind that she would not marry, such constriction may have worried her, as well as a wary view of the fickleness of attractive men, evident in the character of Zamorna, and reinforced during 1840 by her shrewd observations of her father's attractive, flirtatious curate, William Weightman. At one stage he paid court to Ellen, and a letter from Charlotte, warning her of his fickleness, is signed in a spirit of revolt, 'Yours sincerely "Ça ira"', recalling the song sung in the French Revolution:

Ah! ça ira, ça ira, ça ira,
Les aristocrates à la lanterne.

Already, her rebellion against women's vulnerability in the power structure stirred her underclass roots, as against her apparent affiliation with Tory conservatism in line with her father. A spirit of revolt may have shaped her resistance to the idea of marriage as much as her lack of looks and fortune. Florence Nightingale, who had both looks and money, also abjured marriage. She believed that her active nature unfitted her for marriage even though her passionate nature impelled her towards it. Charlotte endorsed the active life: in theory, she thought it better to be a governess than to linger in dependence at home. In practice, she had no wish to teach and, like her sisters, was unsuited to it, as Ellen recalled:

> . . . They had no power of asserting themselves, while they had the most acute and lively sensibility to any act in another which jarred on their exquisite under-heartedness, their refinement, or sense of justice. They suffered intensely from what to another would have been a mere trifle . . .

It was Ellen's view that had Mr Brontë lived more in his family circle and given more thought to his children, he would have advised them against teaching: '– there never could have been temperaments *less adapted* to such a position.' Though they had 'a marvellous amount of self-abnegation firmness and endurance, they could not take measures to repel or avoid what hurt them'. The result was that complacent, hardy natures condemned what appeared to them weakness and infirmity, not perceiving the 'fine susceptibilities beneath the surface'. The bad health which aggravated these susceptibilities accounted for 'the dismal aspect' they put upon their experiences, 'sharpening every pang, in an overwrought suppression of their feelings . . . and giving additional darkness to every shadow that crossed their path when away from home. *At home* they were the bravest of the brave – suffering *there* was nobly met'.

Ellen confirmed that the worst aspect was the obligatory facade: 'Charlotte had a painful conviction that living in other people's houses was to all of them, an *estrangement* from their real characters. It compelled them to adopt an exterior which was a bona fide suppression, an alienation from themselves'.

Their adopted covers took their cue from the norms to which their class aspired, ladylike variations on Amelia Walker. It was by such class standards that Charlotte judged a new suitor, David Bryce, who arrived fresh from Dublin as curate to Mr Brontë's former curate, Mr Hodgson, now Vicar of Colne in Lancashire. Mr Bryce visited Haworth Parsonage, in the company of his vicar, soon after Charlotte's return from Stonegappe, early in August 1839. He proposed immediately after hearing Charlotte talk, that evening, with the freedom of home. Though he was witty and ardent, Charlotte did not consider an Irish curate her social equal. She declared him 'deficient in the dignity and discretion of an Englishman'. Here, once again, is that touchy question of class: only one generation away from Ireland, Charlotte could look down on the Irish. Mr Bryce died soon after this incident.

Scorning Amelia as she did, Charlotte nevertheless visited her again in the autumn of 1839. A year later, she expressed renewed scorn for the artifice of ladyhood: she was vastly entertained by a visit from a south-of-England cousin called Eliza Branwell Williams who cultivated a languishing, saintly air so 'utterly out of keeping with her round rosy face and tall bouncing figure – that I could hardly refrain from laughing as I watched her –'. Throughout the rest of her life, the ambivalence remained. Charlotte practised the manners of a well-bred lady – the modesty, the decorum, the reserve – and, at the same time, exploded the artifice of tameness.

Another norm of the middle classes was to appear benevolent. This was the Sidgwicks' reputation. Their niece, Mary, married a distant cousin, Edward White Benson, future Archbishop of Canterbury, and their son, A. C. Benson, a respected writer, defended the Sidgwicks, as 'extraordinarily benevolent people, much beloved, and would not wittingly have given pain to any one connected with them.' All we learn from this is how they appeared to relatives and other social equals.

Charlotte, on the other hand, penetrates what she described to Mrs Gaskell as the dark side of respectability, 'under no great temptation to crime, but daily giving way to selfishness and ill-temper, till its conduct towards those dependent on it sometimes amounts to a tyranny of which one would rather be the victim than the inflicter.'

It is then fair to say that to be a governess was to lay oneself open to victimisation of this subtler sort which was, literally, annihilating to the Brontës whose commitment to gentility compelled them to assume the mask of compliance. Twenty-five years earlier, Jane Austen, a single woman of meagre income, fortunate in the support of her family, had deplored the fate of the governess through the reluctance of poor accomplished Jane Fairfax to take posts urged on her by smugly secure Mrs Elton. Jane dreads the 'evil day' when she must 'retire from all the pleasures of life, of rational intercourse, equal society, peace and hope, to penance and mortification for ever.'

To a woman of Mary Taylor's advanced views, there was only one solution: leave England. Charlotte wrote to Ellen on 3 January 1841 that 'Mary alone has more energy and power in her nature than any ten men you can pick out in the united parishes of Birstall [Ellen's home] and Gomersal [Mary's home]. It is vain to limit a character like hers within ordinary boundaries – she will overstep them. I am morally certain Mary will establish her own landmarks . . .'

In April, Charlotte wrote again to say that Mary had fixed on New Zealand. Only a year before, in January 1840, the first group of settlers had landed in Wellington. In the event, it took some years before Mary eventually left England in 1845. To emigrate, she said in retrospect, was to take 'a desperate plunge' and to come up 'in another world'. She was careful to be honest. 'The new world will be no Paradise but still much better than the nightmare', she wrote to Ellen from Wellington on 9 February 1849. In 1857, she claimed to be in better health than at any time since leaving school. This she ascribed to the interest of running her own business, the difference between everything being a burden and everything being more or less a pleasure: 'Half from physical weakness & half from depression of spirits my judgement in former days was always at war with my will. There was always plenty to do but never anything that I really felt was worth the labour of doing.'

The one solution which Mary ignored was writing. Of course, public writing was improper – immodest – in the way Southey made clear, but Mary's dark view of women's prospects in England was, in fact, countered by Charlotte's eventual triumph. As Charlotte had long been aware, her way forward depended on a resolve to wrench herself finally and completely from her absorption in Angria. This had the drawn-out difficulty of ending an obsessive love affair. One attempt to free herself was to write a formal 'Farewell to Angria' late in 1839.

In forming her resolve, she was influenced by two novels of the late 1830s. On the back of the 'Farewell to Angria', she notes a new and quite different theme in *Nicholas Nickleby* which she read as soon as it appeared in monthly numbers in 1838–9:

> Boy-destroyer
> Mr Squeers
> Dotheboys-Hall Greta-Bridge
> Yorkshire
> Favoured by Chas Dickens Esqre.

The subject of a child's suffering in a cruel school may have suggested The Clergy Daughters' School and its destruction of Maria as possible material for fiction – an early source, perhaps, for *Jane Eyre*. If this turns out to be true, it might be reasonable to infer it was at this moment that Charlotte Brontë perceived her own life as the material of art. At the same time, she would have been alerted to Dickens' derision of worthless aristocrats (Sir Mulberry Hawk and Lord Frederick Verisopht) and his satire on fashionable tosh (when Kate Nickleby reads from *The Lady Flabella* to Mrs Wititterly).

Charlotte was also impressed by Harriet Martineau's *Deerbrook* (1839) whose hero is a surgeon and whose heroine comes from Birmingham, an industrial town not unlike those familiar to Charlotte in Yorkshire. Martineau herself believed that this novel helped to overcome a prejudice against middle-class life in fiction at a time when readers looked for lords and ladies in every page of a new novel. In *Deerbrook* a disabled governess opens up the experience of unrequited love as women bear it in shamed silence: she claims that though marriage is a constant topic, young women are totally unprepared for the impact of passion, and that the silencing of this tumult in order to present a socially acceptable facade is worse than death. *Deerbrook*, then, links what Charlotte called 'infernal' dreams with a confident reaction against shallow society novels, and in this instance the author was a woman – 'the cleverest woman that ever lived' says the heroine of Charlotte's story, 'Caroline Vernon', written in the second half of 1839. The story also remarks on the unusual freedom of Miss Martineau's investigations of America in 1836: 'she travelled like a man – to find out the best way of Governing a country.' It is impossible to say with any exactness where contemporary influence converges with a writer's latent impulse. But it is clear that after ten years' immersion in dreams of vapid beauties, Charlotte resolved to move on, and that by the time she articulated this resolve, she had already conceived her own antithesis to titled ladies in the shape of a teacher much like herself: intelligent, passionate, and barely seen – much less, known or defined.

Charlotte was twenty-three when she wrote the well-known words: '. . . We must change, for the eye is tired of the picture so oft recurring . . .' The society-dream had become a drug that consumed her mind. To abandon dream-people was, in a sense, the greatest challenge of her creative life:

When I depart from these I feel almost as if I stood on the threshold of a home and were bidding farewell to its inmates.

When I strive to conjure up new inmates I feel as if I had got into a distant country where every face was unknown, and the character of all the population an enigma which it would take much study to comprehend and much talent to expound. Still, I long to quit for awhile that burning clime where we have sojourned too long – its skies flame, the glow of sunset is always upon it.

How did Charlotte reach this 'distant country'? What was the nature of its unknown inmates?

Soon after the 'Farewell to Angria', Charlotte drew on her Roe Head experience in a fictional fragment of 1839 about Mary Percy, a motherless, isolated pupil at 'Mrs Turner's Seminary at Kensington'. Mary's father seldom came to see her. When he did, his appearance and style impressed shallow ladylike Mrs Turner. Charlotte then rewrote the fragment as part of an unfinished novel, known as 'Ashworth'.* Much of this work still has the flaws of Angria: it wallows tediously in high society; the talk is, for the most part, vacuous; the plot meanders. But the dormitory scene in the second chapter, from the view of an exploited teacher called Miss Hall, renews the introspective energy of the Roe Head fragments and the portrait of Elizabeth Hastings. For a brief space, we glimpse, again, the elusive character of an obscure woman: bent to her task as she packs pupils' trunks at the end of term, lit by a single candle, vanishing into shadow – then absent from the text as it returns to routine dramas of society ladies.

Ellen Hall, or 'Hall' as she is called by the snobbish schoolgirl,

---

* CB may have derived the name, Ashworth, from a West Yorkshire beauty, Phoebe Ashworth, who eloped with a man whom she soon discovered she did not like. Rather in the manner of an Angrian romance, she was rescued by the martial gentlemanly Revd Hammond Roberson (see ch. 1), who then married her himself. Phoebe Ashworth was the niece of Dr Joseph Priestley, the scientist, who belonged to a notable family in the area.

Amelia De Capell, is one of those poor, educated, estranged girls who fall between the two nations of rich and poor. As a half-boarder, 'Hall' must work for her education. And as another pupil, Mary Ashworth, observes, 'Hall' is kept so busy by Mrs Turner that she has no time for her studies. The school destines her for a future as nursery governess or companion, a lower grade of employment than her abilities merit.

To notice 'Hall' at all requires a deliberate swerve from the usual material of fiction: 'I am not going to descend into . . . the brilliantly lighted drawing-room of Mrs Turner's establishment – where . . . twenty young ladies elegantly dressed were showing off their accomplishments . . .' As in the case of Miss West, a public downstairs display is set off against the recess of consciousness, and the scene that follows prefigures the lone consciousness of the teacher, Lucy Snowe, in *Villette*. The new fictional focus is the silence that fills the upper chambers of the school where a lone half-boarder bends over a half-packed trunk. When she moves away to seek missing articles 'her candle then vanished with her[;] all behind was left in total darkness & silence' – before a burst of girlish voices sounds through the passage, and party frocks of satin sweep past the 'Drudge' kneeling on the floor in her dark merino gown made high and bordered only with a narrow tucker. The girls gather by their dressing-tables which stand in the window recesses (a revival of the scene in the 'Roe Head Journal' where Charlotte was jolted from her dream by the chatter of pupils at the window as they curled their hair). Amelia De Capell, who speaks to the Drudge only to convey her orders, contrasts with Mary Ashworth who says to Hall: 'Of all the Slaves of Industry you are the most indefatigable –'.

That final school night, in the sleeping darkness of the dormitory, Mary makes Hall a present of Scott and Byron. Their communion registers, briefly, a rapport women might share in the interstices of the plots laid down for them by their society. Hall and Mary go different ways: Hall fades into obscurity, Mary enters her lady-of-the-manor destiny. As the novel progressed, Charlotte became increasingly caught in Angrian elaboration: Mary, the daughter of a financial rogue (Percy, the Angrian 'Rogue', was the original name of Ashworth in the manuscript) is in line to marry the prospective hero, Arthur Ripley West (the wild son of General West, derived from Arthur Wellesley/ Zamorna in the Angrian tales), after he has toyed with and destroyed the little snowdrop girl, here called Marian Fairbourne (Marian Hume in Angria).

Ellen Hall did not belong in these Angrian tangles, and her author seems to intimate that she could not as yet pursue character at that depth: 'a mind of another order – one that could see farther – feel deeper – look higher, One whose nature was not all known at once – . . . a subject of protracted interest – that might give you employment for many months before you learnt to read its indications correctly – . . . one liable to more varied & profound impressions – perhaps also to more numerous & rooted defects.'

Too complex, too authentic for the 'novel' in its present form, Hall exists only briefly, by the light of a single candle that fades from our sight as we watch her move away into a further room. But that communion between Hall and Mary, derived from the nightly rapport of the Brontë sisters, foretells other suggestive scenes in fiction where women murmur to each other in the darkness, almost without words: Rachel Vinrace and her aunt, Helen Ambrose, in the dark garden of Virginia Woolf's *The Voyage Out*; mother and grandmother on the shadowy verandah in Mansfield's *Prelude*; and Lily Briscoe and Mrs Ramsay in the midnight bedroom in *To the Lighthouse*.

Charlotte Brontë probably began to write 'Ashworth' in the winter of 1839–40. During the first six months of 1840, Branwell was a tutor at Broughton-in-Furness in the Lake District. On 1 May he visited Hartley Coleridge, the eldest son of the poet, at Ambleside. A few weeks later Branwell sent him translations of Horace's *Odes*. His encouragement of Branwell may have persuaded Charlotte to send him her manuscript of 'Ashworth' – it is not clear exactly when, but it is certain from the stamps on the wrapper that he returned it some time between May and late November 1840. On the inside of this wrapper, Charlotte drafted a reply to some criticisms, which she rewrote as a letter sent, eventually, on 10 December 1840.

Charlotte, like Branwell, was in search of a mentor, but Hartley Coleridge was more suited to Branwell. Eloquent, poetic, he had lost his Oxford fellowship for intemperance and had failed as a schoolmaster. Later, he had redeemed himself with much-praised sonnets, published in 1833, and contributions to *Blackwood's Magazine*. In 1836 he had brought out the biographical *Worthies of Yorkshire and Lancashire*. When Charlotte wrote to him, she had not forgotten Southey's lesson: she did not reveal her sex, and signed herself 'CT' (Charles Thunder). In fact, she rather enjoyed teasing Hartley Coleridge that he could not tell whether CT was a milliner called Charlotte Tomkyss or a clerk called Charles Tims. Both the draft and final letter were written in an assumed style – offhand, ironic – in order to suggest a level of social confidence at odds with the humble status of the personae CT assumes. Obviously, 'he' was challenging Hartley Coleridge to perceive 'his' superiority through language alone.

It is clear from Charlotte's reply that Hartley Coleridge was far from enthralled with 'Ashworth'. In a self-mocking tone, CT owns to Richardsonian pretensions. Arthur West was to have been a Sir Charles Grandison, Ashworth a Mr B——, and the ladies variations on Pamela, Clarissa, and Harriet Byron – only, they were to improve on Richardson: they would reject perfect virtue and total depravity for characters who were naturally mixed. But, of course, all this was over-ambitious to a ridiculous degree. CT seems able to accept the criticism that 'Ashworth' was far too diffuse. In truth, the young writer had not yet discarded the digressions and indulgences of Angria. There is more of an edge to 'Ashworth' in its critique of women's manners, but it is still entranced with beauties in satin. Realising that Hartley Coleridge was not being unreasonable, Charlotte set to work to revise 'Ashworth' over the winter of 1840–41, and then abandoned it when she left Haworth to be a governess once more.

The most interesting comment in her letter to Hartley Coleridge was a hint of unshaken determination, almost lost amidst the off-hand gestures: CT had resolved to wait patiently for 'some Maecenas [patron of artists] who shall discern and encourage my rising talent'.

The four chapters of 'Ashworth' do not promise a great novel: on the contrary, they show how very difficult it was for Charlotte to leave Angria, despite her 'Farewell'. They show, too, the tenacity of this material for the mature Charlotte Brontë who was to effect a brilliant transformation of this story, thirteen years later, in the beginnings of a final novel, 'Emma'.

At the beginning of 1841, Charlotte steeled herself to find a new post. By March she was teaching a girl of eight and a boy of six at Upperwood House, Rawdon, six miles from Bradford, at a salary of £16 a year (while Branwell was paid £75 as an assistant railway clerk at Sowerby Bridge on the Leeds-Manchester line, rising to £130 a year when he was promoted to a new station at Luddenden Foot in April 1841). Charlotte accepted half the normal salary in a less grand house in the hope of unsnobbish employers. She preferred John White, a Bradford merchant, to the Sidgwicks but had to 'try hard' to like Mrs White who, again, loaded her with sewing to fill spare hours.

'Well I can believe that Mrs White has been an exciseman's daughter,' Charlotte wrote contemptuously to Ellen after she had witnessed her employer's bad grammar and 'very coarse and unladylike' temper. Mr White too, she decided, was of 'low' extraction despite his affected hauteur towards 'trades-folk'.

A visitor to the Whites saw her sitting apart from the family in a corner of the room, poring in a short-sighted way over a book – an ill-at-ease young woman of twenty-five. Years later, in *Villette*, Charlotte Brontë revealed what might lurk within the bent head of a young teacher: a rather soothing thought that where she could never be 'rightly known' it might be an actual 'pleasure' to be wholly misjudged and ignored. This superior thought might have alleviated Charlotte's aversion: for the 'rude familiarity' of the children and for her own mask – the 'cold, frigid–apathetic exterior' she had to adopt, an 'estrangement from one's real character'. She could not adapt to the Whites 'whose ideas and feelings are nearly as incomprehensible to *me*, as probably mine (if I showed them unreservedly) would be to *them*.'

The nub of the problem was not really the Whites nor even the odious Sidgwicks, but her need to expand her mind. During the leisure of the previous year she had devoured numerous (unidentified) volumes in French, borrowed from the Taylors, which she found 'clever wicked sophistical and immoral – the best of it is they give one a thorough idea of France and Paris – and are the best substitute for French Conversation'. Then, there was always the problem of affinities at home which nothing, it seemed, could replace. 'My home is humble and unattractive to strangers,' Charlotte wrote in May 1841, 'but to me it contains what I shall find nowhere else in the world – the profound, the intense affection which brothers and sisters feel for each other when their minds are cast in the same mould, their ideas drawn from the same source – when they have clung to each other from childhood . . .' It was during 1841 that Charlotte decided that some solution would have to be found to intolerable separations.

One solution seemed to present itself when Miss Wooler offered Charlotte the school at Dewsbury Moor, including equipment and furniture for a start. This coincided with Charlotte's idea that she and her sisters should run a school together. Miss Wooler seems to have hesitated over the inclusion of Emily and Anne in her scheme: these were girls who had sickened and collapsed. There was a long silence. In the meantime, a letter arrived from Mary who had been travelling as much as she could while she waited to realise her plan to emigrate. She was now completing her education in Brussels and urged Charlotte to join her. Mary wrote of exquisite pictures and venerable cathedrals. As Charlotte read, an irresistible thirst swelled her throat: 'such a vehement impatience of restraint and steady work. Such a strong wish for wings – wings such as wealth can furnish – such an urgent thirst to see – to know – to learn – something internal seemed to expand boldly for a minute – I was tantalized with the consciousness of faculties unexercised . . .'

In October she refused Dewsbury Moor, that 'obscure and dreary place'. She spoke of a 'fire' for attainments, which she could not quench once Mary had cast oil upon the flames.

To take the school on offer, and eventually, when she was in a stronger position, to bring in her sisters: this would have been a logical course. If Charlotte had chosen this course in September-October 1841, the Brontës' lives might have been different: more secure, more independent of their father and brother, and also more limited to the circumscribed world of school. But as the months passed in the confinement of the schoolroom or in that dim corner of the drawing-room at Upperwood House, Charlotte could think only of another world of art and learning. She must grasp the chance to leave the House of Bondage. Brussels was her 'promised land'.

There was 'still the wilderness of time and space to cross before I reach it', she told Ellen on 10 December. Emily, she decided, was to go with her; Anne to stay behind as the daughter at home. For some reason, perhaps the wish to earn her keep, perhaps a wish to gather material for her first novel on the life of a governess, Anne decided to remain in her second post, as governess to the spoilt, flighty Robinson girls, at Thorp Green Hall, near York, where she had worked since March 1841. Charlotte's comfort for Anne was no more than a vague promise of a similar opportunity for her in the future. At the same time, Charlotte secured Aunt's financial help with a businesslike letter which disguised the promised land as a market where future school-owners would buy the skills — French, German, music — required for their prospectus. She asked for fifty or a hundred pounds. The letter lifts from its solid argument only when Charlotte dares to put herself in the position of her father: 'When he left Ireland to go to Cambridge University, he was as ambitious as I am now.'

At the beginning of 1841, Charlotte had looked back on a 'poetical' adolescence, followed by a cooling period of sober duty, the 'intermediate years' from nineteen to twenty-five which had robbed life of some of its superfluous colouring. She took this as necessary discipline. 'At this age it is time that the imagination should be pruned and trimmed — that the judgement should be cultivated — and a *few* at least, of the countless illusions of early youth should be cleared away. I have not written poetry for a long while.' Southey's denial of her ambition in 1837 had been succeeded in 1840 by Hartley Coleridge with his reasonable disparagement of 'Ashworth'. Her reply assured him in studiedly indifferent tones that she could put away a vast enterprise. There is no evidence that she wrote fiction for another four years.

It might appear that the teacher had ousted the dreamer, but a new and more tangible dream replaced the old. The juvenile fantasies of high life were over; in their place was a real venture in an unknown country and the prospect of mental expansion (in the shade of legitimate duty). Château de Koekelberg, the finishing school attended by Mary and her sister, Martha, proved too expensive, and after much debate, the Brontës settled on the Pensionnat Heger, on the recommendation of Mrs Jenkins, wife of the British Chaplain in Brussels. On 8 February 1842, Charlotte and Emily set out via London and Ostend, fortified by Mr Brontë,

Mary (who had returned briefly to England), and her brother, Joe. In Brussels, the divide between dream and duty would close, briefly, under the inspired teaching of M. Heger at the school on the Rue d'Isabelle.

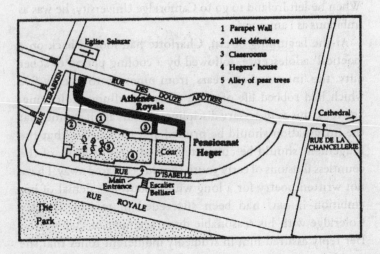

4

LOVE'S LANGUAGE

When Charlotte left for Brussels, nothing in her reading, dreams, or meagre experience had prepared her for the exhilaration of M. Heger: a born teacher who could engage with her gift. At the age of twenty-five she had turned down proposals from wooden Henry Nussey and airy David Bryce. She had discounted the charms of 'Celia Amelia' as she called her father's flirtatious curate, William Weightman. She had felt the temptations of the promiscuous Zamorna and the cold William Percy, and dismissed their destructive games. Parting finally from Angria, she crossed the border from dream to reality as the diligence bowled through flat fields with belts of cut trees on the horizon, past painted farmhouses and narrow canals gliding slow by the roadside, en route to the Pensionnat Heger.

The school was in a narrow, cobbled street, sunk below the fashionable Rue Royale and park. Steep steps led down to the Rue d'Isabelle which no longer exists. Nearby was the Cathedral of St Michel and St Gudule. In a mansion built about 1800, the school occupied the ground of what in the middle ages had been a hospital (in the medieval sense), a charitable institution for housing the poor, infirm, or aged. It had been run by a religious order who had cultivated a herb garden and orchards. The garden, including an ancient pear tree, remained part of the Pensionnat, secluded behind the shutters and high walls. There, Mr Brontë left his daughters in the care of the Hegers.

M. Heger was professor of rhetoric, as Charlotte called him 'a little black ugly being' who soon revealed himself to be 'a man of power as to mind, but very choleric and irritable in temperament.' He contemplated her errors with the face of a 'delirious Hyena'; a stray English word ('fishing-rod') in her French translation seemed to pluck the eyes from his head. Her Anglicisms were 'barbarisms'. She cried as he tore aside the veil of manners with scathing comments on her careful *devoirs*, transcribed with decorative headings in her most immaculate hand. The master set a new standard of logic, grace, and power: no inapt phrase, none of the vagaries of 'Ashworth', must break the developing line. He taught her to 'sacrifice, *without pity*, everything that does not contribute to clarity'. Start with calm, almost prosaic control, he told her, but once the mind is racing, let go the rein.

Some of Heger's directives were curiously seductive. His actions also. Charlotte mentioned a recurrent scene: the way he would smoke into her desk when he left his surprises – books, sometimes with cryptic notes. As she opened the lid, she smelled the tell-tale aroma of his cigar. She recreated this scene in *Villette*, renewing the stir of physical excitement, stronger than her dreams, in the bent of her teacher's body, his intentness, and the searching movement of his hand: 'his olive hand held my desk open, his nose was lost to view amongst my papers . . . Now I knew . . . that that hand . . . was on intimate terms with my desk; that it raised and lowered the lid, ransacked and arranged the contents, almost as familiarly as my own . . . Now, as he sat bending above the desk, he was stirring up its contents; but with gentle and careful hand'.

His fury, she came to see, was a mark of his regard: it singled her out. 'From others of the studious band, / Erelong he singled me', she pencilled in her German Notebook of May 1843. 'But only by more close demand, / And sterner urgency.'

When Charlotte discursed on a longing to exercise her powers ('. . . *parcequ'il y a dans certaines natures*, une ardeur *indomptable qui ne leur permet pas de rester inactives* . . .'), Monsieur told her curtly to keep to the subject of Pierre l'Hermite: '*vous êtes entrée dans le sujet: marchez au but.*'

He rebuked her indulgence in imagery: any image that did not illumine and interpret was a fault of style. He insisted on the decorum of form as the sole route to immortality: '*étudiez la forme — Poëte vous serez plus puissant — vos œuvres vivront*' ['study form — if you are a poet, you will be more powerful — your works will live']. At the same time, he insisted on '*le mot juste*' and introduced her to foreign felicities of expression, screwing up his face with the urgency of his demand, then relenting when she cried. A Brussels poem set out the fierce challenge of this election:

> The task he from another took,
> From me he did reject;
> He would no slight omission brook,
> And suffer no defect.
>
> If my companions went astray,
> He scarce their wanderings blamed;
> But if I faltered in the way,
> His anger fiercely flamed.

One draft of this poem refers to 'nameless bliss' as she dreamt that she might be loved in the way she loved: a 'mighty feeling' she could define only through metaphors of space — the pathless wilderness or dangerous waves that 'lay our lives between'. These dangers she would court with characteristic impetuosity.

This love does not fit the usual terms of infatuation or affair. It was a lifelong attachment, rooted in her writer's being through which 'the tide of life did pour'; it impelled the flow of words, generating the surge of her mature prose. Her teacher was not a man to write books, but he offered her an array of ideas with almost careless abundance: 'his mind was indeed my library, and whenever it was opened to me, I entered bliss'. Though communications were blocked by Mme Heger, Charlotte had no expectation of physical adultery, and she seemed astonished when Madame's suspicions eventually broke on her during 1843. What she most wanted was original and, in its way, more enthralling than adultery: a union of minds in which her *maître* would make her a writer. Her deepest response to him turned on language: the words of her *devoirs* exploding in fury and tears; the words they exchanged through letters; and eventually, when these forms of communication were closed, the novels growing in that unspoken space of 1844–6, after Charlotte's return to the dull routines of Haworth when she closed her lips even to Emily, an act of deliberate silence which she saw as self-punishment for her folly, but which was, all the same, the fertile silence of creativity.

In 1842–3, Constantin Heger was thirty-three, seven years older than Charlotte. He was stocky, with black hair, and always dressed in black. A portrait done twenty-five years later looks much as Charlotte described him: a tigerish tension in his blue eyes, a confrontational readiness in the way he seats himself, a square-faced intentness that suggests a challenge at once dramatic and severe. His '*Écoutez!*' was like a blast on a trumpet. He lacked the calm of force, Charlotte said, 'but its movement and its fire he signally possessed'. Whatever he read became 'a vessel for an outpouring'. Another of his pupils remembered the 'veritable dramas' of these readings inspired by visits to the Comédie Française as a young man in Paris: 'You saw, you felt . . . you went through a riot of emotion, exactly in proportion as he wished . . . In talking perhaps he made his profoundest impression by a steadfast often mocking gaze at the person . . . I believe he liked to watch the emotions he could produce with his ever-changing facial expression and amazing turns of thought and temper.' He could wither a pupil with a scarcely perceptible movement of lip and nostril or exalt her with the faint flicker of an eyelid. He harangued the girls on the way they used their noble tongue, mincing words between their teeth as though they were ashamed to open their mouths. Was this really modesty? Or was it vile affectation? Girls began to weep. There was a passion in his anger that excited rather pleasurable tears. The vast majority who responded in this way venerated the master; a few who did not melt did not much care for him.

For Monsieur, as his pupils called him, teaching was a vocation. Apart from his post at the main boys' school, the Athénée Royale, supplemented by classes at his wife's Pensionnat, he also gave evening classes for factory workers. His strength as a teacher shows in the way he studied the needs and characters of his pupils. In June 1842, by which time he had grasped the extraordinary potential of the Brontës, he devised what was then a new method of instruction. Though, on arrival, their French was not particularly good, he decided that instead of stressing grammar, he would read aloud classic extracts of French literature so that his English pupils might discern an author's motive and 'principle' and, at the same time, catch the feeling and rhythm of French. He asked them to write '*Imitations*' in the same style, with the same subtlety of 'nuance'. The master-stroke was to demand that they apply this feeling, rhythm, and nuance to subjects of their own choosing.

He told them: 'It is necessary, before sitting down to write on a subject, to have thoughts and feelings about it. I cannot tell on what subject your heart and mind have been excited. I must leave that to you.'

Charlotte accepted this challenge; Emily objected. She did not wish to imitate anyone (any more than she would accept the passing dictates of fashion: 'I wish to be as God made me', she is reported to have said at the Pensionnat). Monsieur overrode her objection, but where Charlotte chose Pierre l'Hermite for her *Imitation*, Emily showed her native fist by choosing the Anglo-Saxon leader, Harold, who resisted the Norman invasion. In turn, M. Heger showed his mettle as a teacher unthreatened by manifestations of Emily's will. He must have been a man of unusual judgement, for he was the first outside the Parsonage and for decades to come, to recognise the genius of Emily. He thought she would have made a great navigator with the power to deduce new spheres of discovery and a will never to be daunted by difficulty. He could see beyond what Charlotte called her sister's 'singularities' – Emily's indifference to the *maître's* opinion, or to that of anyone else – and her complete detachment from any concession to femininity. It is to Monsieur's credit that, susceptible as he was, he could see a woman's character and promise rather than her ornamental aspect.

M. Heger transformed Charlotte's ideas of manhood. Unlike Papa, Southey, or Hartley Coleridge, here was a man who wished her to write – wished truly and urgently to perfect her gift. Charlotte's Angrian characters had been hopelessly thin: Monsieur gave her and Emily exercises in character synthesis by exposing them to conflicting portraits, a further training in nuance and insight. Unlike the Byronic nobleman of juvenile fantasy, Monsieur backed work and merit, reflecting their own middle-class and religious values. Many of the *devoirs* Charlotte wrote for him were on religious topics: '*Portrait de Pierre l'Hermite*', '*L'Immensité de Dieu*', '*Lettre d'un Missionaire, Sierra Leone, Afrique*', and '*La Mort de Moïse*' on Moses' sighting of the promised land on Mount Nebo, the visionary's leadership and death, a topic suggested by Monsieur's dramatic reading of a poem on Joan of Arc. Monsieur said of her, '*Elle était nourrie de la Bible.*' Through him, the alternating extremes of pilgrimage and passion were united – all too briefly in Charlotte's life, but permanently in her work.

M. Heger's letters to Charlotte have vanished, but forty years later, writing to another English pupil, his engaging ways remained undimmed. In this later letter we hear his voice as he talks to a favoured pupil: his enlivened response to English reserve, his bristle at the independence of a Protestant. His belief in the silent communication of 'two distant hearts' and his wish to penetrate the emotional guard, had the cover – and licence – of a firmly married man. M. Heger was adept at verbal caresses:

I have only to think of you to see you. I often give myself the pleasure when my duties are over. When the light fades I postpone lighting the gas lamp in my library, I sit down, smoking my cigar, and with a hearty will I evoke your image – and you come (without wishing to, I dare say) but I see, I talk with you – you with that little air, affectionate undoubtedly, but independent and resolute . . . demanding to be convinced before allowing yourself to submit . . .

This voice is like Rochester's as he contemplates Jane in his library and becomes aware of a resolute woman who does not deny feeling but who will not allow it to shake her reason.

The Heger encounter, central to Charlotte's writing, had to be suppressed in Mrs Gaskell's biography, and began to emerge only after Heger's death in 1896. When Frederika Macdonald (who had been at the Pensionnat) spoke to his daughter, Louise, in 1894, she commented to a correspondent how absurd that such an ordinary man should have been in a position of power over a child of genius. But Heger was, in fact, exceptional. Despite his lip service to women's domestic destiny – the refrain of his day – his wish to induce expressiveness in his pupils was special in the context of contemporary norms of feminine passivity.

It was a measure of confidence in Monsieur as her first sympathetic reader that Charlotte was ready to give him some of her private writings. She left three booklets, 'The Spell', 'High Life In Verdopolis', and 'The Scrap Book', behind in Brussels. But why she chose these works of 1834–5, rather than more recent fictions, remains a puzzle. One answer might be a wish to show Monsieur the precocious professionalism of her youth before she had subjected herself to the grind of teaching. She would not, in that case, have offered the booklets as a token of her *present* abilities, but as part of her *past* self. It was the most precious gift she had to confer in exchange for her *maître*'s favour and presents. Another answer could be a lingering attachment to Angria (as she wrote to Branwell on 1 May 1843: 'I always recur as fanatically as ever to the old ideas, the old faces, and the old scenes in the world below'). But the most plausible answer is renewed ambition: the plan to draw on the Cain and Abel theme of rival brothers, originating in Branwell's story, 'The Wool is Rising' (1834), taken up by Charlotte's fiction of that year, and finding its way eventually into her first mature novel, *The Professor* (1846). When she returned to the Pensionnat, after a brief stay in Haworth, in January 1843, it is conceivable that she already had the idea of bringing together the Angrian material of 1834 and the autobiographical material of her Brussels experience in a new fictional venture – but in the course of 1843 became too depressed to pursue this at once.

Yet all the while she tested her belief in interior experience as the basis of art: 'I believe that all real poetry is only the faithful impression of something which happens or has happened in the soul of the poet'.

'Very good', said Monsieur. 'Very true.'

'To write', she pressed him, 'is anything else needed beside genius, converging with some sentiment, affection or passion? . . . Together, will they not be like a cut diamond for which language is only the wax on which they stamp their imprint? . . . It is in sharpening sensibility, in giving a great vivacity to the passions . . . that [genius] announces his presence and shows his power.'

Monsieur checked her: 'Genius without study, without art, without the knowledge of what has been done, is strength without the lever', he said, 'it is the soul that sings within, and cannot express its interior song save in a rough and raucous voice'.

Genius must be rash and daring, Charlotte insisted, excessive by its very nature. 'The distinctive quality of mediocrity is moderation: a precious quality, but cold; the result of gentle temperament, . . . rather than strenuous efforts of the self.'

So, she confided in Monsieur through her *devoirs*. A poem written at the time of their encounter records the convergence of love and ambition. A pupil, 'Jane', puts up with her master's temper and grudging praise because she has 'learnt to read/ The secret meaning of his face'. She feels the laurel descending on her brow, a recognition that pierces the pupil's reserve:

> The strong pulse of Ambition struck
> In every vein I owned;
> At the same instant bleeding broke
> A secret, inward wound.

The consummation of art comes through love – a pedagogic form of love in which the deepest bond lies in surrender to guidance. Monsieur grasped some link between expression and passion of the greatest importance to Charlotte. He could attend to a passion that had an imaginative base in words and character, what Charlotte called 'genius' – the pre-uttered, in part unutterable. The 'black Swan', as Charlotte called him, reached out to this undefined thing. The letter to his pupil speaks of his own 'precious and more convenient methods of communication, spiritual, magnetic, or by suggestion . . .' His wife played this down in her politic way as 'respectful avowal of tender sentiments', but she did allow that Monsieur could, on occasion, be moved by touching eyes (as Charlotte had) to make 'a sort of discreet declaration'. All this suggests his appeal to the young Charlotte Brontë and why passion was not wholly a figment of her need but part of the contact-power he consciously exercised and enjoyed – and from which he could withdraw at his convenience by virtue of the fact that whatever he suggested could not, of its very nature, be stated. Even when he withdrew, his 'spiritual, magnetic' communication was designed to persist in the mind of a pupil to whom he had said those gripping words, 'I see you', and who was conscious that he evoked her memory in the acrid smoke of his cigar when she was gone. If Monsieur behaved in this way to Charlotte, it is no wonder she found him irresistible.

It is clear from her *devoirs* that she either initiated or reciprocated this kind of unspoken exchange. She used her portrait of

Napoleon ('*La Mort de Napoléon*', dated 31 May [1843]) as a rather unsuitable pretext for speaking of the misery of exiles and of a humiliation they may have to bear: overtures of friendship inspired by no warmer motive than pity or charity. This, the exile, in all self-respect, must repulse: 'contempt is charity's brother, and charity herself, though good, is cold.' Monsieur was not a man to have missed such a blatant invitation to convince his pupil of his warmest interest.

Charlotte wondered why this man of intuitive sensibility should have married a cold, calculating, and in Charlotte's view, unamiable woman like Zoë Heger, head of the Pensionnat. In fact, she was pretty, with a white neck and arms, which showed to advantage in evening dress, and abundant hair of a striking colour. A hairdresser was frequently called to the school to attend it. Mme Heger epitomised the mannerly, well-dressed Continental woman, and ran her school with serene efficiency. She had the composed deportment of her émigré French family, in particular that of the irreproachable aunt, an ex-nun, from whom she had inherited her school. When Claire Zoë Parent had married Constantin Heger, he had been absorbed into her flourishing school, after a stressful youth when his family had lost their wealth, followed by fighting in the 1830 revolt against the Dutch, and the death of his first wife and child in the cholera epidemic of 1833. The second Mme Heger, five years older than Monsieur, gave him security and a new family. In *The Professor*, Charlotte's first novel to grow out of the Brussels experience, the head advises the professor against the attention he gives his star pupil, Frances Henri. Zoraïde Reuter, the head, takes the view, in the same terms as Southey, that young women must be schooled to the social scheme. Frances delights in composition: 'such occupation seemed the very breath of her nostrils'. She smiles shyly and her eyes rest on the master's hand which, stretched over her shoulder, is writing some direction in the margin of her book. Mdlle Reuter, who sees all, warns Monsieur that Frances has too much self-love: 'celebrity has a tendency to foster this sentiment and in her it should be rather repressed; she rather needs keeping down than bringing forward; and then I think, Monsieur – it appears to me that ambition – *literary* ambition especially, is not a feeling to be cherished in the mind of a woman; would not Mdlle. Henri be much safer and happier if taught to believe that in the quiet discharge of social duties consists her real vocation, than if stimulated to aspire after applause and publicity? She may never marry; scanty as are her resources, obscure as are her connections, uncertain as is her health . . . it is more than probable she never will; . . . but even in celibacy it would be better for her to retain the character and habits of a respectable, decorous female.'

This is a jealous fiction. The real head was too discreet to articulate such explicit resistance. All Charlotte knew was that Monsieur gradually withdrew from her during the second year at the Pensionnat, wrote her fewer and fewer letters, and eventually, by the end of 1845, no longer replied to her increasingly desperate pleas. This denial Charlotte ascribed wholly to Madame, in line with her contempt for women as women's chief enemy. In *The Professor* and again in *Villette*, she cast Mme Heger as a caricature Catholic: sinister, devious, smooth – in this, deeply unEnglish – and unEnglish above all in her sly methods of surveillance in order to produce the school's model of robust obedience.

Charlotte's contempt for her sex is nowhere more insistent than in her comments in her 'Roe Head Journal' and in her treatment of Belgian schoolgirls in *The Professor*. It is easy to understand her antagonism to girls at Roe Head where her hours left no time for writing; and it is easy, too, to condone her dislike of snobbish employers. But Charlotte's antagonism for women in Brussels is a different matter. She and Emily held aloof; they told each other that Belgians hated the English. There were eighty to a hundred girls at the Pensionnat, and of them, only Emily's admiring music pupil, sixteen-year-old Louise de Bassompierre, and the English Wheelwright sisters befriended the Brontës or were befriended by them. The Wheelwrights, especially the eldest, Laetitia, were drawn to Charlotte, but disliked Emily whom they described as lanky, untidy, and unsociable. They particularly resented her music lessons, given during playtime so that this did not infringe on her own working hours. 'We are completely isolated in the midst of numbers', Charlotte told Ellen. Between lessons in French, German, and music, the sisters walked alone, Emily – though taller – leaning on Charlotte and, in Monsieur's view, exercising some sort of unconscious tyranny over her. Of course, given Emily's history of breakdown at Roe Head and Law Hill, Charlotte, alert to the dangers of Emily's homesickness, watched over her anxiously; yet an exclusive bond with Emily was something she always wanted.

Were they rejected for their odd clothes, defiant Protestantism, and awkward reserve? Or did they estrange themselves through proud contempt and anti-Catholic intolerance (despite – or because of – their own Catholic origins in Ireland)?

Many of their schoolmates came from social backgrounds above that of the Brontës, and the question of class cannot be ignored. That Charlotte and Emily took their touchiness with them to Belgium is evident in their recoil from certain kindnesses that were *not* foreign: invitations from the Revd and Mrs Jenkins of the British Embassy, when Emily would sit through holidays and Sunday afternoons uttering no more than an occasional monosyllable. Charlotte's habit was to wheel round in her chair so as almost to conceal her face from the person who addressed her. At school, they did not associate with the only other English boarder, the fashionable, dashing Maria Miller, and they deplored the 'hard' and 'heavy' Belgians, the society girls whom Charlotte dismissed as alien creatures of lead and iron.

The Professor examines girls as specimens drawn from a multitude of countries, in order to explode the nineteenth-century myth of womanhood. 'Let the idealists, the dreamers about earthly angels and human flowers, just look here while I open my

portfolio and show them a sketch or two, pencilled after nature.'
The English observer, Crimsworth, teaching the second class (as
Charlotte taught the second class in 1843) has before him about a
hundred specimens of the genus '*jeune fille*', similar in dress and
manners. One by one, platitudes of femininity are demolished:
the majority was 'rough, boisterous'. Aurelia was slovenly and
even dirty; her hair 'glossy with gum and grease'. Juanna Trista
spat and used brutal expressions. Each pursued her needs, indifferent to those of others. And far from the usual equation of
ignorance and innocence, almost no one over fourteen was not a
flirt. The subversion of femininity is uncompromising: 'Doubtless
it will be thought that I ought now, by way of contrast, to shew
something charming; some gentle virgin head, circled with a
halo, some sweet personification of Innocence, clasping the dove
of peace to her bosom. No — I saw nothing of the sort and therefore cannot portray it.' Here is the second explosion, more
controlled, more assured as the novelist's voice of truth: a fresh
spurt, from the same source as the 'Roe Head Journal', but
brought into the open by the inviting vehemence of Monsieur.

Initially, Charlotte and Emily went to the Pensionnat in
February 1842 for six months only, though Charlotte meant to
stay for a year in Brussels by finding a post. In the event, posts
came their way smoothly through Mme Heger: in July 1842 she
proposed that the sisters extend their stay at the Pensionnat as
teacher-pupils for another half-year. Charlotte was to teach
English, Emily music where she continued to show brilliance.
Madame offered no pay, but the sisters were to have their lessons
and board free. Towards the end of 1842 came news that Aunt
Branwell was dying, and they returned to Haworth to find her
dead.

They were dismayed to hear of another, more untimely
death, that of William Weightman, the flirtatious curate whom
Charlotte had called Celia Amelia. Mr Brontë's succession of
curates was almost all Irish, and there seems to have been a prejudice in the Parsonage against the Irish which may have been

part of Mr Brontë's effort to distance himself and his children from their social origins. We might contrast Charlotte's flat refusal of the offer from the Irish curate, Mr Bryce, with Willie's immediate popularity at the Parsonage when he had arrived in the same month, August 1839. His unusual popularity with all the Brontës may have been due as much to the fact that he was born an Englishman as to his engaging manners and soft good looks with his blue eyes, curly auburn hair, and pink and white complexion. He came from a brewer's family in Appleby, Westmoreland, and had studied theology at Durham University where he had also read some classics. He proved delightful company, sweeping the sisters off to Keighley to hear him lecture at the Mechanics Institute, and sending them and Ellen charming valentines beginning 'Fair Ellen . . .', 'Soul divine . . .', and 'Away, fond love'; in return, Ellen, with mock-tender solicitude, would ask after 'his young reverence'. He was warm, engaging, but soon proved inconstant. At the age of twenty-eight, he died suddenly of cholera in September 1842 while Charlotte and Emily were in Brussels and Anne away at Thorp Green. There is no evidence to support the suggestion that Anne was in love with him beyond the fact that once, in church, Charlotte saw his glance fall on Anne who averted her face. In Anne's first novel, *Agnes Grey*, the heroine has the same first name as Agnes Walton, the girl to whom Weightman claimed, for a while, to be engaged. The narrator says that she began the novel with the intention of concealing nothing, but when she falls in love with a local curate, Mr Weston, reserve seals her lips: '. . . we have *some* thoughts that all the angels in heaven are welcome to behold, but not our brothermen . . .' This long-suffering governess is finally rescued by her marriage to the discerning Mr Weston. Dark, grave, unsmiling, he does not look or act like the fair, merry Weightman but, like him, is surprisingly attentive to the poor and sick.

While the family was united at Haworth, a warm joint letter, full of praise, then arrived from the Hegers, inviting Charlotte to return to the Pensionnat to take over English teaching. Afterwards, Charlotte told Ellen that in January 1843 she was prompted by 'an irresistible impulse' for which she was punished by a total withdrawal of peace of mind for more than two years. Part of Charlotte's temptation in returning to Brussels for a second year was a change in her position: Emily would remain at home to run the Parsonage. During Charlotte's first year in Brussels, Emily had possessed her eldest sister in a way that excluded an outsider's advance, and it is likely that Charlotte's attachment to Monsieur could have flourished only in Emily's absence. From January 1843, back in the sunken street below the Rue Royale, behind the shuttered windows of the Pensionnat, Charlotte now had lessons in French and German alone with M. Heger. As so valuable a member of staff, so liked by the Hegers, she expected to be friends. At first, this seemed to happen: the Hegers invited Charlotte to join them in their private sitting-room after school hours. Soon she was giving English lessons to Monsieur.

The master, now her pupil, made rapid progress. She was teaching her own language, while Heger taught his, and for about two months, there was this reciprocity. In English, Charlotte could give the full measure of her mind. Her licensed expressiveness with a man she had grown to love was a new experience which, in time, she would bring to bear on the ringing tones of Jane Eyre in her speeches to Rochester and on the acid heat of Lucy Snowe in *Villette*, whose surprising competence as a teacher in Brussels is an index of unfathomed flair. Lucy, teaching English to the Belgian master, Paul Emanuel, ventures to call him 'friend', aware that he would grant it the connotations of *mon ami*, though the English word 'did not breathe the same sense of domestic and intimate affection'. The word awakens a smile of content and pleasure she has not seen before – before she had witnessed only the sarcastic or disdainful or passionately exultant smile. This new smile changed his aspect from a mask to a face; his darkness lightened. This may have been the

time when he learnt certain useful phrases like 'I – love – you'
with which, decades later, he delighted to confront an English
pupil, in his staccato tone, half-embarrassed, half-amused.

Suddenly, in April, lessons were terminated. Monsieur
harangued Charlotte on 'universal *bienveillance*' and advised her to
befriend the fellow-teachers she despised. Then he withdrew
'the light of his countenance'. A book he gave Charlotte soon
after may have been a consolation-present, *Das Neue Testament
unsers Herrn und Heilandes Jesu Christi*. She noted in German script:
'*Herr Heger hat mir dieser Buch gegeben Brussel May 1843*'. He also gave her
the *Pensées* of Pascal, a book of poems, the works of Bernardin de
Saint-Pierre, and two of his own prizegiving lectures at the
Athénée Royale.

Charlotte always believed that Monsieur withdrew at the
instigation of Madame. This was indeed a betrayal of the fond
terms in which the couple had urged her to return to Brussels.
Charlotte reacted with rage and rebellion: the other teachers
were 'nothing', she fumed to Branwell in June. She wearied, as at
Roe Head, of 'caring nothing, fearing nothing, liking nothing,
hating nothing, being nothing, doing nothing'. Teaching, for
her, was empty, and she found the pervasive correctness of the
Pensionnat Heger even more unendurable than Roe Head. In
Brussels, if she were to speak as warmly as she had spoken sometimes to Miss Wooler, 'they would think me mad.'

The rest of the year she spent in solitude. 'I lead an easeful,
stagnant, silent life', Charlotte told Branwell on 1 May, aware
that he had joined Anne as tutor at Thorp Green. 'I get on
from day to day in a Robinson Crusoe-like condition – very
lonely', she told Emily at home in the Parsonage. In *Villette*,
Lucy's isolation, as Englishwoman and Protestant, follows the
downhill course of Charlotte herself when the Hegers left her
severely alone. As Lucy leans out of the school window, she lis-
tens to a band, 'thinking meantime my own thoughts, living
my own life in my own still shadow-world . . .' In the deserted
school during the *grandes vacances*, beginning 15 August 1843,

Charlotte's shadow-life dwindled to a point of despair. There came a day when she sought relief in the nearby Cathedral of St Gudule. 'I actually did confess', she wrote to Emily on 2 September, '– a real confession', but she did not explain that her love for Monsieur had taken as complete a hold of her mind as Angria had once done – and if love-dreams had once seemed 'infernal', leaving her 'polluted', the more immediate eroticism of a real man, his intimate looks during private lessons, his hand reaching over her shoulder to correct her writing, his smell in her desk, must have made her even more guilty. Sexual arousal, uninvited as it may have appeared to her, was so shaming to a woman of her faith and class that it was to some indeterminable degree buried, even from herself, but is likely to have surfaced in that moment of extremity when she was driven to a 'real confession' in the Catholic church, and it was to surface again, later, in her fictions.

During this wretched vacation, Charlotte also confided in Mary who was then teaching in Germany. Possibly, she confided more than she owned to Emily, for Mary urged her to leave at once. If she stayed any longer, Mary said, she would not have the strength to go. Afterwards, Charlotte spoke of this advice as a 'service', but she stayed on another two months, living for rare contact with Monsieur – she cared for no one else – while she watched Madame turn into 'a rosy plum' before the birth of a fifth child in November. Madame was no more than 'coloured chalk', she thought bitterly. Though jealousy is obvious, it is also clear that Madame had used and ignored her, in much the same way, in fact, as previous employers. After appearing to offer a special friendship, Madame had argued (via her husband) that Charlotte must find other associates. It must be remembered, too, that though Madame continued to praise her teaching, she drove a mean bargain, paying her employee only £16 for the year, out of which Charlotte had to pay for German lessons with Monsieur. (She was driven to ask her father to cover the extra ten francs a month, which means that, frugal as she was, she

could not subsist on this salary, much less save.) Later, in a letter
to Monsieur, Charlotte could not resist mentioning a £100 offer
from a school in Manchester. It is possible that her combined
sense of personal betrayal and economic exploitation disturbed
her as much as her muted need for Monsieur's continued interest.

Charlotte Brontë's *devoirs* show great leaps in imaginative control as well as verbal range and polish. The final fruit of this
flowering were four longer *devoirs* for M. Heger, written during
1843: 'La Chute des Feuilles' (30 March); 'La Mort de Moïse' (27 July);
'Athènes Sauvée par la Poësie' (6 October) and 'Lettre d'un pauvre Peintre à
un grand Seigneur' (17 October). Charlotte's outrage at her *maître's*
withdrawal might be seen not only in terms of her emotional
need but in the context of the unmistakably gifted work she
produced for him, writing a French that was already 'the language of an artist'. It was also the language in which she judged
and defied her master, using her *devoir*, again, to speak to him,
most urgently in the last two, written in quick succession.

'Détail remarquablement! heureux', M. Heger exclaimed in the
margin of the more ambitious piece, where she recreates a scene
from Plutarch in which a captured Athenian poet is invited by
the victorious Spartans, at the end of the Peloponnesian War, to
celebrate the sack of his city planned for the following day. The
poet, knowing his song would be futile, at first refuses to sing. In
Charlotte Brontë's version, the Spartan leader, Lysander, hurls a
lance at the poet; it misses, and instead cuts the rope which holds
the tent flap closed. It falls back to reveal the moonlit city
beyond, with the columns of the Parthenon gleaming in the distance. It was this poetic detail that impressed Monsieur, but he
disliked what followed. In Plutarch, the poet touches the hearts
of his listeners with his love for the doomed city. In Charlotte
Brontë's version, his listeners, far from spellbound, go to sleep. In
bitter amusement, the poet flees.

Charlotte spelt out her reproach to Monsieur through the
disillusion of the poet: he, like Charlotte, performs to indifferent

ears. As her verbal powers expanded, she must have known how far she surpassed any pupil Monsieur had known, so that his withdrawal – she demonstrates through her analogy – is to seal himself off from genius.

Monsieur turned the reproach: '*On ne doit pas se moquer de son lecteur.*' It was not good manners to tease your reader with unexpected disillusion. The poet's *morale*, he insisted, should be sustained.

But Charlotte was to have the final word, nine years later, in the disillusioned conclusion to *Villette*, her most autobiographical treatment of their relationship. Contrary to nineteenth-century expectations, the reader is wrenched away from facile hopes. The eccentric Belgian master proves unexpectedly weak when it comes to his own happiness. Though he does love the young English teacher, he permits the head of the Pensionnat to force them apart.

A week after Charlotte spelt out her parable of neglected genius, she gave notice to Madame. She contrived to think positively of her departure as an escape from the chill October classroom and from the grey urban scene, to climb once more the Yorkshire hills. Monsieur, characteristically, called her to him 'and pronounced with vehemence his decision' that she should not leave. He was warm, compelling. Charlotte found she could not resist 'without exciting him to passion'. It is likely that he did care for her, so long as it did not annoy his wife, and in this instance, Madame must have agreed, for it would have been inconvenient to lose an accomplished English teacher at the start of the school year. So Monsieur persuaded Charlotte to remain, against Mary's urgent advice, against her own better judgement which she scrawled into one of her textbooks on 14 October: 'First Class. I am very cold – I wish I were at home with Papa – Branwell – Emily, Anne, and Tabby – I am tired of being among foreigners – especially as there is only one person in this house worthy of being liked'. Three days later, she made her last and most dramatic effort to bare her soul to Monsieur through a *devoir* which takes the form of an urgent letter from a poor artist called Howard (Charlotte's word for Haworth in her juvenilia) to *un grand Seigneur*. It is easy to extract the bold message – '*Milord, je crois avoir du Génie*' ['Milord, I believe I have Genius'] – from the thin fictional shell of a young painter who leaves his native land to perfect his art in Italy:

My purpose in writing to you is to solicit your patronage . . . You are my equal in intellect and my superior in virtue and experience, so I will render you homage from the heart, pure and real . . . [The artist abroad is one who] arrives in this country without acquaintances and without family, and who has no other fortune than . . . the love of his art. Such is my position; I know how . . . suspect, even how contemptible it is in the eyes of certain people who regard as shameful everything that is perilous and uncertain . . . What right have I to hope to succeed . . . ? Milord, I shall answer those questions frankly. I entered upon this career because I believed that it was my vocation. I hope to succeed in it because I sense in myself the courage to persevere despite all obstacles I may encounter. [The artist declares some testing experience in Adversity: this test was passed because] the love of my art was a passion in me which rekindled the fire in my veins . . . Milord, I believe I have talent. Do not be indignant at my presumption or accuse me of conceit; I do not know that feeble feeling, the child of vanity; but I know well another feeling, Respect for myself, a feeling born of independence and integrity. Milord, I believe I have Genius.

That declaration shocks you; you find it arrogant. I find it very simple . . . Throughout my early youth the difference that existed between myself and most of the people around me was, for me, an embarrassing enigma that I did not know how to resolve . . . I believed it my duty to follow the example set by the majority of my acquaintances, an example sanctioned by the approbation of legitimate and prudent mediocrity, yet all the while I felt myself incapable of feeling and acting as they felt and acted . . . In what I did there was always excess; I was either too wrought up or too cast down; unintentionally, I showed everything that passed in my heart and sometimes storms were passing through it. In vain I tried to imitate . . . the serene and even temper of my companions . . . ; all my efforts were useless. I could not restrain the ebb and flow of blood in my arteries, and that ebb and flow left its mark upon my physiognomy and upon my harsh and unengaging features; I cried in secret. Finally, a day came (I was eighteen) when I opened my eyes and glimpsed a heaven in my own soul. Suddenly I realized that I had a force within . . .

[After a period in thrall to dreams] I do not know what voice it was that cried in my ear, 'Rouse yourself! leave your world of phantoms, enter the real world, look for Work, confront Experience, struggle and conquer!' I arose, I wrenched myself away from that solitude, those dreams that I loved, I left my country and went abroad.

. . . I did not lack courage or fortitude; immediately I set to work. Sometimes, it is true, despair overwhelmed me for an instant, for when I saw the works of the great masters of my art I felt myself only too contemptible; but . . . from that deep consciousness of inferiority, I derived new energy to work . . . I won what I wished to possess: an intimate knowledge of all the technical mysteries . . . a taste cultivated in accord with the rules of art. [But underlying this is the natural genius which is God's gift and which] within my soul I carefully guard . . .

Milord, it is to put myself in a position to exercise that faculty that I entreat your help . . . I know that in the long run true merit always triumphs, but, if power does not offer a helping hand the day of success can be a long time in coming. Sometimes, indeed, death precedes victory . . .

Milord, excuse me if this letter seems long to you. I did not count the lines, I thought only of speaking to you sincerely.

Here, in this torrential 'letter', Charlotte spelt out in the clearest terms an indomitable conviction of her potential greatness,

and invited her teacher to participate and promote it. She was
alternately self-possessed, defiant, exhilarated – and always self-
absorbed. It took enormous daring and trust to exhibit her
ambition so nakedly. M. Heger, unusually, refrained from comment, making only light pencil corrections of wording and
punctuation. There are several 'B's' (for *Bon*?) in the margins, but
it was not the response a confession demands. So, this last bid for
attention failed: Charlotte could not compel Monsieur to renew
the stimulating exchanges that had followed her return earlier
that year. She could not draw her teacher any further into her
private drama, and she offered no more *devoirs*.

All through the second half of October, through November
and December, she lingered – and deteriorated. 'I am not ill in
body', Charlotte explained to Emily on 19 December. 'It is only
the mind which is a trifle shaken . . .' Finally, on 1 January 1844,
she tore herself away. Determined to prevent a parting scene,
Mme Heger, on her own, escorted this troublesome
Englishwoman to the ship at Ostend.

'I suffered much before I left Brussels. I think, however long I
live, I shall not forget what the parting with M. Heger cost me',
she owned to Ellen that January. She had come back to Haworth,
she felt, changed in ideas and feelings. She could not recover, as
in the past, her enthusiasm at home. She was 'tamed and
broken'.

But was she? The pathos has obscured the consolations.
Charlotte's letters to Ellen, the main biographical source, say
nothing of her wish to write. She seems to tell Ellen so much
that it is easy to overlook what she did not say. The shadow of
despair and apparent stagnation was also the shadow in which
her mind moved, in which she had copied out old poems and
had begun, already, to use the Brussels experience, possibly in
plans for a novel, certainly in the new poems she wrote there.

Charlotte's correspondence with Monsieur in 1844–5 was central to this shadow-life that flickered on and off in the grim
post-Belgium years when Haworth seemed to her a place of

burial. Her letters tell Monsieur repeatedly that the letters *are* her life, together with the memories that beat behind their reach for words. This reach had an ambiguous purpose: to veil urgency as the enthusiastic but respectable gratitude of a pupil and, at the same time, to infuse her words with French expressiveness: '*— encore une fois adieu monsieur cela fait mal de dire adieu même dans une lettre . . .*',* she wrote six months after her departure from Brussels, on 24 July 1844.

One recurrent message was the importance of French. It is easy to assume that she spoke as devoted pupil or yearning lover, but she may have cared as much for language. Each day, she learnt a passage of French literature by heart, as well as reading French books and papers regularly. Translation, as a form of writing open to ladies (in their handmaid capacity), was the route to independence for many Victorian women: Mary Ann Evans took her first public step en route to George Eliot with a translation of Strauss's *Life of Jesus* which appeared in 1846 without her name. She followed this with a translation of Feuerbach's *The Essence of Christianity*, the only work she ever published under a woman's name, 'Marian Evans', in 1854. Catherine Winkworth, whom Charlotte met later, became a well-known translator of German hymns; her sister, Susanna, translated *Theologia Germanica*, a handbook of devotion dating back to the fifteenth century. In this context, Charlotte's continued pursuit of French might be seen as her route to professional writing, aiming beyond translation itself, in pursuit of new frontiers of expression. Is it conceivable that her letters to Monsieur were part of a language exercise which lay behind scenes of bilingualism and translation in Charlotte Brontë's novels? Shirley covets language through her French tutor who becomes her husband at the end of *Shirley* (1849). As he recites in French, her face turns towards him: 'she took the word up as if from his lips: she took his very tone; she seized his very accent; she delivered

---

* '— once more goodbye, Monsieur; it hurts to say goodbye even in a letter'.

the periods as he had delivered them: she reproduced . . . his expression.' The exchange of language bonds them in a quickening reciprocity that seems all the more erotic for its varied translations. When she entreats him to recite from Racine, he says it 'for her' and at once 'she took it from him; she found lively excitement in the pleasure of making his language her own'. They move on to one of La Fontaine's fables which brings their union to a climax: 'a simultaneous feeling seized them now, that their enthusiasm had kindled to a glow'. Repeatedly, in Charlotte Brontë's novels, a man extends a woman's power of expression in a way that extends and frees her desire. If this reflects Charlotte's own ambition, trained expressiveness in a foreign tongue prompted a liberation, perfectly timed to replace the unreal extravagance of Angria. While Branwell remained addicted to Angria in his continued identity as Northangerland, it was part of the cure of the Angrian drug for Charlotte to continue to experience genuine passion, genuine pain.

Day after day she waited for the post as one waiting for vital sustenance: '*je dépéris*', she cried when she could not forget her teacher through the silent summer and autumn of 1845. Instead of vicarious thrills, she had touched '*la vie*', and was trying to compel *la vie* to communicate with remote Haworth vegetating dully, it seemed to her, at the outposts of existence.

Charlotte was obliged to put Papa's needs first, earning her living second, and ambition last – or, at least, to reassure herself that she adhered to received priorities. What comes down to us through surviving documents are her dutiful statements to contemporaries. Those close to her felt compelled to destroy whatever conflicted with Victorian proprieties, in view of her reputation for unwomanly fire. In all good faith Charlotte spelt out the discourse of obedience, to her friends, to Monsieur himself (stressing her father's increasing blindness or her renewed intention to start a school), as once she had made the correct gestures of self-abnegation to Southey. And yet, she could not relinquish the need to write, if only letters.

The Parsonage at Haworth.

Mrs Brontë (*née* Maria Branwell).

Mr Brontë in 1825.

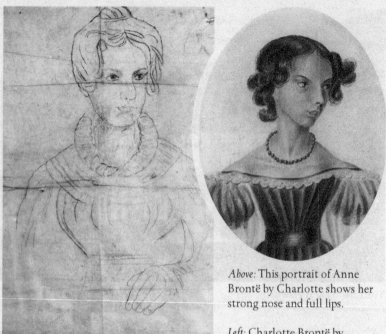

Above: This portrait of Anne
Brontë by Charlotte shows her
strong nose and full lips.

Left: Charlotte Brontë by
Branwell Brontë.

Emily Brontë writing in her room, 1845, with her dog, Keeper, and Anne's
spaniel, Flossy.

Branwell: 'A pair of spectacles garnished his nose'.

Jack Shaw the guardsman, and Jack painter of Norfolk'.

Question — "The half minute time is up, so come to the ~~last~~ scratch; wont you?"

answer — " Blast your eyes, it's no use, for I cannot come!"

Branwell's self-image as a prostrate young man haunted by Death.

Charlotte Brontë's watercolour copy, at age 14, of a portrait of her mother.

'Aunt' Elizabeth Branwell.

'Our Land of Silence': a favourite place on the moor.

'She is good; she is true; she is faithful, and I love her.' Ellen Nussey in a
watercolour attributed to Charlotte Brontë.

Miss W— in the back-ground. Stupidity the
atmosphere, school-books the employment, asses the
society. What in all this is there to remind me
of the divine, silent, unseen land of thought, dim
now & indefinite as the dream of a dream. The shadow
of a shade.

I wanted to speak
to Miss — it was impossible. I felt that
this was a frightful predicament.

Main picture:
Brontë heroines long to over pass the horizon of their constricted existence. Anne's drawing while a governess in November 1839.

Left: The hot words still scald the pages of Charlotte's 'Roe Head Journal'. Her mature vehemence may be traced back to these outbursts. (A transcription reads: Miss W[oole]r in the back-ground, stupidity the atmosphere, school-books the employment, asses the society, what in all this is there to remind me of the divine, silent, unseen land of thought, dim now and indefinite as the dream of a dream, the shadow of a shade.

I wanted to speak, to rise – it was impossible – I felt that this was a frightful predicament –).

Above: Roe Head School, drawn by Charlotte.

Above: 'Thick sewn with the germ of ideas her mother never knew' (*Shirley*, ch. 9). The only photograph of Mary Taylor was taken decades after Charlotte knew her.

Right: Mary's well-travelled father, Joshua Taylor (1760–1840), who encouraged Charlotte's taste for Continental art and French literature, and was a model for Mr Yorke in *Shirley*.

At first, she wrote to Monsieur every fortnight; then, when Madame intervened, she accepted a restriction to one letter in six months. The fact that Madame pieced three of Charlotte's letters together from torn fragments she found in her husband's bin suggests that Madame did not consider this tie negligible. She mended the first surviving letter with strips of paper; and the second and third she patiently sewed. It has often been suggested that Madame did so to preserve evidence of her husband's innocence. This is unconvincing in view of Charlotte's torrential feeling which prompts inevitable speculation, as it must have provoked Madame: to what extent was Monsieur responsible, if inadvertently, for this passionate response? There has been much debate whether the four surviving letters of 1844–5 were adulterous or innocent. This is a misunderstanding of Charlotte's capacity for an indefinable form of love that did not demand enactment but thrived all the more on imagination and words: the exchange of English and French in the Brussels classroom; the exchange of fury and tears, and Charlotte's laughter at Monsieur's absurd pronunciation of 'Williams Shackspire'; the books and notes he secreted in her desk; the letters she sent from England, pursuing his language as she sought his response: '*quand je prononce les mots français il me semble que je cause avec vous*' ['as I pronounce the French words it seems to me as if I were chatting with you']. This verbal engagement was to find expression in poems and novels, not embraces. Though Charlotte suffered greatly in parting with M. Heger, it was to her advantage to have to imagine a relationship, not enact it, for this freed her to imagine from a woman's point of view. The notion of sublimation seems reductive: a way of dismissing what we cannot understand. The idea of 'courtly love' – which never really existed but was supposed to find expression in words and bravery – is closer to the truth, but where 'courtly love' is encased in a code of manners, what is striking about Monsieur's classroom conduct and Charlotte's epistolary style is the excitement they generate when manners are abandoned.

On 24 October 1844, when she broke the six months rule, she tried to elicit a quicker reply with a calmly correct letter, almost an exercise in politeness, to be delivered by Mary's brother. When he and then Mary returned empty-handed, she wrote explosively on 8 January 1845 that after a silence of eight months she could no longer measure her words: '*On souffre en silence tant qu'on a la force et quand cette force manque on parle sans trop mesurer ses paroles.*'*

The suppressed power of a writer's voice was breaking through the veneer of humble gratitude in a dramatisation of Charlotte's expectant queries and the Taylors' regretful denials. She reminds Heger that he once had a *little* regard for her to which she means to hold as to life: 'un peu *d'intérêt quand j'étais votre élève à Bruxelles — et je tiens à conserver ce* peu *d'intérêt — j'y tiens comme je tiendrais à la vie.*'**

To understand the rise of Charlotte Brontë is to keep the phantom of potentiality in view during this apparently unpromising time: the author's almost ruthless invention of the life that will feed the art and, too, the rise of the art itself as we hear the pulse of Brontë passion break through the language of the letters — a pulse perhaps foreign to English. It has long been customary for English readers to see these letters in translation, but this falsifies them, for English was a language in which they could not have been written. Charlotte's repeated link of French with her attachment to her '*maître*' suggests, as Sara Dudley Edwards put it, 'she was speaking not French but Heger: he has given her the words to make love to him. It is his idiom; she cannot escape it. To speak French is to love him — it is the expression of his words.' Jane Eyre says: 'I looked at my love: that feeling which was my master's — which he had created . . .' Charlotte herself had called the man she loved '*mon maître de*

---

* 'One suffers in silence so long as one has the strength so to do, and when that strength gives out one speaks without too carefully measuring one's words.'
** 'You once showed me a *little* interest, when I was your pupil in Brussels, and I hold to the maintenance of that *little* interest — I hold to it as I would hold on to life.'

littérature – [le] seul maître que j'ai jamais eu . . .' When women like
Charlotte Brontë, Emily Dickinson, or Gwen John speak to their
'*maître*' or 'master' it has no connotation of self-abasement. To
them a master is a teacher – one confident enough to engage
with genius and to shape whatever it came to be. The erotic
energy of an Abelard, a Rodin, or an Heger has to do with an
understanding that discards the 'artificial thing' to engage with
whatever the woman knows to be the authentic source of her
intelligence or art. In the Bible it is always the man who 'knows'
the woman, and though mutuality may be implied, the man's
act of 'knowing' is potentially more dramatic because a woman
is harder to know – veiled in biblical times and obscured since
by her social position. The 'master' is not a man to whom she
defers, but that person who would rescue her from unknowability by sharing some fruits of his advantage.

If we think of Charlotte's letters to her teacher in view of the
great novels to come, these letters might be seen as the source of
a new model of manhood: a hero who will engage with the
hidden 'other' in women; who does not exclude it as alien. This
future fictional enlargement on Constantin Heger gains its imaginative licence from distance – from the correspondent's very
invisibility as her reader, her *lecteur*. In this sense, what Charlotte
undertook was not quite a real correspondence which reflects
the correspondent; it was more an *invented* correspondence, close
to an imaginative act and supplemented, probably, by many letters which Charlotte composed (in her mind or even on paper)
but did not send. For, so long as women, unheard lovers, under-
classes, despised races, or other excluded people live in unseen
spaces of the mind, they will 'speak' privately to chosen inter-
locutors who occupy public space. The difference of Charlotte
Brontë or, say, Emily Dickinson, is that private speaking ventured into the arena of public language, boldly appropriating
that language for alien use.

* 'My literature master – the only master I have ever had'.

In Charlotte's letters to Monsieur, she alternates between two modes. When she writes as the person he has known (in spirit), her French rises to grandeur, punctuated by the rhythm of her dashes. In this mode, she speaks as monumentally as Diderot might have done about the career of letters. In fact, she appropriates this language of men to declare that, as a woman, '*la carrière des lettres m'est fermée*'.*

Her alternative mode is that of the English schoolgirl writing a careful exercise. This is her cover, when she adopts the manner of the grateful pupil and asks woodenly after Mme Heger and the children, Maria, Louise, Claire, Prospère, and Victorine, about their family vacation and the teachers at the Pensionnat, and sends the respects of her father and Emily. The whole letter of 24 October 1844 was in this stilted mode, and the obvious reason was that she was breaking the six months ban. A letter of model politeness prods M. Heger to reply at once.

She recognised the danger of an exercise in passionlessness: she might bore him. At this point, Monsieur exceeded the six months' gap and when, by January 1845, he still failed to reply, she broke into an eloquent letter of frustration and fury – returning to the passionate mode. She plunges in, without her customary address, as though continuing an argument. It seems Monsieur had reproached her for mad and morbid thoughts. Her dreams now torment her – he appears severe, incensed. Reproach her he may, call her what he will, he *must* write. All she begs is a letter – a crumb from a rich man's table. She cannot survive if she must lose the 'friendship' of her master. Her script abandons its usual neatness. Her tones are pitiful, embarrassing, but the words contain a challenge: why should a relation so innocuous as 'friendship' be denied? If she appears '*exaltée*' – and this her logic refutes – is she not suffering from her master's incomprehensible betrayal of a pupil's devotion that asks only a regular, written exchange that would sustain the work which is her life?

* 'the career of letters is closed to me'.

Si mon maître me retire entièrement son amitié je serai tout à fait sans espoir —
s'il m'en donne un peu — très peu — je serai contente — heureuse, j'aurais un
motif pour vivre — pour travailler. [If my master withdraws his friendship from me entirely I shall be altogether without hope — if he
gives me a little — just a little — I shall be satisfied — happy; I
should have reason to live — to work.]

Without his voice, she felt imprisoned for life in the 'narrow cell'
of her own mind, a mind which had lost its creative powers:
'Dark — imageless — a living tomb'.

She wrote to Monsieur again on 18 May, a letter which has disappeared. Punctually, she wrote her final letter on 18 November
1845. Monsieur's last letter had sustained her, she said, for half a
year. She now begs another, resigning the claim to 'friendship'
and asking only for his compassion. Her idea of the relationship
seems to have changed over the disappointing waits for the post
through the summer and autumn. She has become humiliated
by the increasing abasement his silences force upon her and by
her own capacity to love when hope fails. She has become, after
all, a slave — *'esclave à un regret, un souvenir, esclave à une idée dominante et*
fixe qui tyrannise son esprit' ['the slave of a regret, of a memory, the
slave of a fixed and dominant idea which controls the mind']. In
short, by the end of 1845, it seemed that the knowing bond had
deteriorated into terms of subjection.

In a postscript to this last letter, Charlotte gave way to an
impulse to utter her feelings just once in English: 'According
to the words of the Bible: "Out of the fullness of the heart,
the mouth speaketh".' After the slavishness of her pleas in
French, she recovers her dignity at the last with a full
declaration in her own language, rooted in the seventeenth-
century eloquence of the King James Bible. Her French was
Heger's; in English she expresses what is wholly her own.
Returning to Haworth from a visit to Ellen, she had fallen
into conversation with a Frenchman. The French, she wrote
in the postscript, 'sounded like music in my ears — every word

was most precious to me because it reminded me of you – I love French for your sake with my heart and soul.' This frank declaration of love in English, where no excuse for foreignness could be made, went too far. According to his daughter Louise, it was at this point that M. Heger decided to end the correspondence.

Charlotte's last words to her *maître* bless him in her own language: 'Farewell my dear master – may God protect you with special care and crown you with peculiar blessings'. He never replied, and tore up the letters, not because they meant nothing but to protect Charlotte from misunderstanding. Madame's habits of surveillance may well have increased with her husband's trying susceptibility: all through their marriage, even when Monsieur was old, she would have had to guard the decency of her school. Charlotte's excited response to her husband's attentions would have been exactly what she feared when she pieced together the fragments of Charlotte's imploring letters, and her understandable annoyance must have ensured the end of the correspondence. She would have been alert to Charlotte's naive ardour, not to her more subtle passion for language.

Charlotte offers her own misinterpretation of the correspondence in a poem that begins, 'He saw my heart's woe'. Where her letters assert her right to a response, the poem presents a more conventional, pathetic view of a woman who speaks only in 'a whisper low and dreary'. She is forced to conclude that she had worshipped an idol. 'My Baal', as she calls him, would not have seen or understood if she had slashed her wrists. This would seem to bear out the charge of morbidity.

Posterity has so far backed the righteousness of M. Heger's position. There is uncontrolled resentment in Charlotte's letters not found in the passions she recreated in fiction. A Victorian heroine could not allow herself so much insistent argument. But looking at the letters at this distance in time, there seems a reasonable basis for Charlotte's patent anger. For

Monsieur had, in fact, invited response – as he habitually played on the emotions of his girl pupils. There was a danger in a man of his susceptible and histrionic temperament let loose in a girls' school, which provided a realistic basis for Madame's watch on what he threw away, and for the paternal image they constructed in formal letters to pupils and parents. In an age when virtuous women were perceived as innately passive, they would not be expected to respond to any signal short of a proposal of marriage. The whole onus of misinterpretation would therefore fall on the woman, as it fell on Charlotte when she confessed in the cathedral as the sinner she felt herself to be and, afterwards, when she punished herself with deliberate silence at home in 1844–5. Sadly, she blamed herself as much for her lack of feminine charm as for her persistent one-sided attachment:

> Devoid of charm, how could I hope
> My unasked love would e'er return?
> What fate, what influence lit the flame
> I still feel inly, deeply burn?

The two questions do not quite match: where the first castigates herself for offering an 'unasked love', the second question simmers with veiled anger at some ill-defined 'influence' which lit her flame. This anger was directed at Monsieur himself – until he put an end to this awkward correspondence.

The righteousness of Charlotte's demands turns on an unanswerable question: emotionally aware as he was, did Constantin Heger not realise that this pupil had active desires of her own, unlike Flemish girls whose blood (said Charlotte) was 'too gluey to boil' – did Monsieur not realise that, with this woman, he played with real fire? In a poem of about 1845, defiantly called 'Reason', Charlotte describes a fire burning with the continuous, unresolved action of the present participle – a fire now part of her life:

>   . . . Even now the fire
>   Though smothered, slacked, repelled, is burning
>   At my life's source.

There is another connotation to 'burning' from Charlotte's point of view. If we are prepared to unlock desire from sexuality, to see desire as a longing for something as yet unformulated, which is other, and more, than what is available, if we are willing to put aside our simplistic categories of eros, adultery, and madness, and lend ourselves to Charlotte's particular desire for a voice in whose presence her own might rise, then her anger and gloom at its withdrawal is understandable, as is her repeated plea for the continuance of that voice, however minimal. That voice was, indeed, her life. So long as it continued, she could sustain the resonance of a writer; to lose it was to collapse back into that silent womanhood that existed only to serve Papa. In the letters to Ellen, in conversations with Mary, and in wan poems during these two years, she played out this collapse. All that was left was duty to care for Papa whose eyesight was failing; even the stake in life that teaching would offer, was an alternative she must forego.

Mary urged Charlotte to leave Haworth. Mary herself was about to join her youngest brother, Waring, in New Zealand. In February 1845, Charlotte made a farewell visit to Hunsworth Mill, Cleckheaton (where Mary lived temporarily with her brother Joe). During their final talks, Charlotte owned to being buried where she was.

Mary declared that to stay in Haworth would ruin her. 'Think of what you'll be five years hence!'

Such darkness came over her friend's face that Mary stopped short. 'Don't cry, Charlotte!'

She didn't cry, but went on pacing up and down, then said after a while, 'But I intend to stay, Polly.'

A space resonates here with unspoken intent. The words are resolute, not pathetic. Her intent, I imagine, was complementary

to Mary's 'plunge' into 'another world': a writer's plunge into a
world of her own. I don't believe that she relinquished this intention for a moment, however daunting her domestic obligations,
her lack of means, and depressive solitude. At this time, Emily
withdrew from Charlotte into a private world of her own. Anne
and Branwell were still seventy miles away at Thorp Green.

After Mary sailed on 21 March 1845, Charlotte's spirits sank.
She wrote to Ellen on 24 March that 'one day resembles
another – and all have heavy, lifeless physiognomies – Sunday –
baking day and Saturday are the only ones that bear the slightest
distinctive mark – meantime life wears away – I shall soon be 30 –
and I have done nothing yet . . . I feel as if we were all buried
here – I long to travel – to work to live a life of action . . .' She
and Ellen visualised Mary's ship tossed by winds, Charlotte with
envy of Mary's initiative: 'Mary Taylor finds herself free – and on
that path for adventure and exertion to which she has so long
been seeking admission – Sickness – Hardship – Danger are her
fellow-travellers . . . Yet these real – material dangers when once
past, leave in the mind the satisfaction of having struggled with
a difficulty and overcome it – Strength – Courage – experience
are their invariable results – whereas I doubt whether suffering
purely mental [h]as any good result unless it be to make us by
comparison less sensitive to physical suffering – I repeat then,
that Mary Taylor has done well to go out to New Zealand.'

Mary's active trial was easy to see; her own trial remained
invisible and perhaps unproductive. She feared, above all, the
lethargy that could descend on the daughter at home, as she
put it to M. Heger: *'quand le corps est paresseux, l'esprit souffre cruellement.
Je ne connaîtrais pas cette léthargie si je pouvais écrire.'** Here is a glimpse
into the shadow: if only she could write. Another glimpse comes
when she confides her dream: to write a book which she would
dedicate to him, the only teacher of literature she had ever had:

---

* 'when the body is idle, the spirit suffers painfully. I should not know this lethargy
if I could write.'

'*savez-vous ce que je ferais Monsieur? — j'écrirais un livre et je le dédierais a mon maître de littérature — au seul maître que j'ai jamais eu — a vous Monsieur.*'*
Then she conceals the hope beneath the disclaimer that the career of letters was closed to her.

All the same, the exercise book filled up with poems and plans for fiction. A plot for a future novel picks out autobiographical themes which, in time, she did use: 'loss of relatives'; 'crosses in the affections'; 'going abroad and returning'. It was all as yet unimagined, and seems more an attempt to pull herself together through a resolve to write. Plot lines peter out in a set of injunctions:

Characters   . . . Avoid Richardsonian Multiplication . . .
Mem —   To be set about with proper spirit —
             To be carried on with the same —
             To be concluded idem
Observe —   No grumbling allowed.

The poems, too, have something of the feared lethargy in them: they are conventionally melancholic, a soggy literariness far from the hot vehemence of the Roe Head fragments and the letters to Monsieur which are close to the compelling voice of the novels to come. One of the dreariest poems calls up a shadowy other self in the twilight of an autumn day: 'Her veil is spread, her shadow shed over stair and chamber still/ And now I feel her presence steal even to my lone fireside/ Sit silent Nun — sit there and be/ Comrade and Confidant to me'. Years later, when the buried nun haunts the lonely teacher in *Villette*, she comes as a subversive figure, a cue to Miss Snowe to recognise the fiery nature of her buried self, but at this earlier stage the nun embodies only the feared attenuation of a single life.

---

* 'do you know what I should do, Monsieur? — I should write a book, and I should dedicate it to my literature master — to the only master I have ever had — to you, Monsieur.'

As she approached the age of thirty she was considering the prospect of the single woman. In the light of Miss Wooler, she tried to envisage the ripening contentment of the woman 'who makes her own way through life quietly, perseveringly, without support of husband or brother; and who . . . retains in her possession a well-regulated mind, a disposition to enjoy simple pleasures, and fortitude to support inevitable pains . . .' But her own experience of unrequited love made her fear that increasing heartlessness might be the fruit of self-control. Silencing, in deference to feminine custom, could fester in a way that depletes the character: 'A lover masculine so disappointed can speak and urge explanation; a lover feminine can say nothing: if she did the result would be shame and anguish, inward remorse for self-treachery . . . Take the matter as you find it: ask no questions; utter no remonstrances: it is your best wisdom.' Her advice is shot through with irony: with sealed lips and placid dissimulation, you will pass through paleness to 'a convenient stoicism' or perhaps 'apathetic exhaustion after the rack'.

At the Pensionnat, she had watched an alternative scenario: the shameless conduct of one of the teachers who made offers to eligible men via her father and brother. She told Charlotte that otherwise, if teaching failed, she would have to become a sister of charity.

'She declares there is nothing she can turn to, and laughs at the idea of delicacy', Charlotte had reported to Mary, 'and she is only ten years older than I am.'

Mary had failed to see a connection with Charlotte.

'Well, Polly, I should hate being a sister of charity. I suppose that would shock some people, but I should.'

'You would have as much feeling as a nurse as most people, and more than some', Mary said.

Charlotte replied that she did not know how people can bear the constant pressure of misery, never to change except to a new form of it. 'It would be impossible to keep one's natural feelings.'

Mary promised her a better destiny than to go begging anyone to marry her or to lose her natural feelings, but Charlotte went on: 'My youth is leaving me; I can never do better than I have done, and I have done nothing yet.' She feared that the pressure of earning her living would lead her to lose one faculty and feeling after another 'till they went dead altogether. I hope I shall be put in my grave as soon as I'm dead; I don't want to walk about so.'

Burial certainly appeared her likely future in 1844–5. To live reclusively, she believed, was not a matter of choice: it was her duty to stay with her father who increasingly depended on her to read to him. She believed in duty and self-sacrifice with all the conviction of her time. And yet, though she continually deplored the conditions of her life – her isolation as a teacher, the remoteness of Haworth from the stir of ideas and action – these conditions did open the invisible space in which her art was made.

A force for recovery appears in a poem called 'Frances' (the name of the heroine of Charlotte Brontë's first novel). A fresh drama of effort and expansion opens between the usual passive dramas of longing and futility:

> The very wildness of my sorrow
> Tells me I yet have innate force;
> My track of life has been too narrow,
> Effort shall trace a broader course.

She looks ahead to new scenes, new language, and new faces to hide that face she can never forget:

> Defined, and fixed, and fading never,
> Stamped deep on vision, heart, and brain.

It was a courageous resolve to turn deprivation to gain. There is no way to fix the inward moment of this turn, but soon after July

1845 Charlotte put aside a passing plan to emulate Mary by travelling to Paris, and settled instead to write a novel in emulation of Anne who was turning solitude to effect with *Agnes Grey*. There had always been the long shadow of this possibility. The later stanzas of 'He saw my heart's woe' take us deeper into shadow. In 'darker shame', the woman resolves to withdraw into the remote spaces of the mind, 'a solitude sought where mortal never came.' It was in this space that Charlotte conceived 'The Master' (renamed *The Professor*).

Her first idea was called 'Lucia'. It takes for its setting a ladies' school, called Gateshead, in the north of England. Obviously, she intended to draw on Roe Head as she thought of a schoolroom with a bay window, a group of three or four pupils conversing and curling their hair, while another, faceless figure is wrapped in a 'night's dream'. Her scanty notes (in the Brussels notebook) return to the contrast of distinctive dreamer versus mundane pupils in the 'Roe Head Journal'.

In 'Lucia' there is no further indication of the nature of this woman, but she returns, briefly, at the end of *The Professor* as the kind of woman a man might remember all his days – but not a woman to marry. Yorke Hunsden shows her picture to Frances Henri who has channelled her own talent into an acceptable blend of marriage and teaching. Frances, who is half-foreign (half-Swiss), recognises in Lucia a wholly foreign (Italian) woman who has broken her social chains. The picture shows a 'very individual-looking female face' with an eye that looked straight into you, 'and an independent, determined eye it was'. Frances divines further:

'– the face is that of one who has made an effort, and a successful and triumphant effort, to wrest some vigorous and valued faculty from insupportable constraint – and when Lucia's faculty got free, I am certain it spread wide pinions and carried her higher than –' She hesitated –

'Than what?' demanded Hunsden.

'Than "les convenances" permitted you to follow.'

'I think you grow spiteful – impertinent.'

'Lucia has trodden the stage,' continued Frances. 'You never seriously thought of marrying her – you admired her originality, her fearlessness – her energy of body and mind, you delighted in her talent whatever that was, whether song, dance or dramatic representation – you worshipped her beauty – which was of the sort after your own heart – but I am sure she filled a sphere from whence you would never have thought of taking a wife.'

At an early point, it is possible that Charlotte's subject may have been the plight of the talented woman, as she herself had known it, first in a ladies' school, and then in relation to a natural mate who would not allow himself to see her in the same light. There is an obvious link between a school which trains girls to fit a social scheme in which they must remain subordinates and the kind of women who are seen to be fit for marriage. Charlotte had a growing conviction that what men looked for was a ladylike decorum with 'a touch of phlegm'. Phlegm is her recurrent image for Belgian women, and this would fit, too, the calculating manner she deplored in Mme Heger, the chosen of Monsieur. In short, Charlotte, at thirty, was facing an issue central to her future existence: how was a woman of talent and passion to conduct herself in a man's world?

The Professor works out a plausible compromise through the first of her ambiguous heroines, Frances Henri. The unambiguous Lucia, with her blaze of talent, was put to one side. She must remain unplotted, the intractable material in the shadow of which Frances stores her unused desire as she moves between the acts of domestic and professional wife. Though 'real', Lucia cannot step forward in respectable fiction, rather as the Italian singer in George Eliot's 'Mr Gilfil's Love-Story' (1857), the passionate Caterina, cannot survive within the phlegmatic scenarios of rural England. Frances, on the other hand, like Charlotte herself, conceals the blaze behind a respectable front. Mrs Gaskell thought Frances the most appealing of Charlotte Brontë's heroines. With her down-bent head, silent compliance, and vulnerability, she appears closest to the Victorian ideal, and consistent with the image of Charlotte which Mrs Gaskell wished to promote.

In her Preface to *The Professor*, Charlotte set out a new aesthetic which foreshadows the realism of George Eliot: she would prefer what was 'plain and homely' rather than unusually handsome people and unrealistic turns of fate. The speaker, Crimsworth, must work his way, and before he finds his measure of happiness, must master at least half the Hill of Difficulty. Crimsworth is an honest soul who resists the dictates of aristocratic relations, the exploitation of his brother, a factory lord, and finally the solicitations of the well-to-do Continental female, Mdlle Reuter. The speaker's values are Charlotte's own: integrity, honest toil, genuine feeling in preference to worldly gain.

Crimsworth blends Charlotte and Heger with his own more fastidious temperament and moderate expectations. He has Charlotte's dogged sense of duty as he works for his brother; he has her need to overpass the limits of a constricted life when he resolves to go abroad; and, like Charlotte, he seeks the stimulus of a foreign city. He teaches English to thick, coarse girls, and discovers the devious character of the directress of the pensionnat. At the same time, the portrait of Crimsworth draws on M. Heger, the teacher. He is contemptuous and stimulating. As Frances, his pupil, declares, he is '*toujours un peu entêté, exigeant, volontaire*'. Frances writes a love poem, a version of Charlotte's Brussels poem about love born of ambition. In the poem, the master begrudges praise and sets his pupil the hardest tasks. She responds to his temper, his quick relenting words, and need to share 'some precious book'. The laurel descending on her brow provokes an almost instantaneous passion which outstrips the tutelary relation where the master correctly stops short. For the pupil, it provokes an irretrievable commitment which, given the passivity of feminine conduct, festers as an inward wound. The drama of Charlotte's love for Monsieur suffuses this poem, a source for the novels to come: a lone, obscure but fiery woman; a wilful, knowing man who sees through her meekly conformist exterior; a love that grows through understanding – teachers' love; then, the agony of parting. This poem-master, unlike Heger, fulfils his pupil's dreams: at the moment of parting, he holds her fast, wonders if others will bear his darling so 'deep a love', calls himself her 'true shelter', and asks her to return to him as to a haven. When Crimsworth reads this poem, he is impelled to declare his love for Frances.

Though Frances has her source in the author, she presents an image of model womanhood. She is Charlotte Brontë crossed with theories of what an able woman might be, at that point in time, given a reasonable mate. Increasingly, it becomes Frances' story as the plot outstrips the wedding. For this particular woman there is to be no dream of terminal bliss, but a continued development.

Life, for Charlotte, was not simply a riot of emotion; it was activity as against stagnation. In this, *The Professor* speaks past its own time and directly to ours, especially in its idea that work, marriage, and motherhood might be combined. When Crimsworth proposes to Frances, she says: '. . . I should like of course to retain my employment of teaching . . . Thus we shall have both the same profession – I like that – and my efforts to get on will be as unrestrained as yours . . .'

Crimsworth asks her doubtfully if she is 'laying plans to be independent of me'.

Frances replies: 'Think of my marrying you to be kept by you, Monsieur! I could not do it – and how dull my days would be! . . . I should be lingering at home unemployed and solitary; I should get depressed and sullen and you would soon tire of me.'

Crimsworth argues that she could read and study perfectly well at home.

Frances will not have it: 'I must act in some way, and act with you.' What she wants is a partnership, not dependence. She believes that people who get together only for amusement never esteem each other as much as those who work together.

'You speak God's truth', Crimsworth agrees at last, 'and you shall have your own way, for it is the best way.' Having chosen an exceptional wife, he has no wish to subdue her:

> I knew she was not one who could live quiescent and inactive or even comparatively inactive. Duties she must have to fulfil, and important duties; work to do, and exciting, absorbing, profitable work; strong faculties stirred in her frame and they demanded full nourishment, free exercise: mine was not the hand ever to starve or cramp them; no, I delighted in offering them sustenance and in clearing them wider space for action.

Frances becomes directress of her own school. In this, Charlotte sets up an ideal which owed something to Mme Heger moving effectively between daytime control and domestic compliance. As with the Hegers, the presence of the husband-professor supports the school. His wife attends his final class of the day, in deference to his accomplished performance. As they pass, at six o'clock, from the schoolroom to their private quarters, she becomes more respectful and attentive – something Charlotte might have witnessed early in 1843 when she was still welcome in the Hegers' sitting-room. The difference is that Frances is not cold. After eight years of marriage, there comes an evening when she dares to express a passion of her own rather than reflect the mood of her husband. When she throws her arms around him, he has a glimpse of an unknown creature. The energy of her whole being glows for a moment in her eye and animates her cheek: 'her look and movement were like inspiration; in one there was such a flash, in the other such a power.'

Half an hour later, when she is calm, he asks where all that 'wild vigour' has gone which had 'transformed her erewhile and made her glance so thrilling and ardent; her action so rapid and strong.'

She answers softly and passively. "'I cannot tell where it is gone, Monsieur," said she; "but I know that whenever it is wanted it will come back again.'"

Crimsworth does perceive a flame that burned latent, a fire that shot up 'a moment high and vivid'; and he saw reason reduce 'its blaze to embers.' To him, once or twice, 'she had in intimate conversation, uttered venturous thoughts in nervous language'. But moderately sympathetic as he is, Crimsworth never elicits the fire nor does he ask what these words mean, and he can ignore what he does not initiate: 'it came of itself and of itself departed'. The relative oblivion of the narrator-husband leaves this in shadow.

The more obvious radicalism is made explicit. Frances, like Lucia, is prepared to break society's rules. She tells Crimsworth that she would abandon a tyrannical or profligate marriage and, if forced by law to return, she would die. Would it be a voluntary death, asks her curious husband. No, it would simply happen. She is explicit about the inevitability of revolt:

'Monsieur, if a wife's nature loathes that of the man she is wedded to, marriage must be slavery. Against slavery all right thinkers revolt — and though torture be the price of resistance, torture must be dared.'

Charlotte Brontë joins others of her time when she links slavery with the plight of women. Others in the 1840s also used the novel to open up the truth of social facts: Geraldine Jewsbury dared to state in *The Half Sisters* (1848) that a woman's adulterous love was 'a real feeling, deep as life, and overpowering as death'. In the same year, Mrs Gaskell demonstrated in *Mary Barton* the connection between poverty and prostitution. But the most radical import of *The Professor* is, even now, unrecognised because it looks beyond the feminism of the nineteenth and twentieth centuries when women saw a struggle against men who blocked rights: their right to vote in the nineteenth century; their right to professional advance in the twentieth century. Charlotte Brontë accepts what was sometimes put aside in the urgency of this struggle: the inescapable biological need to mate and reproduce. This most theoretical of her works restores the institution of marriage in a new form. *The Professor* does not have the conclusiveness of *Jane Eyre* or *Shirley* which offer ideal solutions. Here, she foresees a continuing effort as part of a cure for maddening revolt or unrealistic expectations of men. It is an ending worthy of *Middlemarch* or *Night and Day* which refuse the nonsense of constant bliss and offer instead a plan for rational living. Charlotte Brontë was not capitulating to the master; she was inventing a viable model for the future.

A PUBLIC VOICE

During the years from 1842–5, reality struck through the residue of dreams. Charlotte's passion for her teacher, and the words they exchanged, fuelled her writing. In some way, M. Heger gave credence to the promise of Miss West, Miss Hastings, or Miss Hall; at last, the external sanction she had craved. From now, she pursued such women, ignoring the stock beauty in defiance of her sisters who argued that beauty was essential to heroines.

Charlotte replied: 'I will prove to you that you are wrong. I will show you a heroine as small and as plain as myself who shall be as interesting as any of yours.'

This subject emerged from the post-Brussels years of apparent penance when she closed her lips to Emily – at the very time, as it happened, that Emily herself was secreting new poems in her desk, convinced they were too strange to share: 'So hopeless is the world without; / The world within I doubly prize . . . / Where thou, and I, and Liberty, / Have undisputed sovereignty.' It is impossible to define the quality of this mutual silence: the depth and weight of it, the burial of words – even from sisters as close as they – in the space of patient, obscure years when all three were making independent leaps from juvenile 'play' to classic works. In February 1844, while Charlotte was struggling against inertia after her return from Brussels, Emily began to collect, recopy, and add to her 'Gondal Poems'. Eighteen-forty-three and especially 1844 were, for her, prolific years. When Charlotte

came upon Emily's poems in the autumn of 1845, her astonishment was a measure of a leap unforeseen.

In the summer of 1845, before Charlotte's discovery, there
appear three disparate women, each enclosed in 'the world
within'. As children and adolescents their imaginations flourished together; between 1843–5 they had to separate, each to find
her individual voice. At this ripening moment Charlotte was
twenty-nine, Emily turning twenty-seven, and Anne twenty-
five. As Charlotte recalled, 'formerly we used to show each other
what we wrote, but of late years this habit of communication and
consultation had been discontinued; hence it ensued, that we
were mutually ignorant of the progress we might respectively
have made.' Anne was aware that Emily was writing 'some
poetry' apart from Gondal 'play': 'I wonder what it is about?'
Emily's diary-paper (dated 'July the 30th' to coincide with her
birthday, but actually written the next day) was a self-portrait in
domestic placidity ('I must hurry off now to my turning and
ironing'). She declared she had 'learnt to make the most of the
present and hope for the future with less fidget[i]ness that I
cannot do all I wish . . . and merely desiring that every body
could be as comfortable as myself and as undesponding' – a hint
at some discontent in the Parsonage. This was likely to have
come from Charlotte, tight-lipped as she awaited the post day by
day, and despondent with Branwell who, after a series of dis-
missals, finally, that July, exploded the hopes of his family.

With each successive post, Branwell would begin on his best
behaviour, then try to recover his leadership, eloquence, and
dreams of glory as the centre of an admiring circle of drinking
companions. After unsuccessful efforts to establish himself as a
portrait-painter in Bradford, he had been dismissed in June 1840
from a post as tutor with the Postlethwaite family in the Lake
District. During this period he had met Hartley Coleridge whose
praise for Branwell's poetry and translations of Horace had
renewed his literary ambition. It may have been in this mood
that he rebuffed Mary Taylor who visited the Parsonage at the

time of his return, and to whom he had been attracted on previous visits. Unfairly, Charlotte blamed Mary for showing her
feelings too freely – a man, Charlotte thought, was bound to
back away. But Branwell's dismissal of Mary showed his caprice
or inability to discern Mary's calibre, and perhaps the unrealistic
greatness of his expectations. Three months later, in September
1840, when he took up his next, in Charlotte's view, demeaning
post, she wrote sarcastically to Ellen: 'A distant relation of mine,
one Patrick Boanerges, has set off to seek his fortune in the wild
wandering, adventurous, romantic, knight-errant-like capacity
of clerk on the Leeds-Manchester Railroad.' Following his dismissal in April 1842 (for careless accounts), Branwell's self-pitying
but accomplished sonnet, 'On Peaceful Death and Painful Life',
was published in *The Halifax Guardian*. Anne then arranged for
Branwell to join her in January 1843 as tutor to an eleven-year-
old boy, Edmund Robinson, at Thorp Green. Anne must have
hoped to watch over her brother, but could not prevent his
fancy for his employer, Mrs Robinson. This led to a humiliating
dismissal by her husband in July 1845, preceded by Anne's abrupt
departure from the same household a month earlier, on 18 June.
Back home for good, Branwell subjected his family to violent
tempests of self-pity, while he drowned his sorrows every night
at the Black Bull. Addicted to gin and opium, he cadged money
from his father and anyone else who would oblige. His increasing
uproar may have been a source for the fictional frenzies in the
attic of *Jane Eyre* (October 1847), which, Charlotte claimed, was no
gothic fantasy: it was 'but too natural', a form of 'moral madness,
in which all that is good or even human seems to disappear from
the mind and a fiend-nature replaces it . . . All seems demon-
ized.' Branwell was to be a source, also, for Anne's fictional
exposé of the degrading effects of dipsomania on family life in
her second novel, *The Tenant of Wildfell Hall* (June 1848).

Branwell's story was that Mrs Robinson 'showed me a degree
of kindness which, when I was deeply grieved one day at her
husband's conduct, ripened into declarations of more than

ordinary feeling. My admiration of her mental and personal attractions . . . although she is seventeen years my senior, all combined to an attachment on my part, and led to reciprocations which I had little looked for.' He remained convinced that all Mrs Robinson wanted on earth was to give him herself – and all her property. How much was truth, how much was fantasy is not known, but the Brontës' attitude to Branwell's disgrace was not, at first, unsympathetic: he was seen as the gullible game of his employer. Their view of Mrs Robinson would have come to them through Anne's clear-eyed contempt: they judged her a frivolous woman, whose blend of weakness and deceit had warped her daughters beyond Anne's powers of counsel, and whose careless play with a deluded young tutor had been allowed to gain a destructive hold on him.

Anne's diary-paper, dated 'Thursday, July the 31st, 1845', a month and a half after her return to Haworth, is a self-portrait in weary endurance ('I for my part cannot well be flatter or older in mind than I am now'). As governess, she had endured well over four years in the social shade at Thorp Green, forced at length to witness a 'very unpleasant and unforeseen revelation of human nature.'

None of these self-portraits was true. What they presented to one another and even, to some extent, to themselves, were constructs of current modes. Branwell played out his Byronic drama, while his sisters practised what Charlotte called the 'ceaseless art' of the protective cover. In time, these covers became the décor of Brontë legend, but the facts of creativity tell a different story. On 9 October 1845, Emily's refusal of humility to dare 'the final bound' from life to 'eternal liberty' expressed the reverse of domestic calm. Anne's weary self-effacement is belied by the energy of her satire on the manners of the rich and the gentry in the novel she had been writing in the shadow of the Inghams and the Robinsons. It was 'the mirror of the mind of the writer', Charlotte said later, a story of an obscure governess whose grace of spirit is invisible to her gross employers, and

whose moral sense and capacity for love survives intact in the
unseen space of her private life. By the time Anne 'escaped' from
Thorp Green, in June 1845, she had completed two-thirds of
'Passages in the Life of an Individual', and in fact, at the very time
she referred to her flatness, was at work on the last third.
Renamed *Agnes Grey*, it was eventually published with *Wuthering
Heights* in December 1847. Charlotte's allusions to Agnes Grey in
two of her later novels suggest that she was, for Charlotte, the
definitive governess: in *Jane Eyre*, 'Mrs Grey' is the name of a governess baited by the Ingram children (as Anne was baited by the
insufferable Inghams in her first post, as related in *Agnes Grey*);
again, in Charlotte's next novel, *Shirley*, the maiden name of the
companionable governess is 'Miss Grey'.

During 1847–8, when Branwell became an increasing torment
to his family, Anne absorbed herself in a second novel with its
portrait of the degenerate Arthur Huntingdon whose self-
indulgent abuse of his family becomes demonic. Unlike Emily's
hero, Heathcliff, who ruins family relationships, Arthur is morally
incapable of any transcendent attachment. In this sense Anne's
more worldly novel may be something of a reply to *Wuthering
Heights*.

Charlotte, too, condemned Branwell, and all the more so for
her father's continued absorption in his only son. Her growing
estrangement from the brother who had been her mental partner has its aura of Victorian moralism, but that is less distorting
than attempts to put Branwell's writing more on a par with the
greatness of his sisters. Even as a youth, he had wallowed in the
prospective graveyardism of his own legend, which Charlotte
had caricatured in her teens with sarcastic wit. Emily, who took
a line of practical tolerance, was forced to own in the end he
was 'a hopeless being'. From 1845 his sisters could invite no one to
the disrupted Parsonage, and relinquished their plan for a school
in their own home – in any case, pupils had been hard to find.
Charlotte drew closer than ever to Ellen as she confided
Branwell's dramas, sure of Ellen's understanding, for Ellen's

'dissipated' (alcoholic) brother, Joseph, brought distress to the Nusseys*, while another brother, George, was unstable and eventually diagnosed to be insane. Branwell indulged posturing emotions and fed them further on drink and drugs until he brought himself into a hopeless confusion of dream and reality.

Here, enacted before his sisters' eyes, was a reckless abandon to feeling that came uncomfortably close to what Charlotte let out in rationed words to Mary and Ellen and in her curtailed correspondence with Monsieur. In this sense, Branwell remained her emotional counterpart – amoral, anarchic, bent on self-destruction through surrender to passions that, for Branwell, were unashamedly adulterous. (Branwell wrote to a friend that Mrs Robinson had given him 'all' her love 'for years'.) Charlotte believed that sin was 'a species of insanity', and distanced herself through strict control and repeated commitments to duty. Her letters stress her father's increasing blindness, his dependence on his eldest daughter, his need for her to read aloud to him, and the larger need for her to remain at home. Yet home, of course, was the only place where she would have been free to write. Whatever she said publicly about despair and duty, this alternative existence – the continued life of art – remained. Though her words to Monsieur declare that to pursue 'the career of letters' was impossible, this was what she was doing, in her German notebook and, soon, in two novels between 1845 and 1847. Though she continued to groan to Ellen that she had accomplished nothing ('I shall be 31 next birthday – My youth is gone like a dream – and very little use have I ever made of it – What have I done these last thirty years – ? Precious little –'), at the very time she wrote this lament on 24 March 1847 she had begun (on 16 March) a fair copy of her second novel, *Jane Eyre*.

How much did she question in private? The absolute priority of womanly duty? The refusal of Monsieur to use the words she willed on him? Love was denied her in the usual form of

---

* Joseph Nussey died of a combination of alcoholism and tuberculosis in 1846.

response, but though this did torment her as a woman, as a writer she remained convinced of their unique rapport and the essential blessing that one authority beyond the Parsonage had seen the powers that seethed in her. She had, then, an imagined audience. In this way, she remained emotionally partnered between the daylight world of stagnant duty and the dark world of anarchic attachment. There was danger in this divide – the restless stasis of 1844–5 – but it was in this speechless chasm that she evolved a strategy of survival: to be quiet on the surface where the public gaze falls, yet to rise from within, a writer.

She was exploring the result of her experience abroad in the work she prepared for publication. Even in the thick of denial in Brussels, she had revised and collected earlier poems, learning to exorcise deadness, shame, or loneliness through the act of writing. So we might see her as poems accumulate, as *The Professor* proceeds. Here, alone, she could vent her voice as she exposed the silencing of women's strongest needs: Frances Henri bent over her sewing; Jane Eyre, mute and half-hidden by the curtain in the back seat of the drawing-room, while Rochester sings with Blanche Ingram; and later, in *Shirley*, Caroline Helstone pressing the scorpion into her palm as it bites her – pressing in the urgency of active desire until it depletes the spirit. As Charlotte Brontë spoke up for silenced thoughts, her voice offered the reader a shared experience, compelling, confessional, moving from the lush trappings of high-society romance into the bared truths of the interior life.

Such truths had long echoed in the recess of consciousness, as far back as the 'Roe Head Journal'. But how did she effect the transition to a public voice and who was to hear it?

A turning point in the sisters' lives came in the autumn of 1845. At the very time that Emily dared 'the final bound', Charlotte came upon her poems, which she read alone and in secret. A quick excitement forced her to confess her discovery. She was 'sternly rated at first for having taken an unwarrantable liberty.' This Charlotte expected; her first task was to convince

Emily of an audience, starting with her sisters. By the dint of entreaty and reason, she at last wrung consent to have the 'rhymes', as Emily called them, published. Emily never referred to them, or only with scorn, but Charlotte's conviction never flagged:

> ... They stirred my heart like the sound of a trumpet ... I know no woman that ever lived ever wrote such poetry before. Condensed energy, clearness, finish – strange, strong pathos are their characteristics; utterly different from the weak diffusiveness, the laboured yet most feeble wordiness, which dilute the writings of even very popular poetesses. This is my deliberate and quite impartial opinion, to which I should hold if all the critics in the periodical press held a different one ...

The publication of *Poems* in May 1846 followed an act of reading, reinforced by a torrent of persuasion: Charlotte's repeated conviction that Emily's work was 'unlike the poetry that women generally write.' Her own poems appeared, in contrast, 'crude and rhapsodical'. Struck by a voice starker and more dauntless than her own, fortified by her certainty of Emily's genius, ambition leapt. She knew, in that flash of recognition, that each must now emerge from privacy to join as readers and, more boldly, as voices which would combine to speak beyond the Parsonage. Emily, left to herself, would have secreted her poems through her lifetime. Her unbending will would not have furthered her worldly interests. Her daring was private, a will to shed her contemporaries, and the 'world' as she knew it, to address an absolute; Charlotte's daring was to face the exposure of publication. This kind of public daring was fortified by Mary's repeated exhortations that women must act for themselves. Above all, Mary said, women must learn about business. Accordingly, Charlotte resolved to act for the sisters as businesswoman. To do this, she would have to defy the current icon of fragile womanhood unsullied by contact with the sordid dealings of public life.

Anne agreed with an offer of her own poems. Though Anne had all the tenacity of high ambition, she was too retiring for business, as Charlotte knew: 'a constitutional reserve and taciturnity placed and kept her in the shade, and covered her . . . with a sort of nun-like veil, which she rarely lifted.'

So it happened that an act of reading initiated a reciprocal venture, both private and public. From now on, they renewed their bonds and shared work once again as creatures of the night in the darkened dining-room when Papa retired. Branwell was not part of this scene, and he was not included in his sisters' plans, though he had been as prolific as they and the only one of the four who had published a poem. Was his exclusion a joint decision? Was it Charlotte's decision as leader into the public world? Given the relative weakness of Anne's and Charlotte's poems, Branwell's exclusion is not likely to have been on aesthetic grounds. It may be that Branwell was set apart by his mental state, as he described it at the age of twenty-eight in October 1845: 'I have lain during nine long weeks utterly shattered in body and broken down in mind.' But the most obvious reason for his exclusion was more mundane: Branwell was simply too talkative (especially while drinking) in view of his sisters' insistence on secrecy.

Their first act was to name themselves: 'Averse to personal publicity', Charlotte explained later, 'we veiled our own names under those of Currer, Ellis, and Acton Bell; the ambiguous choice being dictated by a sort of conscientious scruple at assuming Christian names positively masculine, while we did not like to declare ourselves women, because – without at that time suspecting that our mode of writing and thinking was not what is called "feminine" – we had a vague impression that authoresses are liable to be looked on with prejudice; we had noticed how critics sometimes used for their chastisement the weapon of personality, and for their reward, a flattery, which is not true praise.'

Their assumed surname, Bell, was the middle name of Mr Brontë's new curate, Arthur Bell Nicholls, a handsome Irishman, tall and bearded, who had arrived in Haworth six months before, in May 1845, and was said by Charlotte to be a 'respectable young man' who read well in church. The appropriation of his name shows a joking awareness of this eligible man whom the sisters affected to ignore as a nonentity. (Three months after 'Bell' appeared on the cover of *Poems*, Ellen teased Charlotte with a rumour that she would marry Mr Nicholls. She denied this indignantly: 'A cold, far-away sort of civility are the only terms on which I have ever been with Mr Nicholls', she replied on 10 July 1846. She saw herself, in his eyes, as an 'old maid': to mention such a rumour, even as a joke, would be to become the laughing stock of all the curates whom she calls in defensive tones, 'highly uninteresting, narrow and unattractive specimens of the "coarser" sex.')

The continued cover of Currer was necessary, as Charlotte explained to Mrs Gaskell, at the time her third novel, *Shirley*, was published at the end of 1849: 'Currer Bell will avow to Mrs Gaskell that her chief reason for maintaining an incognito is the fear that if she relinquished it, strength and courage would leave her, and she should ever after shrink from writing the plain truth'.

So it had to be that 'Currer Bell' detached herself from Charlotte Brontë, and began her separate existence. This phenomenon is perhaps most pervasive in the Victorian period when a domestic ideology reached its height, claiming women's spirit as well as their service: some ghostly alternative detaches itself, and comes into being. Eighty years later, and nearly ten years after women gained the vote in Britain, Virginia Woolf speculated on the trials of Currer Bell as descendant of a woman born to write or act in earlier centuries. Shakespeare's hypothetical 'sister' would have been so pulled apart by contrary obligations to truth and womanhood that she 'would certainly have gone crazed, shot herself, or ended her days in some lonely cottage outside the village, half witch, half wizard, feared and mocked at'. Had she survived, what she wrote would have been deformed, and would anyway have gone under cover.

That refuge she would have sought certainly. It was the relic of the sense of chastity that dictated anonymity to women even so late in the nineteenth century. Currer Bell, George Eliot, George Sand, all the victims of inner strife as their writings prove, sought ineffectively to veil themselves by using the name of a man. Thus they did homage to the convention, which if not implanted by the other sex was liberally encouraged by them (the chief glory of a woman is not to be talked of, said Pericles, himself a much-talked-of man) that publicity in women is detestable. Anonymity runs in their blood.

For Virginia Woolf, who belonged to the first generation to make it customary for women to publish under their own names, the exposure often brought her close to breakdown. 'Is the time coming', she wrote just before submitting *Night and Day* to Duckworth in March 1919, 'when I can endure to read my own writing in print without blushing & shivering & wishing to take cover?' Virginia Woolf and Sylvia Plath suffered the same attack that was meted out at the end of the eighteenth century to Mary Wollstonecraft who had no cover: Godwin's ill-judged *Memoirs* (1798), revealing her affair with Gilbert Imlay and the illegitimacy of her elder daughter, led to the reactionary attacks of the 1790s, sustained through the following century. It was said that the improper private life of the author of the *Vindication of the Rights of Woman* must discredit the book itself. So it was in other cases: readers, regaled with the flaws of the woman's life are invited, on that basis, to discount her work, as in 1989, the official biographer of Sylvia Plath, as agent of Plath's estranged in-laws, castigated the poet for excessive – that is, unfeminine – 'ambition', without giving due weight to the greatness of the poetry. Often, the most eager detractors of great women have been lesser women hoping to win favour as agents of conventional opinion. There was the journalist, Elizabeth Rigby, who led the attack on Currer Bell for 'coarseness' and cast over her the damaging aspersion that if *Jane Eyre* were written by a woman, it must be one 'who has, for some sufficient reason, long forfeited the society of her sex'. A century later, Queenie Leavis advanced the attack on Virginia Woolf's exclusiveness. Such detraction, designed to strike at the centre of the life, its acts of creation, is almost unheard of with men of distinction. It is unthinkable that a commentator on Dickens or Tolstoy would be allowed to underrate their achievements on biographical grounds – that, say, their humanity at home left much to be desired. The fact that this sort of biographical weapon is still levelled at women writers a hundred and fifty years after Charlotte Brontë's lifetime, justifies the inflexibility of 'Currer Bell' and the associated womanly cover of shrinking modesty and plaintive moralism. As far back as 1837, Southey had dictated the part, and Charlotte had rehearsed it in her replies, with a correctness so keenly mimicked, so perfectly styled, that her glibness verged on caricature.

Truth demanded that she flex the vehement voice Southey had denied. Southey had taught her that its spontaneous, unmediated accents could not be received – not as a woman's voice. She had to develop the unplaceable voice of Currer Bell who could direct her 'plain truth' through the fictional persona of 'I': the 'I' of a man, the cool Crimsworth; the 'I' of a survivor, Jane Eyre, who learns to curb her rage and desire with the rein of reason. The intimacy of this voice had the advantage of the writer's distance from the metropolitan voice of the age; a directness undeflected by fashion. Unlike Thackeray or Dickens, this voice spoke not through public life, but beyond it, as Jane declares herself to Rochester from a site beyond the social order of the time.

The modest, shrinking Miss Brontë, who was eventually on exhibit in London, would never have borne up against the apparent failure of *Poems*, which sold two copies, and the repeated rejection of *The Professor*, but Currer Bell was a creature of more determined resilience: 'Ill-success failed to crush us: the mere effort to succeed had given a wonderful zest to existence; it must be pursued.' She finished the novel on 27 June 1846. In the course of 1846–7, she sent it out six times, not stopping to consider that the scratched-out names of publishers on the front of the parcel were hardly a commendation to her newest choice. She sent the manuscript to Henry Colburn on 4 July 1846. It was returned the next month, on the very morning that sixty-nine-year-old Mr Brontë underwent an operation for cataract. Charlotte was with him in Manchester, and there, within days of the manuscript's rejection, she began her second novel, two months after completing her first.

The gripping story of *Jane Eyre* had its source in a bizarre event that happened near Leeds at the time Charlotte was teaching at Roe Head: it had excited much curiosity at the school. A certain governess had married a gentleman employed by the family in which she held her post. A year after her marriage, by which time she had given birth to a child, it was discovered that her husband had another wife. This wife was said to be mad, which was the husband's excuse for bigamy. Charlotte may have recalled this story in July 1845 when she visited the Eyre family seat of North Lees during a three-week stay with Ellen in Hathersage, Derbyshire. The first mistress of North Lees was said to have become insane and confined to a room with padded walls on the second floor, and to have died by fire. These dramatic details ripened into a story of a young, innocent governess who falls in love with her employer who intends to marry her despite the fact of a dangerous, mad wife secreted in the uppermost floor of his country house. The suspense and horror of the plot owed something, perhaps, to Charlotte's familiarity with the most widely popular of gothic novelists, Ann Radcliffe (1764–1823), whose macabre scenes turn out to have rational explanations. But *Jane Eyre* stands out from many predecessors in the gothic or romance tradition for its unusual heroine: no swooning beauty, no fragile model of sensibility, Jane is a plain, intelligent governess who tells her story with compelling honesty.

Charlotte wrote fast, under unlikely conditions, as she lay

awake with toothache and nursed her father in the month following his operation, August-September 1846. The surgeon, Mr Wilson, ordered 'utter privation of light' and 'perfect quiet'. What happened as she sat with Papa in that darkened room in Boundary Street remains in shadow. All we know is the fact that she sat in darkness and silence, and from that darkness and silence there poured a voice that combined the rational coolness of Crimsworth with the ardour of the letters to Monsieur and the truth-telling conviction of the 'Roe Head Journal'. It was a voice strong enough to cross the spaces that cut her off from the world. Closing with the faceless reader, speaking intimately from private life to private life, the voice passed the outward barriers of reserve. The reader was like the listeners in the dark dormitory at Roe Head as Charlotte gripped them with ghosts; now, the reader was to hear a revelation of a woman's life.

For Jane Eyre, Charlotte Brontë turned to the life of the outwardly meek, inwardly fiery governess. Having worked off the Brussels experience, for the time being, in *The Professor*, she turned back to the tales of 1838–41 which had explored the nature and fate of a Miss West, Miss Hall, or Miss Hastings, drawn largely from her own character and circumstance. Jane Eyre evolves as a new kind of woman, based on a more complex blend of herself with her sisters and Mary Taylor. Mary's far-off life in New Zealand was much on her mind during that fertile month in Manchester.

Mary's latest letters showed her 'in her element – because she is where she has a toilsome task to perform, an important improvement to effect . . .' As *Jane Eyre* gestated in Charlotte's mind, she recalled her friend's sturdiness and self-reliance, ignoring convention, status, and the middle-class norms of comfort to which she had been accustomed: 'She sits on a wooden stool without a back in a log-house without a carpet and neither is degraded nor thinks herself degraded by such poor accommodation.' Here is a model for Jane when she abandons her past to become village schoolmistress in a simple cottage. Mary was the first to know the secret of Currer Bell's identity: Charlotte sent her a copy of *Jane Eyre*, not from Currer Bell but from herself – a unique gesture at a time when even Ellen was not told.

Ellen, who came to know Charlotte's sources, reported later that she had been a blender of character. There is a quiet endurance in Jane that was neither Charlotte (who took relief in plaintiveness) nor the vociferous Mary, but came possibly from Anne Brontë, the only one of the Brontës to endure 'exile' for any length of time in the inhospitable world through which Jane must pass. Back home, when Charlotte looked up from her manuscript she saw her sisters, each bent over a book. They 'looked thoughtful almost to severity.' Grave and slender, 'both possessed faces full of distinction and intelligence.' So she described them in the form of two studious sisters, Diana and Mary Rivers, who shelter Jane when she runs away from biga-mous Mr Rochester. Nor must we forget Maria Brontë who lives on in the shape of the transcendent Helen Burns, Jane's first model – unlike Jane in self-abnegation, yet a profound influ-ence for resolute integrity. The flat exemplars of the past, the stainless saints and the good dying children of Evangelical tales, fade before the palpable impact of her living, aspiring, failing breath. Later, when critics questioned the perfection of Helen Burns' character, Charlotte insisted that she was 'real enough. I have exaggerated nothing there. I abstained from recording much that I remembered respecting her, lest the narrative should sound incredible.'

Though Charlotte drew on actual women in order to create a new figure, she had to imagine circumstances in which such a creature might be driven to emerge from the shadow of the mind on to the platform of action – not, as Mary, in some remote outpost of empire, but in the placid drawing-rooms and repressive schools of the north of England. The transit from life to invention is a shift from one kind of truth to another. Which, we might ask, is better: documentary or imaginative truth, fact or fiction? Jane Eyre is too honest, dauntless, and ultimately too

fortunate to exist in nineteenth-century England; she is a creative truth: not woman as she is, but as she might be. As
potential exemplar, Jane sets before us her trials and possibilities.

Jane Eyre is, above all, a pilgrimage. It follows child and woman
through pitfalls en route to her new Eden: a love which unites
goodness with the dream of sustained passion. In this new map
for the soul, the Fall is not disobedience; it is obedience –
unthinking obedience. Mrs Reed, Jane's guardian aunt, com-
plains that she has never seen a child like her. What sets Jane
apart is that she is incapable of not thinking for herself; the
brutal acts of repression in the Reed household happen because
Jane thinks, and also because, as a child, she blurts out what she
thinks with blunt acumen: '*Speak* I must . . .' A full-formed
speech pours out in self-defence against misrepresentation, and
at this, Jane feels her soul begin to expand 'with the strangest
sense of freedom, of triumph, I ever felt. It seemed as if an invisible bond had burst . . .' As Jane grows, she learns that she may
not use language in this way: she must mute truth and mediate
it through the low voice of schooled politeness, but the search
for truth goes on.

In her journey through a social world, the temptation to fall
is ever present in a variety of plausible forms. Jane is lost should
she once succumb to any of the plots on offer. There is the plot
for the dependent orphan whom the Reeds would fix in her
place as poor relation. There is the plot for the charity girl whom
Lowood would fix in postures of humility, leading to servitude of
the upper classes. There is the plot for a grown-up Jane, devised
by a married gentleman: to be his mistress in a Mediterranean
hideaway where Rochester, according to habit, would confer
sultan smiles, erotic stupefactions, and material rewards. Finally,
there is the most plausible plot of all, traditional marriage, on
offer from that figure of marble beauty and impeccable rectitude, St John Rivers: the temptation of the mature Jane to come
under the sway of an egotistical missionary. Can she distinguish
the valid demands of altruism from the cant of sacrifice which

tempts her to lose her life – worse, to lose her very self – in distant service to pure principle, unwarmed by any concession to human need?

These plots, the pilgrim must see for the played-out fictions they are: all are posited on a false premiss about women's nature as biddable and inferior. The pioneer of a new Progress must break through the encrustations of language, lover's and religious cant, to see, to *see* in the sense of revelation, the destructive self-interest of persons in positions of power. As Christian once did battle with Obstinate or the Giant Despair, so Jane must outface the deceptive faces of nineteenth-century Benevolence. Mrs Reed, the Revd Mr Brocklehurst, Mr Rochester, and the Revd Mr Rivers believe themselves benefactors. For Jane to succumb to Mrs Reed, to the founder of the charity school, to her lover (in his sultan aspect), or to her apparent saviour, would be to lose her soul. When Rochester, thwarted in his bigamous plan, pleads with Jane to live with him, if only to keep him from 'lust', 'vice', and 'despair', she is tempted to 'save him'. When he asks her to transgress 'a mere human law', Conscience and Reason turn traitors against her and Feeling clamours:

'Who in the world cares for *you*? or who will be injured by what you do?'

Still indomitable was the reply – '*I* care for myself.'

This indomitable '*I*' sustains her through the scene that follows, when Rochester seizes her physically – physically, she is powerless, as Rochester, driven by possessive fury, allows himself to lose control. Her eye meets his devouring glance and calls him back to what she is: '– mentally, I still possessed my soul, and with it the certainty of ultimate safety.'

Many have criticised Jane for her resistance. Mary Ann Evans (later, George Eliot) wrote to Charles Bray on 11 June 1848: 'All self-sacrifice is good – but one would like it to be in a somewhat nobler cause than that of a diabolical law which chains a man soul and body to a putrefying carcase.' Eventually, when Miss Evans chose to live with George Henry Lewes, who was locked in a licentious marriage, she did not require a legal tie in circumstances which made this impossible. This is Rochester's line, and he reproaches Jane for her 'difficult' nature – 'flinty', Jane agrees. Morals apart, her 'difficulty' is that she cannot put herself in the power of a man who has used her untruthfully. Passionate as she is, she cannot be subdued to stale schemes of seduction which lead to the weak position of a mistress. In retrospect Elizabeth Hastings' denial of her loved seducer was a rehearsal for this supremely difficult renunciation.

Jane charts her Progress through a world in which gains are precarious, while danger threatens almost to the end. The pilgrim must retain her clarity at all costs – her keen awareness of injustice and the exploitation masked as benevolence – but she must see all this without that rage she had known as a child, screaming and beating on the door when she was locked in the Red Room until frenzy collapsed into illness. That early extravagance teaches her to track a middle course: to gain knowledge without capitulation to the regimented aspect of schooling; to retain strength of feeling without capitulation to licence; to become self-sufficient and economically independent without a chilling degree of purpose. If she is to survive, she cannot afford, either, to succumb to the internal temptations of despair, when she is locked in the Red Room, when she is humiliated at school, and – most difficult – when she cannot marry Mr Rochester.

To follow such a course requires more strength than was usually allowed women in the nineteenth century. In short, such a course could only proceed on a novel premiss about the nature of the 'weaker sex'. This was derived from Charlotte's discoveries about herself, her sisters, and friends, and it was the heat of these discoveries that made the book so revolutionary to its time and ours. 'The standard heroes and heroines of novels are personages . . . whom I could never . . . believe to be natural, or wish to imitate.' When Charlotte Brontë theorised, her appeal

was to Nature: 'Were I obliged to copy any former novelist, even
the greatest, even Scott, . . . I would not write . . . Unless I can
look beyond the greatest Masters, and study Nature herself, I
have no right to paint. Unless I have the courage to use the language of Truth in preference to the jargon of Conventionality, I
ought to be silent.'

Rochester shares the language of truth. He, alone, has the
insight to know Jane, and the confidence to encourage her to be
what she is: 'An unusual – to me – a perfectly new character I
suspected was yours: I desired to search it deeper, and know it
better.' This had been validated by Monsieur's capacity to know
Charlotte; in fact, Rochester's words to Jane are close to Heger's
style:

> 'You entered the room with a look and air at once shy and
> independent . . . I made you talk: ere long I found you full of
> strange contrasts. Your garb and manner were restricted by
> rule; . . . yet, when addressed, you lifted a keen, a daring, and a
> glowing eye . . . : there was penetration and power in each
> glance you gave . . .'

At length, he perceives that what he is seeing has the permanent
stamp of nature. It 'was no transitory blossom; but rather the
radiant resemblance of one, cut in an indestructible gem.'

As new-found creature, Jane will not permit any lapse into
reductive terms. When Rochester casts Jane as comforting angel,
she laughs at him:

> 'I am not an angel,' I asserted; 'and I will not be one till I die: I
> will be myself. Mr. Rochester, you must neither expect nor
> exact anything celestial of me, – for you will not get it, any
> more than I shall get it of you; which I do not at all anticipate.'

When Rochester calls his mad wife 'that demon . . . that fearful
hag', Jane will, again, refuse his language:

'Sir,' I interrupted him, 'you are inexorable for that unfortunate lady: you speak of her with hate – with vindictive antipathy. It is cruel – she cannot help being mad.'

The reductive view that Jane resists is rooted in theology with its categorisation of women as saints or sinners. Unlike Jane, Charlotte herself was not exempt from the glib phrase that guarded her self-protective distance and carefully preserved gentility when she took the view that Branwell was a lost soul. Emily, unconcerned with refinement, could afford to pity Branwell, to see a Fall, not a demon.

Emily went further than her sister in questioning the codes and language of religion, with her assault on heaven, dogmatism, and false humility. Organised religion has held the monopoly on souls; Emily reclaimed them. When Heathcliff cries, 'I *cannot* live without my soul!', he means the undying love he had shared in youth with Catherine Earnshaw. *Wuthering Heights* was completed just before Charlotte began *Jane Eyre*, and almost certainly formed part of the nightly talks. Charlotte shared with her sister an ideal of sustained passion which they defined in part through its failures. Where *Jane Eyre* explores the danger of erotic oblivion, *Wuthering Heights* explores a stranger passion warped by social plots: Catherine's Fall into a tepid marriage with Edgar Linton; Heathcliff's Fall into plots of power, especially the revenge plot, which brutalise his nature. In betraying Nature, both lovers lose themselves and wander in the wilderness – Heathcliff as scheming monster, Catherine as ghost. In the end, Catherine and Heathcliff recover their souls, their heaven – which is not a resting-place for the smugly obedient; it is union in spirit. For Emily, this union can be sustained only through death. She took a more extreme position than Charlotte: she saw the impossibility of spiritual wholeness in a shallow world which she despised and utterly shunned. Like Maria Brontë, Emily longed for the freedom that death could bring. For her, wholeness had an absolute existence beyond life; within this world, it remained a possibility immanent in the rocks of the immutable moor, the landscape closest to Emily's heaven.

Charlotte said of *Wuthering Heights*: 'It is moorish, and wild, and knotty as a root of heath. Nor was it natural that it should be otherwise; the author being herself a native and nursling of the moors . . . Her native hills were far more to her than a spectacle; they were what she lived in, and by, as much as the wild birds, their tenants, or as the heather, their produce.' When Charlotte wrote these words she was constructing her sister's legend after her death. Central to this legend is Emily's complete reclusiveness: Charlotte claims that Emily had no more knowledge of the people amongst whom she lived than a 'nun' has of those who pass her convent gates. What Emily knew of their ways, language, and family histories, was known only at secondhand, Charlotte insists, because she wished to separate her sister from the rudeness, the cruelty, the almost diabolical hate and vengeance Emily recounts when she goes to the moors for her heroes. There is no doubt that Charlotte wished to placate the pervasive disgust of the first readers of *Wuthering Heights*, but she was also covering up something that remains unexplained.

Emily may not have been quite as reclusive as Charlotte argues. She seems to have visited the Heatons whose old family had lived since 1513 across the moor; family hearsay has it that it was Emily, of all the Brontës, who sustained some measure of contact with their forebear, Robert Heaton, who died in 1846 (the year Emily finished *Wuthering Heights*), and his five retiring and musical sons. Their home, Ponden House (now Ponden Hall), was built in 1541, and an additional dwelling, confusingly called Ponden Old House, was built in 1634. Ponden has often been considered a source for the grand Thrushcross Grange in Emily Brontë's novel, but, though it did have a magnificent library (which the Brontë children are said to have used), the long, low building is more of a farmhouse, more like Wuthering Heights, particularly the Old House where there was a tree with a branch which beat against a window, as in the novel. The main house was rebuilt in 1801, the date over the door, and this date opens *Wuthering Heights*. The novel's plot suggests that it was not only the Hall that interested Emily but also the family and its history: at one stage, the family had been ousted by Henry Casson, the second husband of a young Heaton widow, who gained control of the property for nearly twenty years from the 1640s to the 1660s. The rightful heir, his stepson, was left uneducated. The name, Heaton, is obviously close to Hareton, the uneducated orphan heir in Emily Brontë's novel who, for the space of his boyhood and youth, loses his inheritance to the usurper, Heathcliff. Heathcliff's callous union with his social superior, Isabella of Thrushcross Grange, may have one source in a more recent Heaton tragedy, that of Elizabeth Heaton who fell in love with a delivery boy called John Bakes. Their marriage was a disaster, and Elizabeth returned to Ponden to die at the age of twenty-one in 1816, followed rapidly by the death of her small daughter. This tragedy would have been alive for Robert Heaton of Ponden and Michael Heaton of Royd House, Oxenhope, who were Elizabeth's surviving brothers.

Connections with *Wuthering Heights* must remain supposition, but one certain and curious fact is that there was some rift between the Heatons and Mr Brontë. Robert and Michael Heaton were hereditary trustees of church lands, the main source of the stipend for the incumbent of Haworth. Mr Brontë's letters to the Heatons were coldly formal, with no sign that the families were on visiting terms. When Michael Heaton died at the age of seventy on 5 March 1860, Mr Brontë refused to bury him in the ground adjoining the Parsonage. Nor would he permit his curate, Mr Nicholls, to do so. The immediate reason was that the burial ground had been declared full, but an order was obtained from the Secretary of State (dated 7 March) to bury Mr Heaton with his ancestors, and here is the puzzling fact: Mr Brontë still refused. In the end, Michael had to be buried by Mr Grant of Oxenhope. It is possible that Mr Brontë was being stubborn, but this would have been an irrational position since Mr Brontë himself expected to be buried there with his wife and children. The member of family Mr Brontë would have opposed most directly was Michael Heaton's son and heir, Robert, an exact contemporary of Branwell and a year and a half older than Emily. In 1842, while Emily was in Brussels, this Robert had married Mary Ann Bailey who gave birth to a child soon after, in September of that year. In the Heaton archive there is, unusually, no record of the exact date of this marriage. Had there been a seduction of which Mr Brontë disapproved? (Mrs Gaskell records that a Heaton did seduce a girl.) Yet another possibility could be some slight that wounded the Brontës' thin skin when it came to their recent rise in the class system. I have wondered if the slight could have been analogous to Catherine Earnshaw's refusal to marry Heathcliff, despite her affinity for him, because of his social inferiority. This single event propels Catherine to early death, and sets in motion Heathcliff's extended downhill course of degradation, which ends only when the lovers meet to haunt the moors after their deaths.

Charlotte had more in her of the social concerns of the Old Testament prophet; Emily more of the New Testament reach beyond death. Emily practised a loneliness that Byron at times felt but could not live with and could not purify:

> From my youth
> My spirit walk'd not with the souls of men,
> Nor look'd upon the earth with human eyes.

She shed plots more ruthlessly than Charlotte, the 'hope of youth' and 'fancy's rainbow', for what she called 'infinity'. Like her admirer, Emily Dickinson, she lived for a rising life beyond death.

Charlotte would not concede the impossibility of sustained passion within this world. Jane Eyre will not settle for anything beyond or less than a transformed Rochester. He is the educable man. Though blinded in the fire that destroys his wife, he can learn to 'see' his true mate who is not to be his grateful dependant but his equal. Rochester rides out of darkness, and is largely a creation in the dark. His appearance – whether ugly or not – is irrelevant because what Jane sees is his promise to know *her*. This knowing is blocked, to some extent, by sultan habits (the wrong sort of masterfulness which presumes to think for her, in fact to trick her into false union). Rochester must learn to see Jane's right to her integrity: this 'seeing' is a triumph, not a loss. To deride Rochester as an impossible dream is to misread Charlotte Brontë. She was a reformer. Where Emily terminates in 'infinity', Charlotte is closer to contemporaries like Dickens and Mrs Gaskell who look to a society improved through reformed characters. Rochester is not meant to represent men as they were, but a man as he might be.

Charlotte Brontë denied any identity with Jane beyond plainness. With contemporaries, it was prudent to preserve her detachment from that passionate voice. In fact, the author had not the overt rage nor quite the unflinching strength of Jane. But her story sets out an exemplary pattern which realises the deepest structure of Charlotte's own life. The subtitle, *An Autobiography*, is true, not in the literal way that *The Professor* drew on events in the author's life, but in its polarities: the tensions of pilgrimage and passion, of chill and fire, the iron grip of rational control and the anarchic abandon that Charlotte had known in the shadow of Branwell. 'The action of the tale is sometimes unnatural', said a reviewer, 'but the passion is always true.' 'It is an autobiography,' said George Henry Lewes in *Fraser's Magazine*, '– not, perhaps, in the naked facts and circumstances, but in the actual suffering and experience.'

Autobiography is an attempt to distil from the life a form and meaning. Charlotte's letters to Ellen and Monsieur insist on her atrophy in Haworth, her loss of her '*maître*', and her despair over 'doing nothing yet' at nearly thirty, at nearly thirty-one. And to Ellen she confides, too, the impossibility of marriage: the men she met in West Yorkshire were either 'narrow' curates or worldly cynics like Mary's brother, Joe, who demanded looks and means when they came to marry. No Englishman she encountered could have conceived of knowing a woman in the way she wished, or could have said those liberating words that Rochester says to Jane: '. . . in time, I think you will learn to be natural with me, as I find it impossible to be conventional with you'.

It would be easy to dwell on futility and sadness, yet this would not explain Currer Bell's command: her will to convert life into meaning. *Jane Eyre* selects for those trials that emerge as gains. The loss of Maria, retold through Helen Burns, is an instructive episode in a Progress. The loss of Monsieur and the ensuing depression drives Jane into the wilderness near Whitcross. Her gain is Charlotte's in the aftermath of Brussels: a determined endurance, dramatised in the final volume where Jane must part with Rochester to devise another fate. Whitcross was derived from the stone pillar known as the Moscar Cross, close to the Hallam moors in Derbyshire which Charlotte would have seen when she vacationed with Ellen in the village of Hathersage in the summer of 1845. The pillar marked the cross-roads where the old east-west road from Sheffield to Manchester crossed the north-south road from Yorkshire. It might be said to mark a moment, a year and a half after Charlotte's flight from Monsieur, when she conceived for herself a new story.

In *Jane Eyre*, Currer Bell found ways of dramatising desires and principles, so as to speak to all readers, not only women. Through the hidden alien in all women we discover the singularity of all members of our species and beyond this, our dualities, our plural languages, beyond the horizon of Jane's repeated gaze, beyond sight. One reviewer, William George Clark, hearing extravagant praise, resolved to be 'as critical as Croker'. But as he read on, he forgot commendations and criticism, identified with Jane in all her troubles, 'and finally married Mr. Rochester about four in the morning.' What carries the reader, as Lewes recognised, is the book's voice: 'it is soul speaking to soul; it is an utterance from the depths of a struggling, suffering, much-enduring spirit: *suspiria de profundis!*'

Though Charlotte Brontë wrote at the onset of a long and still-advancing period when women must question the abuses of power – sexual power, violence, militarism, and the evils these perpetuate – from an objective distance, men and women belong to the same species, sharing the same fundamental pattern of existence. Have we attractions as a species, we might well ask, and shall we go on? Jane, as survivor, with unflinching moral courage, reason in command of passion, and vigour which derives from vivacity of mind, embodies a principled resilience all can share. As orphan, she stands for all who are dependent and alone, who are vulnerable to abuse, both crass abuse of child, class, or woman, and also that more subtle abuse explored in all Charlotte Brontë's work: denial of feeling.

The bully, John Reed, cuffs Jane because she will not show him due deference. Brocklehurst humiliates Jane, and starves the girls at Lowood in order to break their spirit; but, when Jane looks back, it is his words – repressive, threatening, sanctimonious words – that remain the focus of resentment. What draws Jane to Rochester, despite his dubious past, his growls, and gloom, is that Rochester invites the opposite of this denial: 'I have not been petrified', Jane tells him when she explains her attachment. 'I have not been buried with inferior minds, and excluded from every glimpse of communion with what is bright, and energetic, and high.'

In contrast, Mr Brocklehurst and St John Rivers are pillars of a structure that denied the right of feeling to those it designed for service. The danger of this emotional imprisonment is the depletion of character, as Anne Brontë feared when she went 'flat' after her years with the Robinsons, or as Jane fears when Mr Rivers (saying 'I . . . I . . . I . . .'), insists on marriage to support his spiritual ambition.

Jane and Rochester both pass through their periods in the wilderness: Jane begging for food and shelter near Whitcross;

Rochester a blind recluse at Ferndean, after the fire that destroys his house. Jane's self-reliance is tested under conditions of extremity when she is bereft of protection, money, the means for cleanliness, even the reserve dear to her pride. Rochester, in turn, is stripped of the sultan aspect of power – the power that had charmed the parasites (Céline, Giacinta, and Clara) of his licentious past. Sultan largesse had been an irritant to Jane: it would make her a ridiculous doll. Worse, it had presumed to think for her, to plan a false wedding: '. . . I would not say he had betrayed me: but the attribute of stainless truth was gone from his idea; and from his presence I must go'. Yet all that is desirable in Rochester's power does survive this parting and their subsequent ordeals. Still retrievable beneath his encrustations of bitterness are his knowing, his verbal play, his ready engagement with Jane. The final chapter, which follows the pair through the first years of their marriage, asserts the success of sustained compatibility: 'We talk, I believe, all day long'.

This resolution of freedom and bonding comes about only when Jane has purged herself finally of two forms of tyranny. First, she must free herself of the tyranny of licence: the child's abandon to rage, and the adult's abandon to appetite that leads to the concealed frenzy in Rochester's home, Thornfield Hall.*

Bertha Mason Rochester, the mad woman on the third floor, is a warning more than a character: a warning of mindless passion. Jane veers closest to her in one cancelled sentence in the manuscript which admits an underlying recklessness in her susceptibility to Rochester during their engagement: '. . . if he was subjugated so was I – and that by a strange and resistless sway'. This is checked after the disclosure of attempted bigamy, followed by the visit to Rochester's mad wife. Jane, alone in her

* Based on Ellen's old home, The Rydings, near Birstall, and on the Eyre family seat of North Lees which CB visited during her stay in Derbyshire in 1845. Another candidate is Norton Conyers with its legend of a mad woman in the attic, an old hall which Charlotte could have visited when she accompanied her employers, the Sidgwicks, to Swarcliffe, to the east of Harrogate.

room, stops the momentum of shared passion with the words (heavily underscored in the manuscript), 'but *now — I thought*.' Her reassertion of reason separates her sharply from the madness in which Rochester continues to remain implicated. Bertha embodies the anarchic element in Rochester, rampant until she is dead. Dying in her blaze of fire, she leaves him scarred and, to a degree, disabled. It is suggestive that it is Rochester she disables, not Jane. He has been scarred by his part in a long tradition of flawed judgement. For Bertha Mason never was a promising woman; she was thick, with slow, unmoving eyes, like those of her brother.

The creative madness that Charlotte Brontë and other writers — Emily Dickinson, Olive Schreiner, Virginia Woolf, Sylvia Plath — experienced, in one way or another, is different from the vicious madness of Bertha. She is stupidly violent, like capricious fighter dogs with rending teeth. As Charlotte Brontë conceived her, Bertha was the cause of her misfortune, not her husband. It will not do to infuse Bertha with feminist sentiment if we care at all for what is there on the page as an emanation of its time and place. I see it as part of Charlotte Brontë's greatness that she will not simplify truth as truism. Women are not simply victims; they have, within them, the agency to discover gains in the most restrictive life. This is what Charlotte sought to show.

Bertha is not to be aligned with such able, aspiring women, rather with the showy female type Charlotte deplored: the rich, thick, insensitive beauties. Men trail after them, abandoning their better natures to lust and greed, as Rochester degraded himself through his union with Bertha. She is most threatening as a relic of dangers in Rochester's nature, hidden and for a long time unknown to Jane, who finds herself susceptible to a man who has accustomed himself to the shallowness that can treat a succession of bodies as passing pleasure. This is what Bertha means as Rochester's mate, a part of him that may be invisible but lives on. Rochester travels between passion in its debased form and passion as he knows it with Jane, which can redeem and heal him because (he sees as he reads her face) it has the grace of reason.

Rochester occupies an ambiguous position. In part he represents the traditional man who constructs 'woman' as opposite and alien, a defective 'other' to be shut away if he is to assert his autonomous existence. To relegate Bertha to a separate region of the house is to deny some part of himself, a bestial lust and rage, which he expels beyond the domestic boundary he must police with strict rules – unsuccessfully, for Bertha is liable to break out and invade her husband's bedroom with furious incendiary attentions. And yet Rochester is also a man who can learn to cultivate the 'other' in the form of Jane whom he comes to recognise as his better self. He can promote genuine knowledge of this alien 'sprite'. Confident in his manhood, he can admit the 'other' to intimacy, but he can do so only by a love that confronts his controlling habits of force and lust.

The tyranny of licence is no more dangerous than the tyranny of self-constriction, that denial of the right to feeling that Mr Brocklehurst and St John Rivers seek to impose through their brands of religion. To succumb to Rivers with his high-flown discourse of sacrifice would be, Jane sees, to lose half her self. She prays in a different way to St John's, but effective in its own fashion. As Jane had claimed her right of communion with what is bright, energetic, high, so, with Rivers, she claims what Helen Burns had practised, a religion of her own. The real daring of this book lies not in Jane's moments of anger and rebellion, nor in the loveplay of Jane and Rochester, nor even in replacing cant with a purer Christianity, but in Jane's claim to think for herself – not only as a woman and worker but as a spirit equal to any other spirit, and with the same right to exist and experience:

'– I have as much soul as you, [Jane tells Rochester] – and full as much heart! . . . I am not talking to you now through the medium of custom, conventionalities, nor even of mortal flesh: – it is my spirit that addresses your spirit; just as if both had passed through the grave, and we stood at God's feet, equal, – as we are!'

Part of Jane's experience is to know the extremes of a seething chaotic life and one of disciplined order. It is here that Charlotte Brontë gave form and meaning to the private extravagance of her own life tugged between the claims of the self and the claims of society. Here is the 'inner strife' that Virginia Woolf perceived in Currer Bell and George Eliot – and presumably in her own 'night and day'. To what extent Charlotte Brontë resolved the 'inner strife' remains to be seen; but Currer Bell lays down the path to resolution in 1846–7 as she follows Jane Eyre in her transitions from the restrictive Lowood to the tempestuous Thornfield, and from Thornfield to the bare testing-ground of Whitcross, to her final habitation in the fertile landscape of Ferndean where the broken hall, inhabited by a damaged Rochester, might be restored. In the course of her journeys, Jane learns to guard herself against the excesses of heat and frigid self-discipline. These extremes are embodied in two men: Rochester who offers passion without marriage, and Rivers who offers marriage without passion.

As Jane moves from place to place, the pattern of her life emerges. She is oscillating between the dangers of passion and restraint. Gateshead, her point of origin, the gate from which she issues on her journeys, is a place of physical savagery, concealed by a veneer of middle-class gentility. The indulged John Reed injures Jane. The heat of Jane's answering rage leads to further violence when she is locked in the Red Room. There, rage burns out as gothic terrors reduce the child to insensibility.

Lowood is the counterpoise. The temperature is low: chill to freezing. A single fire is surrounded by rows of big girls so that the smaller are cut off from any source of warmth. The water in the basins is frozen in the mornings; as a result, Helen is birched for not cleaning her nails. Helen. Miss Temple. Their names suggest the classics. Helen is reading a neo-classic work, *Rasselas*, a rational dialogue on the vanity of human wishes, which is conducted with serene forbearance. It is from Helen and Miss Temple that Jane learns to accept the decorums of social conduct and the virtues of humility, poverty, servitude, and self-denial. By the time she leaves Lowood eight years later, she appears a changed character: 'I had given in allegiance to duty and order . . . I appeared a disciplined and subdued character.'

Discipline is a counter to futile rage. The graces of decorum prove essential to Jane's progress through a public world. At Lowood she learns French and other subjects which will give her the means to earn her keep. In short, there are benefits at Lowood, and, in the end, it is not the pains but the gains that matter – if they can be distilled and used. Jane owes it to Lowood that she holds her own with dignity as she engages – as she must, if she is to survive – with the ephemeral norms of her age: the artifice of bloodless dolls, Adèle and Blanche; the self-absorption of vain Georgiana Reed; the mercenary snobberies of Aunt Reed and Lady Ingram, blind to the woman forming in the double-enclosure of the window seat and in the back shadows of the drawing-room. The insistently visible Blanche Ingram epitomises the taste of the age as she holds the floor with her props on show – her ringlets, her trinkets, her stock of accomplishments – while Jane, the unrecognised portent of the future, slips away. Rochester follows and commands her to remain. His refusal to let a genuine woman vanish up the stair is a gesture towards what lies beyond his time. Jane is called back – drawn into the light – for Rochester alone recognises her authenticity. To place Blanche in apparent competition is to fan Jane's love in cruel Zamorna fashion, but it also goads her out of silence to make her famous declaration of a soul equal to his own.

Jane had left Lowood to seek 'a new servitude' but, at Thornfield, without the model of Miss Temple, she finds herself again in her 'natural element' as she awakens to needs unsubdued. It is heady to be told by Mr Rochester that she is 'not naturally austere'. A trained restraint has muffled her voice and restricted her limbs – these he will free. Yet this liberator is also the keeper of his wife. The Thornfield scenes rework the Richardsonian story of the rakish Mr B— and his high-principled servant, which Jane had heard as a child when Bessie read aloud from the pages of *Pamela* (1740). But more influential than this specific parallel is the closed-in world of Richardson's heroines: women as captives or in frantic flight, their fear of sexual injury, and their tense debates of response versus self-preservation. At Thornfield, raging fires signal passion in its erotic and destructive aspects. The fire around Rochester's bed warns of his licentious past; this is matched by Jane to the rescue. In so far as this act foretells their future, it is something of a practical answer to futile emotional abandon in *Wuthering Heights* where the dying Catherine pulls feathers from her pillow. Immured in domesticity and pregnancy, shut by her own rebellion in her room, she flings open the window as though she might fly in spirit towards the moors. The wildness of Catherine's nature has its point of reference in Peniston Crag, the refuge of her childhood. Her need to escape the stuffy marriage to a kind but closed-off gentleman is propelled by her need to recover the nature her soulmate, Heathcliff, shares. For he, in a more distilled form than Catherine, is Nature itself: exhilarating and often anarchic. In *Wuthering Heights*, passion and society are incompatible; in *Jane Eyre*, Charlotte Brontë challenged this view, but for a long time Rochester remains a lawless character.

Thornfield exposes Jane to a thorny path – when she tries to suppress her longing for a response to her love, and later when she must face up to the perversion of passion in Rochester's past, represented by the biting animal secreted on the top floor or escaping, with malevolent intent, along the passages of the night. The most painful thorn is the alteration of a pure feeling for Mr Rochester, when she discovers his deception: 'Mr Rochester was not to me what he had been; for he was not what I had thought him.' The greatest pain is loss of trust: the loss of that direct, even abrasive truth that had provoked Jane's love.

As Thornfield presented a subtler temptation than Gateshead to live by feeling alone, so Moor House, the home of Rivers, provides the final temptation to renounce the flesh – a subtler version of the spirit of Lowood than Mr Brocklehurst. 'There are no *good* men of the Brocklehurst species', Mary wrote from New Zealand when she received the book. But Charlotte did make a small distinction: Mr Brocklehurst is a 'black pillar'; Rivers a 'white pillar'. As missionary, Rivers does offer Jane work, a fulfilment of part of her nature – but at the cost of that vital part she had discovered at Thornfield.

In the end, the two lovers, tried by their ordeals, are reunited in their retreat at Ferndean, a place based on the ruins of Wycoller Hall, in a remotely beautiful spot, with a pebbled stream and large trees, across the moors above Haworth. This reunion could have been a bath of sentiment, but both speak with a blunt, almost brusque directness that marks their assurance: they have found a perfect mean between passion and restraint.

The last of the publishers to turn down the one-volume *Professor* was Smith, Elder, and Co. who wrote an encouraging letter intimating that a work in three volumes would meet with careful attention. Three weeks later, on 24 August 1847, Charlotte sent them the manuscript of *Jane Eyre*. The head of the firm, George Smith, read it throughout the following Sunday, cancelling a riding engagement, bolting his dinner, and refusing to go to bed until he had finished the book. On Monday he offered Currer Bell £100 (later adding extras amounting to £500). Six weeks later, on 16 October 1847, he published it.

An explosion of praise followed. Ugly men gave themselves 'Rochester airs'. Most pleasing to Charlotte was the remark of a writer, Miss Kavanagh, that the book had been '*suggestive*' to her. This went with a report of Miss Kavanagh's character as one 'rarely found except where there has been toil to undergo, and adversity to struggle against: it will grow to perfection . . . in the shade.' Reflected in Charlotte's words, she sounds like Jane. Of all contemporary writers, Charlotte most admired William Makepeace Thackeray, the author of *Vanity Fair*, who wrote at once to William Smith Williams, her first supporter at Smith, Elder: 'I wish you had not sent me *Jane Eyre*. It interested me so much that I have lost (or won if you like) a whole day in reading it at the busiest period with the printers I know wailing for copy.'

Another established writer, John Gibson Lockhart (the biographer of his father-in-law, Sir Walter Scott), wrote on 29 December 1847: 'I have finished the adventures of Miss Jane Eyre, and think her far the cleverest that has been written since Austen and Edgeworth were in their prime. Worth fifty Trollopes and Martineaus rolled into one counterpane, with fifty Dickenses and Bulwers to keep them company; but rather a brazen Miss.'

This 'brazen Miss' explains why the novel was regarded, for three more decades, as 'dangerous' in the words of Anne Mozley, writing in the *Christian Remembrancer* in April 1853. She complained of 'outrages on decorum' and saw 'no . . . true insight into the really feminine nature. Such [as Currer Bell] cannot appreciate the hold which a daily round of simple duties and pure pleasures has on those who are content to practise and enjoy them.' Lady Herschel, visiting Mrs Smith, mother of the publisher, was shocked to see the novel in the drawing-room. Were not the Smith daughters to be guarded from its dangers? And, strangely, even Mrs Gaskell's daughter had to ask her mother's permission to read it. 'I am afraid I never told you that I did not mind your reading *Jane Eyre*', Charlotte's future biographer told Marianne, aged twenty, in 1854. Mrs Oliphant, the foremost opponent of emancipation, said that 'this furious love-making was but a wild declaration of the "Rights of Woman" in a new aspect.' She warned of 'grossness' and 'refined indelicacy'. It was often women who feared the novel, and used it as a text on which to hang warnings about a rebellious temper.

Such women particularly resented insights about desire. It is now emerging that active desire in women was taboo for reasons that were more covert and disturbing than truisms about Victorian prudery. Rochester's double standard was, of course, a norm in nineteenth-century England, and the concomitant fear was, of course, the spread of venereal disease. What is less known is that an influential body of medical and quack opinion, from the seventeenth to the early twentieth century, warned men that 'a woman was more likely to transmit such an infection the nearer she approached to orgasm herself.' This belief shaped the secret attitudes of several ages which saw women's arousal in terms of disease. This taboo may have hovered behind the double standard of reviewers of *Jane Eyre* who were anxious to determine the sex of the author: the *North British Review* which argued that 'if "Jane Eyre" be the production of a woman, she must be a woman unsexed' and *The Economist* which praised the book if written by a man, and pronounced it 'odious' if by a woman. These were the reviews most distressing to the author: 'To such critics I would say, "To you I am neither man nor woman – I come before you as an author only. It is the sole standard by which you have a right to judge me – the sole ground on which I accept your judgement."'

In the mid-twentieth century it was common to read *Jane Eyre* as an expression of gender antagonisms, and to point to Rochester's blindness as 'emasculation'. Such readers were descendants of those first reviewers who misinterpreted Jane's longing for experience as a feminist threat. Mary Taylor wrote to Charlotte: 'You are very different from me in having no doctrine to preach.' She was surprised, she owned, to find *Jane Eyre* 'so perfect as a work of art'. This separation of doctrine and art is too rigid. Charlotte, it is true, was not a polemical feminist. At the same time, she did not abrogate ideology: she was broadening it from the arena of public rights to the more difficult, hidden, and even taboo arena of private feeling – those spaces in the mind where, as Mill perceived, women were more insidiously and deeply enslaved than through more obvious restrictions to do with work, property, and the vote. This form of emancipation is yet to come; Jane portends a future we might realise. She may not be a preacher, but is something of a prophet.

The novel is prophetic in Jane's search for independence, and above all in its claim of her right to feelings of her own. She finds, in the end, the domestic union society approves, but in the process she has refused to violate her nature. *Jane Eyre* was a triumphant assertion of the inviolability of the individual soul.

TO WALK INVISIBLE

'It is a woman's writing, but whose?' A week after *Jane Eyre* was published on 16 October 1847, Thackeray was wondering about the identity of Currer Bell. So was everyone else who read the novel.

By the start of 1848, *Jane Eyre* reached Yorkshire. Charlotte, secure in her cover, overheard the comment of a local clergyman.

'Why,' he exclaimed, 'they have got Cowan Bridge school, and Mr Carus Wilson here, I declare! and Miss Ann Evans* [Miss Temple in *Jane Eyre*].' The portraits were just, he went on, and Carus Wilson 'deserved the chastisement he got.'

Charlotte recounted this to William Smith Williams, her correspondent at Smith, Elder. 'He did not recognise Currer Bell', she gloated, '– what author would be without the advantage of being able to walk invisible?'

With *Jane Eyre* now circulating close to home, Emily and Anne urged Charlotte to disclose her identity to Papa. Three months after publication, she ventured to disturb him in his study.

'Papa, I've been writing a book.'

'Have you, my dear?' And went on reading.

---

* Miss Evans, like Miss Temple, left the school to be married. She became the wife of the Revd James Connor of Oswestry on 6 July 1826. He gave evidence in favour of The Clergy Daughters' School during a controversy, later, in 1857.

'But, Papa, I want you to look at it.'

'I can't be troubled to read manuscript.'

'But it is printed.'

'I hope you have not been involving yourself in any such silly expense.'

'I think I shall gain money by it. May I read you some reviews?'

She read them; then asked, again, if he would read the book. He said she might leave it in his study, and he would see.

That day he sent his daughters an unusual invitation to tea, and towards the end of the meal said: 'Children, Charlotte has been writing a book — and I think it is a better one than I expected.'

Why did he expect so little? Had he no awareness of his daughters' gifts? They never dared tell him of unpraised novels by Emily and Anne, published two months after Charlotte's. He may have known nothing of their publications until the autumn of 1850 when William Smith Williams proposed a new edition of *Wuthering Heights* and *Agnes Grey*, to be edited by Charlotte, an occasion for her to break the news to their father that there had been other writers in the family. This indifference to daughters' minds suggests the domestic background to the Revd Mr Helstone, a formidable slighter of women in Charlotte's next novel, *Shirley*, which raises the Woman Question.

To her publishers she remained unseen. It had been a dream to enter the metropolis, but this she deferred. She declined to attend a dramatisation of *Jane Eyre* in February 1848: it was 'not in my power', she said. As her fame swelled and *Jane Eyre* went into second and third editions, her excuse was the work to be done before she might allow herself a 'treat' on so grand a scale as a visit to London.

She knew that to go into society would unsettle the central action of her life, which was to stay at home and write. This was a practical line, not a gesture of Romantic solitude. Avid, as Charlotte owned herself to be, for the stir of public event in the world beyond the moors, she sustained her seclusion, partly

because she wished to begin a new novel, and partly because visibility itself was a challenge she could not face at once. In the
meantime, she secured her connection with her publishers
through frequent correspondence. Every letter established her
character, taste, and values: her critical view of the 1848 revolts in
France; her admiration for qualities of endurance and exertion;
her backing of *Vanity Fair* (then reaching its last number),
Ruskin's *Modern Painters*, and the letters of the essayist, Charles
Lamb (1775–1834). In view of her dismay at the increasing disturbance of Branwell, she was intrigued by Lamb's choosing to live
with his intermittently mad sister. She did not hesitate to dismiss
the ephemera of mere 'book-makers' like George Henry Lewes.
In this way, before revealing her uneven mouth and slight form
to inevitable scrutiny, she might be known, first, on her own
terms. For a time, then, she would continue the disembodied
Currer Bell who used 'his' voice with confident ease and said, 'It
would take a great deal to crush me'.

At length, early in July 1848, Charlotte, together with Anne,
ventured to London. They stayed at the Chapter Coffee House
in Paternoster Row, panelled and low-ceilinged, in the eighteenth century a meeting-place for Dr Johnson, Chatterton,
and Goldsmith, then a base for university men and clergymen
passing through London. Mr Brontë had stayed there thirty
years before, but it was not thought to be a place for ladies.
There, in February 1842, Charlotte (accompanied by Papa, Emily,
Mary, and Joe Taylor) had awaited the packet for Belgium.
Upstairs, in a dingy bedroom along the warren of passages, she
had heard the great bell of St Paul's strike midnight 'with colossal phlegm and force. From the small, narrow window of that
room, I first saw *the* Dome, looming through a London Mist.'
During the three days they had climbed to the dome and seen
the spread of London with its river, bridges, and churches, and
Charlotte had inspected as many paintings as she could before
they sailed from the wharf at London Bridge. Back in London,
six and a half years later, on a summer morning in 1848,

Charlotte and Anne made their famous, unannounced advance on Smith, Elder, and Co.

The immediate concern was to clear up the truth about their separate identities. In June 1848 Anne published *The Tenant of Wildfell Hall*, a novel in which she had refused to be dissuaded by Charlotte from drawing a revealing portrait of alcoholism and loss of feeling in her brother. As Charlotte put it: 'She had been called on to contemplate, near at hand, and for a long time, the terrible effects of talents misused and faculties abused . . . What she saw sank deeply into her mind . . . She believed it a duty to reproduce every detail . . . She must be honest; she must not varnish, soften, or conceal.' The novel imagines the effect of such a man on a wife whose hidden ordeal is exacerbated by laws which give her no rights whatever, even rights to her child. When we meet Helen Huntingdon she has fled her husband and is living, quietly resolute, under an assumed identity at Wildfell Hall: the horrors of her life as a wife are told in a long flashback through the diary she lends Gilbert Markham who befriends her, falls in love, and eventually marries her after her husband dies. The detailed report of what it is like for a woman of moral refinement to live in the same house with a fiendish man, and the questioning of the helpless legal position of married women (a problem not addressed in Parliament until the late 1850s) gave the novel an immediate *succès de scandale*, despite, or perhaps because of, antagonistic reviews. The demand for it was second only to *Jane Eyre*.

When it seemed about to become a bestseller, the unscrupulous Mr Newby, publisher of Ellis and Acton Bell, gave out that Acton was the author of *Jane Eyre*, and tried to sell *The Tenant of Wildfell Hall* as Currer Bell's new novel to the American firm of Harper Brothers. In other words, he was claiming that all three Bells were one person. George Smith, who expected Currer Bell to give his next novel to him, had written to ask whether he was or was not the author of *Wildfell Hall*?

Outraged at Newby's deception, Charlotte and Anne had

walked four miles through a thunderstorm, past the dull-coloured rows of stone cottages thrown up by factories, until they reached the station at Keighley. From there, they had 'whirled' up to London on the night train from Leeds. At about eight in the morning, they arrived at the Chapter Coffee House (they had no idea where else to go), washed, had some breakfast, and set off to expose their identities 'in queer inward excitement'. They were resolved to outface Newby, once and for all, by visible proof. Ellis Bell had declined to leave Haworth, so it was two Bells, not three, who stood, next morning, in their homemade dresses and pale with fatigue, under the skylight in the office at 65 Cornhill.

At the time they arrived, George Murray Smith was absorbed in his Indian correspondence. He was surprised to hear of a visit from two ladies who would not send up their names. How could he connect the vehemence of *Jane Eyre* and the uncrushable judgements of Bell's letters with this anxious little woman of thirty-two, rather quaintly old-fashioned, looking up, through her spectacles, at the tall, urbane young man who came out to the bookseller's shop to investigate?

'Did you wish to see me, Madam?' he asked politely.

'Is it Mr Smith?'

'It is.'

Silently, she handed him his letter to Currer Bell. He looked at it – then at her – then at the letter again – then again at her.

'Where did you get this?' he asked sharply.

'From the post office. It was addressed to me.' She laughed suddenly at his puzzlement. Here was her moment. 'We are three sisters,' she blurted, forgetting as she took that leap into visibility that Ellis Bell had refused any part in this act of exposure.*

Hurriedly, Mr Smith brought in William Smith Williams, a

---

* George Smith's memory of this first exchange differs from CB's. I draw on both, but give preference to CB's because her version was written immediately after the event, while Smith's was published over fifty years later in December 1900.

mild, stooping man of forty-seven who shook the Brontës' hands for a long, silent time. He understood better than his employer their wish for secrecy. Mr Smith, excitedly, made swift plans: 'You must allow me to introduce you to my mother and sisters – How long do you stay in London? You must make the most of the time – to-night you must go to the Italian opera – you must see the Exhibition [at the Royal Academy] – Mr Thackeray would be pleased to see you – If Mr Lewes knew "Currer Bell" was in town – he would have to be shut up – I will ask them both to dinner at my house –'.

Charlotte stopped him, saying gravely that she and her sister were determined to preserve their 'incognito': 'We have only confessed ourselves to my publisher. To all the rest of the world we must remain "gentlemen" as heretofore.'

Mr Smith did not at first take to this quiet plan. He suggested they meet a literary party incognito, and would introduce them as 'country cousins'.

As Charlotte told Mary afterwards, a desire to see some of the personages he mentioned 'kindled in me very strongly – but when I found in further examination that he could not venture to ask such men as Thackeray etc. at a short notice, without giving them a hint as to whom they were to meet, I declined even this – I felt it would have ended in our being made a show of – a thing I have ever resolved to avoid.'

The quick fame of Currer Bell; the speculation about the author's identity; the secrecy; the deferral of the visit to London; the modest countrywomen who appeared from nowhere, asking for the head of the firm without explaining their business: these were the ingredients of drama. Yet a private drama coexisted with their public emergence. Privately, Charlotte and Anne did not reveal themselves at all.

They showed only their public image, the long-practised image of the governess: Charlotte, shrinking and watchful; Anne, calm and silent. In this sense, they remained as obscure as ever. The report of this scene, which has entertained readers for a century and a half, is only what George Smith saw, reinforced by Charlotte's comic version of what he saw (in a letter to Mary).

George Smith had a cream-brown complexion with dark, close-trimmed side-whiskers and candid dark eyes, glancing from face to face a bit quickly but with a pleasant mirthfulness. He was energetic and talkative — the only one to talk as the Brontës sat before him. What he called 'impish humour' as a boy had led him to join The Row Society at Blackheath School: its aim was to stir up as many rows as possible. He had been expelled from school and soon joined his father's publishing firm. There remained a niggle beneath his confidence in his powers as a businessman. A private belief that he 'might have made a scholar' was to be fortified throughout his life by keen friendships with writers. In a two-volume 'Recollections of a Long and Busy Life', he looked back on such friendships as 'the happiest and most characteristic feature of my business life'. He owned to 'constitutional shyness' with men of the world like Thackeray, but was far from shy with women authors who, unsure of their public position, allowed him scope for his buoyant encouragement.

George Smith's father had been a Scotsman of the purest integrity — too unworldly, his son implied, for success in business. After a stint with John Murray, the elder George Smith began a bookselling and stationery business in 1816. His partner, Mr Elder, who began publishing in 1819, was erratic in his efforts and had poor judgement: if a book made a success he would publish almost everything on offer which, of course, produced a harvest of disasters; then, for a while, nothing was published. Young George was keen to take over publishing, and before he was twenty persuaded his father to give him £1,500 to see what he could do. Soon after, his father became ill in 1844 (he died in 1846), and at the same time Mr Elder retired, so that, at the age of only twenty, George Smith found himself in charge, with a mother and younger brothers and sisters dependent on him. He set to work with zeal, supported by mutton chops and green tea at stated intervals, but sustained most of all by his devoted mother who spoilt him just enough to make him happy and confident. As a youth he had been painfully thin, and was still not vigorous – he often fainted – but, determined to be strong, he put himself through a course of riding which, he claimed, had the desired effect. It was typical of his optimism and drive that he saw a problem in terms of a solution which he instantly put into practice and expected to work, and any mistaken judgement he put behind him matter-of-factly, without much reflection or self-criticism. There was therefore almost no waste of directed energies, but he never appeared driven – he had time for dinners and balls, and enjoyed the humour of the Museum Club where he got over his shyness and exercised his flair for anecdotes. Cheerful, genial, courteous, he was not rash – a man to beat down adversity with smiles.

The firm he inherited had published a fashionable annual called 'Friendship's Offering', Sir Andrew Smith's *Illustrations of the Zoology of South Africa*, Leigh Hunt, and Darwin's *Journal of Researches into the Geology and Natural History of the various countries visited by H.M.S. Beagle* (1839). One of George Smith's first successes was to acquire Ruskin's *Modern Painters* (volume one published in 1843 and volume two in 1846); another was Sir John Herschel's *Astronomical Observations made at the Cape of Good Hope* (1846). At this stage, the firm had banking and export interests in Calcutta which had been the main arena of another partner, Patrick Stewart, who had embezzled more than £30,000 over the years. It took George Smith seven or eight years of hard struggle to save the firm, but as Charlotte later pictured him in *Villette* (he had no difficulty recognising himself), he was something of a champion – an attractive champion with a full cleft chin which she thought the acme of male beauty.

He was only twenty-four when he encountered Charlotte Brontë and, already, showed the judgement and practical sense that were to make him the leading publisher of the Victorian age: Thackeray, Hawthorne, Mrs Gaskell, Matthew Arnold,

Ruskin, George Eliot, and Browning were amongst his authors. He also established the foremost literary magazine, *The Cornhill*, in 1860, edited initially by Thackeray, later by Leslie Stephen, publishing Hardy and Henry James. Eventually, in 1882, he founded the *Dictionary of National Biography*, with Leslie Stephen as its first editor.

His early judgement showed in his unhesitating acceptance of *Jane Eyre* from an unknown author, and in his appointment of a fine reader, William Smith Williams, who alone spotted promise in the manuscript of *The Professor*. Williams had done his apprenticeship with Coleridge's and Keats' publishers, Taylor and Hessey (in fact, it had been Mr Williams who had seen Keats off when he departed from England in 1820). In middle age Williams, supporting a large – and, in Charlotte's view, rather lowering – family, had declined into inefficiency as book-keeper with Hullmandel and Walter, the firm of lithographers who had printed the illustrations for Darwin's *Beagle*. Mr Williams' accounts were in total confusion, but Smith saw a man of sound taste (he reviewed, especially plays, for *The Spectator*, *The Athenaeum*, and other weeklies), wasted in inappropriate work. Smith had the discernment to make him literary adviser in the publishing department. He held this post for thirty years.

Smith's strength, in his own view, was his judgement of men as well as a flair for quick decision. He also had a gift for eager listening and ready laughter.

For all this, the publisher was a Victorian when it came to women: his taste did run to sweetness in a plumed bonnet. His first impression of Charlotte was her woeful lack of feminine charm; he could not imagine that she did not crave this above all things. Her head looked too large for her body; she had fine eyes but her face was marred by her mouth and complexion. He noticed that she had 'a pretty little foot' and 'too small a waist', by which he meant that she was laced too tightly, or so he thought. To George Smith, she appeared pathetic. This is what was visible at Cornhill, at the Smith family dinner six miles away at 4 Westbourne Place in Bayswater, and at a fashionable performance of *The Barber of Seville*: the odd little creature in a high-necked country dress – 'clownish', Charlotte reported to Mary – walking up the crimson-carpeted stair of the Opera House beside Eliza and Sarah Smith and their 'distinguished, handsome' elder brother in evening dress and white gloves, while town women in splendid, low-cut gowns ('such as we had not in the world', said Charlotte) glanced at the Brontës with graceful superciliousness at the box door. It was a scene worthy of Elizabeth Hastings, who remains triumphantly unknown in the glare of society.

'I smiled inwardly', Charlotte confided to Mary, 'I felt pleasurably excited'. She was secretly entertained again next day when Mr Smith brought his fine portly mother to fetch them to dine. Neither Mrs Smith nor her daughters knew who they were and, as Charlotte phrased it, 'their strange perplexity would have been ludicrous if one had dared to laugh – To be brought down to a part of the city into whose obscure streets they said they never penetrated before – to an old, dark strange-looking Inn – to take up in their fine carriage a couple of odd-looking country-women – to see their elegant, handsome son and brother treating with scrupulous politeness these insignificant spinsters must have puzzled them thoroughly'.

As further cover, she insisted on yet another pseudonym: George Smith was required to introduce her and Anne as 'the Misses Brown'. In impenetrable nonentity and voiceless modesty lay their protection. This image did prove entirely convincing, both to their time and to the soggy proprieties of subsequent legend. In short, the visible woman and invisible author became, from this point, separate. The passion and vehemence that were part of the author, but inadmissible in women, were given the lie.

Locked in their incognito, awed by the elegance of the Smith residence and the Sunday dinner, the two sisters felt constrained and awkward. Neither could eat, and both were glad when it was over. Dining out in London would be a hideous bore, Charlotte concluded.

In this way, she deepened her disguise with an anti-metropolitan bias which went back to the 1830s. This common bias was shaped by scripture. London was 'Babylon' or 'Nineveh', a place of shallow glitter, contamination, and inauthenticity, to which she would concede nothing, but nothing, of her authentic self. Caroline Vernon, in her novella, has a 'wholesome contempt' for society and passes through it with the secret superiority of those brought up in retirement, who often 'retain a notion . . . that it would be a letting down . . . to give the slightest glimpse of their real nature & genuine feelings to the chance associates of a ballroom.' For many years, Charlotte's only knowledge of society had been as a governess at the mercy of provincial snobbery. Some of her most miserable moments had been in drawing-rooms full of strange faces: 'At such times, my animal spirits would ebb gradually till they sank quite away, and when I could endure the sense of . . . solitude no longer, I used to steal off, too glad to find any corner where I could really be alone.' In those corners, she had concluded that society turned Nature 'upside down'. To such people, a lie was truth; truth a lie. All coteries, whether scientific, political, or religious, must have a tendency 'to change truth into affectation. When people live in a clique they must, I suppose, in some measure, write, talk, think, and live for that clique; a harassing and narrowing necessity.' As she saw it, the power of her voice depended on her distance from fashion, and she went to London wary of its encroachments.

'Ellis . . . would soon turn aside from the spectacle in disgust', Charlotte said. 'I do not think he admits it as his creed that "the proper study of mankind is man" – at least not the artificial man of cities.' As Charlotte turned towards the metropolis, it appeared to her that she and her sister travelled 'different roads'. Though she shared Emily's 'disgust' and honoured the self-sufficiency of genius, though Charlotte too would concede nothing of herself to the metropolis, still – she wanted something from it:

art, theatre, public issues. To encounter sophisticates was a trial to be born for the sake of material. She wanted to look in the face of her Reader with whom she lived in intense intimacy, and see for herself the events of her day. She envied city writers, Dickens and Thackeray, their easy access to the Condition of England. As she left the interior and absolute issues of *Jane Eyre* behind, she saw progress in terms of engagement with the great public issues of the century: industrial unrest and the Woman Question. Emily's continued refusal of the public arena struck Charlotte as 'more daring than practical'. To keep Emily abreast with the talk and taste of the age, she brought back a copy of Tennyson's latest volume, *The Princess* (1847). Emily's response remains unknown, but Charlotte may have reflected her opposition when she told Mrs Gaskell, later, that she did not care for Tennyson.

Charlotte's notion of fame, according to Mary, was 'a passport to the society of clever people'. Clever men now wrote to Currer Bell. She was determined to learn from them, above all from her hero, Thackeray (1811–63), who had begun to make his name as a writer in the course of the 1840s. In the 1830s he had been a struggling journalist and art student in London and Paris. In the early 1840s he wrote under the pseudonyms of Michael Angelo Titmarsh and George Savage FitzBoodle – FitzBoodle was 'editor' of *The Luck of Barry Lyndon* (1844). In 1847 his first major novel, *Vanity Fair*, began to appear in monthly numbers, illustrated by the author. *Pendennis* followed in 1848–50, as well as a series of Christmas books. Thackeray responded warmly to *Jane Eyre*: 'the love passages made me cry', to the astonishment of his servant, John, who came in with the coals. Thackeray declared it the first English novel he had been able to read for many a day. When Charlotte ventured to dedicate the second edition to him, Thackeray wrote to say that this was the greatest compliment of his life. At first, he had the politeness not to mention the embarrassment it caused; afterwards he explained his situation: his wife, Isabella, had become mentally ill in 1840, following childbirth, and had been put away. The dedication provoked rumours that Currer Bell's novel had been written by the governess to Thackeray's two daughters – in fact, Thackeray was deep in a different problem: from 1841 he was increasingly in love with Jane Brookfield, the wife of an old Cambridge friend. But all that mattered to Charlotte was her wish to learn from Thackeray as from another *maître*: her continued urge to go on developing.

Reading the conclusion of *Vanity Fair*, she envied its 'quiet'. This reflected a renewed wish to curb her vehemence. In *Vanity Fair*, she marked the flow of the story to an end that remained 'as quiet as reflection, as quiet as memory . . .' Thackeray's genius was his 'servant' – it worked no fantastic changes at its own wild will. Charlotte wrote this after the reviewer, Lewes, criticised her 'melodrama'. Attentive to his advice, she was turning to social realism for her next novel. It was to be about industrial unrest in the north of England. Her first start, 'John Henry', was an attempt to recast the opening scenes of *The Professor* in the more detached mode of *Vanity Fair*. It opens with extensive sparring between newlyweds, a bully of a manufacturer and his vain wife. Neither, we are told by a satiric voice, is going to evoke the slightest sympathy. They are starting their life with well-matched appetites for wealth and power. This is silently challenged by the arrival of a superior poor brother like Crimsworth, the John Henry of the title.

Charlotte put 'John Henry' aside at the start of the third chapter. The attempt to fuse *The Professor* with Thackeray was one of those abortive starts which, she said later, happened with every book. The sparring of the Helstones (as the couple was called) is plausible enough, but too predictable. What endured from 'John Henry' was the turn to documentary truth: 'Something real, cool, and solid, lies before you; something unromantic as Monday morning'. If she controlled her imagination, as Lewes advised, she would put behind her, finally and for good, the fits and furores of Branwell, her double.

From 1846 communication between her and Branwell had virtually ended. When she spoke to him, he would often appear not to hear and make no reply. She found it scarcely possible to remain in the same room. As Branwell's health declined, Charlotte continued to show little pity, in contrast with Emily. Where Charlotte saw 'a life perverted', Emily (in Charlotte's view) saw 'The Wanderer from the Fold'. Charlotte's similarities to Branwell – with their slight forms and wide, superb foreheads, their protracted imaginative bond, and susceptibility to forbidden passion – made her more anxious to detach herself. Before her, day by day, was an example of 'the inadequacy of even genius to lead to true greatness if unaided by religion and principle.'

Eighteen-forty-eight, the year of revolts in Europe, was also the year Charlotte Brontë became more radical. 'I often wish to say something about the "condition of women" question,' she told William Smith Williams, 'but it is one respecting which so much cant has been talked, that one feels a sort of repugnance to approach it.'

Mary, the only other person to whom Currer Bell was not invisible, urged her, as always, in the radical direction: 'Has the world gone so well with you that you have no protest to make against its absurdities? . . . I will scold you well when I see you.'

At the same time, Charlotte was feeling the impact of critical opinion on her 'very slender' stock of materials. George Henry Lewes had said: 'Almost all that we require in a novelist she has: perception of character, and power of delineating it; picturesqueness; passion; and knowledge of life.' He seemed to understand her gift for creating romance out of real experience. But his subsequent letters to Currer Bell were more challenging. Though the greatest English novelists of her time, Thackeray, Dickens, and later George Eliot, all recognised her gift, she had to contend with the voice of the critical establishment, as it seemed to her, in this series of letters. Back and forth, Lewes and Charlotte Brontë debated the ideal novel at a time when serious criticism of novels had only recently begun in quarterlies and monthlies, with Lewes as the most prominent reviewer, first in *Fraser's Magazine* and later in the *Westminster Review* and the weekly *Leader*. Where Lewes had the advantage of visibility – a public assurance impossible for any 'lady' – Charlotte Brontë had the advantage of the proven practitioner.

In 1848 we see an earlier, slightly different Lewes from the supportive 'husband' of George Eliot, who wrote a durable *Life of Goethe* (1855) and took an informed interest in physiology and psychology: in these earlier days he exercised amazingly varied talents as comic dramatist, actor, and essayist, as well as writing a popular history of philosophy and a novel in imitation of Goethe called *Ranthorpe* (1847). He and his wife, Agnes Jervis, were followers of Shelley's ideas on free love (a year later Lewes would condone Agnes' decision to take his best friend, Thornton Hunt, as lover). Lewes also went in for the rather personal, bludgeoning repartee favoured by early Victorians who were members of the Museum Club where men entertained one another with anecdotes of public personalities. Here, Lewes showed off his dramatic gifts, mimicking dialect and gesture with an accuracy that made him highly popular. He could be condescending to women (declaring that the best women to distinguish themselves as writers were 'second only to the first-rate men of their day') and, having guessed Currer Bell was a woman, decided to put himself in the position of adviser-in-chief. He urged her to put vehemence aside in favour of dispassionate studies of manners on the model of Jane Austen.

When the imagination 'speaks rapidly and urgently in our ear,' Charlotte asked, 'are we not to write to her dictation?' Pointing (inaccurately) to Jane Austen's 'mild eyes', Lewes counselled Currer Bell 'to finish more and be more subdued'.

At first, she was uneasily attentive. This was not far from Southey's advice, more than ten years before, to calm herself – the only aspect of Southey's letters she had taken to heart. To what extent did this advice lead her to begin a novel as cool as Monday morning? When she read *Pride and Prejudice*, she thought it wanted 'fresh air', nature, poetry. When she read *Emma*, she concluded that 'the Passions are perfectly unknown' to Miss Austen – 'what throbs fast and fully, though hidden, what the blood rushed through, what is the unseen seat of Life'. She did acknowledge 'Miss Austen's clear common sense and subtle shrewdness. If you find no inspiration in Miss Austen's page, neither do you find there windy wordiness'. But she preferred George Sand, especially *Consuelo* (1842), for her 'grasp of mind'. She also admired Sand's *Lettres d'un voyageur*, 'full of the writer's *self*'. She identified with a mind which can register tragedy and can transmute suffering into an art that gains from blows, so that 'the longer she lives – the better she will grow.' Charlotte's portrait of George Sand is virtually a self-portrait. Her insistence on '*self*' and resistance to Jane Austen must be seen in context. Lewes had used a model of restraint to challenge the passionate voice of Charlotte Brontë, in effect her distinctive gift. It was a case of the didactic reader who can see only one route to excellence. Jane Austen was heir to Augustan decorums; Charlotte Brontë was heir to Romantic and Gothic traditions. By posing Jane Austen in opposition, as it were, Lewes was harping on stale categories of criticism, not seeing a common convergence on what is hidden in lives. Charlotte did not see Jane Austen's more shaded works, *Sense and Sensibility*, *Mansfield Park*, and *Persuasion*, but had she encountered the stifled scream of Marianne when her passion is denied, had she read into the silence of Fanny Price, or into the unspoken recess of feeling in Anne Elliot, had she heard Anne Elliot speak of 'senseless joy' in *Persuasion*, and witnessed her sacrifice to politeness in a suffering spirit, she might have acknowledged common ground. It remained for Virginia Woolf to bring them together in 1909 when she noted that nineteenth-century novelists 'disclosed the secret that the precious stuff of which books are made lies all about one, in drawing-rooms and kitchens where women live'.

In his next letter, Lewes warned of 'sentiment', eloquence, and 'the enthusiasm of poetry'. There is no knowing how far

the attempt at solidity and coolness in *Shirley* was affected by
these strictures as they met Charlotte's hidden fear of
Branwellian extravagance. The increasing heat of Charlotte's
replies to Lewes, both written and silent, suggest how strongly he
struck at her art; how difficult it was, in practice, to resist his con-
victions. Her reply held her ground: she flung back poetry as
'the divine gift'. She flung back sentiment as she understood the
word: 'sentiment' is 'deep feeling' for one's kind. She *will* have it.
At the same time, she ventured to judge Lewes (believing herself
safe from detection as a woman). His *Ranthorpe*, she told him, as
man to man, was not a total success. Currer Bell would await his
next novel to see how well he, himself, fulfilled his theories.

There were withering retorts to Lewes in the following
months as she struggled with his strictures. 'You have a sound,
clear judgement as far as it goes,' she told him silently, 'but I
conceive it to be limited . . . To a certain point, Mr Lewes, you can
go, but no farther. Be as sceptical as you please on whatever lies
beyond a certain intellectual limit; the mystery will never be
cleared up to you, for that limit you will never overpass.'

What occasioned this was Smith, Elder's publication of Lewes'
Rose, Blanche, and Violet in April 1848, a novel based on the three
lovely daughters of Swynfen Jervis, the loveliest of whom he
had married. It was nothing more than a trashy melodrama.
Charlotte scorned the citations from Greek, Latin, French, and
German authors, displays of learning to awe a common reader.
'Not all your learning, not all your reading, not all your sagacity,
not all your perseverance can help you over one viewless line –
over one boundary as impassable as it is invisible', she went on.
She dared not loose this torrent, but (she confided to Williams)
it was what she *thought* both of Lewes 'and many others who have
a great name in the world.'

Her agitation was understandable if she sensed that Lewes was
only posing as her friend. Charlotte did perceive clearly that her
art was at stake, for Lewes willed an end to daring. She was aware,
too, of the danger of denying him the right to be her master: 'I

submit to your anger, which I have now excited . . .' Sure enough, Lewes savaged her in his next review, saying now that the 'overmasculine' vigour of *Jane Eyre* 'often amounts to coarseness, – and is certainly the very antipode to "ladylike".' Women, he argued, might write fine novels, but they were only half-educated, and in any case, breeding was their prime purpose. Lewes has been excused on the grounds that, when he wrote this, his wife was having the first of four children by his friend, but why take it out on Currer Bell? She did not foresee such 'brutal' publicity.

When Charlotte Brontë wrote her first two novels far from the impact of public opinion, she knew that no life was too marginal for the material of art. But she did shift ground as she began *Shirley*, early in 1848: she spoke enviously of men's access to public event. As she read of the 1848 revolts, she was trying to align herself with the foremost writers of the day who concerned themselves with the condition of England. She decided on a historical novel set in 1811–12. This was the time when Luddites, supposedly under the leadership of 'General Ludd', a Nottinghamshire weaver, tried to resist the mechanisation of the weaving process by smashing machinery. The unrest spread to the woollen mills of the West Riding of Yorkshire, the area of Gomersal and Birstall which Charlotte knew personally from visits to the Nusseys and Taylors, especially Hunsworth Mill, Cleckheaton, where the Taylors manufactured their army cloth and where Mary had lived temporarily with her brothers, John and Joe (in a cottage at the back of the mill). This is where Charlotte bade goodbye to Mary in February 1845. Since childhood, she had known of the area's history from her father's reminiscences of his years at St Peter's Church, Hartshead, which lay in the centre of industrial action. The workers' riots were a by-product of the Napoleonic Wars and the Continental trade embargo which hit the Yorkshire woollen trade at the very time that new machinery was introduced to the mills, causing unemployment. For two years Yorkshire seemed on the edge of

revolution, as *Shirley* explains: 'Misery generates hate: these suf-
ferers hated the machines which they believed took their bread
from them; they hated the buildings which contained those
machines; they hated the manufacturers who owned those
buildings.' The countryside was rife with rumours of men on
the march to destroy the machines, and every man (including
Mr Brontë) had his gun to hand.

The original title of Charlotte Brontë's novel was 'Hollow's
Mill', but the workers' attack on the mill (based on the Luddites'
attack on Rawfolds' Mill near Hartshead, as reported in the *Leeds
Mercury* for 18 April 1812) is seen from the perspective of two
women hiding themselves at a distance from the action, and this
comes to be the perspective of the novel as a whole.

'Details – situations which I do not understand, and cannot
personally inspect, I would not for the world meddle with, lest I
should make even a more ridiculous mess of the matter than
Mrs Trollope did in her "Factory Boy" – besides – no one feeling
on any subject – public or private, will I ever affect that I do not
really experience . . .' So wrote Charlotte at the outset. She put
the visible wrongs of the labouring class in relation to the invisible wrongs of women. 'This world's laws never came near us –
never!' exclaims the abused wife, Mrs Pryor, in the privacy of
her daughter's bedroom. 'They were powerless as a rotten bul-
rush to protect me! – impotent as idiot babblings' to restrain
her vicious husband.

Shirley is a revolutionary novel. It questions men's power over
women and workers. A mill owner, Robert Moore, is a relentless
man, but no Bounderby*: he is out of touch with his workers,
not wilfully, but in part because he is half-foreign and in part
because he himself struggles for survival against the laws of the

---

* Mr Bounderby (in Dickens's *Hard Times*) is the self-inflated, oblivious mill-owner
who declares, when his workers complain of exploitation, that they want to eat off
golden spoons.

land, specifically the controversial Orders in Council which put war before the needs of trade and populace. The author treats Robert Moore with cool justice: he is unpleasantly hard, but is not inhuman or irredeemable. All the same, Robert remains a wooden bore, possibly a result of an author's excessive attention to peers and advisors.

Far more memorable are peripheral clergymen, in particular, the misogynist Rector, Mr Helstone. According to Ellen, he was a blend of Mr Brontë and his admired acquaintance, Mr Roberson of Liversedge, the martial clergyman who, like Helstone, had been fierce against rioters. Where Helstone's brother, James, had abused his wife (who took the cover of 'Mrs Pryor' when she left him), Helstone himself had destroyed his wife in more subtle fashion – it must be said, unintentionally – by oblivious neglect. She had soon faded away. At the time of the novel's events, the Rector is guardian to his brother's daughter, Caroline, whom he treats with similar oblivion. What he has in common with Mr Brontë is that he is a clever, forceful man, charming to women on public occasions, but withdrawn at home. He intends no unkindness, but a low opinion of women guards a nature that is emotionally evasive, a flaw of which he is unaware.

Worse than the Rector are the curates who, as the minor agents of power, caricature its excesses: vanity, condescension, snobbery. Beneath lowered lids, certain women mark it all. They are what Charlotte Brontë calls 'soul-readers'. The point is that official soul-readers are unequal to the task. While clergymen preach their interminable sermons, two women sit outside talking to a worker who alerts them to the fact that a riot is about to erupt.

When Charlotte sent her publishers a draft of her first volume, they disliked the attack on the clergy, and when the novel was published, reviewers concurred and churchmen, like Charles Kingsley, were offended. The curates may appear gratuitous in a novel of industrial unrest, but in so far as *Shirley* is about the abuses of power in its domestic aspect, the curates are telling. Ineffective as agents of God, despised by intelligent women whom they bore, and hated by the poor whom they neglect, the curates display their complacency (when they talk only of themselves), their gracelessness (when they gobble their tea), and cowardice (when they are chased upstairs by the dog, Tartar – based on Emily's intimidating dog, Keeper). Charlotte told her publishers she would not withdraw the curates 'because, as I formerly said of the Lowood part of "Jane Eyre", *it is true*. The curates and their ongoings are merely photographed from the life.' Her satire draws on an unexpected tea-time visit by three curates in June 1845, mentioned in a letter to Ellen: the three had begun 'glorifying themselves and abusing dissenters in such a manner that my temper lost its balance and I pronounced a few sentences sharply and rapidly which struck them all dumb – Papa was greatly horrified also – but I don't regret it.' The younger clergy of this time were mostly Puseyites who embraced the High-Church principles of the Oxford Movement, but they show themselves to be no less unenlightened in their attitudes to women than the old Yorkshire clergy, represented by the sombre Revd Helstone. Local readers at once recognised the vulgar, insensitive Mr Malone as James William Smith, curate to Mr Brontë from 1842–4, then curate at Keighley until 1846; the presuming, begging Mr Donne as Joseph Brett Grant, curate to Mr Brontë from 1844–5, then incumbent of the neighbouring parish of Oxenhope; and affable Mr Sweeting as James Chesterton Bradley, curate at Oakworth (near Haworth) from 1845–7, then curate of All Saints', Paddington. Afterwards, it was their amusement to call one another by their names in *Shirley*. When Mr Nicholls read of their antics, he laughed so loudly, clapping his hands and stamping his feet as he sat alone, that Mrs Brown, the sexton's wife, thought he had gone mad – very gratifying for Charlotte.

Shirley retains the two brothers from 'John Henry', the hard industrialist and the poor scholar. Caroline Helstone is secretly in love with the industrialist, the mill-owner Robert Moore. She combines facets of Anne Brontë and Charlotte herself: Anne's reserve and rectitude, Anne's poor state of health, both sisters' longing for some wider experience, and Charlotte's suppressed passion transmuted into Caroline's silent pining for a man who is too preoccupied with his troubled mill to give her more than passing attention. Caroline, like Charlotte again, questions the fate of peripheral single women who have no outlet for their energies. Fortunately for Caroline, another model presents itself in the shape of a fearless young woman called Shirley, modelled on Emily Brontë. Shirley's closest attachment is to her intelligent governess, now companion, Mrs Pryor, who turns out to be Caroline's mother. Despite Charlotte's disapproval of *The Tenant of Wildfell Hall*, she did draw on its gripping central story of wife-abuse, but with fewer shocking details than Anne had shown. Like Helen Huntingdon, Mrs Pryor is a runaway wife, supporting herself under an assumed name. For a long time Caroline does not know Mrs Pryor's true identity but benefits from her support as she benefits from her friendship with Shirley.

Meanwhile, Louis Moore, the poor scholar who is Robert's brother, arrives on the scene and tutors Shirley in French. She falls in love with him as she reveals the unknown nature of authentic womanhood through her *devoir*, in the way of Charlotte and Monsieur – though Shirley is more reluctant to surrender an iota of her proud freedom. The two young women, who understand subjection, are in sympathy with rising workers in a way that is unthinkable for the hard industrialist and High Tory Revd Helstone.

During the summer of 1848, Charlotte was writing the first volume which brings out Caroline's vulnerability in relation to impervious men – curates, guardian, and mill-owner – as well as the emptiness of her workless days and her unwilling identification with single women in the parish. Charlotte's portraits of Caroline's pallor and thinness are likely to have been drawn from Anne Brontë whose poor health had been causing

Charlotte some anxiety since the end of 1846: 'Poor Anne has suffered greatly from asthma . . . She had two nights last week when her cough and difficulty of breathing were painful indeed to hear and witness . . . She bore it, as she does all affliction, without one complaint . . . She has an extraordinary heroism of endurance.' Again, Charlotte had worried over Anne's health during the autumn of 1847 as her sister stooped over her desk, intent on writing *Wildfell Hall*: 'It is with difficulty we can prevail on her to take a walk or induce her to converse.' This determined diligence continued until the novel was published in June 1848: a more substantially radical work than *Agnes Grey*, as ambitious in its way as *Jane Eyre* and *Wuthering Heights*.

In September 1848 Charlotte finished a fair copy of her first volume of *Shirley*. The contrast between the ambitious dissipation of Branwell and the ambitious diligence of his sisters could not have escaped her. Francis Grundy, a friend of Branwell's from his railroad days, described their meeting at an inn in Haworth: '. . . the door opened cautiously, and a head appeared. It was a mass of red, unkempt, uncut hair, wildly floating round a great, gaunt forehead: the cheeks yellow and hollow, the mouth fallen, the thin white lips not trembling but shaking, the sunken eyes, once small, now glaring with the light of madness'. Once Branwell was warmed by a glass of brandy 'he looked frightened – frightened of himself.'

Grundy also met Mr Brontë who spoke affectionately but hopelessly of his son. Mr Brontë had Branwell in his bedroom at night, despite Branwell's threats that one or other would not emerge alive next morning. In Mr Brontë's much-used manual on *Domestic Medicine*, he made notes next to the entry on 'Insanity or Mental Derangement': 'There is also "delirium tremens" brought on sometimes by intoxication – The patient thinks himself haunted . . . If intox[ication] be left off this madness will in general, gradually diminish.'

After his drawn-out wreckage, Branwell died suddenly on

24 September 1848, crying out to his father's sexton and his friend, John Brown: 'In all my past life I have done nothing either great or good.' He was thirty-one. Chrlotte said that she could not weep from any sense of bereavement, 'but for the wreck of talent, the ruin of promise, the untimely dreary extinction of what might have been a burning and a shining light.'

Other comments of Charlotte after Branwell's death bristle with jealousy for Papa's favour: 'My poor father naturally thought more of his *only* son than of his daughters, and, much and long as he had suffered on his account, he cried out for his loss like David for that of Absalom – my son! my son! – and refused at first to be comforted.' Mr Brontë never showed the same anguish at the deaths of his daughters, whatever he may have felt. Curiously, amidst his copious notes in *Domestic Medicine* next to various treatments for indigestion and cataract, as well as next to 'Nightmare' and 'Insanity', there is almost nothing next to the disease which caused the deaths of four of his daughters: Consumption [Tuberculosis]. It was Branwell to whom he had looked for achievement, Branwell who went to his death ignorant of what his sisters had achieved in his place. Their 'unhappy brother', Charlotte said, 'never knew what his sisters had done in literature – he was not aware they had ever published a line. We could not tell him of our efforts for fear of causing him too deep a pang of remorse for his own time misspent and talents misapplied.' She talked of pain; but there was triumph, too. It was a comment directed, mentally, at their father who must now depend on the strength and fame of a daughter to whom he had looked only for dutiful care.

But now Charlotte's strength was to be tested to its limits. By the end of October, she was gravely worried about the frail health of both her sisters. She wrote later: 'My sister Emily first declined . . . She sank rapidly. She made haste to leave us. Yet while physically she perished, mentally, she grew stronger than we had yet known her. Day by day, when I saw with what a front she met suffering, I looked on her with an anguish of wonder and love. I have seen nothing like it; but, indeed, I have never seen her parallel in anything.'

Emily's end came swiftly between late October and mid-December 1848. Charlotte could not accept, or fathom, the strength of a spirit inexorable to the flesh. Emily would not rest: she retired at the usual time of ten each night and came downstairs punctually at seven each morning, to the day of her death; with paroxysms of coughing and pain in her side, a hastening pulse, and panting after the least exertion, she would not concede illness. If Charlotte asked about her health, she did not reply. She refused any 'poisoning doctor'. Charlotte had to witness 'the conflict of the strangely strong spirit and the fragile frame before us – relentless conflict – once seen, never to be forgotten.'

After Emily died, unexpectedly soon, on 19 December 1848, Charlotte would wake at night to 'crushing' loss as she entered a 'lone wilderness', one of the great trials of her pilgrimage:

> Weary, weary, dark and drear,
> How shall I the journey bear,
> The burden and distress?

'Torn' was the word she repeated, as Emily's loss seemed to paralyse her being. She asked why Emily was 'torn from us in the fullness of our attachment, rooted up in the prime of her own days, in the promise of her powers; why her existence now lies like a field of green corn trodden down, like a tree in full bearing struck at the root . . .'

Papa had to beg her almost hourly: 'Charlotte, you must bear up, I shall sink if you fail me.'

Emily was buried on 22 December in the vault of St Michael's Church where her mother and Branwell lay. At the age of thirty, she was wasted by consumption. Her coffin measured her height, five feet, seven inches, but was only seventeen inches across – the narrowest adult coffin the local carpenter had ever made.

With Anne's progressing consumption, not helped by Papa's dread of sickrooms, Charlotte wondered if she could ever be Currer Bell again. The first five months of 1849 felt like crossing an abyss on a narrow plank: she could afford to look neither forward nor back. 'My literary character is effaced for the time', she wrote to her publishers. 'Worse than useless did it seem to attempt to write what there no longer lived an "Ellis Bell" to read.'

After Emily's fierce race into death, Charlotte had to witness Anne's slower but inexorable fading between January and the end of May 1849. Emily's death seemed to draw on Anne's: their sympathies had always been completely entwined. Emily's belief in the reach beyond death – the power of the spirit to reach the living – may have tugged Anne in a way that made it impossible for Charlotte to stay the course of her sister's decline. She felt powerless to alleviate Anne's 'nights of sleeplessness and pain and days of depression and languor which nothing could cheer.' During her last days, Anne did recover happiness in visiting York Minster which gave her an overwhelming sense of omnipotence, and in travelling on to Scarborough on the Yorkshire coast where, at her wish, Charlotte and Ellen took her for a last look at the sea. On the evening of Sunday 27 May, after a walk near the beach, she watched a brilliant sunset from her chair at the window. Ellen remembered how the ships in the distance glittered in the rays of the sun and how Anne's face became illumined as she gazed out across the horizon. Was it a realisation of her drawing at the age of nineteen: the longing reach of a woman gazing across a sea into a radiant horizon? There, in lodgings looking out to sea, Anne died, next day, very calmly; her last words were for her sister, trying to hold back her tears: 'Take courage, Charlotte.'

Afterwards, Charlotte looked back at the past nine months: 'A year ago – had a prophet warned me how I should stand in June 1849 – how stripped and bereaved – had he foretold the autumn, the winter, the spring of sickness and suffering to be gone through – I should have thought – this can never be endured. It is over. Branwell – Emily – Anne are gone like dreams – gone as Maria and Elizabeth went twenty years ago. One by one I have . . . closed their glazed eyes – I have seen them buried one by one – and – thus far – God has upheld me. From my heart I thank Him.'

It was not only faith which sustained her. Despite her fear that 'Currer Bell' would die with her sisters, she managed to go on writing – even sharing her work with them, when it was possible. In the second volume of *Shirley*, written after Emily's death with Emily much in mind, Shirley follows Jane Eyre as a new exemplar – but so much a forerunner of the feminist of the present time that it is hard to believe in her actual existence in 1811–12. She is a theoretic possibility: what a woman might be if she combined independence and means of her own with intellect. Charlotte Brontë imagined a new form of power, equal to that of men, in a confident young woman who inherits a local estate and who, as a member of the gentry, is deferred to by all. The extraordinary freedom of Shirley's position has accustomed her to think for herself.

Shirley embodies an authentic woman who is totally at variance with the cherished illusions of even the acutest men, including, it seems, most writers:

'If men could see us as we really are, they would be a little amazed; but the cleverest, the acutest men are often under an illusion about women: they do not read them in a true light; they misapprehend them, both for good and evil: their good woman is a queer thing, half doll, half angel; their bad woman almost always a fiend. Then to hear them fall into extasies with each other's creations, worshipping the heroine of such a poem – novel – drama, thinking it fine – divine! Fine and divine it may be, but often quite artificial – false as the rose in my best bonnet there. If I spoke all I think on this point; if I gave

my real opinion of some first-rate female characters in first-rate
works, where should I be? Dead under a cairn of avenging
stones in half an hour.'

Unlike other women of her time, Shirley speaks out, and she
speaks most freely when she and her new friend, Caroline, are
alone. Their very position, outside the church where the whole
community is at prayer, is an act of spontaneous defiance against
the elaborate constructs of authoritarian eloquence, the curates
who will 'hammer over their prepared orations'. Nature's holiness is more inviting: 'Nature is now at her evening prayers: she
is kneeling before those red hills.' In this moment, Shirley envi-
sions something of what Emily experienced in her mystical
moments: a daring to contend with Omnipotence, with the
strength to bear a thousand years of bondage, a woman-Titan
whose robe of blue air 'spreads to the outskirts of the heath',
whose eyes are full of worship as, kneeling, 'face to face she
speaks with God.' Nature, alone, is 'the mighty and mystical
parent of Shirley's visions'.

Shirley rewrites scripture. 'The First Blue-Stocking' is her
parable of Eva, a child of Nature who, in her innocence meets
and mates with Genius to become a Woman God. Her mode of
communication undercuts language as a construct alien to the
signs of Nature: 'she heard as if Silence spoke. There was no language, no word, only a tone.' Eva speaks of her Genius as an
elusive and indefinable communication: 'The dark hint, the
obscure whisper, which have haunted me from childhood'. She
asks, was she to burn out unseen, when her life beat so potent,
'when something within her . . . restlessly asserted a God-given
strength, for which it insisted she should find exercise?' The
parable tells how the marriage of Woman and Genius is defiled
by the Father of Lies who put poison into passion. The parable,
which ends with the death of the Woman-Genius, is a prophetic
re-creation of Emily's end: '. . . Genius still held close his dying
bride, sustained her through the agony of the passage, bore her

triumphant into his own home . . . and at last . . . crowned her with the crown of Immortality'. Shirley knows 'a genii-life', as did the young Brontës. Theoretic possibility and the actuality of the Brontës, the prophetic proto-feminism of Charlotte and the visionary nature of Emily, meet in Shirley. Her parable sets up a model for the feminist parables, called *Dreams*, which Olive Schreiner published in 1891: reprinted twenty times in England, translated in eight countries, they sold 80,000 copies. One of the Dreams was read aloud by Lady Constance Lytton to fasting suffragists in Holloway prison in the early years of the twentieth century.

This is part of the polemic in the novel which, as a genre, has always fused with other genres. It might be said that, with *Shirley*, Charlotte Brontë furthered the form of the polemical novel which explores the position of women, a mode begun by Mary Wollstonecraft in *Mary* (1788) and *The Wrongs of Woman* (1798). In this mode, truth comes most directly through the essay element which draws on the writer's life. Truth is better than Art, Charlotte Brontë said in the midst of the second volume. The truthful essay-novel was continued by Olive Schreiner in *The Story of An African Farm* (1883) and by Virginia Woolf in *The Pargiters* (1932) and *The Years* (1937). In *The Years*, the dutiful Victorian, Eleanor, thinks: 'When shall we be free? When shall we live adventurously, wholly, not like cripples in a cave? . . . She felt not only a new space of time, but new powers, something unknown within her.'

In the abundance of her strength, Shirley supports Caroline who embodies the other half of womanhood: not the unknown agency awaiting release, but conditioned diffidence and low expectation, leading to loss of hope and atrophy. This is an idealised and distorted version of Emily's relation to Anne. Truth blends with a good deal of fiction. Shirley like Emily is a law unto herself with the eye of a she-eagle, but Shirley has a social aplomb Emily lacked. She talks a great deal, while Emily hardly talked at all. But it is the closeness of the bond between two women on which Charlotte dwells, stressing the generosity of

Shirley's power (as distinct from agents of public power) which she confers on the frail Caroline. Unfortunately, Shirley remains unreal. It might be said that the idealised portrait of Shirley was the fruit of Charlotte's struggle – partly a posthumous struggle – with a sister who refused her lead, refused intimacy, and often refused to speak. Shirley is least convincing when the author chains her in marriage to her French tutor: it is as though Charlotte were at last asserting control over Emily, posthumous control, by forcing a free Shirley into her own mould.

Caroline's pathos is based partly on Anne as her health waned in 1848–9, partly on Charlotte's own depression in 1844–5 but, unlike Anne and Charlotte who were determined and effective, Caroline is seen to be rather helpless and in this she manifests something of well-bred Ellen Nussey. Caroline represents all women whose energies were unused by a society that relegated them, by law and custom, to ineffectual positions. Caroline's unspoken love for Robert Moore festers in a stagnant existence. Love, she tells Shirley, 'burns away our strength'. The explosiveness of the book is not primarily the actual attack on the mill, the broken windows, and the wounded; it ferments in the destructive force of feeling that may not be stated. It warps the health and character of a society, but does so invisibly. Caroline observes that to those grievances society cannot readily cure, 'it forbids utterance', and from the vantage point of her own weak position in relation to a tyrannical guardian who keeps her demoralised, dependent, and idle, she examines the atrophy of her sex as it dwindles into sterile forms of respectability or silent endurance. Custom also forbids a woman to declare her love so that Caroline is compelled to close her fist upon the scorpion's bite as she stands in her characteristic posture, shrinking a little to one side. Seated beside Robert Moore, 'screened by the very closeness of his vicinage from his scrutiny, and sheltered further by the dusk which deepened each moment, [Caroline] soon regained, not merely *seeming*, but *real* mastery of the feelings which had started into insurrection . . .'

There are links, then, between public and private revolt. We are shown a society which backs those with loud opinions – the employer, the Rector, the useless curates – while it denies voice to the educated governess, 'Mrs Pryor', or the tutor, Louis Moore, whose faculties 'seemed walled up in him, and were unmurmuring in their captivity.' Shirley and Louis are drawn together in a society which draws back in suspicion from expressiveness of any unfamiliar kind, as when Shirley sings with dramatic passion: 'The Misses Sympson and the Misses Nunnely looked upon her, as quiet poultry might look on an egret, an ibis, or any other strange fowl. What made her sing so? *They* never sang so. Was it *proper* to sing with such expression, with such originality – so unlike a school-girl? Decidedly not: it was strange; it was unusual. What was *strange* must be *wrong*; what was *unusual* must be *improper*. Shirley was judged.'

Women are hardest on their own sex. A closed-minded mother, Mrs Yorke, will not attend to the protest of twelve-year-old Rose who prefigures a woman of vigour – an exact portrait of Mary Taylor as Charlotte had first known her. Rose claims a life that shall not be a long, slow death, like Caroline's in Briarfield Rectory, but a life of travel and exploration. The portrait of Rose has its complement in a letter Mary wrote from New Zealand illustrating a physical vigour unthinkable in middle-class women in Victorian England: 'How we work! I lift, & carry & knock boxes open as if we were carpenters by trade, & sit down in the midst of the mess when we're quite tired, & . . . find it is the middle of the afternoon & we've forgotten our dinner!' She and her cousin, Ellen Taylor, would not 'give over working till bedtime, & take a new number of D[avid] Copperfield to bed with us & drop asleep at the second page.' It is not known whether Mary read Mary Wollstonecraft, but her actions seem an answer to the ineffectual lives of women described in *A Vindication of the Rights of Woman* (1792): 'How many women thus waste life away the prey of discontent, who might have been physicians, regulated a farm, managed a shop, and stood erect, supported by their own industry, instead of hanging their heads surcharged with the dew of sensibility . . .'

Mary took issue with *Shirley*'s qualified plea that women need work: '. . . This great necessity you seem to think that *some* women may indulge in – if they give up marriage and don't make themselves too disagreeable to the other sex. You are a coward and a traitor.'

Mary was too ideological, and perhaps too strong, for the compassion Charlotte felt for Caroline. Mary had only contempt for feeble women: 'Probably they are not worse than other women, but never called upon to stand alone or allowed to act for themselves, of course they lose their wits in time.' The child, Rose, prefigures Mary when she defies her mother: 'I will *not* commit it [her strength] to your work-table to be smothered in piles of woollen hose. I will *not* prison it in the linen-press to find shrouds among the sheets: and least of all, mother – (she got up from the floor) – least of all will I hide it in a tureen of cold potatoes, to be ranged with bread, butter, pastry, and ham on the shelves of the larder.' To Mrs Yorke this is a lot of 'ranting and spouting', the result of 'conceit' and undaughterly 'boldness'. Rose answers in the measured tone of absolute purpose: 'I utter it and leave it; it is for you, mother, to listen or not.'

'What a little lump of perfection you've made me!' Mary wrote when her copy of *Shirley* arrived in August 1850, after a long voyage via Constantinople. 'There is a strange feeling in reading it of hearing us all talking. I have not seen the matted hall & painted parlour [of the Red House] so plain these five years'. In the same letter, Ellen Taylor reports that they evoked much astonishment, as two women setting up shop on their own: 'Some think we shall make nothing of it, or that we shall get tired; and all laugh at us, before I left home I used to be afraid of being laughed at, but now it has very little effect upon me.'

In the essay-chapters of *Shirley*, Charlotte Brontë drew close to the issues of her own life. What were women to do when they could not marry and when they could not endure the position of the governess? Would inactivity deplete or embitter the character, or could the 'old maid' give worth to her existence, like Miss Ainsley, through helping others? Charlotte takes a bleak look at this alternative through the eyes of Caroline. Although she tries to emulate Miss Ainsley and fill time with charitable action, she remains blighted and nearly dies.

As Cary passes through the Valley of the Shadow of Death, Charlotte drew on the deaths of her sisters. The two illness chapters, at the start of the third volume, were the first to be written after Anne's death, while Charlotte lingered with Ellen on the Yorkshire coast. Giving words to mourning, she often appears to be thinking of her sisters and only obliquely of her heroine. At once, even before her return to Haworth, she picked up her pen to recount the wasting illness of Caroline and the dire effects of self-suppression. At first, there is no other focus but the sickroom, a girl's nerveless hand on her chest, her perpetual thirst, the watcher's wrestle with God throughout the night, pleading by the sweat of her brow — only to be denied at dawn by the changed face of the sufferer: the marble withdrawal and glassy eye — 'a certain look, dread and indescribable' — of those approaching death.

Not always do those who dare such divine conflict prevail. Night after night the sweat of agony may burst dark on the forehead; the supplicant may cry for mercy with that soundless voice the soul utters when its appeal is to the Invisible. 'Spare my beloved,' it may implore. 'Heal my life's life. Rend not from me what long affection entwines with my whole nature. God of heaven — bend — hear — be clement!' And after this cry and strife, the sun may rise and see him worsted.

This passage was written in the agony of recent event, but in fiction Caroline recovers (when her mother reveals her identity) and marries the man she loves, while Shirley and Louis Moore find in each other improbable mates.

In the midst of this, Charlotte returned to the emptied Parsonage where the grandfather clock ticked and ticked at the turn of the stair. Hearing the silence, she wondered: 'Can spirits, through any medium, communicate with living flesh? Can the dead at all revisit those they leave? Can they come in the elements?. . . What are all those influences that are about us in the atmosphere, that keep playing over our nerves like fingers on stringed instruments . . . ? *Where is* the other world? In *what* will another life consist?'

Charlotte framed her own answer in a letter to William Smith Williams: 'Faith whispers [Ellis and Acton Bell] are not in those graves to which imagination turns – the feeling, thinking, the inspired natures are beyond Earth – in a region more glorious. I believe them blessed.' She alone remained to her father, 'the weakest, puniest, least promising of his six children'.

What life remained for her? As she brought *Shirley* to 'The Winding-Up', another curate crossed her mind: reliable Mr Nicholls, always there.

Shirley's satire on curates may not be unconnected with the fact that, for the Brontës, curates were the only eligible men with whom they came in contact. It was therefore disappointing to find so many unacceptable. Willie Weightman had been one exception: the only curate whose company they all enjoyed. As *Shirley* came to an end, it occurred to Charlotte that Arthur Bell Nicholls was another possible exception. Making a brief appearance in the last chapter is the newly arrived Irish curate called Macarthey. Breaking the satiric vein in which the author, aware of the reader's expectation of sweet endings, struggles in vain to varnish the curates, she turns with relief to Macarthey who is worthy of '*truth*':

> I am happy to be able to inform you, *with truth*, that this gentle-
> man . . . proved himself as decent, decorous, and
> conscientious . . . He laboured faithfully in the parish: the
> schools, both Sunday and day-schools, flourished under his

sway like green bay-trees. Being human, of course he had his
faults; these, however, were proper, steady-going, clerical faults;
what many would call virtues: the circumstance of finding
himself invited to tea with a Dissenter would unhinge him for
a week; the spectacle of a Quaker wearing his hat in the
church – the thought of an unbaptized fellow-creature being
interred with Christian rites – these things could make strange
havoc in Mr Macarthey's physical and mental economy;
otherwise, he was sane and rational, diligent and charitable.

This portrait, with its teasing candour, was a bouquet which
Nicholls did not miss. In January 1850, he delighted in reading the
curate scenes aloud to Mr Brontë, and, as Charlotte put it, 'triumphed in his own character'. It was ever her habit to speak
covertly to specific people through her writing: to M. Heger in
her *devoirs*, to Mr Nicholls at the end of *Shirley*, later to George
Smith in *Villette*. To them she said through the medium of fiction
what she could not say outright. And there is adequate evidence
to suggest that all responded in one way or another to these mes-
sages. Although Mr Brontë and Mrs Gaskell had the impression
that Mr Nicholls made the first, amazing advances at the end of
1852 without the slightest encouragement, it seems that Charlotte
made the first move, even before the advent of Macarthey in the
late summer of 1849. In an earlier chapter, written some time
during the winter of 1848–9, Shirley weighs disillusion with marriage against the possibility of a suitable husband. The man she
defines here could mirror Mr Nicholls, and is consistent with his
acknowledged image as Macarthey: 'we watch him, and see him
kind to animals . . . to poor people. He is kind to us likewise –
good – considerate: he does not flatter women, but he is patient
with them, and he seems to be easy in their presence, and to find
their company genial . . . Then we observe that he is just – that he
always speaks the truth – that he is conscientious.'

Charlotte warmed to Mr Nicholls through her novel at a time
when she had lost two sisters in six months. She pictures

Macarthey as considerate and kind, at a time when she herself was in great need of kindness, as she returned from Scarborough to an empty Parsonage, to lonely evenings in the dining-room with Papa still immured in his study across the hall. Could some feeling for Mr Nicholls have begun in some awareness of shared bereavement (for Mr Nicholls' father also died in 1849), in gratitude for unobtrusive help, as he walked the dogs, Keeper and Flossy, when her sisters were dying, and in his participation in her griefs when he conducted the burial service for Emily at the end of 1848 and when he held Flossy in his arms to prevent her from running after the carriage when Anne left the Parsonage on her last journey in May 1849? He may have offered to look after Mr Brontë when Charlotte hesitated over their departure for Scarborough. Though Mr Brontë refused when Charlotte made this suggestion, we can infer that Charlotte trusted Mr Nicholls. She did continue to think him narrow: he did 'groan a little' over Charlotte's flippancy towards High-Churchmen like himself. She would deride 'the present successors of the apostles, disciples of Dr Pusey' who had undergone instantaneous 'regeneration by nursery baptism in wash-hand basins' wearing 'the Italian-ironed double frills' of their net caps, and who now flourished the white surplice 'aloft' in their pulpits, to the consternation of old-fashioned country vicars. Mr Nicholls was not amused. Sternly doctrinaire, there was nothing in him of the imaginative rapport Charlotte had lost in her sisters. But she did mark his goodness.

Though she was thankful for the affectionate kindness of her father and the two servants, Tabby and Martha Brown, her nights remained wakeful as she relived the deaths. By day, the expected pieties rolled off her lips: another two sisters have died in quick succession – how great and good is the Power above. To her correspondents she declared this pathetic acceptance; by night, she faced uncontained 'rebellion'. Her real salvation was work: the challenge of the final volume of *Shirley*. To write, she told herself, is to 'give your soul its natural release.'

The novel's message of secret strength gives her rationale for survival. However quiet and meek a writer may appear, there is 'a truculent spirit' that scorns pathos. 'While strangers, perhaps, deem his existence a Polar winter never gladdened by a sun', he maintains the creative glow. 'The true poet is not one whit to be pitied, and he is apt to laugh in his sleeve, when any misguided sympathizer whines over his wrongs.' Written before the deaths of Emily and Anne, she is thinking of their shared defiance of adverse opinion. Of course, she had far less to contend with than the authors of _Wuthering Heights_ and _Wildfell Hall_, who provoked the hostility of incomprehension. Ellis and Acton had met this in silence. Ellis had smiled half-amused and half in scorn to hear the _North American Review_'s opinion that he was dogged and brutal. Acton, sewing, had dropped one word of calm amazement to hear of the darkness of his character. To what extent public opinion undermined them cannot be known, but Charlotte was able to cultivate 'hard derision' and 'merciless contempt' for critics. Her true poet was, in her view, so fierce that 'he' might merit blame, not sympathy. Her tone was exultant, not the least apologetic. For a moment she revealed the home character: tart, outspoken, formidable in the act of judgement. Her power amused her, invisible as it was. For her, the true writer pre-empts the world's displeasure, turning from the world before the world can turn from her. Nature, alone, is her friend.

This creed spoke for Emily. It is perhaps a measure of how much Charlotte had gained from her sister whose 'genius' she never doubted for one moment in the face of public disgust with the ruder elements of _Wuthering Heights_. Shirley entered Charlotte's novel just before or just after Emily died, and at once Shirley defines herself through her memories of a landscape identical with Emily's habitat: 'a boundless waste of deep heath', purple black on a stormy day with nothing to be seen 'but wild sheep; nothing heard but the cries of wild birds.' On the day Emily was dying, Charlotte had searched the moor in vain for a sprig of heather. Afterwards, she defended Emily against contemporary taste for the voluminous and detailed: 'Because Ellis's poems are short and abstract, the critics think them comparatively insignificant and dull. They are mistaken.' Emily's sublimity was a law to itself. In her, Charlotte lost a fearless character who had, to some indeterminable extent, shaped her own. '. . . I think a certain harshness in her powerful and peculiar character only makes me cling to her more', she said just before Emily's death, and two years after she said: 'Stronger than a man, simpler than a child, her nature stood alone.' From now on Charlotte would carry the banner for her sister's unflinching strength.

Charlotte's plan had been to bond with Emily as authors whose 'true' voices would carry through their society, attentive or not, hostile or not. But Emily's mission had been to bond with the divine spirit of the nightly visitations, carried by the glorious wind that swept the world aside, the essence of the Tempest's roaring:

> A principle of life, intense,
> Lost to mortality.

Emily gone, Shirley rose before her: a free creature. She had pressed on with the second volume of *Shirley*, her script jagged and hasty, unlike the neat hand of earlier manuscripts. Here, she began her practice of excising with scissors, as though it were not enough to cancel bad lines; she must eliminate them. Volume two was completed by the time Anne died at the end of May. Anne's patient, Christian death did not rend her as Emily's swift, unyielding end. 'I let Anne go to God, and felt He had a right to her. I could hardly let Emily go. I wanted to hold her back then, and I want her back now.' She had lost her secret sharer, but *Shirley* shows that she had gained enough to go on alone.

With incredible resolution, hampered – or was it fortified? – by nightly rebellion, Currer Bell revived. In less than three months, between June and the end of August 1849, a third

volume of *Shirley* was written. 'The fact is my work is my best
companion', she told William Smith Williams on 26 July, 'hereafter I look for no great earthly comfort except what congenial
occupation can give.' As Charlotte pushed the book to its end,
she realised that Currer Bell was stronger than ever, for this
character had now become her only stake in life: 'The loss of
what we possess nearest and dearest to us in the world produces
an effect upon the character', Charlotte wrote again to Williams
on 21 September, 'we search out what we have yet left that can
support, and, when found, we cling to it with a hold of new-
strung tenacity. The faculty of imagination lifted me when I was
sinking, three months ago; its active exercise has kept my head
above water since; its results cheer me now . . .'

By the time Charlotte Brontë completed *Shirley*, she no longer
walked entirely invisible. In January 1848, she had revealed her
authorship to Papa. In May 1848 Ellen had voiced suspicions and
spread them. Charlotte did not actually lie, but refused publicity
with fury at Ellen's suspected betrayal: 'I have given *no one* a right
either to affirm, or hint, in the most distant manner, that I am
"publishing" – (humbug!) Whoever said it – if any one has,
which I doubt – is no friend of mine. Though twenty books were
ascribed to me, I should own none. I scout the idea utterly . . .
The most profound obscurity is infinitely preferable to vulgar
notoriety; and that notoriety I neither seek nor will have.' Then,
in July 1848, the Bells' identities had been revealed to Charlotte's
publisher in London, who had been restrained with difficulty in
his first transports of excitement.

   Now, more than a year later, a parcel of proofs from Smith,
Elder was opened in transit – by prying gossips in Keighley,
Charlotte guessed. When she visited Ellen in October 1849, she
could not be unaware of new deference from old schoolfriends
– nor of clerical brows lowered against her. The Yorkshire setting
of her new novel, the easily identified characters – the curates
and the Yorkes – invited inevitable speculation. The Haworth

sexton, John Brown, heard of Charlotte in Halifax; Mary's brother, George, heard of her in Bradford. Yet she could not bring herself to regret one line she had written.

At the end of November, she returned to Babylon (as she still called London). This time, a month after the publication of *Shirley*, she no longer enjoyed the anonymity of 'Miss Brown', though her publisher did what he could to protect her modesty. When Thackeray came to dine on 3 December, Smith had the tact not to force an introduction. She saw an immensely tall man, ugly (she thought) with a peculiar flattish face, rather stern and satirical in expression, but capable of kindness. Before they went down to dinner, as Charlotte was allowed to linger in shadow, she saw Thackeray look at her through his spectacles. Soon, he came across very quietly and said, 'Shake hands.' At first there seemed no need for name or pseudonym; only this simple act of recognition. But after dinner and cigars, when the gentlemen joined the ladies in the drawing-room, Thackeray advanced on Charlotte quoting the passage from *Jane Eyre* about 'the warning fragrance' of Mr Rochester's cigar. Thackeray was careless of reticence; in the familiarity of friendly talk, he never stopped to consider what ought not to be said. Refusing to be lionised, Charlotte guarded her gift with silent refinement. She never played the celebrity; she was playing another role.

Her intention was to separate the fiery writer from the well-bred lady. Her mouselike demeanour, her trembling timidity, were vital to social survival. This put her always at risk of exposure; she was vulnerable because the author might give the lie to the lady — who must allow evident vulnerability to strengthen her claim to ladyhood.

At the same time, she was bent on material: she had to observe and assimilate. She did tremble, according to Thackeray, but she lifted her eyes to judge for herself: 'New to the London world, she entered it with an independent, indomitable spirit of her own; and judged of contemporaries, and especially spied out arrogance or affectation, with extraordinary keenness of vision.' She had bright eyes which could blaze with meaning. Thackeray's elder daughter, Anne, recalled how Charlotte sat gazing at her father 'with kindling eyes of interest, lighting up with a sort of illumination now and then as she answered him. I can see her, bending forward over the table, not eating, but listening to what he said as he carved the dish before him.' Thackeray did not wholly please her: though she liked his simplicity, his taste for flattery and the way he danced attendance on great ladies showed a weakness — 'not unamiable'. Nor was she overawed by the seven leading critics who came to dinner, neither by the 'loud swagger' of Mr Forster, nor by the grimaces of Mr Chorley. She examined Mr Chorley as a specimen, 'uncertain whether, when you had probed the small recess of his character, the result would be utter contempt and aversion, or whether for the sake of some latent good you would forgive obvious evil. One could well pardon his unpleasant features, his strange voice, even his very foppery and grimace, if one found these disadvantages connected with living talent and any spark of genuine goodness. If there is nothing more than acquirement, smartness, and the affectation of philanthropy, Chorley is a fine creature.'

To understand the kind of woman that Charlotte was bringing into being, we must therefore see more than pathos. We must watch the play of shrinking femininity for which the brilliant verbal glide of her abjection to Southey had been the first practice run; we must note the subversiveness of her retreat; and we must listen to comments of London literati who could not make her out. For her silence posed an incomprehensible gap between writer and woman. How could fashionable London reconcile that impetuous voice they heard between the covers of *Jane Eyre* and *Shirley* with this quivering mouse? At the Smiths, she resented being drawn out. Mrs Smith and her daughters found her a difficult guest, silent and self-absorbed. This was far from the 'home character': the self-effacement was designed to obliterate, for public purposes, the woman of passion and the volume of her utterance.

When public appearance became inevitable, Charlotte was on guard against the image of 'rather a brazen Miss': every gesture, every movement and facial expression declared the opposite. She could not prevent, therefore, the alternative image – equally crude, yet springing easily to the lips of men of the world like Lewes and Thackeray: the sad spinster, hungry for sex, who would cease to bother her head with writing if she could find herself a common 'Tomkins' with whom to mate. This automatic conclusion came as readily to Thackeray, who genuinely admired her mind, as to lesser men, but it was a gross misunderstanding of Charlotte who declined four offers: from the Revd Mr Nussey in March 1839; from the impulsive Irish visitor, Mr Bryce, in August 1839; and two still to come. Between these events, she went sensibly armed against the charmer who had 'the art of impressing ladies by something apparently involuntary in his look or manner – exciting in them the notion that he cares for them while his words and actions are all careless, inattentive and quite uncompromising for himself. It is only men who have seen much of life and of the world and are become in a measure indifferent to female attractions that possess this art'. No worldly-wise woman could have been shrewder. But she had, at the same time, sympathy for the susceptible of her sex. She understood the warping effect of the emptiness of women's lives. Compulsory inactivity opened women to delusive excitements: 'while their minds are mostly unemployed, their sensations are all unworn and consequently fresh and keen . . . I only wish I had the power to infuse into the soul of the persecuted a little of the quiet strength of pride – of the supporting consciousness of superiority . . .'

The descendants of Thackeray's thinking on Tomkins were twentieth-century feminists who deplored Charlotte's need for a master. This was a reductive position which did not allow for the writer's discriminations: Shirley's capitulation to her tutor, Louis Moore, may not fit our taste, but at least she is choosing inward and intelligent authority over the material power, brutality, and mere status of other suitors. Nor may we pass by

Charlotte's sharp comment on a friend's wish for a husband with a will of his own, even if he be a tyrant: '. . . If her husband has a strong will, he must also have a strong sense – a kind heart – a thoroughly correct notion of justice – because a man with a *weak brain, chill affections* and *strong will* – is merely an intractable fiend – you can have no hold of him – you can never lead him right. A tyrant under any circumstances is a curse.' Privately, to Ellen, she showed this strength; publicly, her manner gave no hint of judgement and superiority. Yet, under all that nervous reticence, they were there.

During the London visit of December 1849, and on her return six months later, what most tried Charlotte was when Thackeray, who scorned pretence of any kind, challenged the discrepancy between author and woman. Ostensibly, this was cruel. Yet she had, in truth, set it up. Thackeray called her bluff by refusing to play her game. On 12 June 1850, at a party in her honour at Thackeray's house at 13 Young Street, Kensington, Charlotte was exposed to society. Guests included a novelist called Catherine Crowe, the Carlyles, and a poet, Adelaide Anne Procter, who was connected with the Sidgwicks of Stonegappe. All eyed her – especially when Thackeray called her 'Currer Bell' as she came down to dinner on his arm, barely reaching his elbow. Outraged, she pulled her cover closer.

'I believe there are books being published by a person named Currer Bell,' she replied, 'but the person you address is Miss Brontë – and I see no connection between the two.' Then, with prompt and amusing ruthlessness, she defeated Thackeray in his own home.

Single-handed, she wrecked his party. George Smith recalled how she blocked society women.

'I hope you like London,' said Thackeray's special friend, Mrs Brookfield, by way of an opening.

'I do and I don't,' said Charlotte curtly.

Refusing to be drawn by a single question or initiate the brilliant conversation all awaited, the guest of honour abandoned the drawing-room and retired to the dimmest corner of the study with the governess, Miss Truelock. She would not converse with anyone else, not even Jane Carlyle. The room darkened as a lamp began to smoke. Silence fell; awkwardness prevailed. Anne Thackeray caught her father as he disappeared through the front door with a finger to his lips. Escaping from his own party, he fled to the safety of his club. Charlotte's insistence on invisibility – placing herself with the governess, when she was meant to play the celebrity – seemed to George Smith a fit of pique caused by his attentions to attractive Miss Procter – he did not know of her unfortunate link with Charlotte's employers. To the mannerly publisher, Charlotte Brontë's withdrawal was an act of social ineptitude. But it was also an act of revolt: a vindication of the obscure.

THE LIMITS OF FRIENDSHIP

When Charlotte heard the clock tick through the emptied Parsonage on her return in the summer of 1849, two alternatives lay before her. As the last of six to remain alive, was she to see herself as the relic of a doomed family, their constitutions eroded (she believed) by The Clergy Daughters' School? That summer, when she called herself the 'puniest' of Papa's children, was she calling attention to her unlikely survival, or was she hopeful of continued life against all odds? Perhaps something of both, but her actions suggest her wish to make the most of the second possibility. This position is distilled in her next novel, *Villette*: 'I saw myself in the glass, in my mourning-dress, a faded, hollow-eyed vision. Yet I thought little of the wan spectacle. The blight, I believed, was chiefly external: I still felt life at life's sources.'

Hope, she told George Smith, could not flower easily in her northern climate, but it did put forth buds; 'Fortitude' pulled her through rebellious nights, through what she called 'the weird', when the dead claimed her, and Fortitude was what she called on when letters from Cornhill became too necessary to those buds of hope.

At first, in the summer of 1849, she managed to turn loneliness to effect as creative solitude. In that silent house, with reminders of the past about her, she might have faded with grief, as Emily and Anne had faded, but within a few days of Anne's death she was holding grief at bay with a tremendous, sustained burst of work. And though she did have household duties and care of Papa, she had, now, liberty: no longer need she watch the sick or earn her living against the grain and, of course, she was free of the perpetual child-bearing, factory grind, or social obligations that used up the initiative of all but the most resourceful women of her time. In this way, she was more fortunate than Florence Nightingale, rich, young, beautiful, surrounded by family and suitors, but almost maddened in the early 1850s by the sistering, visiting, and obligatory parties which, for years, deflected the purpose that lurked within her. Portionless and lonely as Charlotte was, her time, that most necessary thing, was her own. A few intrepid lion-hunters did find their way to Haworth, but its remoteness, much lamented by Charlotte, was also her protection. Her determined completion of *Shirley*, and the testing responsiveness with which she engaged in new ties between 1849 and 1853, reinforce the image she had presented in *Jane Eyre* of a survivor or pilgrim who does not shrink from renewed effort.

In a continuous effort to go on with life, this phase was one of unwonted activity: visits to London, the Lakes, Edinburgh, and Manchester; quickening friendships with George Smith and his forceful manager, James Taylor; and overtures to other women writers, Harriet Martineau (whose *Deerbrook* had influenced Charlotte in 1839 when she was struggling to free herself from Angria) and Elizabeth Gaskell, whose first industrial novel, *Mary Barton* (1848), preceded *Shirley*. Charlotte had read *Mary Barton* when her sisters were dying, and later she told Mrs Gaskell, 'There are parts of "Mary Barton" I shall never read a second time', parts that had pierced her with 'too keen-edged emotion'. Charlotte sent copies of *Shirley* to Mrs Gaskell and Miss Martineau, and both replied appreciatively, Mrs Gaskell saying that she would 'treasure' Currer Bell's works to give to her daughters. In the years that followed, a vast number of letters kept these ties expanding during the long periods when Charlotte remained in Yorkshire.

The widening of her correspondence as she became a celebrity

makes it hard, in this phase, to see her direction. Until the publication of *Shirley*, there was always the centrality of imaginative
work, but she did not begin another novel for at least a year and
a half. She had the patience of high vocation, and believed that
every serious delineation of life ought to come from personal
experience of a normal, not a forced kind.

She said, 'I have not accumulated since I published *Shirley* what
makes it needful for me to speak again, and, till I do, may God
give me grace to be dumb.'

Many now wrote for her opinion of their deplorable books
or simply to gain acquaintance, often flatterers 'who utterly
mistake all about me.' Was the centre of her attention new
friendships with writers with whom she might discuss, say, the
article on 'The Enfranchisement of Women' (published anony-
mously by Harriet Taylor Mill) in the *Westminster*? Or was the
centre the bleak silence of the Parsonage and her longing for
domestic talk? Day after day, clockwork arrangements repeated
themselves: breakfast with Papa at nine, housework, dinner at
two alone, tea at six, prayers at 8.30. Then, after the household
retired at nine, she walked in the dining-room for an hour with
the memory of her sisters. (In 1853, when Mrs Gaskell visited the
Parsonage, she heard Charlotte walk every night: 'that slow
monotonous incessant walk in which I am sure I should fancy I
heard the steps of the dead following me.') Papa remained, as
ever, in his study. When James Taylor was due to fetch the manuscript of *Shirley* in September 1849, Charlotte had to make her
father's excuses: she could not invite Mr Taylor to stay the night,
as she wished, since Papa could not 'spare time' for visitors. Nor
did she expect him to change at his age. What was wrong with
'The Enfranchisement of Women', she and Mrs Gaskell agreed,
was that it posed a shallow-hearted demand for power against
the deep emotion of selflessness. She saw her father, at seventy-
two, as a very old man whose health it was her duty to guard
with caring anxiety. 'When we have but one precious thing left
we think much of it,' she said. It was her habit to join her father

for tea; if Mr Nicholls were there, she soon retired to the dining-room across the hall. Between eight and nine, Mr Nicholls would let himself out: as she sat on alone, she heard the footsteps depart and the front door close. Then she had to get through those evening hours when she and her sisters used to share their work; and then, night vigils when she could not sleep, except on rare occasions when Ellen came and shared the bed. As she confided to Ellen, her problem was not that she was a *single* woman and likely to remain *single* – but that she was a *lonely* woman and likely to be *lonely*.

The extremity of this loneliness led her to consider James Taylor. Somewhere between the end of 1849 and the end of 1850 it became apparent that he could make her an offer. From the time she submitted the first part of *Shirley*, in February 1849, he began to correspond, first to comment on the strengths and flaws of that novel, then to discuss the non-fiction he began to send her. His high-minded selections showed his regard for her mind and character, and Charlotte wrote back about the books she read like *The Soul: her Sorrows and her Aspirations* (1849) by Francis Newman (brother of the century's most famous convert to Catholicism, John Henry Newman, later, Cardinal Newman). 'Have you read this work?' Charlotte asked James Taylor. 'It is daring – it may be mistaken – but it is pure and elevated.' Mr Taylor's replies were earnest, dry, but intellectually compatible; and his top managerial position at Smith, Elder was the result of his probity and command. He had forty men under him, whom he ruled with a will of iron – 'iron' was a word that rose spontaneously to Charlotte's lips whenever she thought of him.

The relationship was not unlike that of Jane Eyre and St John Rivers, except that Taylor was no Apollo: he was a sandy-haired Scot whom she called, in private to Ellen, 'the little man'. There was respect without attraction. In this situation, there is often the possibility that respect and common interests could promote affection. Repeatedly, Charlotte probed the character Taylor revealed in letters and in person. Whenever he kept his distance, she was reassured; but there was something pushy about his person that showed itself when they met in London in December 1849 and from which she recoiled instinctively. She wanted to like him, but her body would go rigid, and nothing softened her except 'a perfect subduing of his manner.' She feared that he would turn out to be a man of the Helstone order: able, dominating – and unfeeling to women. After her long commitment to passion in the form of M. Heger, an imaginative kind of passion projected in all her fictions, she now contemplated a rational union, and for obvious reasons: the relief of loneliness; security when her father died; and more, perhaps. To entertain this possibility was not an aberration, though it may appear so, but part of that sensible, Monday-morning self who strove to push back passion within the bounds of reason.

Charlotte's manner to Taylor was sober and civil, forthcoming with moral opinions, but otherwise rather stiffly correct. It is impossible to detect any nuance of liking. Whether, with her honesty, she could not feign liking where it did not exist, or whether she was guarding herself from the impropriety of expressiveness with a controlling man, who can say? But if Taylor was capable of sensitivity, she made it hard for him. Not a chink of 'home character' did she reveal – yet, from her side, the testing continued. When he sent her Stanley's *Life and Correspondence of Thomas Arnold* (1844), she posed the idea that though Dr Arnold was a hard-driving man, he was not deficient in domestic affections. How would Taylor respond – *would* he respond? Would he allow for reciprocity or was he closed to suggestion? The good sense and principle in Taylor's letters fertilised the buds of hope. But when Charlotte met him again in London in the summer of 1850, he 'cut into' her soul when he poked his determined nose in her face. To turn from him to his master, George Smith, was to exchange cold iron for soft fur.

Where Taylor provoked a combination of hope and recoil, George Smith liberated in Charlotte a dancing humour. This burst out immediately after her triumphant visit to London as author of a second successful novel at the end of 1849. She took pride in the fact that she was now a 'prop' to Smith, Elder, and Co. which had entered the front rank of publishers with the huge success of *Jane Eyre*. Through her, Thackeray and then Mrs Gaskell joined the firm. Staying for the first time with the Smiths at 4 Westbourne Place, she was surrounded by attentions: fires and two wax candles in her room, and the reassuring surveillance of Mrs Smith when Charlotte stood surrounded by gentlemen, including George himself – George who was tall, well-knit, self-reliant, with the vigour of a keen rider and chivalrous 'to the backbone'. At first, he had thought Charlotte lacking in complexion and charm, but as he came to know her better he found her 'quick and clear' intelligence a delight. 'When she became excited on any subject', he said, 'she was really eloquent'. She would gaze with kindling interest as her eyes lit. Yet, Mrs Smith, guarding her 'cherished one', was satisfied that Charlotte was too shy to be an adventuress. She was, in fact, like Elizabeth Hastings, whose wits grant her entrée to a public world which she cannot approve but whose more enlightened approbation she cannot but enjoy.

This stay with the Smiths was the first of a series of visits to London between November 1849 and January 1853. Over this time, she allowed herself to become visible, in a limited way, meeting fellow-writers on her own terms. She sent a note (signed 'Currer Bell') to introduce herself to Harriet Martineau who, at forty-seven, was the leading woman writer of the day, more established at this point than either Charlotte Brontë or Mrs Gaskell or the poet, Elizabeth Barrett Browning, and in 1849 at the height of her fame as indefatigable critic of the punitive Poor Law, and as an advocate of women's education and professional advance. In her twenties, her fiancé had died and the family business had collapsed. Her deafness made it impossible for her to become a governess and she had resolved to earn a living through writing. She had first gained fame in the 1830s for a twenty-four-part series, *Illustrations of Political Economy*: George

Smith remembered his father reading these 'tales' to him while he was growing up. At the age of thirty-five, Miss Martineau had been offered the editorship of a new economics periodical, but her beloved brother James disapproved, and she had refused it. Instead, she wrote *Deerbrook*. On 7 November 1849, Currer Bell sent her *Shirley* with a note acknowledging that *Deerbrook* had 'rectified his views of life.'

On 9 December, Charlotte, in her usual deep mourning, went alone to Westbourne Street (around the corner from Westbourne Place), where Miss Martineau was staying, to meet this respected and outspoken woman. Coming on a family party in the drawing-room, Charlotte at once identified Miss Martineau as the robust woman with the ear-trumpet. Her own identity, she told Miss Martineau, was to be kept secret.

'What did you really think of *Jane Eyre*?', she wanted to know. She was puzzled by the critics' talk of coarseness.

'I thought it a first-rate book', said Miss Martineau, noticing that her visitor had beautiful hair, smooth and brown. 'I have ever observed', she went on, 'that it is to the coarse-minded alone *Jane Eyre* is coarse.' This was the smallest creature she had ever seen outside a fair, but full of power.

Currer Bell went red with pleasure. Seated beside Miss Martineau, she gave her a look 'so loving and appealing' that the reformer was astonished and touched. Charlotte was willing to overlook the brusque manner and major differences of opinion – Miss Martineau's atheism, in particular – for the sake of a heartening model: an independent woman who wrote book after book with a sturdy sense of purpose. The attraction of Harriet Martineau was not based on likeness; she had 'no bump of secretiveness at all', Charlotte later told Mary. She did not expect Miss Martineau to understand her own 'Quakerlike waiting on the spirit'. Her new friend's Dissenting background and practical, economic concerns may have encouraged Charlotte to find in her a bracing substitute for Mary, but she could not confide in Harriet Martineau – in any case, how could you bellow 'the spirit' into an ear-trumpet? It was certain antithetical qualities that drew Charlotte: the very absence of shade, the purpose of a woman who models herself on the kind of no-nonsense professionalism which ignores the distractions of feeling. Charlotte thought of Harriet Martineau as a stubborn character who would harden in the face of opposition, but imagined that she detected also a 'rough' kindliness which might be touched by patience and tolerance. For Miss Martineau's part, she welcomed a projection of herself: a strong vocation, an absence of 'feeble egotism', and indifference to applause. She said that Charlotte's 'moral strength fell not a whit behind the intellectual force manifested in her works.' Accurate enough, but because Miss Martineau had come to despise passion, she overlooked, at first, this core of Charlotte's nature and work. Her eye fastened approvingly on her visitor's composure: she saw a sensible face indicating a habit of self-control.

In London, Charlotte avoided fatiguing large parties and the lionising Thackeray enjoyed. Thackeray, once her model, continued to disconcert her with cynicism and misogyny. After his *Rebecca and Rowena* came out at Christmas 1849, she discussed 'our cause' with Mrs Smith, declaring that Thackeray should be punished for his 'abuse of Rowena and of women in general'.

'I will tell you my dear Madam what I think he deserves', she said, '– first to be arrested, to be kept in prison for a month, then to be tried by a jury of twelve matrons . . . and I trust they would not spare him.'

Mrs Smith, born Elizabeth Murray, had been the daughter of a wealthy glassware manufacturer. A woman 'of quite exceptional shrewdness and strength of mind', as her son called her, she had never been less than sturdy when her father and her husband lost money. Strong, healthy, and rather tall, she was dark for an Englishwoman, with a rosy glow in her cheeks and alert black eyes. She made Charlotte welcome with the same easy alacrity as her son's. Charlotte, who had no experience of mothers, who had been forced to contend with the indifference of Mrs Sidgwick and Mrs White, to endure the prolonged ostracism of Mme Heger, and whose godmother had rejected her after reports of coarseness in *Jane Eyre*, treated Mrs Smith at first with cautious reserve. But over the course of two successive visits in November-December 1849 and May-June 1850, she warmed to Mrs Smith's cheerful attentions. In pilgrim's terms, to visit Mrs Smith was like the sojourn of Hopeful beside a pleasant stream (as Lucy Snowe describes visits to her godmother in *Villette*). Such a visit was no more than a 'sojourn', and because Charlotte knew it could never be a terminus, it became increasingly painful to depart on her own more arduous pilgrimage. But during those sojourns Charlotte allowed herself to unfold in the salubrious climate of the Smith household, propped by Mrs Smith's decided bearing and prompt hand under Charlotte's arm as they moved through London society. Though Charlotte preserved a demeanour of modest restraint, the Smith women found her disconcerting: too watchful for their entire comfort, as though she were assimilating observations for future use – as in truth she was. In her next novel, George Smith noticed that some of his mother's expressions were used 'verbatim' in the mouth of Lucy's godmother, Mrs Bretton, who guards her handsome son. A few years later, when Mrs Gaskell called on the Smiths in 1856, she found Mrs Smith '*exactly* like Mrs Bretton. Mr Smith said (half-suspiciously, having an eye to [her son] Dr John, I *fancied*), "Do you know, I sometimes think Miss Brontë had my mother in mind when she wrote Mrs Bretton in 'Villette'?"'

Charlotte also disconcerted fashionable opinion at the select dinners she attended: her modesty did not colour her honesty about the extravagance of Macready's acting in *Othello* and *Macbeth*. 'Hollow nonsense', she said: such staginess was fit only for farces. 'The actors comprehended nothing about tragedy or Shakespeare, and it was a failure.' Silence fell. The consternation of socialites, accustomed to raptures over London idols, spurred Charlotte to further dissent. With the genius of Emily in mind, she had a poor opinion of Elizabeth Barrett Browning whose

Poems (1844) were so highly regarded that when Wordsworth died in 1850, many proposed her as his most appropriate successor as poet laureate. Since her father was a tyrant who forbade his children to marry, she had eloped to Italy with a fellow-poet, Robert Browning, in 1846. There she was to produce her *Sonnets from the Portuguese* (1850) and her magnum opus, *Aurora Leigh* (1857). Her only child was born in 1849, the year Charlotte delivered her opinion in London: she could not admire the wordy, obscure style of this favourite. Again, silence.

She was audible, then, as well as visible. In her only authenticated photograph she appears sensible and not in the least plain. Her profile is neatly regular, her hair drawn down over her wide forehead and cheeks to cluster in her neck. With the twist of her mouth turned away from the camera, her round chin and throat set off by a neat frill, she is more than presentable. She is attractive in her simple, dark dress with its round neck and buttoned front, with the manner of an unpretentious person who is sure in her views and resting within them.

At home, George, talkative, humorous, was more likeable as a son and brother than as a businessman. In a delightfully witty letter, Charlotte soothed Smith with what she came to call, in their private language, one of her 'comfits' (a conviction that there were aspects to his character that would redeem the merchant). These comfits were supposed to sweeten her doses of 'medicine': here, her ridicule of his conventional taste in women. She imagines a comic scene in which various solemn men of business, including Smith, select bonnets for export:

December 26, 1849

My dear Sir

Your note reminded me of the 'cross portrait'; it is exceedingly wayward. You shall have the full benefit of the character you give of yourself; I am willing to look on you as a 'hard-headed and close-fisted man of business', only — remember —

your conduct must be consistent with the claim you prefer to these epithets; if you are 'close-fisted', shut your hand against Currer Bell, give him no more books; we are apt to judge people very much by what they are to ourselves, and to derive our impressions of their nature from the side we chiefly see . . . One should study human nature under all aspects; one should see one's friends, for instance, in Cornhill as well as in Westbourne Place; one should hear them discuss 'discounts' and 'percentages' as well as converse at their own fireside. I think if a good fairy were to offer me the choice of a gift, I would say – grant me the power to walk invisible; though certainly I would add – accompany it by the grace never to abuse the privilege. And I would not count it an abuse to watch the proceedings of gentlemen commissioned to make a selection of ladies' bonnets for the East-Indian exportation. You do not know the anecdote . . . The bonnets were carefully chosen, and subsequently – with a conscientious desire to have all right – they were *tried on*, and judgment duly passed as to their merits. Imagination cannot resist the impulse to picture the scene – it rises before her, and she looks at it with delighted eyes. She sees a back-room crowded with bonnet-boxes; she sees three umpires whom she knows well; P— stands in the back-ground waiting to pack. Opinions vary and tastes differ just sufficiently to give interest to the discussion. A gentianella blue satin is found most becoming to Mr T–y–r; Mr W—m's artist's eye finds special charm in the rich tint of . . . a garnet-coloured velvet bonnet while Mr G—e S–th divides his preference between the prettiest little drawn-silk and the neatest white chip with a single drooping ostrich feather . . .

Of course it is very wrong to make any allusion to topics so frivolous in a letter to a 'hard-headed, close-fisted man of business' but it is to be hoped the error will be pardoned on promise of non-repetition.

Offering my kindest regards to your Mother and Sisters and wishing you and them a happy Christmas,

I am, my dear Sir,
    Yours sincerely
        C Brontë

Though Charlotte spoke of 'friendship' to James Taylor and George Smith, it was in this phase that she tested the limits of friendship with the kind of man she might have married. Since she professed to despise curates as a lower species, the most likely partner would seem to come from the publishing world she had recently made her own, someone whose regard for her gift might outweigh her drawbacks. I would guess that Charlotte fixed her attention on the less-desirable Mr Taylor, not only because he was 'deficient neither in spirit nor sense', but to hold at bay any temptation to be drawn to Mr Smith. It was Charlotte's resolve, projected in the character of her new heroine, Lucy Snowe, that a woman without looks, means, or connections must not raise her eyes to one of fate's 'curled darlings'. To entertain any illusion of love from a worldly, pampered man, would endanger peace of mind. To wait again for letters, as Charlotte in fact found herself waiting in February 1850, was to risk the depression she had suffered over Monsieur in 1844–5. So, Charlotte was on her guard against the gallantries and invitations of George Smith, even as she responded to his amusing, mildly confidential letters with replies in the same vein. This determined guard, even with herself, makes it impossible to know exactly what Charlotte felt about Smith; or, indeed, what Smith felt about her. I imagine that George Smith was a kind of test following her emergence as an author: could he allay her anxiety about appearing in public? Could she emerge from the shadow of her heroines? His tact and chivalry had already conducted her safely through a publicity she had never thought possible in the fastness of Haworth. And, in the light of this, was she tempted to any further public story which, sense told her, could not be? Though reason warned against her new longing for letters from 'Cornhill', she remained susceptible, like Elizabeth Hastings who requires more of society than acceptance: she requires an emotional tie.

Charlotte's visits to London were 'rewards' for work, but also try-outs of a dream which Smith seemed to encourage – now and then. As a young man, with his way to make, he could have married one of the most celebrated writers of the day. As her astute judgement of his publications, her warmth and integrity, and playful humour presented themselves through prompt letters, he had the discernment to recognise how much she had to offer. Long after Charlotte's death, in December 1900, just before Smith died, he said something which would have pleased her: he said that her personal quality had interested him even more than her books. Because he had accepted her so enthusiastically in her character as Currer Bell, he freed that aspect of Charlotte Brontë that *was* Currer Bell; and it cannot have been other than heady for her to venture to close the gap between woman and writer. What Smith had in common with Heger is that both seemed to offer the opportunity Rochester offers Jane: the freedom to become visible.

Without much imagination himself, George Smith had an intuitive sympathy with imagination in others and a respect for those who pursued intellectual ideals rather than mere prosperity. Smith's pride in his association with what Leslie Stephen called 'the upper world of literature' drew him to Charlotte Brontë who revealed more of the wit in her home character than to anyone else outside the Parsonage – but exactly how far he was drawn was a matter for play and testing. Both shifted back and forth in their approaches to the border of friendship, with Charlotte more or less convinced that her sanguine, rising publisher was destined for happiness beyond her lot. Her self-control and withdrawal, her shifting view of George Smith, she transmutes into fiction: the reserve of Lucy Snowe in relation to the chivalric Graham Bretton or, as he was called abroad, Dr John. One contemporary reader noted that Lucy 'scarcely gave him a chance.' In his memoir of Charlotte Brontë, George Smith owned that he had 'stood for' Graham Bretton, and recalled that she had confirmed this to Mrs Gaskell.

A month after Charlotte's first stay with the Smiths, on 23 January 1850, she wrote her first fragment of the novel which became *Villette*. It shows that from the start the speaker is a woman who has not known herself. She thinks herself 'by nature enduring and forebearing', serene and unimaginative, despite 'a gift for inventing tales'. Her attempt to recount her life is to be an 'experiment' – perhaps an experiment with the spinster-bogey which had haunted Charlotte as far back as *The Professor*: the effect on a woman of persistent serenity, submission, and self-control. In the third (undated) fragment, which looks back to childhood, a younger child [Paulina] confides to a boy, Graham [Bretton], that the narrator 'is something strange – I think a witch.' In lines added at the foot of the page, she is called 'the silentest watchingest girl that ever lived'. In the final (also undated) fragment, Paulina and the narrator, Lucy Snowe, now grown up and living abroad, discuss Graham, who has become their focus of interest. They speculate about his flirtation with Miss Liddell (a discarded name for the shallow Ginevra Fanshawe), and they go on to speculate about the extent of Graham's careless levity:

> 'Lucy –' she asked presently 'Do you think Graham inclined
> to be of a fickle nature?'
> I replied that I was not sure whether he was fickle or not.
> 'I believe he is' She went on 'many ideas come into my mind
> about him – perhaps some of them unwarranted. I believe it
> would not be wise in any person to – to – what is called – to *love*
> him. I found in a book the other day what I have a secret con-
> viction is his exact picture – it was a description of one who
> > *Laughed* at the flame he felt or lit
> > Replied to tenderness with wit –
> and there is more of the passage and it is all like him – I know
> it is – I know that he too when he discovered and fully felt he
> was cared for would all

      Calm – supine – but pleased no less
      Softly sustain each soft caress
and *only* sustain it.'

'How strong' I remarked 'is the impression on your mind of
Graham's independence of sympathy and proud heartsease.'

'Ah! I remember my childhood' – said she – 'how gay and
hard – how good and cruel – how dear and pitiless he was to
me . . .'

'And what would you find him now?' asked I. And I
answered myself. 'You would find him gay – good and dear.
The hard, the pitiless – the cruel have all melted away –'

I am afraid I did not quite believe what I said – but I *did*
believe that if there had been sometimes a relentless levity in
his manner to me – Lucy Snowe – there would be none to
Paulina – Countess de Bassompierre. She need not fear it – the
powerful charm of beauty as well as the legitimate influence of
rank warranted security on that head.

And now I entered into details about his general character – and communicated proofs of his bounties and charities his
tender mercies & loving-kindnesses I had seen with my own
eyes . . .

To what extent did these ambiguities derive from Charlotte's
knowledge of George Smith? A light half-caressing, half-ironic
shone aslant in his eyes. He had a sweet smile, a face beaming
with health and energy, and an assurance that showed in the way
he carried his head and body. Leslie Stephen likened him to a
captain of a sound ship as he welcomed an author aboard. He
invited a joking relationship. He liked to call Newby (the devious
publisher of Emily and Anne), 'the Nubian Desert' – for Newby
yielded nothing. When Cardinal Wiseman was appointed
Archbishop of Westminster, Charlotte entertained Smith, in
turn, with comic sketches on the Catholicising of Cornhill.
Thackeray always played the role of penitent, limping to Smith
'with peas in his shoes', for a long delay with his Christmas book.

Another time, as punishment for idleness and gourmandising, he was made to work all day on bread and water.

As Charlotte played this back with keen enjoyment, she did wish Smith more serious. His mirth did not reassure; his raillery was too at the ready. But when she withdrew, he did have the awareness to pick up a scarce-thought reproach. His pleasant directness calmed her; his advice was to do as he and his mother: cultivate happiness. Mrs Smith was never in the least downcast; she carried anxieties easily. In the same way, no stroke of misfortune ever shook her son's confidence. If Charlotte knew the venom of critics like Lewes in the winter of 1849–50, she found in George Smith consolations too fine not to welcome his beneficence.

Curiously, it was George Smith himself who suggested Cornhill – by implication, himself – as a subject for a novel. He came to figure as a decent, urbane, princely man, on the border of sympathies and understanding that lie beyond the conventions of the age. Could he cross that border? George Smith's chivalrous but rather shifting relation to Charlotte bears on her exploration of a woman's buried needs in the course of *Villette*, between January 1850 and the end of 1852.

The play on the border of friendship was renewed with Charlotte's next visit to the Smiths, six months after the visit in 1849, from the end of May until the end of June 1850. When George Smith escorted Charlotte to the House of Commons, she was seated in the Ladies' Gallery, behind the Strangers' Gallery, from which only the eyes of the women could be seen. Smith instructed her to signal with her eyes when she grew tired. As Smith scanned the gallery above him, it seemed to the handsome young man that not one pair of eyes but all were flashing responses to his attention. As much as he admired Miss Brontë's luminous eyes, he could not distinguish hers from the others.

'I looked so earnestly from one pair of eyes to another', Smith recalled, 'that I am afraid more than one lady must have regarded me as rather an impudent fellow. At length I went round and took my lady away.'

When he apologised for his delay, he said something about the difficulty of getting out after he saw her signal.

'I made no signal', she replied. 'I did not wish to come away. Perhaps there were other signals from the Gallery.'

She was glad to relinquish invitations from a persistent lioniser, Sir James Kay-Shuttleworth, in favour of Mrs Smith's calm hospitality. And it gratified Mrs Smith that Charlotte preferred the cheerful middle-class comfort of their new home at 76 (later 112) Gloucester Terrace to the grandeur of Sir James with his forcefulness and nervous fuss. Mrs Smith took the cue from her son – her easy kindness touched Charlotte, and from this time she began to write separately to Mrs Smith, warm, joking letters on a more domestic note, about, say, the baby's socks which Charlotte had undertaken to knit but which did not progress in a bottom drawer, or about Charlotte's vain promise of working a cushion for the Smiths and having embarrassed recourse to one given her by her prolific acquaintance, Amelia Ringrose.

In keeping with Charlotte's wish, there were again no parties, only meetings with select writers of her choice. During a two-hour call on Thackeray on 12 June, she told him his faults – presumably, her opinion that his novels abused women and that his susceptibility to aristocratic attentions wasted his gifts. 'The giant sat before me – I was moved to speak to him of some of his shortcomings (literary of course). One by one the faults came to my mind and one by one I brought them out . . . He did defend himself like a great Turk and heathen – that is to say the excuses were often worse than the crime itself'. To Charlotte, a writer had a vocation; she wanted to persuade Thackeray that he was a man with a mission, but Thackeray, with many jests, declined to recognise that mission – her heroics asked to be deflated. Meeting Lewes for the first time, she forgave a crass review of *Shirley* because there was something about his looks, his rather prominent mouth, that recalled Emily. But when Lewes proposed that they had both written 'naughty' books, she answered this impertinence with a torrent of indignation. George Smith watched 'with mingled admiration and alarm' as 'the fire concealed beneath her mildness broke out.' He acknowledged that Lewes could say very coarse things in a soft, gracious voice as if he were totally unconscious of the bearing of his remark.

When George Smith learnt of Charlotte's childhood fixation on the Duke of Wellington, he took her to the Chapel Royal, St James's which the Duke attended every Sunday. According to Smith, they 'followed the Duke out of the Chapel and I indulged Miss Brontë by so arranging our walk that she met him twice.'

The Smiths pressed Charlotte to extend her visit, and she stayed another week. One of Smith's reasons was to fulfil a present which he wished to make Mr Brontë: a drawing of his famous daughter. Accordingly, on Thursday 13, Saturday 15, and Monday 24 June, Charlotte went to 10 York Street, off Baker Street, to sit for the artist, George Richmond. He saw a short woman who was 'not remarkable in appearance except for having eyes of extraordinary brilliancy and penetration.' Richmond did not allow sitters to see portraits in progress. On the last day of the sittings, Charlotte came with Mr Nicholls (Richmond recalled) and the picture was shown to them. (How did she come to be going about London with Mr Nicholls? In London did she feel safe from ridicule for chasing a curate, which she feared in Haworth? There are no further facts beyond this one memory, but it suggests the possibility of a closer contact between Charlotte and Arthur Bell Nicholls than anyone knew. It did require a certain degree of closeness to take him to see her portrait which she had not yet seen.) To Nicholls, the likeness was admirable, particularly the great breadth of Charlotte's forehead (it was so broad, he remarked later, that she often tried to cover it with her hair). Her shining hair, parted in the centre, is drawn in smooth swathes over her ears. The breadth of her forehead is balanced by a swan neck which perhaps owed its length to artistic invention.

But the focus of the portrait is the intent look in her large brown eyes, a look that is at once observant, level, and visionary.

Richmond, standing at Charlotte's side, waiting for her verdict, noticed that tears were running down her cheeks.

She turned to him, half in apology and said: 'Oh, Mr Richmond, it is so like Anne!' The artist had slimmed down Charlotte's broader features so that she looked more like her sisters.

The inward beauty suggested by this idealised drawing shows nothing whatever of Charlotte's awkwardness and reddish complexion, nor of the plainness that both Charlotte and her contemporaries remark. Possibly, the plainness lay chiefly in her irregular teeth and the set of her mouth when she spoke, but here in the portrait it is neatly closed: it is not a rosebud mouth, beloved by Victorians, but its wide line, with a slightly fuller and firmer underlip, has resolution. In reconsidering the reputed 'plainness' of Charlotte Brontë, we might bear in mind how far images of female beauty change with fashion. In the context of doll-like figures in stiff skirts, many petticoats, and featureless faces, Charlotte Brontë in limp silk or wool (Mr Brontë would not permit more fashionable materials, like taffeta, because of his fear of fire) may well have appeared odd: it was not fashionable for a woman to be thin and expressive. We might contrast the imagined inward life in Richmond's portrait of Charlotte Brontë with his more external portrait of Mrs Gaskell. She has a gracious mildness but, at this distance in time, the animation of Charlotte Brontë is more attractive.

George Smith pressed her to join him and his sister when they went to Scotland to collect their brother from school. At first Charlotte refused on account of Mrs Smith. But the son was master of his mother: Mrs Smith bowed to his wish, and begged Charlotte to accept. She told Ellen that she and George Smith understood each other – in other words, Mrs Smith had nothing to fear.

En route to the north, Charlotte stayed at Brookroyd, near

Leeds, with Ellen, and for some reason prolonged her stay. To Smith's annoyance she did not join him for a tour of the Highlands (this may have been Charlotte's concession to Mrs Smith), but she did meet him for two days, 4–5 July, in Edinburgh. A flurry of letters speak of Edinburgh as of paradise: its history, its graces, she owned, were suffused by congenial company. These days were 'as happy almost as any I ever spent' – an unprecedented statement from Charlotte Brontë. George Smith rejoiced in what he called 'a certain faculty for reading men'. What he and Charlotte had in common was an astute observation of character, a relish for detail, and a willingness to speak directly from experience without any tedious parade of learning. He rarely generalised and never prosed. When he spoke of books, though he never pretended to be a connoisseur, what he said was fresh and pithy, bending his head to gather her 'adroit' advice, with no sense that to do so might imperil his manhood. At the same time, she noted, he enjoyed a sleek self-regard, striding forward in the pink of his mother's pampering: the rare happiness of this gifted woman entertained and pleased him, and he had some recklessness in exciting, some vanity in reflecting it. (Later, in *Villette*, describing the effect of Dr John on the still, shadowed life of the teacher-heroine, she would draw on the forest imagery of the Sleeping Beauty: 'Conceive a dell deep-hollowed in forest secresy; it lies in dimness and mist'. An axe clears a way: 'the breeze sweeps in; the sun looks down; the sad, cold dell becomes a deep cup of lustre . . .') In this interlude, Charlotte journeyed on, in George Smith's company, to Abbotsford (the property near Melrose on the Tweed which her beloved Scott had bought in 1811), enjoying 'a lyric, brief, bright, clear and vital as a flash of lightning'. Edinburgh was 'mine own romantic town'.

At the end of this idyll, she and George Smith travelled on the same train south, Charlotte alighting at York. It was hard to part, and to find her father highly agitated on her arrival at the Parsonage: as he put it, she had 'received some overtures' which could lead to marriage. Charlotte herself became agitated: her need to hear from George Smith was so urgent, she confided to Ellen, that to protect herself, she should 'close all the correspondence on some quiet pretext'.

She preferred Scotland to the Lakes where she went unwillingly, at Papa's insistence, to join the Shuttleworths in August. Twelve years older than Charlotte, Sir James Kay-Shuttleworth was one of those strenuously energetic Vctorians: starting his career as a teacher among the poor, he was an advocate of free libraries and free national education, his efforts culminating in the Education Bill of 1870. He was also keen to promote the higher education of women, but like many reformers, too overbearing for domestic comfort. In between his tireless projects (for he was also a doctor interested in sanitary reform) he wrote novels, and part of his interest in Currer Bell may have been a wish for an introduction to a publisher. In his role as a practical man he tended to go on at length on 'the beauty of expediency' and how artists should 'bring themselves down to a lower level', flashing his Carker-teeth in terrible smiles, while his captive guest was obliged to listen with resignation. Privately, she told George Smith, that at the very time 'Sir James was warning me against the faults of the artist class, all the while vagrant artist instincts were busy in the mind of his listener.' At Briery Close, Windermere, she had to hide the 'she-artist' who might jar her host's egotism. He was one of the powerful, she perceived, who are nine parts utility to one part artistic interests. Drawn to artists, he was touchy about not being one himself. She suspected that he would not forgive unless an offender grovelled. With such hardness, Charlotte was most divorced from her home character: politely half-at-ease. Trapped in his carriage as they viewed lakes and fells, she longed (she confided later to Miss Wooler) 'to slip out unseen, and to run away by myself in amongst the hills and dales. Erratic and vagrant instincts tormented me, and these I was obliged to control, or rather, suppress — for fear of drawing attention to the "lioness" . . . — the she-artist. Sir James is a man of ability – even of intellect – but not a man in whose presence one willingly unbends.' But she did, to some extent, unbend with another guest, Mrs Gaskell.

Elizabeth Cleghorn Gaskell was six years older than Charlotte, just forty when they met, and had recently published her first novel, *Mary Barton*, in 1848, which Charlotte had read during her most terrible year of three family deaths while she wrote *Shirley*. In fact, Mrs Gaskell had written her first novel in not dissimilar circumstances: as a distraction from grief at the death of her only son. These two novels share a humanitarian plea for better understanding between employers and workers, and warm-hearted sympathy for the needy at the periphery of society: where Mrs Gaskell dwelt on the poor and the outcast, Charlotte Brontë dwelt on the social plight of single women. Though *Mary Barton* had won an ally in Dickens, in the summer of 1850 Mrs Gaskell was still at the outset of her career with her best works still to come: *Cranford* (1853); *North and South* (1855); *Wives and Daughters* (1866); and not least her celebrated biography of Charlotte Brontë in 1857, published by George Smith. Most of her work was first published by Dickens in his periodicals, *Household Words* and *All the Year Round*, alongside contributions from Wilkie Collins, Meredith, Coventry Patmore, and Dickens himself, but she and Dickens were not congenial – she did not always do as he wished. He once exclaimed: 'If I were Mr G. Oh Heaven how I would beat her!' In fact, Mrs Gaskell was a good and helpful wife of a Unitarian minister, endlessly active in her care of the needy in his parish. She was also thought a very beautiful woman.

Where Mr Nicholls saw the great span of Charlotte's forehead, Mrs Gaskell saw an overhanging brow, missing teeth, and hands like birds' claws. Though Miss Brontë had open, expressive eyes looking straight at you, a sweet, slightly hesitating voice, and just, well-phrased views, Mrs Gaskell thought her fellow-guest 'altogether *plain*'. At the same time, Charlotte's reticence about her great losses, as well as her modest refinement reassured Mrs

Gaskell as to coarseness. Mrs Gaskell had a queenly manner that was engaging, not condescending: this was the effect of her flow of talk. She talked readily about her present feelings and passed on her rather colourful stories of others, in a way that communicated her strong curiosity, but she did this disarmingly, without hurry or pressure, disseminating a mood of ease, leisure, and playful geniality which encouraged response. Deftly, she drew from Charlotte the story of her life. This 'life of desolation', as relayed by Mrs Gaskell to friends, at once formulates the image of a shy, silent Charlotte Brontë who had 'gone through suffering enough to have taken out every spark of merriment'. This was Mrs Gaskell's first and lasting impression: a sterling, nervous 'poor thing' who could hardly smile – a far cry from Charlotte's merry correspondence with George Smith (the full scope of which was not known till the 1980s).

In her biography of Mrs Gaskell, Jenny Uglow observes that in some ways Charlotte was 'tougher' than her new friend. Though Mrs Gaskell gave the impression of vigour, with her liveliness and all-encompassing busy-ness, her reddish-brown complexion, and tall, full figure, she tended to give in to stress with migraines, neuralgia, and spells of lassitude, propped by opiates. In contrast, Charlotte (who never took one grain of opium at a time when it was widely used) had been able to write the first book of *Jane Eyre* under the stress of her father's unanaesthetised eye operation in Manchester in 1846 (she was present at his wish), during the uncertain weeks of his recovery, and plagued at the same time by toothache. Yet despite such amazing feats in adverse circumstances (we might recall, also, the final book of *Shirley*), she continued to look childlike and tiny. Emphasising this vulnerable image, Mrs Gaskell was responsible for circulating the rumour that Charlotte was 'already tainted with consumption', a view that took root in literary circles and proved damaging in that it convinced Mrs Smith that Charlotte was unmarriageable and her son in need of protection. Over the next year, crucial to her happiness, Charlotte tried in vain to deny this rumour. 'Poor Miss Brontë' was the echo when Catherine Winkworth, the recipient of Mrs Gaskell's outline, passed the letter to her sister, Emily, who was moved just enough to concede: 'One feels that her life at least *almost* makes one like her books, though one does not want there to be any more Miss Brontës . . .'

From the perspective of Mrs Gaskell's domestic content, with her kind husband, four daughters, and warm ties with her husband's parishioners, she was struck by the wretchedness of Charlotte's life: the loneliness, genteel poverty, illness, deaths, and the passive aspect of filial duty. The future biographer at once slid her subject into the sentimental slots of the time: the woman as victim, self-sacrificial, and beset by deathbeds. In *Ruth* (the novel Mrs Gaskell was writing at the same time as *Villette*), she did speak out for a fallen woman, but when Charlotte read the outline she asked why Ruth had to *die*? This query challenged a morality which decreed that Ruth could atone only through death. In a similar way, Mrs Gaskell's eventual biography would redeem Charlotte's reputation for 'coarseness' through the sadness of doom. Sensing misapprehension, Charlotte asked Mrs Gaskell not to pity her too much. After all, she still had Truth and she still had her father.

But Papa could not fill the loneliness of her return to Haworth after this active summer. In September, she was afraid to write to Cornhill in case she did not get the reply she wanted – wanted too badly for her own good. This waiting for letters was always a sign of suppressed feeling that rose to a fever of expectation as the time for the post came, and then slumped when nothing arrived. The post seems to have been the only event of the day.

She told Miss Wooler that she did not wish to fill this void with visiting ('indiscriminate visiting tends only to a waste of time and a vulgarizing of character'); what she wanted were a few strong ties and domestic talk.

The least allusion to marriage was most offensive to Papa. She believed she could marry – she meant James Taylor – but so far she had not met any man who would marry her whom she thought 'truly desirable'. What she implied in this confidence to Ellen was, first, that she could not desire Mr Taylor. She may already have been aware of Mr Nicholls in the wings, but he remained, as yet, too available, too familiar, no more than a reliable oak in contrast with base fellow-curates. It is possible that Charlotte's words also implied the existence of a desirable man who would not marry her: George Smith, who was eight years younger and protected both by his mother and by his own vein of Scottish caution which Charlotte at once detected.

The autumn of 1850 was a time of 'bad days, weeks, months', as Charlotte wrote to Miss Martineau, envying her even productivity. In September and October, loneliness deepened into renewed mourning as she edited *Wuthering Heights* and *Agnes Grey* for Smith, Elder. In the course of describing her sisters in a 'Biographical Notice', she realised that her own bitter pain would only be 'soft pathos' to readers. Grief was not communicable. When she read Tennyson's newly published *In Memoriam*, a long poem on the loss of the friend of his youth, Arthur Hallam, she said: 'It is beautiful; it is mournful; it is monotonous.' She was sceptical of a grief that could command such a flow of words; Tennyson could not have written in this way of a brother. Nor would she have stuck in helpless melancholy: she preferred a mind like George Sand's which 'disastrous experience teaches without weakening or too much disheartening' so that the longer you live, the better you grow.

Alternating between renewed grief and relief in her own resilience, she brooded over her sisters' achievements. Her introductory Notice to their novels is curiously apologetic and critical, even competitive, as though she wished the public to dissociate Currer Bell who understood manners, good taste, and appropriate subject-matter, from Ellis and Acton Bell who chose such deplorable material as the demonic Heathcliff and the dipsomaniac husband of the estranged tenant of Wildfell Hall. Her

Notice is a blueprint for Mrs Gaskell: it separates Emily and Anne from their works, assuring the public that they were ladies of the utmost refinement. Charlotte interpreted her sisters to the world – the instigator of Brontë legend – interposing herself between her family and future readers. Her sisters, she claimed, were innocent of the savagery of their subjects, which befell their pens as the inevitable result of living out their lives in darkest Yorkshire. In her most ladylike manner she turned away the nastiness of Anne's close-up of a disrupted marriage. Anne, she insisted, was a delicate and gentle creature who hardly knew what she did. She bent over backwards to see Emily's fiction through the shocked eyes of its first readers: 'Men and women who, . . . with feelings moderate in degree, and little marked in kind, have been trained from their cradle to observe the utmost evenness of manner and guardedness of language, will hardly know what to make of the rough, strong utterance, the harshly manifested passions, the unbridled aversions, and headlong partialities' of *Wuthering Heights*. Yet, as she reread this novel two years after Emily's death, that autumn of 1850, it is possible that she herself took on more of the intransigence of Emily's nature. This was to find a voice in a more contemptuous heroine who puts truth before lovability – a frosty heroine whom Charlotte did not expect others to like, whom she professed not to like herself, and yet a woman of hidden substance, at a remove from all contemporaries, especially the artifice of her female acquaintance.

A new asperity sounds in her own voice from this time, her 'indignation and contempt' for reviewers and her sarcasm with Lewes over the *Leader*'s tolerance towards Catholicism. Eighteen-fifty was the year of the so-called 'papal aggression', when the Pope's establishment of territorial bishoprics in England, and his appointment of Wiseman as Archbishop, led to fierce anti-Catholic outbursts in which Charlotte participated with an intolerance she reserved for Catholicism alone – an intolerance which may have derived, in part, from fear of her own susceptibility. In her most sarcastic manner, she congratulated Lewes on his likely conversion: 'There is something promising and touching in the tone you have lately assumed – a something which will kindle the glow of holy expectation in the heart of Cardinal Archbishop Wiseman when his chaplain reads to him your lucubrations.' She went on to imply that Wiseman was a hypocritical Jesuit, and finally wished Lewes and Thornton Hunt 'much facility of speech in your first experiment in auricular confession'.

During a restorative visit to Miss Martineau's home, The Knoll at Ambleside, from 16 to 23 December, she met Matthew Arnold at Fox How, a house which looked to her like a nest half-buried in flowers and creepers. Matthew, at twenty-eight, was the eldest son of the eminent Dr Arnold of Rugby who, during his years as headmaster from 1828 to 1842, had changed the idea of the public school, subduing brutality in favour of manliness and cricket. The year before his meeting with Charlotte Brontë, Matthew Arnold had published his first volume of poems; the year after their meeting he married and became an inspector of schools. He is best remembered for later work: his poem 'Dover Beach' (1867) and as a critic of the 1860s–1880s who resisted cultural 'Philistinism', and set out as 'touchstones' the high points of thought and literature. He walked into a room with a grand air, his chin aloft in a way that explained why he had been known at Rugby as 'the lofty Matt'. He had an impressive presence, over six foot high, very upright, and crowned with abundant hair.

He liked to be thought younger than he was. If Arnold had a sneer for Miss Brontë ('past thirty and plain'), it was nothing to the more subtly caustic view she formed of him: 'Striking and prepossessing in appearance, his manner displeases, from its seeming foppery . . . Ere long a real modesty appeared under his assumed conceit, and some genuine intellectual aspirations . . . displaced superficial affectations.'

Arnold's notorious slight that Charlotte Brontë was nothing but 'hunger, rebellion, and rage' would not have surprised her.

Rude reviews had already taught her the willingness of people to slander a woman in a way from which men were exempt. Dickens was able to limit the talk when he dismissed his wife of many years for a nineteen-year-old actress, Ellen Ternan. False rumour, on the other hand, pursued Charlotte Brontë as soon as she became famous: one report was that in London she did not attend church but went to balls all week; another was that she had been jilted by one – no, three – curates in succession. She was aware of vindictiveness against the 'she-artist' who dared abandon the model of passivity and silence enjoined on women.

With relief, she returned to the unconventional company of Harriet Martineau: harsh she was, abrupt, despotic, but invigorating too, a model of industry. She rose at five, took a walk by starlight and was at her desk by seven. They spent the afternoons together, had dinner at five, and discussed work with frankness. In this bracing atmosphere, her guest soon recovered.

In January 1851, George Smith invited Charlotte to accompany him on a Rhine journey the following summer. The prospect brought on a 'fever' of anticipation though she feared Mrs Smith would resist and London would gossip. It was impossible not to respond to the 'excitement' of Smith's letter: 'I am not made of granite', she excused herself. Ellen, with whom she shared her more interesting letters, detected 'fixed intentions' on Smith's part, backed by an 'undercurrent' of feeling.

Charlotte replied as sensibly as she could: 'I think the "undercurrent" amounts simply to this – a kind of natural liking and a sense of something congenial. Were there no vast barrier of age, fortune, etc. there is perhaps enough personal regard to make things possible which are now impossible. If men and women married because they liked each other's temper, look, conversation, nature and so on – and if besides, years were more nearly equal – the chance you allude to might be admitted as a chance but other reasons regulate matrimony – reasons of convenience, of connection, of money. Meantime I am content to have him as a friend – and pray God to continue to me the common sense to look on one so young, so rising, so hopeful in no other light.'

At this time, Ellen was pursued capriciously by Mary's brother, John. Both women needed 'wisdom', Charlotte warned as Ellen teased her about 'Venus' and 'Jupiter' (Ellen's name for George Smith). Charlotte, furiously rejecting the 'heathen' innuendo, insisted that his manager, James Taylor, was the likely suitor. Taylor continued to woo her with books but was, alas, 'not bothered by much vehement ardour'.

The contrast between an unpredictable 'Jupiter' and a dependable Taylor might be said to be the main plot of a drama whose subplot began early in February 1851, when George Smith rejected *The Professor* a third time. Altogether, as Charlotte pointed out, this novel had been rejected nine times. Smith then made the extraordinary suggestion that he would take *The Professor* 'into custody' in lieu of publication. Perhaps he thought this would release Charlotte from an obstinate attachment.

She refused the offer categorically. 'Ah, no!' He might, she pictured, make tapers with the manuscript to light his cigars. No, she would lock it safely in its own cupboard at Haworth, for she remained partial to it 'as a doting parent towards an idiot child'.

Her tart voice came into being more fully that month as she talked of the need to begin her novel. Far from putting *The Professor* aside, she recast the professor in a form closer to his Belgian source. She began with the youthful aspect of a pampered, humorous Briton (called Bretton), so as to set up a contrast between him and the Belgian. One organising idea was to measure two potential heroes: the light-spirited Bretton (based on George Smith), and the vehement teacher, Paul Emanuel (based on M. Heger). In setting up this experiment, the author deferred the outcome. The structure of the test allowed her the freedom to follow the course of emotional truth as it evolved.

The go-ahead came early in March 1851 when George Smith

proposed that Charlotte use 'Cornhill' as material for a novel. This was, she replied, 'most dangerously suggestive'. She felt like the serpent at the opening of Paradise. Already, she was gliding to the entrance – her luminous eyes on George Smith, as she marked his assent to an idea that lurked, already, in two of the fragments. Plans, undefined possibilities, seemed, like their letters, to play together.

'Don't be alarmed.' It was the snake speaking. 'You are all safe from Currer Bell – safe from his satire – safer from his eulogium.' Ignoring past practice, the snake claims that Currer Bell could not write if his subjects knew the hand that sketched them. 'So – I repeat it – you are *very* safe.'

Charlotte's letters to George Smith in 1850–51 were not letters to an editor; they were playful offers of transformation. Without higher education, he had doubts about his intellect: this one buried aspect to George Smith was the main source of his susceptibility to Charlotte Brontë who waved a creator's wand over him. Attentive, analytical, her letters treated him like one of her more promising characters – and this, too, may have been one reason why he was more drawn by her letters than by her physical presence (in person, she tended to reticence, except for the odd flare of eloquence). Her letters invited him to see himself as a man of artistic and generous potentialities who could transcend the 'hard-headed, tight-fisted man of business' which he claimed to be. After their Scottish holiday, she urged him to write a poem on the Highlands; when Thackeray tried Smith's temper with delays, she suggested he write a book on the trials of 'a spirited publisher'. When Charlotte awaited Smith's replies, she was awaiting the results of her creative powers. (For the writer-heroine in the manuscript of *Villette*, a letter will prove a better form of 'utterance' than her 'weak' bodily presence and faltering lips.) Since Charlotte could not expect to hold her publisher through personal graces, could she hold him through her pen? In a sense, she set up the same test with George Smith, almost against her volition, against her own repeated self-warnings, as she had set up with another man responsive to writing – Monsieur.

When Smith knew Charlotte he was still in his twenties, yet in the making. He was drawn to her idea of his nature, as lengthy letters on this unbusinesslike subject raced back and forth between Yorkshire and London. 'You happen not quite to know yourself', she told him.

The fictional version of Smith's character is explored more freely than in letters: in the form of a doctor abroad, he is observed through the detached eyes of an apparently insignificant teacher who has no claim on his attention. The fact that he helps her in distress testifies to a genuine gallantry. In the light of a lamp she saw 'that he was a young, distinguished, and handsome man; he might be a lord, for anything I knew: nature had made him good enough for a prince, I thought. His face was very pleasant; he looked high but not arrogant, manly but not overbearing.' Here, clearly, is a potential hero. Or is he? He is winning to all – Lucy sees that his eye 'glanced from face to face rather too vividly, too quickly, and too often, but it had a most pleasant character . . . As to his smile, . . . there was something in it that pleased, but something too that brought surging up into the mind all one's foibles and weak points: all that could lay one open to a laugh'. His unfailing courtesy, his air 'of good-natured amenity' has a dash of indifference. Where the letters from Charlotte Brontë to George Smith were educative, the novel was testing – it tested both an individual man and the nature of a potential hero.

A great novel emerged from this interplay of writer and publisher. This was not the work of a victim. As victim, Charlotte Brontë would have surrendered to grief, depression, and the pattern of family doom, but in the face of this possibility she bestirred herself to act according to her powers. This is reflected in her heroine who may appear blighted and passive, but is strong, severe in judgement, and ultimately, creative. The truth of this portrait, as it derives from its author when she had to face life alone in the early 1850s, was an act of defiance against what fate denied her: family and love as she once glimpsed its fullness through an exchange of letters.

For some the most intense feeling, whether it be erotic or religious, requires mystery, concealment, privacy, and a sense of the unspeakable. This was true of all the Brontë sisters. There is no truth which does not include lost facts and silence – the question of what is *not* said. Where does the abundant speaking voice of Charlotte Brontë meet the silent flight of her feeling? Does language exist for passion as she experienced it? And how much does even an exceptionally candid writer conceal when she puts pen to paper? Her 'Reader' is the person who responds to the stimulus of secrecy, the tension between the snowy social self and the ardent inner self. Without secrecy, there would have been no art. For advancing women in the nineteenth century, the gap between public and private was so great that the pressure of art (in the sense of truth, utterance, exposure) was the more explosive. We cannot gauge Charlotte Brontë's life without this gap, what she called 'shadow'. And the prevalence of 'shadow' – not attenuated as grief, but in the fullness of desire and subversion – would have been exactly what was suspect in her life, and therefore not allowed to survive when certain of her papers were destroyed after her death. Still, the novels remain to tell us about the shadow in which Charlotte Brontë lived, and which she interpreted for her 'Reader'. Gaps have the interest of suggestion; the works can define their meaning. And if Charlotte Brontë was deprived in many unhappy ways, she was not bereft of work and the shape art finds in the amorphousness of daily experience. As Charlotte conceived this novel, she directed an enquiry into definitions of women and men, which lent meaning to her solitude, deprivation, and need. Though these sufferings did exist undeniably, they existed (in her own terms) not as pathos but as Truth.

The visible drama took over at the end of March. Smith,

Elder had entered a shaky period which was to affect Charlotte in two ways. George Smith, now working often till three in the morning, had to cancel the Rhine journey. Also, he was sending James Taylor to India to open a branch of the firm called Smith and Taylor. This was not a measure of buoyant expansion but a manoeuvre to prop the firm. When Taylor came to visit Charlotte at Haworth at the beginning of April, she noticed that he never mentioned his employer's name but spoke only of 'the firm'. Was there some tension between him and Smith?

It was clear that James Taylor had made the journey to Haworth to propose to Charlotte before he sailed. Charlotte was disposed to like him for his vigour and 'pith' of mind, but in person, again, found his manner abrupt and jarring. She was hard put to hold still as he looked at her in his keen way and the inflexible lines of his face came into focus through her spectacles. Whenever he came near – near enough to see his eyes fastened upon her – her veins 'ran ice'. Though she did not wish to be proud, she felt her body stiffen 'with a strange mixture of apprehension and anger'. So Mr Taylor left without declaring himself. Though Charlotte did invite him to write from India, she told Ellen she could not think of him as a husband:

> It would sound harsh were I to tell even *you* of the estimate I felt compelled to form respecting him; dear Nell, I looked for something of the gentleman – something I mean of the *natural* gentleman; you know I can dispense with acquired polish, and [as] for looks, I know myself too well to think that I have any right to be exacting on that point. I could not find one gleam, I could not see one passing glimpse of good-breeding; it is hard to say, but it is true. In mind too; though clever, he is second-rate; thoroughly second-rate. One does not like to say these things, but one had better be honest. Were I to marry him my heart would bleed in pain and humiliation . . . No – if Mr

Taylor be the only husband fate offers to me, single I must always remain.

... With kind regards to all, I am, dear Nell, your middle-aged friend,

C. Brontë.

It was disconcerting to find that Papa had taken a decided liking to Mr Taylor. Many explanations have been suggested, one of which is that, from Mr Brontë's point of view, the most desirable suitor was one who would disappear to the other side of the globe for five years. Another explanation might be that Mr Brontë did genuinely like Mr Taylor because they were both 'of the Helstone order'.

Papa was impatient when Charlotte queried whether Mr Taylor was a 'gentleman'. She thought him indelicate and possibly unfeeling. To Mr Brontë, the worth of hard-nosed rectitude made the issue of delicacy irrelevant. But instinct compelled Charlotte to exclude the idea of Mr Taylor from her mind – only, it left her deeper in solitude.

Two weeks later, Charlotte received an invitation from the Smiths. Though it was against her rule to go to London again before she had done much writing, she told Mrs Smith ruefully that she at once felt 'a great wish to descend from my stilts'. She was not made of granite, she owned a few days later to George. Here, dates tell of subtle pressures that could not be articulated. June was the date the Smiths proposed for the visit, and to this Charlotte quickly agreed. What was unstated was that she would miss James Taylor who was due to sail for India in mid-May. Charlotte had told the Smiths that Taylor's visit to Haworth had been a great pleasure. Such a deliberate lie was out of character. Was it a tease? And was Smith responding with a date which showed that he did not encourage the match?

Mr Taylor then wrote to ask if he might see her in London. Her decision to arrive towards the end of May, soon after his date of departure (20 May), would have told the suitor that she had no desire to see him.

There was a certain flurry to Charlotte's preparation for this visit to London that led Papa, the servants, and Mrs Nussey to think that she was about to get engaged – though she denied this emphatically. She asked Ellen to look in Leeds for lace cloaks, if not too costly, and bought herself a white mantilla, fresh shifts, and a bonnet with a pink lining. She wished she could afford some 'sweet pale silks' at 5s a yard, but had to buy the usual black silk at 3s.

In the midst of this shopping, she let Mrs Smith know that she had 'no ailment'. Ostensibly, she was denying false rumour; certainly, she was reassuring George Smith's mother that she was not, like her sisters, doomed by organic disease; but was she not also hinting that she was no less marriageable, for reasons of health, than Miss Smith whose sickliness necessitated a concerned query?

Amongst the attractions of George Smith were his moves at this time towards something warmer than friendship. His letters probed Charlotte's reserve. Was she prepared to admit that she would be glad to see him?

No, she replied with playful caution on 12 May, not 'glad', only 'pleased'.

Fanning anticipation, he sent back a letter of such impetuous satisfaction that Charlotte was afraid to show it to Ellen in case she mistook what Charlotte insisted was no more than a 'temporary' rise of feeling.

There was always this element of caution in her friendship with Smith, even now as it seemed to cross the border of something stronger. 'I dare not say I am happy – or see before me any very happy prospect in the future', she put it to Ellen. That pilgrim honesty (which never quite abandoned Charlotte to her emotions) scanned Smith's words, often in conjunction with Ellen. The fact that Charlotte once put Ellen down as merely a conscientious woman whom she happened to love, has led to the assumption that Ellen was mediocre. Though Ellen could not offer the critical response of Cornhill, she shared something better with Charlotte: the capacity to read character. Her observations of the Brontës themselves were unfailingly intelligent and empathic. Emily, who liked Ellen, would not have tolerated mediocrity for one moment – Charlotte once told Ellen that Emily esteemed her perhaps more than any other person outside the Parsonage. Charlotte would not have bothered to send Ellen all those sophisticated letters from Cornhill (those from the manager as well as from Smith) if Ellen had been unable to share in the subtle process of 'soul-reading'. To Ellen alone could Charlotte confide that she thought the manager 'second-rate'. They reminded each other of the necessity for wisdom when it came to the marriageable man. Many letters were exchanged on the subject of this challenge: the source, they observed, of much marital unhappiness. Women's 'reading' of men (and vice versa, as Jane Austen and George Eliot amply demonstrate) often takes place prematurely. With Charlotte and Ellen, we see two women, in their mid-thirties, refusing illusions that marriage is necessarily the most desirable situation for their sex. They shared their scepticism of 'the turtle-doves', the obligatory show of domestic bliss (undercut by helpless whining) from Amelia Ringrose who had succumbed to Mary's other unreliable brother, Joe. The flirt, the tyrant, and the fool must be avoided at any cost.

'John Taylor is a noodle', Charlotte warned Ellen against her suitor, as her own insides fluttered before her visit to London. She had a continuous stomach upset, and it concerned her that she was not looking her best.

On 28 May, she boarded the London express at Leeds. When it arrived at ten that night at Euston Square, George Smith and his mother were there to meet her.

He had changed, she saw at once. He was older, graver, more authoritative. His mother and sisters now deferred, it seemed, to every wish.

The fourth day after Charlotte's arrival, 1 June 1851, she marked with a 'white stone'. There is no record of what happened to make her 'very happy', but it was associated with a sermon she heard in the afternoon by a visiting Protestant, D'Aubigny. The sound of French blended with her happiness, unburying what she had felt for Monsieur. It was 'half sweet – half sad – and strangely suggestive to hear the French language once more.'

Years later, in the 1870s, Ellen told a Brontë biographer, Sir Wemyss Reid, that George Smith had proposed to Charlotte. I doubt this happened explicitly, since he was not a man to go back on his word; what seems more likely is that he reinforced the warmth of his anticipatory letter so that, for the space of one particular day, it may have seemed to Charlotte that his rise of feeling would not be 'temporary' after all.

And then, suddenly, hope vanished. Again, it is impossible to know what happened between 7 and 10 June, except for the fact that Smith withdrew into such unremitting work that Charlotte hardly saw him at 76 Gloucester Terrace. One possibility is that the crisis in the firm now took some turn for the worse. Charlotte may have perceived Smith's busy-ness as a withdrawal from the path she presented: with a shaky firm and a sense of responsibility for his large family of dependants, he would have to be more pragmatic from now on. Whatever the facts of the case, it was at this point that Charlotte decided that there was no future to her tie with George Smith beyond the limits of business and friendship, and I think, at this moment, she closed her fist, with resolution, on the sting. She would have behaved impeccably, granting tacit assent to the difficulty of Smith's situation.

Her reaction to Mrs Smith was quite different. After this visit Charlotte said that she wished she could think of Mrs Smith's kindness in the way she used to. As, in Charlotte's eyes, Mme Heger had been the enemy of her innocent feeling for Monsieur, so again she identified an obstruction in the shape of another woman. She concluded that Mrs Smith could not be won, after all; benign and hospitable as the mother was, she would exert her considerable influence on her son to take a prudent course. In a sense, the hidden drama of this visit to London was a struggle for George Smith, a struggle, it could be said, between his higher possibilities which Charlotte wished to elicit and his future as a worldly-wise gentleman. And if we are looking for the sources of creativity in the life, this issue in the making of George Smith lay behind Charlotte's evolving idea of *Villette*: could this kind of public man be redeemed as her hero?

Looking back at the end of his life, George Smith remembered his mother as 'indomitable'. This is also how Leslie Stephen recalled her: 'sanguine' and 'shrewd'. The son she formed was approved by other men of his time as firm and manly – such were the terms they used – extravagantly generous with Thackeray and George Eliot (authors who expected no less), confident and cheery, a commander with his temper under control. Smith recalled also his strong bond with his mother: 'more than ordinarily tender and intimate. Every interest was shared with her and every plan discussed.' Mrs Smith had a habit of coming into her son's room almost every morning for a little talk. He had no secrets from her: 'Few sons and mothers, indeed, have ever been on terms of closer confidence.'

Inevitably, then, Mama won. This is obvious from the cool tone of the bread-and-butter letter Charlotte penned to Mrs Smith after her departure, while her tone to George remained unchanged. She would have judged him in the best light, as a dutiful son. In the memoir written at the end of his life, Smith recalled that once, during a conversation at Cambridge, Sir James Stephen (Virginia Woolf's grandfather) had remarked that he had never met a perfectly just woman, and Smith had reflected that Sir James had not known Charlotte Brontë. Smith recalled further that Charlotte had been critical in her judgements of character, but not of action. 'Generally, I thought, she put too kind an interpretation on the actions of a friend.'

Between 7 and 10 June, flatness and headache set in and grew more violent until Charlotte felt sick and weak. She told Ellen that she had to rebuke the pleasant moments because it was now clear there was no future attached to them, and to indulge this pleasure would 'add to solitude'. Pleasure, she said, was 'no more to be relied on than the sunshine of a summer's day. I pass portions of many a night in extreme sadness.'

London was, once more, 'Babylon'. Though she admired Thackeray's public lectures on eighteenth-century humorists, she was astonished by his willingness to change the date of one lecture so that certain ladies should not be inconvenienced by having to give up Ascot. Thackeray greeted Charlotte audibly as 'Jane Eyre' at his second lecture, on Congreve and Addison, at Almack's Assembly Rooms, St James. Afterwards, Charlotte found herself, far from invisible, walking through two lines of admirers, her hand trembling on Mrs Smith's arm – trembling, it may be, with rage and chagrin to judge from her action, next morning, when Thackeray called to see her. She flew at him as he stood unhappily on the hearthrug.

'If *you* had come to our part of the country in Yorkshire, what would you have thought of me if I had introduced you to my father, before a mixed company of strangers, as "Mr Warrington"?'

'No, my dear, you mean "Arthur Pendennis".'

'*No*, I *don't* mean Arthur Pendennis!' she retorted fiercely. 'I mean Mr Warrington, and Mr Warrington was a gentleman, and he would not have behaved as you behaved to me yesterday.' As George Smith entered the room he heard Charlotte's explosive words like shells dropped into a fortress.

Thackeray concluded they could not be friends. 'There's a fire and fury raging in that little woman, a rage scorching her heart which doesn't suit me', he said in private. Smith saw that Thackeray had not the quickness necessary for repartee and was not fond of the society of what were called 'clever' women – women he felt to be critical and with whom talk involved mental strain. For this reason, he did not like Charlotte. Thackeray liked soft, worshipping women who put him at ease. In his talk with Charlotte he refused to be straight about writing; instead, he would banter, and burlesque their common pursuit as though he were ashamed of it. It vexed Charlotte to be treated in this unserious way.

On 7 June (the date Charlotte's troubles began), she was riveted and appalled by Rachel's acting (as Adrienne in Scribe's *Adrienne Lecouvreur*): 'her soul was in it' she wrote to Amelia Taylor, '– and a strange soul she has – . . . She and Thackeray are the only two living things that have a spell for me in this great London – and one of these is sold to the Great Ladies – and the other – I fear – to Beelzebub.' When she saw Rachel again on 21 June (as Camille in Corneille's tragedy, *Les Trois Horaces*), she saw 'a wonderful sight, terrible as if the earth had cracked deep at your feet . . .' What Charlotte feared was a part of herself: the temptation to expose raw emotions – rebellion, madness, rigid resistance. She saw an actress, a woman like 'Lucia', with her gifts on show, who closed with her public face to face, revealing without fear, with patent exhilaration, storm, rage, fire – the pent-up gamut of feelings. Charlotte set out her ambivalence, repeatedly, in letters as well as in *Villette* where she demonstrates, through an actress called Vashti, the uncomprehending contempt that such exposure must evoke. She believed that publicity was degrading if it were not 'glorious'. Degradation was a fear which never left her. 'There is something divine in the thought that genius preserves from degradation', she had written to Williams, 'were it but true; but Savage tells us it was not true for him; Sheridan confirms the avowal, and Byron seals it with terrible proof.' To see this was part of Charlotte's relentless honesty. She feared anarchic feeling, associated with Branwell, as evil licence. To what extent was creativity bound up with abandon? How far dared she go?

Yet another strand of Charlotte's life converged on that 7 June: on that day, in her third letter to Papa, she first sent her remembrances to Arthur Bell Nicholls. From this time it became her habit to include him in her wishes to the home circle whenever she was away.

Through most of June, low spirits and sickness continued to poison many moments which might have been pleasant. She was not much impressed by the Great Exhibition, a mix of Glass Town palace and bazaar. Then, during the last days of her stay, she appeared to recover.

On 25 June, George Smith took a day off to escort her to Richmond, and they devised a joint escapade. Disguising themselves as Mr and Miss Fraser (brother and sister), they had themselves examined by a fashionable phrenologist, Mr Browne. Immediately after Charlotte left London, Smith sent 'A Phrenological Estimate of the Talents and Dispositions of a Lady' (dated 29 June) as well as the Estimate of Mr Fraser. Mr Browne saw that 'Miss Fraser' was a gifted and acutely sensitive woman, but his portrait lacked 'shadow', Charlotte told George Smith. She asked him to add shadow 'in good broad masses . . .'

Charlotte had left London, on 27 June, resolving to moderate her attachment to Cornhill to avoid the disappointment of not being loved. She decided to inform Cornhill that she would expect no letter for three months, intending to extend her abstinence to six months. This sounds like a repeat of her arrangement with Monsieur, and she warned herself to avoid the misanthropy which accompanies revulsions of feeling. She was in close imaginative touch, now, with the precarious control of Lucy Snowe, who receives an unexpected letter from Graham with 'a glad emotion which went warm to my heart, and ran lively through all my veins. For once a hope was realized.' It was with similar surprise that a swift letter from George Smith caught Charlotte in Manchester where she had broken her return journey to Haworth, for two days, in order to visit Mrs Gaskell in her cheerful, airy house, filled with the perfume of her garden at 42 Plymouth Grove. Smith's letters to Charlotte Brontë have vanished, but she may well have described this particular letter in *Villette* where Graham writes to Lucy after she has spent several weeks in his home: 'he had written in benignant mood, dwelling with sunny satisfaction on scenes that had passed before his eyes and mine, – on places we had visited together – on conversations we had held – on all the little subject-matter, in short, of the last few halcyon weeks. But the cordial core of the delight was, a conviction the blithe, genial language generously imparted, that it had been poured out – not merely to content *me* – but to gratify *himself.*' Once more, George Smith's mirth, turning Charlotte's way, lent attention to their mutual investigations of character. She could not but respond, as before.

On 2 July, she wrote to say that the phrenologist's view of Mr Alexander Fraser accorded with her own highest hopes of him: 'I wanted a portrait, and have now got one very much to my mind . . . It is a sort of miracle – *like* – *like* – *like* as the very life itself . . . I am glad I have got it. I wanted it.' She made a copy, hoping again to redeem Smith and tease out of existence whatever compromising strand in his character she did not approve. Her advice to Mr Smith was to use the intellectual promise Browne, too, discerned: 'Be jealous of a shadow of falling off.' She resumed the bracing tone of Lucy Snowe: in future she would dole out her 'comfits' with an austere hand: she had not been 'at all pleased' to get his first letter; she must now tell him candidly that he had deserved a slap ('a hostile manual demonstration'), yet his own blows were worse than those he received. He took his medicine, she acknowledged, 'with grace beyond all praise', consistent with the phrenologist's report that Mr Fraser was entirely without arrogance.

Charlotte's playfulness was in the English vein of comfortable, not corrosive, humour. Nothing could seem farther from the impassioned French of her letters to Monsieur. With George Smith, the tone was distinctly English: a form of candour that is humorous, subtle, and not unrevealing but controlled through multiple shades of implication which seem to guard confession with the comedy of verbal play. Such candour extends a relationship through mutual amusement without exposure or pressure. So Charlotte responded to Smith's raillery, as he played on his listener as though he were enjoying a silent joke. The clean poise of his manners banished the sting: she discerned 'a touch of Mephistopheles with the fiend extracted.'

Despite this play, Charlotte had a covert message for George Smith which she spelt out even before she left Manchester to pursue *Villette*: if he wished her to get on with this work, he would have to grant her something of himself – not marriage, but the attention of special friendship, an attention – she insists – that must be reliable and regular. This is the deadly serious bargain behind what appears to be no more than a playful fantasy that George Smith would lodge her in a small chamber of her own at Cornhill, where she would labour from dawn to dusk with the sole but reliable pleasure of a dinner alone with him each evening 'of which [we] should partake together in the finest spirit of geniality and fraternity'. This message reappears in the novel where Lucy imagines that Graham keeps a place for her under the skylight (reminiscent of the skylight in George Smith's office) where she might be 'entertained' if she called. It was not the handsome chamber where he lodged his male friends, nor the splendid pavilion for his marriage feast – yet she might be satisfied if he kept 'one little closet' specially for her. She kept a place for him too, of which she 'never took the measure . . . All my life long I carried it folded in the hollow of my hand – yet, released from that hold and constriction [like the hand hiding love's sting in *Shirley*], I know not but its innate capacity for expanse might have magnified it into a tabernacle for a host.'

While his mother was away on holiday in Hastings, George Smith took the initiative in a new bout of correspondence when letters flew faster than ever. It has been noted that these exchanges coincided with the steady progress of the first book of *Villette* and a decided improvement in Charlotte's health. Despite her fear of her letter-obsession, she succumbed to his warmth: 'since you say that you would like to write now and then I cannot say "never write" without imposing on my real wishes a falsehood which they reject . . .'

As she forged on with *Villette* in the late summer of 1851,

George Smith was again giving Charlotte strong signals of liking. His letters gave her vital comfort and she may, again, have referred to these letters when she wrote in *Villette* that Graham's letters to Lucy contained three or four half-tender lines, touched – but not subdued – by feeling. I have wondered whether Charlotte drew on her own practice when Lucy writes two different replies: an ardent one which she does not send; the other, the kind of light letter a lady could post. George Smith's most winning grace was to sanction her voice and draw it out. The easy tone of their correspondence reached its peak in Charlotte's spontaneous reply to what appears to have been a free-spoken note from Smith:

My dear Sir,

People say it is wrong to speak or act on the spur of the moment or from first impulses – but I must do so for once. Your note of this morning is so like yourself – and – I must add – the best part of yourself – the *best* because the most individual – the least like ordinary-minded, ordinary feeling people who hardly ever doubt themselves . . . but how far astray you are! How widely mistaken! NO *indeed* your letter did not displease me – how could it? And you shall not find fault with what I like – for I *did* like the letter – nor shall you imagine me some such paltry-minded, porcupine-souled person as to fancy offence in what is genial, life-like and full of pleasant spirit . . .

I am tempted to say a little more on this subject – an explanatory metaphysical little bit drawing a sort of distinction. You mention the words 'flippancy and impertinent license'. Allow me to say that you never need to mention these words because (it seems to me) that your nature has nothing to do with the qualities they represent – nothing in this world. I do not believe that except perhaps to people who had themselves a great deal of effrontery and hardness – you could be other than kindly and considerate – you are always so to Currer Bell – and always have been, which is the chief reason why he has a friendship for you: you must leave a contrary line of conduct to people of another species – of the Mr Lewes-order for instance. You are not like Mr Lewes – are you? If you are not one atom like Mr Lewes – I will never trust my own instinct again – for I felt what he was through the very first letter he sent me – and had no wish ever to hear from – or write to him again. You appear to me something very different – *not* hard – *not* insolent – *not* coarse – *not* to be distrusted – all the contrary . . .

Never mind my spirits etc I rub on – and only keep grudging myself the manna of an occasional letter from Cornhill and wishing I had the strength of mind to cut off this indulgence and scorning myself pretty heartily because I have not the strength . . .

She knew this correspondence could be no more than good nature on his part, as he dwelt on shared thoughts and jokes. She felt that it was part of his grace to write as though he did this to gratify himself – not to content her. A few days later, on 22 September, she was 'very happy', she told him. 'Can I help wishing you well when I owe you directly or indirectly most of the good moments I now enjoy?' He invited her again to London, but she refused.

'No; if there were no other objection (and there are many) there is the pain of that last bidding good-bye, that hopeless shaking hands, yet undulled and unforgotten. I don't like it. I could not bear its frequent repetition. Do not recur to this plan. Going to London is a mere palliation and stimulant: reaction follows.'

It is possible that no more border-letters came. After September, to judge from Charlotte's replies, Smith's letters became more concerned with business: the absurd, unprintable novel which Miss Martineau had written for Smith, Elder, and the firm's struggles in India. Charlotte refused a renewed invitation from the Smiths for Christmas. In the meantime, she went downhill with the equinox, a season always disturbing to her, as though the elements, wrestling for control, reflected a conflict of body and soul. On 30 October she spoke of respite from some 'painful mental worry . . . Life is a struggle'.

George Smith tantalised Charlotte, not only by conventional chivalry but by seeming, at times, to offer her emergence from her retreat. Could she enter a public life, empowered by her success? To turn away, to shake hands at Euston as she departed once more for the shadows was more painful than never to emerge at all. Like the Lady of Shalott, she could not sustain a real-life sight of the knight riding by to many-towered Camelot. It was better to stay at the interface of life and art; best of all, to hold in her hand a letter, a solid morsel, what human hunger craved: 'the wild savoury mess of the hunter, . . . fresh, healthful, and life-sustaining.'

There is no doubt that George Smith admired Charlotte Brontë for her art and eloquence, but whether he felt more than a strong liking was something neither, it seems, could determine. So much stood in his way: his mother, his family obligations and, given Charlotte's reading of his character, something too easily detached, too satisfied, too comfortable with the assumptions of his age. Many decades later, when George Smith was seventy-four, he told Mrs Humphry Ward that he had been more drawn to Charlotte Brontë when she was in Haworth than when she was in London – in other words, it had been her letters rather than her physical presence which had deepened their tie. As he remembered it, he had never been in love with her, though his mother had been 'alarmed'. Virginia Woolf, whose father had been Smith's friend and his editor for both the *Cornhill* and the *Dictionary of National Biography*, thought she could recall 'old George Smith preening himself' when her mother had said, 'I am sure Charlotte was in love with *you*, Mr Smith'. It is not possible to know exactly how Charlotte came to her conviction that there was no future to this tie, but the fact that she thought of denying herself the 'indulgence' of his letters suggests how very badly she craved them. As summer faded into autumn, and autumn into winter, she was again waiting for the post, with the ensuing depression. This was transmuted into the wary account of the relation of Lucy Snowe to Graham Bretton in *Villette* which Charlotte was writing fast during the second-half of 1851. In her tight-lipped way, Lucy owns to his almost irresistible attractions. She must acknowledge, too, his 'friendship – with its calm comfort and modest hope', restoring her when life seems to be extinguished, and following this with a series of letters which are Lucy's 'treasure'.

Charlotte's letters reflect a more substantial and attractive man than Graham Bretton who is something of a handsome cypher. In transforming man into hero, Graham is less George Smith than a pervasive type. Graham's shifts are close to the caprice of William Percy in Charlotte's novella, 'Henry Hastings'. Percy is capable of a certain 'freak of taste' as he goes about his business, and this will warm him as a 'small soothing amusement'. Such a freak of taste could take hold with a certain tenacity; but it could well prove no more than a whim. In 'Mr Gilfil's Love-Story' (1857), George Eliot observed the same type in Captain Wybrow: a young man of 'calm passions'. He is an obedient son because he has no powerful inclinations of his own. As a tame, well-bred Englishman, he is shown to have not the slightest notion of the foreign tumult of his parents' adopted girl, the Italian Caterina, and he can be thoroughly pleased with a suitable marriage to a woman of class and means. This sort, as both Currer Bell and George Eliot recognised, was particularly dangerous to a feeling woman, an Elizabeth Hastings, a Lucy Snowe, an operatic Caterina. In September 1851, Charlotte reminded Smith of the bargain she had proposed two months before: 'You are to keep a fraction of yourself – if it be only the end of your little finger – for *him* [Currer Bell] and that fraction you will neither let gentleman or lady . . . take possession of, or so much as meddle with.' She was asking him to ensure that neither his mother nor any future wife would diminish their understanding; if Smith would grant this, 'he' [Currer Bell] would ask little in return – the masculine pronoun was a reassurance that her need carried no sexual demand. As with Monsieur, when she had begged a *little* interest, a crumb, she begs only a 'fraction' – not love, not visits, only continuous correspondence to keep her going.

As Charlotte introduced the princely Graham in the first volume of her novel, her vivid letters warmed George Smith, for sometimes he responded in the same vein. At other times, he turned away while Charlotte waited eagerly, too eagerly, for his response. Easily, forgetfully, he turned away because, though he was kind and helpful, feeling on the Brontë scale did not compel him. So he would turn away, encouraged, of course, by his indomitable mama.

Did life dictate the fiction, or fiction the life? Did George Smith beckon her once more with invitations to return to London in September and December? Did Charlotte refuse because she had imposed upon him a more lightweight character than he, in fact, had? Or did she refuse on realistic grounds that she could not afford to expose herself again to false hopes? She might well have concluded that Smith's concern was primarily for a valuable author. His concern was great enough for him to contemplate a winter journey to Haworth at the end of January 1852 when news arrived at Cornhill that Charlotte had fallen dangerously ill. Unfortunately, at just that time, she had gone to convalesce at Brookroyd with Ellen.

The doctor had diagnosed a liver complaint. Winifred Gérin assumes this was jaundice, but the details are vague and the mercury treatment provoked a violent reaction – it was the treatment more than the disease that had brought Charlotte close to death. Charlotte stressed the associated depression to George Smith in a letter of which only the conclusion has survived: Currer Bell, she said, was not writing; instead he was swallowing drugs 'for the purpose of chasing away a low nervous fever which after long annoying him with threats – at last established a somewhat unfair tyranny over his spirits – sleep and appetite – and he had nothing for it but to seek medical advice . . . Meantime pen ink & paper are as much forbidden as if they were three of the seven deadly sins.' This was probably written in December 1851, soon after Charlotte recounted Lucy's collapse at the end of the first volume of *Villette*. Details, here, suggest connections between mental and physical illness, drawn from Charlotte's memory of her deterioration in Brussels in the summer of 1843 and from the present repeat of this: '"my mind has suffered somewhat too much; a malady is growing upon it – what shall I do? How shall I keep well?" . . . At last a day and night of peculiarly agonizing depression were succeeded by physical illness; I took perforce to my bed . . . Sleep went quite away.'

She goes on to describe a 'visitation from eternity' in which the well-loved dead appeared to be alienated from her. In the course of this nightmare, 'galled was my inmost spirit with an unutterable sense of despair about the future. Motive there was none why I should try to recover or wish to live . . . That evening more firmly than ever fastened into my soul the conviction that Fate was of stone, and Hope a false idol – blind, bloodless, and of granite core. I felt, too, that the trial God had appointed me was gaining its climax, and must now be turned by my own hands . . .'

There are simpler versions of this experience in Charlotte's letters. 'I passed such a winter as, having once experienced, will never be forgotten', she wrote to William Smith Williams. To Laetitia Wheelwright, her Brussels schoolmate, she elaborated: 'Some long stormy days and nights there were, when I felt such a craving for support and companionship as I cannot express. Sleepless, I lay awake night after night, weak and unable to occupy myself. I sat in my chair day after day . . . It was a time I shall never forget . . .' She could say breakdown was the result of writing a book in total isolation (*Jane Eyre* and two-thirds of *Shirley* she had shared with her sisters). What she could not say, except through the medium of fiction, was that loneliness was compounded by loss of hope as Smith's burst of lively letters from July to September tailed off into mundanities and as Taylor, after two letters from Bombay (dated 17 September and 2 October), stopped writing altogether. The post became a daily confirmation of hope denied. When Mrs Smith invited her again to London, after her son became alarmed, Charlotte replied meaningly that where there is 'no available remedy' for solitude, she must bear the consequences: the temporary sop, the brief diversion, was no use to her. If George Smith did not get the message in July and September, he could not fail to get it now.

For four months over the winter of 1851–2 Charlotte did not put pen to paper. Then, on 29 March 1852, she bestirred herself to copy the first volume of *Villette*. During the period she was unable to write, she read the first volume of *The History of Henry Esmond*, which Smith sent in manuscript. She thought Thackeray 'unjust to women, quite unjust'. She also deplored the weak 'twaddling' of Dickens' narrator in *Bleak House*: 'an amiable nature is caricatured, not faithfully rendered, in Miss Esther Summerson.' Perhaps the perceived failures of these two most eminent of her contemporaries to give a truthful account of women nerved her to press on with her second volume, the difficult volume that draws most obviously on the Smiths and the recent drama of the letters. As Lucy resumes her tasks after a breakdown, she resolves to subdue her 'insane' need for letters: 'insane that credulity which should mistake the transitory rain-pool, holding in its hollow one draught, for the perennial spring . . .' Looking back, she understands her obsession better, in its dual aspect. Firstly, the crude hunger: 'I suppose animals kept in cages, and so scantily fed as to be always upon the verge of famine, await their food as I awaited a letter. Oh! – to speak truth, and drop that tone of a false calm which long to sustain, outwears nature's endurance – I underwent . . . strange inward trials, miserable defections of hope, intolerable encroachments of despair. This last came so near me sometimes that her breath went right through me. I used to feel it, like a baleful air or sigh, penetrate deep, and make motion pause at my heart, or proceed only under unspeakable oppression. The letter – the well-beloved letter – would not come; and it was all of sweetness in life I had to look for.'

The other, more subtle aspect of her obsession with letters had to do with language. In person, as a visible lady, it would be unseemly to express herself ('privation, penury stamp your language'); but the letter, written from the shadows, untrammelled by bodily presence, offered a fuller medium ('where the bodily presence is weak . . . surely there cannot be error in making written language the medium of better utterance than faltering lips can achieve?'). Reason still warns against any attempt at full emergence, even from this invisible ground between body and author. It was one of the sternest lessons of Charlotte Brontë's life that she could not use the developed voice of Currer Bell in her private capacity as a woman – in other words, she could not use her prime asset. Through her heroine, she exposes the problem:

> 'But if I feel, may I *never* express?'
>
> '*Never!*' declared Reason.
>
> I groaned under her bitter sternness. Never – never – oh, hard word! . . . Reason might be right; yet no wonder we are glad at times to defy her . . . We shall and must break bounds at intervals, despite the terrible revenge that awaits our return.

Speaking here through fiction, Charlotte both blames and defends and finally consoles herself. Fear might have destroyed her voice altogether but for a 'kinder Power' who holds her secret and sworn allegiance, who exists not on the lips but in the 'temple' of interior space: this deity has offered some promised land of futurity. Meanwhile, a silent woman must progress through the wilderness of the present, hushing the impulse to idolatry. Nowhere do Charlotte Brontë, Currer Bell, and the shadow-strength of the fictional model merge more fully than at this complex moment of deferred promise.

Picking up her pen once more in the spring of 1852, looking back to the 'inward winter', Charlotte Brontë was able to comprehend the precarious feat of her survival through the seasonal metaphors of Lucy Snowe. At best, the lone creature will hibernate, preserved 'in ice', holding out for the spring; but the possibility haunts it that the frost may penetrate its heart, especially at the 'mid-blank' of this terrible void.

The second volume of the novel sifts Charlotte's obsession together with other disturbing events of the preceding year: the unfulfilled Rhine journey; the white stone with which she had marked one day in London; the termination of Taylor's letters from India. This last issue became the admissible cover for a renunciation she could not express except through fiction. In this dark period, as depression interrupted the flow of composition, she registered Graham's shifting relation to Lucy as he turns from her:

> That goodly river on whose banks I had sojourned, of whose waves a few reviving drops had trickled to my lips, was bending to another course: it was leaving my little hut and field forlorn and sand-dry, pouring its wealth of waters far away. The change was right, just, natural; not a word could be said: but I loved my Rhine, my Nile; I had almost worshipped my Ganges, and I grieved that the grand tide should roll estranged, should vanish like a false mirage . . .
>
> But soon I said to myself, 'The Hope I am bemoaning . . . did not die till it was full time: following an agony so lingering, death ought to be welcome.'

It is here that Currer Bell rose to the challenge of a trial that must be turned by her own hands. Unlike the Lady of Shalott, her art did not fly apart at the sight of a knight riding towards another life, with a clear, sunlit brow as he sang his merry 'Tirra lirra'. Hers was an art that could look at the hard fact that such a knight was not for the lady apart and alone. At the end of the second volume, her narrator-heroine does not fade away in picturesque despair; she acts decisively, even drastically. She buries his letters — in effect, severs herself from them, as the living must sever themselves from the dead if they are to survive. She buries her 'treasure' which is also her 'grief'. And with this, the voice of the writer finds the strength to go on. In the third volume, she is able to look back on Graham as a buried 'passage of feeling' — her remembered delight in his grace. As she walks and looks back to this, she asks herself if the feeling was dead:

> What was become of that curious one-sided friendship which was half marble and half life; only on one hand truth, and on the other perhaps a jest?
>
> Was this feeling dead? I do not know, but it was buried. Sometimes I thought the tomb unquiet, and dreamed strangely of disturbed earth . . .
>
> Had I been too hasty?

This question recurs on renewed contact with this hero: his kind looks, warm hand, and the pleasant tone in which he speaks her name. 'But I learned in time that this benignity . . . belonged in no shape to me: it was a part of himself; it was the honey of his temper'. He is the sweet fruit on which, for a while, in a time of great need, she had fed — but she must now forge on: '"Good night, Dr John; you are good, you are beautiful; but you are not mine. Good night, and God bless you!"'

In the manuscript, Charlotte Brontë wrote: 'not dead yet — no — to this day it is not dead —'. Here is a possible explanation for her repeated refusals to visit the Smiths: to avoid the intense longing that followed her departures.

In the process of revision, Charlotte excised (literally, with scissors) a lot of material to do with Graham Bretton. Amongst the most heavily revised passages are Lucy's reaction on returning to work after her stay with the Brettons, and her comments on Graham's kindness and imperfections when she receives his letter and when she realises there will be no more letters. In the third volume, Graham fades into the background as Lucy discovers a renewed capacity for feeling in her relation to a Belgian professor, Paul Emanuel, her closest portrait of Constantin Heger.

Charlotte insisted that she did not want *Villette* announced until the publishers had the manuscript: she had always resisted serialisation, and now resisted any pressure to finish quickly. All the same, she worked with some haste (as the manuscript of the third volume shows) in the late summer and autumn of 1852. On 26 October, she sent off the first two volumes of the novel. George Smith would have appreciated the private joke in the second volume where Graham Bretton wins a lady's head-dress in a lottery, 'a most airy sort of blue and silver turban, with a streamer of plumage on one side, like a snowy cloud.' One evening, while he nods off in the drawing-room, his mother slips it on his head. Encouraging responses from Cornhill spurred Charlotte, and after three weeks of difficult decisions over the final chapters, adding titles last, often in pencil, she posted the third volume on 20 November.

There followed an unprecedented silence from George Smith, as he absorbed the critique of the gentlemanly Graham / Dr John, and Lucy's unexpected preference for an ugly, fierce foreigner. The book contained an explicit message to George Smith, that its switch of opinion was the direct outcome of the narrator's experience: 'Reader, if in the course of this work, you find that my opinion of Dr John undergoes modification, excuse the seeming inconsistency. I give the feeling as at the time I felt it; I describe the view of character as it appeared when discovered.' What she discovers is that her first hero cannot be redeemed from the conventionality of a man of the world: he will remain slave to what Fashion, Wealth and Taste decree. She discerns, too, that this sort wants no fire in a wife, only public graces. And with this, Currer Bell shunts him on to his minor track: his predictable romance with a prize angel. As Paul Emanuel takes

Lucy's hand, she thinks: '*His* friendship was not a doubtful, wavering benefit – a cold, distant hope – a sentiment so brittle as not to bear the weight of a finger . . .' George Smith was too alert to have missed the private allusion to Charlotte's old plea for the fraction of his finger, and too discerning not to have picked up the reductive satire in the concessionary phrases that lap round the fallen hero. He would not permit Williams to read the final volume.

Anxiously, on 1 December, Charlotte wrote to ask Smith what he thought: 'I am afraid – as you do not write – that the 3rd Vol. has occasioned some disappointment. It is best, however to speak plainly about it, if it be so. I would rather at once know the worst than be kept longer in suspense.'

Still, silence.

Then a cheque for a poor sum arrived: £500 when Charlotte and her father had expected £700. The amount might be measured against the £1,200 which Smith paid at this time for *Esmond* and the £10,000 he offered later for George Eliot's least distinguished novel, *Romola*. Since no letter accompanied the cheque, Charlotte decided to set off for London 'to see what was the matter, and what had struck my publisher mute.' Just then, the letter came. Smith thought the switch of interest in the last volume peculiar.

Charlotte agreed: 'It is not pleasant, and it will probably be found as unwelcome to the reader as it was, in a sense, compulsory upon the writer.' Her words press her publisher to acknowledge his failure to be her hero, after all. She pointed out that in a romance Lucy would have kept faithfully with a 'paramount hero' who would have been 'supremely worshipful', but the evidence of 'real life' was against it.

She also asked rather tauntingly if she were right in thinking that the beautiful, angelic wife destined for Graham was hopelessly insubstantial: union with her would be like mating with a 'cloud'.

Smith's reply was scarcely legible. This letter, like his others, has vanished, but to judge from Charlotte's communications to Ellen, he seems to have felt the need to explain his actions and feelings, and to have been unable to do so: 'he continues to make a mystery of his "reason" – something in the third volume sticks confoundedly in his throat.' He thought the destined wife was 'an odd, fascinating little puss' but, he protested, he was 'not in love with her.'

That was his last word. He declined to answer further questions. Though Charlotte may have told herself their play had ended, her confidences to George Smith in the text of her novel, and her provocations that followed, opened the way for continued drama.

8

BURIED FIRE

The climax of Charlotte Brontë's creative life was to tell the story of a woman's rise from frozen passivity. This story had its source in her own acts of survival and in her relation to two men: her animating teacher, M. Heger, and buoyant George Smith. Both provoked the same pattern: expressive letters fading into waits for the post; depressive collapse; then, recovery through work. In *Villette*, events and interior dramas in Charlotte's life were transmuted into her most searching revelation of hidden character.

Lucy Snowe talks of her 'heretic narrative'. She speaks in the context of her experience as a Protestant in Catholic Belgium, but the statement implies more than a religious position. Between the publication of *Jane Eyre* in October 1847 and *Villette* in January 1853, their author was called unwomanly and rebellious. Emily's fury when Charlotte revealed her identity as Ellis Bell – including Ellis in her blurted words, 'we are three sisters' – proved justified. The secret was soon about, and after the first wave of praise for the pseudonymous *Jane Eyre*, hostile reviewers judged the Bells less as authors than as women. Charlotte wrote to Lewes on 1 November 1849:

> I wish you did not think me a woman. I wish all reviewers believed 'Currer Bell' to be a man – they would be more just to him. You will – I know – keep measuring me by some standard of what you deem becoming to my sex . . .

Come what will — I cannot when I write think always of
myself — and of what is elegant and charming in femininity — it
is not on those terms or with such ideas I ever took pen in
hand; and if it is only on such terms my writing will be tolerated — I shall pass away from the public and trouble it no more.
Out of obscurity I came — to obscurity I can easily return.

She was outraged that, after this plea, Lewes still attacked
Shirley on gender grounds in a review which betrayed its author's
trust by revealing her sex. It was rare for her to confront a critic,
but she sent him this acerbic retort:

TO G.H. LEWES, ESQ

I can be on my guard against my enemies,
but God deliver me from my friends!

Currer Bell

On 19 January 1850, she wrote to Lewes again. She was hurt, she
said, not by severe criticism 'but because, after I had said earnestly
that I wished critics would judge me as an *author* not as a woman,
you so roughly — I even thought so cruelly — handled the question of sex.'

Nearly three years later, as she completed *Villette*, she suggested to George Smith that she might publish the novel under
a new pseudonym: 'I should be much thankful for the sheltering
shadow of an incognito.' This, Smith could not allow: by then,
'Currer Bell' was a worldwide name. She pressed Cornhill again
when she sent off the first two books of her manuscript on 26
October: 'My wish is that the book should be published without
author's name.'

When Charlotte said that she did not think of herself when
she wrote, she meant the public image of the meek little
woman as she appeared in London — not the invisible author.
The 'heretic' voice came from that shadow: a woman strong
enough to speak to the future: '. . . Though I knew I looked a

poor creature, and in many respects actually was so, nature had given me a voice that could make itself heard, if lifted in excitement or deepened by emotion.' This voice, intimate, passionate, caustic, brings out what was latent in her sex.

It is coming to be recognised that Victorians were frequently less stuffy than Moderns like Lawrence and Strachey liked to believe. Queen Victoria exclaimed in her diary on the deep interest of *Jane Eyre*** which she read aloud to dear Albert, and Marian Evans (not yet George Eliot) thought *Villette* a 'still more wonderful book than *Jane Eyre*.' With its uncompromising realism about the life of an obscure, intelligent woman and its refusal of the usual happy ending, *Villette* was closer to the kind of novel George Eliot would devise. She was speechless as she read it three times: '*Villette* – *Villette* –'. In about March 1853, she and Lewes became lovers. Lewes told her of his meeting with Charlotte in 1850 when he had found her 'a little, plain, provincial, sickly-looking old maid', yet on the strength of the novels, Marian Evans saw more: 'What passion, what fire in her! Quite as much as in George Sand, only the clothing is less voluptuous.' All the same, there remained what always exists in one form or another: the closed mind, as tenacious in the educated reviewer as in the Smallweeds and Podsnaps of every society. The pretension to refinement that marked status in Victorian society had to be seen to resist whatever brought a blush to the cheek of a young person. So, Jane Austen's niece, her beloved Fanny, began to deplore her aunt's directness as the unfortunate product of a less-refined age. So, too, the accusations of 'coarseness' that followed Currer Bell's revelations of passion in good women.

Lucy appears more ordinary than Jane or Shirley, for Lucy is locked in the prevailing mode of feeble womanhood, given to apathy and incipient collapse. In this, Lucy is closer to the author for whom, at the time of writing this novel, there was so little relief from stagnation that she almost clung to it as the

---

* Queen Victoria first read *Jane Eyre* in 1858, and with renewed admiration in 1880.

given mode of being, refusing invitations, including those of George Smith, which offered no real bond. Lucy appears to lack the vigour of Jane Eyre; she presents herself as a helpless creature. As it turns out, this proves a delusion, conditioned by debilitating norms of womanhood. The problem of *Villette* is that a heroine who appears so poor in spirit is not immediately engaging. Less eventful than Currer Bell's earlier novels, *Villette* draws directly on her own buried emotions in Brussels during 1843, her breakdown in the summer of that year, and the repeat breakdown in the winter of 1851–2. Lucy tells her story as an unprotected young Englishwoman who ventures abroad to teach in Villette (Brussels), who experiences various trials in the foreign school – ranging from arrogant pupils to gothic encounters with a buried nun – and whose self-command is tested in relation to two very different men: the best kind of gentlemanly Englishman, Graham Bretton (known abroad as Dr John), and the irascible, ugly Belgian teacher who challenges Lucy's habitual reserve. But this story is no more than a channel for the interior drama of Lucy's transformation. Because this change is realistically slow and because it remains unseen, *Villette* asks more of the reader than *Jane Eyre*: the reciprocal action of a reader alert to secret lives. The weak, helpless facade of Lucy Snowe contains a challenge similar to the breathless flutter of Emily Dickinson: these disarming voices from the feminine repertoire cover their antithesis. In its measured, waiting open-endedness, *Villette* is, in fact, the most suggestive of Charlotte Brontë's novels.

In Brussels, she had known a reckless attachment; she had been ground in the mill of convention by the slights and suspicions of Madame; and she had found how far her need for action diverged from the placidity or hypocrisy of acceptable women. This divergence between private and public woman is the prime link between Charlotte and the subject of *Villette*. Where Charlotte had most affinity with Anne was in detailed ridicule of the manners of women who accept convention, like the calculating Mme Beck, the directress of the foreign school (based again on Mme Heger who for some years after the publication of *Villette* did not admit English girls to her school). Mme Beck is said to be like a superintendent of police: 'acute and insensate'. A typical pupil is the idle beauty, Ginevra (based partly on Charlotte's Roe Head schoolmate, Amelia Walker, whose delicate airs failed to mask her wheedling manipulations). When Lucy and Ginevra look in a mirror, their visible aspects reveal the usual contrast of workaday teacher and decorative doll, but neither, of course, is what she appears.

Villette undercuts female constructs with ruthless acumen, and none more inexorably than the narrator's own mode of feeble coldness. 'Frost' was Lucy's surname in the manuscript sent to Smith, Elder. On 6 November 1852, Charlotte wrote to Williams:

> As to the name of the heroine, I can hardly express what subtlety of thought made me decide upon giving her a cold name; But at first I called her 'Lucy Snowe' (spelt with an 'e'), which Snowe I afterwards changed to 'Frost'. Subsequently I . . . wished it 'Snowe' again . . . for she has about her an external coldness.

It is only external. The fire of feeling and a natural energy propel an authentic Lucy from beneath the chill crust. People about her – Mme Beck, Ginevra – begin to suspect her of secret acquirements, even of secret identity. The most suspicious, and increasingly curious, is a fellow-teacher, Paul Emanuel. Mme Beck comes to see her as a learned blue-stocking; Paul Emanuel, as a creature of wilful independence which he sees as a mark of her Englishness. There is truth to each view: Lucy is certainly a keen reader; she is indeed alien. But the question of her emergence remains. Ginevra who sees Lucy as 'so mysterious', nags her for a social solution. Is she well-born? Has she some advantage of rearing or education?

'But *are* you anybody?' persevered she . . .

'Yes,' I said, 'I am a rising character . . .'

To some extent, Currer Bell treats the disabling conditions which blocked women's rise (and this was her interest for feminists of the past), but primarily she believes that a woman must create herself (and this is where she speaks to generations yet to come). To rise is an imaginative act. It has been assumed that public rights present the toughest challenge and an advance on latent needs, but the reverse may be true. It was so for Charlotte Brontë who concurred with Harriet Taylor Mill's demand for equal opportunities, but thought the writer on 'The Enfranchisement of Women' undeveloped. Public needs are easier to discern and offer simpler targets for reform than private need to come into being, for which (as Florence Nightingale said) there has been no genuine model. For public rights, there is the precedent of what men have achieved. For interior becoming, the only precedents are women like the Brontës and, following them, Emily Dickinson, George Eliot, Olive Schreiner, Virginia Woolf, Sylvia Plath, and vast numbers of obscure women who left no record of their desires and discoveries. They are waiting to be found in the unlit tracts of the past, through new forms of record, as Henry James found in his cousin, Minny Temple, the model of a woman who would 'affront her destiny'. Thirty years earlier, Charlotte Brontë imagined new exemplars who are not saints, who struggle and fail, yet demonstrate a capacity to overpass old limits. They offer the incentive to look for further possibilities in human nature, expressed most gracefully in Tennyson's salute to the rising woman, which Olive Schreiner made her epigraph to *Woman and Labour* (1911): 'Give her the glory of going on, and still to be.'

What Lucy is to be — a woman in command of work and language — seems improbable at the outset. Where Jane starts as a rebel, Lucy starts as a dullard in the making. Where Aunt Reed declares in outrage that she has never encountered a child who answers back as Jane, Lucy appears silent, effaced. Apart from a certain watchfulness, there is not, at first, the slightest hint of an existence beyond bland non-being. But we are looking at different patterns of development. Jane oscillates between increasingly subtle temptations to live by passion or duty alone, while Lucy develops through a linear pattern of successive events which stir another being, active and even fiery, under that frozen facade. It is like a volcano, starting with mild tremors, shaking Lucy's routine life, then breaking the foundations of her onlooker existence until her landscape is remade. This is an inward landscape; the 'new region' will remain invisible to urbane Graham Bretton. Through his eyes, Lucy appears no different after her upheavals, but the confidante-Reader is privy to the process of interior revolution.

Lucy is first seen as a well-conducted Victorian girl paying a visit to her godmother, Mrs Bretton. For the next eight years, she slumbers idle on the deck of non-existence until a storm throws her overboard. The narrator is not concerned with sensational event but with states of being: we learn nothing about the storm, beyond the fact that family deaths deprive Lucy of all future protection.

Her first self-reliant act is one of 'cowardly indolence': she immures herself in the prison of a sickroom as a superior servant to ailing Miss Marchmont: 'Two hot, close rooms thus became my world . . . All within me became narrowed to my lot.' The death of Miss Marchmont forces her to seek a living. To venture abroad is a daring act for a young woman alone, but this is concealed by Lucy's staid manner. Yet, en route, she passes through London and when she looks at the dome of St Paul's, she tells us, 'my inner self moved; my spirit shook its always-fettered wings half loose; I had a sudden feeling as if I, who had never yet truly lived, were at last about to taste life'. Then, she draws 'divine' delight from the heaving Channel waves, seabirds, and sails in the dark distance, and looks to the continent ahead 'like a wide dreamland, far away.' For a moment, we glimpse a mood similar to that of Jane when she gazes at the horizon from the leads of Thornfield and longs to overpass the limits of domestic shelter. This mood had its most perfect expression in nineteenth-century ballets which discover women in dark regions beyond ordinary sight. Giselle and Odette fade into invisibility with the first blankness of day. They and their companions are compelled to conduct a ghostly existence which yet has the instantaneous impact of authenticity as opposed to the social routines of peasant or court.

Lucy takes up her own ghostly existence at the foreign school when she walks in its neglected alley, associating with shades of peculiarity 'no more to be parted with than my identity'. She clears away dead relics of past autumns: 'the hidden seat reclaimed from fungi and mould'. Schoolgirls, in training for conventional womanhood, are forbidden this path which existed, exactly as in *Villette*, at the far end of the walled garden at the Pensionnat Heger, running parallel with the blank stone wall of the neighbouring boys' school, the Athénée Royale. The walk was so neglected and overgrown that the dense foliage cut off the sun. The garden's past connection with a religious order was not forgotten, and a legend flourished in the school of a nun buried alive behind the moss-covered slab still visible beneath the ancient pear tree.

At first, Lucy fears to appear singular, and takes this path only when others are at prayer. In short, she takes the path as Protestant and alien. Lucy perceives her present and future to be fixed and dead, but here in *l'allée défendue* she feels some unknown quickening within her lifeless mould. 'And in catalepsy and a dead trance, I studiously held the quick of my nature.'

It is here, when she walks invisible, that she awakens to a buried being, antithetical to the stupefied Miss Snowe who would settle for twenty years in a nursery or classroom, out of a 'base habit of cowardice' and 'infatuated resignation'. In the dim alley, Lucy finds her counterpart in the spectral nun. Here, among the roots of the old pear tree, dead, except for a few remaining boughs,

> was the portal of a vault, emprisoning deep beneath that ground, on whose surface grass grew and flowers bloomed, the bones of a girl whom a monkish conclave of the drear middle ages had here buried alive, for some sin against her vow. Her shadow it was that tremblers had feared, through long generations after her poor frame was dust . . .

As the nun passes with fierce gestures through a storm, 'the whole night seemed to feel her.' Lucy, too, stays out in the wild hour 'pealing out such an ode as language never delivered to man'. She watches clouds split by 'white and blinding bolts', exulting in nature's manifestation of disruptive power. When nature speaks to her in its own language, Lucy longs to be rescued from her sterile existence.

In the meantime, at the school's fête, Lucy moves nunlike amongst girls in white, wearing a gown of 'grey haze' (in the manuscript, a 'gown of mist', altered to one of 'shadow'). Forced to perform in the school play, she covers her dress with a vest, cravat, and *paletot*. Cold, reluctant, telling herself she acts only to oblige others, she warms to the part as she finds that a 'keen relish for dramatic expression . . . revealed itself'.

This is confirmed by Paul Emanuel who alerts Lucy to a fuller nature she does not, for a long time, acknowledge. After he witnesses the unexpected drama of her performance on stage, he seeks her out: 'I know you!' he exclaims. 'I know you! Other people in this house see you pass, and think that a colourless shadow has gone by . . . I watched you, and saw a passionate ardour for triumph . . . What fire shot into the glance! Not mere light, but flame'. This is the first hint of the fire belied by the name and manner of snow.

The pains of coming to life involve Lucy in two almost annihilating trials: first, a new awareness of acute stagnation during the long, lone summer when the domestic interior of the school stifles her burgeoning life, as the slab of the tomb had sealed off the living nun. As Lucy's life dwindles, she is beset by lurid dreams when she is visited by the alienated dead. In life Maria had presented the Christian ideal of pure spirit rising above her untidy, beaten, and failing body. Emily had met her own ideal of 'a chainless soul, / With courage to endure.' Anne's last emphatic words had been 'Take courage, Charlotte; take courage!' Neither Charlotte nor her heroines could follow her sisters into spiritual grandeur. Lucy falls into a despair that carries her into mental illness, her flesh becomes a 'prison' which the spirit should possess, but unlike the dead, she craves earthly attachment.

Some measure of attachment comes to her through the balm of Graham Bretton's letters. Lucy delays reading them until she is alone in the attic. The delay is not repressive; on the contrary, it is an act of pleasure, close to love-making – a form of sustained desire. Its sequel is a forbidden act: the abandon of the unsent reply. Through this release Lucy can enjoy what many of her contemporaries had to deny: passion in their own terms. Words, as for Charlotte herself, going back to the free, erotic writing of her adolescence, are interfused with the rise of desire. So, Lucy's second trial is the fever of silenced love when letters stop.

In these trials, autobiography is barely transmuted into fiction, as Charlotte recounted her atrophy in Brussels in the summer of 1843 while M. Heger was away; her waiting for letters in 1844–5; and waiting again, increasingly wretched, in the autumn and winter of 1851–2. In the matter of the letters, Lucy shows more composure than Charlotte who sank into depression. Resolutely, Lucy buries Graham's five letters in a sealed box under the nun's pear tree: with this act, she buries potential love for the gentleman whose light, teasing charms guard him from fire. So Charlotte Brontë herself sealed off the unwritten plot of desire, a plot that exists only by virtue of its insistent absence – insistent, that is, in gothic encounters with what lies in shadow, the buried other who calls out sexual disturbance. Self-conceived, this has no social plot, and in so far as fiction is a social form, desire is effaced. There is no man to meet it, with whom the secret nuances of women's need can come to life. Rochester, who lives with fire, can only be, after all, an imaginative possibility. In the more realistic world of *Villette*, it is dangerous for Lucy to relinquish cool control: if hopes knock, 'an inhospitable bar to admission must be inwardly drawn . . . I dared not give such guests lodging.' Desire fulfilled cannot be recorded in this realist text because Charlotte Brontë had not had her desire fulfilled; as she said pointedly to George Smith, the outcome was 'compulsory upon the writer'. Lucy, we are told, prefers books where 'the writer's individual nature was plainly stamped'. The great daring of *Villette* is to flaunt its untold story of buried fire beneath its stories of breakdown and creative promise.

It is crucial to Lucy's remaking that she judge stale models of her sex. This is stimulated by her visit to an art gallery. Cleopatra, painted as gypsy temptress, is a 'piece of claptrap'. Another stale model derives from a triptych of scenes from a woman's life by Fanny Geefs which went on exhibition in Brussels in 1842, during Charlotte's first summer there. In *Villette* four panels represent '*La vie d'une femme*' as pale and lifeless. Lucy denounces the maiden, simulating modesty, as a flagrant she-hypocrite; the bride, showing the whites of her eyes as she prays, is 'exasperating'; and altogether the four ages of women show 'bloodless brainless nonentities!'

Lucy's judgement of her sex is more challenged when she goes with Graham Bretton to see the actress, Vashti. Lucy is drawn and repelled by an exposure of emotions which seem anarchic, exactly as Charlotte had been both drawn and repelled by Rachel in 1851. Her exposure of torrential emotion is 'a mighty revelation' – this is a woman's understanding of the uncompromising honesty of a woman artist more courageous than Charlotte herself; at the same time this self-exposure is immodest – this is the Victorian male judgement internalised by women in a way that enslaved them more profoundly than legal restrictions and made necessary the careful guard with which Charlotte Brontë protected herself on all public occasions, including meetings with other women writers. But she went further when she condemned the actress as 'immoral': this, I think, touched on Charlotte's own divided self, not the calculated duality of shadow and propriety, but her deep fear of an abandon reminiscent of Bertha Mason, the potency of evil in rage unbridled by reason. Behind this fear lay Charlotte's reading of Heathcliff as demon, and behind Heathcliff, Branwell, and that part of Branwell she had shared.

Graham, though, condemns Vashti solely on grounds of convention: 'he judged her as a woman, not an artist: it was a branding judgment'. Here, Lucy learns the bitter lesson which Charlotte had learnt from George Henry Lewes as well as from members of her own sex. Her godmother, Mrs Atkinson, had thought *Jane Eyre* wicked and unwomanly, and had severed relations with Charlotte. Even Miss Wooler was not proud of her former pupil: taking the high moral ground of forgiveness, she felt called upon to reassure Charlotte that the book would make no difference between them.

Lucy defines herself in opposition to constructs of womanhood in art and theatre as well as society. Ginevra Fanshawe, like Blanche Ingram, is a relic of Charlotte's juvenilia, the fashion-plate of the 'silver fork' fiction of the 1830s, crossed with trifling women like Amelia Walker, a Brussels schoolmate, Maria Miller, and Mrs Robinson. There is an intimacy in Lucy's tone to Ginevra that mocks artifice: it takes a woman to call Ginevra's bluff. Lucy is kinder to Paulina Home, a Victorian wife in the making. A worshipper of Graham Bretton, her husband-to-be, Paulina's manner is agreeably modest. Though more observant than her father or suitor, she says only what pleases them. It is not sycophancy but in her nature to reinforce the limpet-attachments of the child. 'I liked her', Lucy owns. It is not an admission she often makes, and her Reader must bear with it for once. Watchful, reserved, Lucy feels that Paulina understands her singularities, as she understands Paulina's surrender to Graham's attractions – to the extent that Lucy cannot allow herself to 'see' him.

Graham, as the Victorian embodiment of manliness, has benevolence, consideration, and all sorts of goodness. But he proves facile: involved; then offhand. '[T]he mood of one hour is sometimes the mockery of the next', he owns to Lucy. His taste in women is banal: he responds to sweet prettiness in dyes of silver and rose; 'for what belonged to storm, what was wild and intense, dangerous, sudden, and flaming, he had no sympathy, and held with it no communion.' Worse, he is locked in blinkered phrases: 'His "quiet Lucy Snowe", his "inoffensive shadow", I gave him back; not with scorn, but with extreme weariness . . . He wanted always to give me a rôle not mine. Nature and I opposed him. He did not at all guess what I felt . . .' He cannot 'see' a woman as she can 'see' him. Graham would not have glanced in Paulina's direction had she not come furnished with the money and status his manhood requires. Modesty, too, is a must, for this man is 'fastidious'. Paulina has to rewrite her acceptance of Graham's proposal, again and again, to cool it to the acceptable degree of frost – frost tinged with the merest zest of sugar. Desire can surface only as unsent letters of uncensored expression and there it must terminate: in unuttered, soon-buried words which may not reach their implied (male) reader. Women's desire has no plot to follow: it comes to these dead ends. In *The Professor*, it seems visible to Crimsworth only as a passing flash which it does not occur to him to question or pursue. It is seen as a mere curiosity of Frances' dual perfection as submissive/working wife. So, desire is faded out of language, including the language of the body; even in marriage it exists in shadow. Lucy can sympathise with Paulina who will accommodate to a husband's taste. For Miss Home, the need to mate is the point of existence; for her, it is simply unthinkable to seek any other form of life.

Lucy, lacking family, finds a sister in Paulina and something of a brother in Paul Emanuel (named perhaps after Monsieur's second son, Paul, born in 1846). Unlike the voyeur of 'Cleopatra' or dismisser of Vashti, M. Paul is a man who can 'see' a woman. Lucy is outraged by what she takes to be his 'Jesuitical' spying. But he is determined to know her, and in the end, she finds it compelling.

Though George Smith and some contemporary reviewers criticised the transfer of interest from one hero to another, it follows logically from Graham's reproof of Vashti. By contrast, M. Paul accepts, even elicits, what Lucy fears to be. Prudery is an emotion he dreads and vindictively detests. Almost rudely, he jolts Lucy: 'What do you start for? Because I said passion? Well, I say it again. There is such a word, and there is such a thing . . . You are no child that one should not speak of what exists'. His directness, infused with choleric vehemence, is a match for Lucy's independence of mind. He is (as he claims) her other self. In this, he is Heger – and not Heger: he looks exactly like Monsieur – with his sallow, grimacing tiger-face – and he responds in Monsieur's abrasive way, yet, as a single man, he is free to care for her. All the same, Monsieur did make it possible for Charlotte Brontë to imagine such a man and make him plausible. Less beautiful, less mannerly than the Englishman, M. Paul is the right partner: the acerbic sloe in the wild thicket rather than the fruit of the Hesperides.

The secret of his appeal is that he puts Lucy physically at ease. In his presence, she finds that she can move her body as she pleases, can laugh, can retort. 'Pink! pink!' she protests when he teases her for wearing too bright a colour. Although he does retain some standard views – that women should pamper men – his pleasure in Lucy's retorts does allow her unusual licence. As Jane finds that she has 'not been petrified' with Rochester, so Lucy finds that she is not 'asphyxiée' with Paul Emanuel who alone perceives 'that mine was a fiery and rash nature' – adventurous, indocile, audacious. For Lucy Snowe, who is habituated 'to be passed by as a shadow', it is 'a new thing to see one testily lift-ing his hand to screen' himself from her 'obtrusive ray'. He projects an image which Lucy does not quite recognise. It is Charlotte Brontë's feat to suggest a mystery of character, which is, to some extent, a mystery to Lucy herself. Where Ginevra harps on a drama of secret rank, Paul Emanuel concocts a different drama of arcane knowledge. Both are silly, as Lucy asserts; only slowly does she come to see that their sense of mystery derives from her untapped potentialities. This is a genuine phenomenon, as opposed to the standard mysteries of fiction: the gothic clap-trap of the nun who turns out to be a prank; the secret rank of romance; the worldly agency which a privileged education might confer: all these would have been predictable plots. Lucy eludes them, as she eludes the school inspectors who have been told she is a prodigy and go away satisfied that she is an idiot.

The inspectors make this mistake because they try to cate-gorise her intelligence as ignorance or learning. Lucy discovers herself in her retort to Paul Emanuel: 'I am ignorant, monsieur, in the knowledge you ascribe to me, but I *sometimes*, not *always*, feel a knowledge of my own.'

'What did I mean?', he enquired sharply.

Unable to answer in a word, she evades the question. Her position is too remote from the proprieties of an examination answer. She has not the attributes to shine in examinations: the quick answer, showmanship, self-confidence. Her mind takes its own course – in 'the fresh silence of morning, or the recluse peace of evening' – at the edges of day. Her 'knowledge' comes from some indefinable fire within; the most active thing in the novel, it has no drama, no plot, no conclusion. The plot of Ginevra's flirtation and elopement, and the elaborate Catholic plot of Mme Beck and Mme Walravens to separate Paul Emanuel from the Protestant alien, are soulless manoeuvres. These plots with their flat social ends offset the burning energy of Lucy's unacted part and indeterminate future.

*

The ferment beneath the silent surface of Miss Snowe is fuelled by language. The words pouring from her pen are provoked by her alien status; we might call them the fruit of exile. In the year *Villette* was published, Charlotte wrote twice to Mrs Gaskell about a woman's need for isolation in order to be true to herself. These letters show a stranger and stronger Charlotte Brontë than the well-known victim of loneliness. She may have used isolation in the constructive way that Florence Nightingale used illness or in the way that Virginia Woolf later used bouts of 'madness'. Charlotte's loneliness became 'illness' at the time she was pouring out these words – though 'illness' like 'madness' is a word that fails to comprehend the condition. Virginia Woolf said that 'illness' was a subversive condition which roots up traditional modes of thought. This is not, of course, peculiar to women: Charles Darwin did a prodigious amount of writing while an invalid. T. S. Eliot, who completed *The Waste Land* during a breakdown, said: 'it is a commonplace that some forms of illness are extremely favourable . . . to artistic and literary composition.' In a similar way, Charlotte Brontë was able to transmute the solitude of 'illness' into creative daring. In June-July 1853, after the success of *Villette*, she could exult in what the isolation of Haworth had given her. She likened her surroundings to some New World to which she invited Mrs Gaskell as to the 'back woods of America. Leaving behind your husband, children, and civilization, you must come out to barbarism, loneliness, and liberty. The change will do you good . . .'

The opposite of heady solitude, as Charlotte hinted to Mrs Gaskell, was the temptation of wives to give in to the husband who feels kindly but sometimes does not see justly as, in *Villette*, Paulina adapts to Graham so entirely that she becomes nebulous. Apologising for her to George Smith, Charlotte owned that Paulina was too insubstantial. Lucy could not distort herself in this way. But Lucy, as Charlotte foresaw, was too awkward, too alien to current norms, to be likeable to George Smith or even to

Mrs Gaskell. The problem for wives, which Charlotte intimated to Mrs Gaskell, was to hold to 'severe Truth'.

Severe is the tone of Lucy Snowe. She sees that Cleopatra, painted as a hunk of flesh, is 'coarse and preposterous'. The astringency of her tone is less obviously appealing than the ardent Jane; her appeal lies in her refusal of the ploys of charm in favour of telling the truth. When Lucy looks forward to seeing Paul Emanuel, she observes tersely: 'He came. Life is so constructed, that the event does not, cannot, will not, match the expectation.' Lucy is determinedly prosaic, a counter to the fictional dreams of Charlotte's youth: she marks the sober fact of inevitable disappointment, to be looked at steadily with what George Eliot would call 'clear-eyed endurance'.

What is striking about Lucy's voice is the gradual emergence of authority, a voice worthy of George Eliot's attention. It is not a cynical voice; it never abrogates feeling. What links Charlotte Brontë with George Eliot is that both were rooted in an early nineteenth-century Evangelicalism which banished cynicism from any respectable position in society and which found its strength in its appeal to the affections. This is the voice that emerges from a muted young woman of twenty-three, developing into the voice of a fully formed writer at the end of _Villette_.

This utterance will not learn the formula for religious confession; it is, in a sense, a Protestant alternative: indwelling and singular. Catholic confession is seen as another temptation: the amenity it offers to mental pain. The confessor, Père Silas, would have Lucy become a nun, one answer for a woman of passion with abilities that unfit her for marriage. The spectral nun, reappearing at moments of trial (when Lucy reads Bretton's letter in the attic, and when she buries his letters under the tree), seems to reveal an aspect of the self buried alive a thousand years ago.

'Why do you come to me?' Lucy asks the apparition who, of course, will not answer – for there is no word for a part of human nature lost to sight. This gap in the given language is integral to the poems of Emily Dickinson, particularly those of her *anni mirabili* 1862–3; it was recognised by Bathsheba in *Far from the Madding Crowd* (1874); and restated by Virginia Woolf in 1920: 'I have the feelings of a woman but I have only the language of men.' In the same way, Lucy Snowe may be articulate in the classroom, teaching standard English to foreigners, yet outside this accepted role, she, too, must struggle for words – words to relay her unacted part.

Her first expression of such a part comes when she rehearses, alone in the attic, in preparation for the school play. The attic is uninhabited and remote. In summer it is as hot as Africa; in winter as cold as Greenland: regions of the globe yet unexplored. It is the perfect haunt for the nun who emerges from a curtain in the darkest corner, part of the lumber of the past. As Emily Dickinson played a cracked Queen in the extreme privacy of her poetry, Lucy in the privacy of this unvisited room, improvises a throne out of boxes. She mounts it, and declaims to her audience of garret vermin – first in a whisper, then aloud, then with force and zest. On the real stage (a forbidden place for virtuous Victorian women, especially one playing a man), what Lucy most fears is her own voice. But when she risks utterance, when her 'tongue once got free', and her 'voice took its true pitch, and found its natural tone', she feels the 'right power come – the spring demanded gush and rise inwardly –'.

The struggle for expression is daunted, almost wiped out, by the difficulty of letters. As the recipient of Graham's letters, Lucy is cast in the role of womanly waiting. This reflects Charlotte's own gloom as she wrote the second volume of *Villette* in the aftermath of her breakdown over George Smith in the winter of 1851–2, when she told various people that, though she was physically better, she had not yet recovered her spirits. Her susceptibility to the passive, and, for her, debilitating role of waiting for the post, was exacerbated by James Taylor's decision to write no more from India, which followed Smith's withdrawal as a further blow in the winter of 1851–2 when her 'illness' worsened. It was unreasonable of Charlotte to expect more from Taylor after her coolness, but when Smith withdrew, Taylor personified a residual hope which now was gone. Charlotte, like Lucy, feared the frozen buds of hope: their actions are designed to guard against this — and, with each, the guard could slip.

At the height of her 'illness', in January 1852, Charlotte was forbidden pen and paper as, later, Virginia Woolf was forbidden to write when she was 'ill'. It was common medical practice to regard mental exertion on women's part as abnormal and therefore a cause of breakdown. Of course, the opposite was the case: writing, as a form of expression, eases the mind; silencing strains it. Charlotte's letters to Monsieur had alternated between her plea for reciprocity and her deliberate, almost exaggerated restraint. M. Heger then placed between him and Charlotte the impassable barrier of silence. Following the attentions she had enjoyed as his favoured pupil, this bar seemed so unkind that she could hardly credit it of the teacher she had known. She contrived to recover when novels replaced letters: *The Professor* in 1846 and *Villette* in 1852. Through the imaginative as opposed to the epistolary mode, Charlotte could legitimise her need for expression. A 'heretic narrative' in the context of 'illness' may suggest that, in certain cases, depression is a form of buried utterance. The denial of words lies not only in buried letters; it is evident in the excisions in the manuscript: in many places Charlotte did not simply cross out; she cut pages and paragraphs, often pasting blank white paper across the back of omissions. In other words, her gaps would have been visible to her publisher's eye, in a curious drama at the intersection of life and literature, in which the publisher had to read his part as it was set down for the public and at the same time perceive privately what the author left out — what he alone may have been challenged to know. The statement that affection was 'not dead yet — no — to this day it is not dead' was cancelled very lightly: the words are perfectly legible. When Lucy says that to bury letters was to bury her grief, the word 'grief' is substituted for three or four words which the author excised. Another gap, about the length of a paragraph, comes in the middle of an analysis of Graham's emotional limitations, presumably along the lines of one of the earliest fragments. Another gap cuts short Lucy's 'struggles with the natural character' in the course of her breakdown, as she tries to quiet her emotional need to a respectable tranquillity. She is cutting short the incommunicable matter of depression: there are no adequate words for a soul-killing vision of the meaningless existence of millions who rise from dust to suffer and pass away to dust again, through blank cycles of time. The manuscript tells us, 'Beyond melancholy – lies madness'; then 'madness' is covered by the more acceptable 'heart-break'. Elsewhere it comments that the world would understand starving to death, but not going mad from solitary confinement. Nerves at first inflamed, sink to palsy – then, following an excision of one and a half lines, the writer exclaims at the incommunicability of this state: 'Speak of it!'

Another matter of depression is self-despair: this is registered by another piece of blank paper in the manuscript where Lucy sees a reflection of herself with the Bretton party: the handsome middle-aged mother, the gentleman-son with the 'best face, the finest figure', and a third person – and here comes the gap as Lucy sees herself as others see her with an uncontrollable pang of regret. She is dressed in the pink silk Charlotte could not afford to buy for her visit to London in May 1851 and the black lace mantle she returned at the same time because it made her dark dress look rusty, yet despite this finery, Lucy must still turn away from the sight of herself: 'No need to dwell on the result.' Chastened as her visible image may be, her invisible self holds firm: heavy corrections show the importance of Lucy's refusal to be an 'appendage' or 'foil' as a paid companion: 'I was no bright lady's shadow' – her shadow, even if it be one of 'dimness & depression', must be voluntary.

The manuscript shows Charlotte's repeated concern with 'shadow' – for instance, en route to the concert with Graham

Bretton, the thought of a return to solitude comes over Lucy as a 'shadow', in the same way as Charlotte herself had to block her need during her stays with the Smiths – until she could no longer bear to go. Graham appears wholly obtuse as to Lucy's shadowed nature; in actual life, George Smith did, to some extent, engage with it. In fact, it was his very leaning for her 'personal quality' – far exceeding usual relations between author and publisher – that made the limits of friendship more disturbing.

Graham's obtuseness has to do with language. A man of good will, he is attuned to whatever the given language can convey, but he will always remain oblivious to what cannot be made explicit through words: 'Put your grief into words, he turned no deaf ear. Expect refinements of perception, miracles of intuition, and realise disappointment.' A hope of more intuitive communication comes through M. Paul. The role he is to play is unclear in the first book: he seems to wait in the wings to see if he is called upon to play a peripheral or central part in Lucy's ultimate fate, and in so far as it falls to Lucy to become a self-sufficient teacher and writer, not a wife, M. Paul comes forward as promoter of her gifts. It is as though at the mid-blank of Charlotte's 'illness' during the winter of 1851–2, her allegiance turned back to Monsieur, and the recovered life she found through her novel derived from her old promise to write a work dedicated in her heart to him, 'the only literature master I have ever had'. No novel was ever written so close to unfolding event, its very course determined, perhaps, by George Smith's decision *not* to make that prospective journey to Yorkshire in the dead of winter. With Lucy's recovery in book two, comes the birth of her peculiar talent. As teacher, Paul Emanuel is alert to its first breath in her essays. He saw the heart beat and discerned a new form of life in her observant eye, and he 'stamped it with his deep brand of approval'. *Villette* has been called the last great *devoir* that Charlotte Brontë wrote for her teacher; it is certainly the longest love-letter in English literature.

In his character in the novel, his pedagogic assumptions do

pose problems: he regards a woman of intellect as a *lusus naturae*. Exasperated by his sneers and goads, Lucy at one point throws his books aside; then, in the manuscript, one and a half pages are cut after Lucy mentions the sweetness of reconciliation, as Charlotte recalled those scenes of tears and warmth in Brussels nine years ago. The teacher does think Lucy too volatile, too ready with obtrusive opinion – like Monsieur, he discerns the hidden range, the brilliant vocal promise in the shadow of the quiet foreigner (a paragraph is cut again, probably to preserve her decorum – Lucy is too English for the exhibitionism of a Lucia or Vashti). Still, he does want her as a prize pupil, to exhibit her talent in a public examination. Lucy retorts that she would rather undergo imprisonment than write in this obligatory way 'for a show and to order, perched up on a platform'. The corollary to her unvoiced 'knowledge of my own' is her creative impulse which is not even and regulated – in the way of the professional writer – but appears at the edges of the day, associated with moods of nature: some cry of the wind or some unseen stream of electricity. Writing seems to her a bloodletting or a heady oracular moment that often fails to fix its message in words. This sort of writing was not for schools and examinations, but Lucy testifies to its existence in a much-revised passage in the manuscript, which is, in essence, a flaming denial of the constraints imposed on Charlotte by Southey's letters. When M. Paul continues to press Lucy to write to order, according to the established system, she cries out to be liberated, to get out into the air; and when his back is turned, she escapes. There followed eight excised pages in the manuscript – possibly, Lucy had more to say on the subject of women's expression which she could not share with Victorians. And yet, the whole book reveals the secret of her creativity, its source in a rising mind of her own, in her fire, in a nature as fierce and tigerish as that of her 'brother', her natural mate.

When the inspectors force themselves on Lucy, answers to their questions surge up fast: 'my mind filling like a rising well, ideas were there, but not words. I either *could* not, or *would* not speak – I am not sure which'. At length, the inspectors set her an essay on 'Human Justice', the subject of one of Charlotte's essays for Constantin Heger.* It is a topic, Lucy says, which 'did not suit'. She writes fiercely – and unacceptably – on Human *In*justice.

Later on, she has to take on another battle of words: Père Silas' attempt at conversion. Again, she cannot argue, and this saves her because, of course, arguments would invoke logical persuasion which is alien to her private mode: '. . . I could talk in my own way – the way M. Paul was used to – and of which he could follow the meanderings and fill the hiatus, and pardon the strange stammerings, strange to him no longer.' In this way, she defends her creed.

When Paul Emanuel leaves to go abroad, he speaks a similar 'wordless language' of communion. After he gives her a school-room of her own, she says, 'you are *too* good!' and comments: 'In such inadequate language my feelings struggled for expression: they could not get it; speech, brittle and unmalleable, and cold as ice, dissolved or shivered in the effort.' They speak only through gesture: his hand strokes her hair; she presses the hand to her lips. These restrained signs are finally given verbal expression through their faithful exchange of letters. Through letters, love takes shape 'in another degree'. Called out by writing, as Lucy puts it, 'he is more my own.' This exchange will do what M. Heger and, to some extent, George Smith, failed to do for Charlotte Brontë: it will console and sustain Lucy through her uncertain future. It will provide the impetus for the 'heretic narrative' which she will write in after years.

The final stage of Lucy's emergence is her three years of happiness as she starts her own school and awaits M. Paul's

---

* *La Justice Humaine* (6 October 1842) was corrected by M. Heger, and marked '*Bon*'. This original essay, too, was defiant: 'What can be loftier than justice in the abstract? – But its administration is subject to gross abuse.'

return from the West Indies. The happiness is derived not from wedding bells but from economic independence and letters.

Here, Charlotte projects her own dream: letters which would speak to the rising woman. She wanted a love which could sustain itself as a spur to action – or spur to art. M. Paul set up Lucy in her career, then 'wrote because he liked to write; he did not abridge, because he cared not to abridge. He sat down, he took pen and paper . . . because he was faithful and thoughtful, because he was tender and true . . . His letters were real food that nourished, living water that refreshed.' This is the inspiring part which Charlotte had devised for Constantin Heger in her projected dual career as schoolmistress and writer. Misunderstood and foiled in actual life, she recreated this possibility nine years later in *Villette*. In a sense, Paul Emanuel's probable loss at sea is irrelevant to the fullness of being Lucy has gained by the end of her narrative.

Villette tests three kinds of women. It exposes the false femininity of high-society romance. Ginevra Fanshawe fought 'the battle of life by proxy, and, on the whole, suffer[ed] as little as any human being I have ever known.' She leans on Lucy, a dead weight emblematic of the burden of feminine artifice. Lucy shoves her off with increasing impatience.

Paulina Home is the domestic dependant who accommodates to Victorian expectations. She has genuine feeling, but her distortion is such that a large part of what she feels will remain unknown. Charlotte Brontë thought her an artistic failure, and ascribed this to the fact that Paulina was not based on a known person. This is what Charlotte told George Smith, assured nevertheless that Graham would enjoy perfect happiness with this more appropriate partner.

Lucy Snowe is the woman to be. Rising from the shadows, she looks to the future. The book ends when she is ready to write it: the work of art to complement an exchange of letters which, at the crest of rapport, shapes character and extends expression. We leave Lucy advancing into a future in which she will record her rise in heretic terms. What is to be the fate of such a woman? This question looms in the 'pause: pause' at the end of *Villette*.

MARRIAGE

For Charlotte herself, fate – or 'Providence', as she put it – was close at hand in the shape of Arthur Bell Nicholls. A vastly different prospect from the mental stimulus of the Belgian professor, Mr Nicholls was a sturdy, steady, practical man, not much given to thought. But he did have honesty and durable powers of feeling – two qualities of first importance to Charlotte.

Mr Nicholls was close enough to events at the Parsonage to know when Charlotte completed *Villette*. This was the moment for which he had waited, and Charlotte herself was not unaware of his regard: for a long time, she had marked his glances, feverish restraint, and threats to take himself away. It seems that she had felt more than seen this: in some corner of her consciousness she had sensed that he wished her to care for him. So, the moment he tapped at the dining-room door between eight and nine one Monday evening in December 1852, she knew 'like lightning' what to expect.

What she had not expected was the sheer force of his feeling: this large man who looked like a statue trembled from head to foot. She had thought him mild and reserved; he appeared, now, in a new aspect: obsessed, determined, and careless that the whole of Haworth should watch his pursuit – and deplore his presumption.

So long as Charlotte held out against Mr Nicholls, from December 1852 to December 1853, she pursued her future as a writer. From April to July 1853, she made several starts on 'The Story of Willie Ellin'. Towards the end of the year, in November, she began a more promising novel known as 'Emma'. But after this last burst of writing, she never wrote again — except letters, and even these eventually became subject to Mr Nicholls' control. Of course, Charlotte had grave doubts about marrying a man whose tastes were 'uncongenial'. It is well known that these doubts were dispelled, after marriage, by increasing fondness for her 'dear boy', but one issue is yet uncertain. Her reasons for domestic happiness are simple — relief of loneliness, closeness, a rocklike fidelity; what remains obscure is the preceding period of inward debate, between her continued dismissal of Mr Nicholls in the spring of 1853 and her continued doubts and need for privacy during their engagement from April to June 1854. How did Charlotte Brontë change in that prolonged period during which she prepared herself to transform her life? It was so customary for Victorian women to think of marriage as the consummation of their existence, and for fathers to oppose poor suitors, that Charlotte — moving between set positions on some course of her own — was necessarily mute.

She had to hold herself '*entirely passive*', she confided to Ellen, wishing her father's red-veined outrage would subside and that the all-too-visibly sulking suitor would go back to his beef and pudding. Mr Nicholls' open distress gave her 'pain'; so did her father's antipathy to the bare thought of anyone seeing her as a wife. When she had told him of Mr Nicholls' proposal, the veins had stood out on his forehead 'like whipcord' and his eyes had grown bloodshot with fury. Fearing for him, Charlotte had made haste to assure Papa that she would refuse Mr Nicholls next day. Mr Brontë had then reinforced her refusal with a note Charlotte thought 'cruel'. If Ellen could see her father in his hard mood, she would 'know something of him'.

When these events reached Mary in New Zealand, she exploded in rage at Charlotte's sacrifice to 'that selfish old man'. Eighty years later, reading these letters, Virginia Woolf opened up the area of daughters' fear and paternal anger which 'prevent real freedom in the private house'. Fathers like Mr Brontë, Mr Barrett, and presumably, at the back of her mind, her own father, Leslie Stephen, had been protected by the assumption that it would be unnatural and unwomanly to oppose fathers' wishes: they had 'nature' as well as the law on their side. 'Thus protected it was perfectly possible for the Rev. Patrick Brontë to cause "acute pain" to his daughter Charlotte for several months, and to steal several months of her short married happiness without incurring any censure from the society in which he practised the profession of a priest of the Church of England; though had he tortured a dog, or stolen a watch, that same society would have unfrocked him and cast him forth.'

What exactly was Charlotte's course during this fraught time, what issues beset her, and how did she reconcile herself, finally, to a lover so different from those of her heroines?

When Mary's companion and cousin, Ellen Taylor, died in New Zealand early in 1852, she wrote to Charlotte of a different kind of fear: that she would now, in her solitude, become 'a stern, harsh, selfish woman'. This struck home for Charlotte: 'again and again, I have felt it for myself', she owned. At that time, in March 1852, she had undergone a breakdown which left its mark. At the end of that year she warned Mrs Smith to expect a change in her appearance since her previous visit to London eighteen months before. Conceivably, the hair that had framed the face in the 1840s was now pulled further back, baring the 'slight astringency' remarked by Mrs Gaskell as well as the resolute aspect of a woman who has sailed close to torrent and iceberg.

After her breakdown, when Lucy Snowe buries Hope with her letters from Graham Bretton, she does not give up. Since food and forage failed in these winter quarters, she must move on and fight another pitched battle with fortune: 'if so, I had a mind to the encounter: too poor to lose, God might destine me to gain. But what road was open?'

When hope had frozen for Charlotte Brontë during her third visit to the Smiths, in the summer of 1851, she may have turned spontaneously to faithful Mr Nicholls to whom she offered an unwonted thought in her letter on 7 June, an attention repeated throughout that month. This may have encouraged him to invite himself for tea at the Parsonage on 27 July before leaving on a visit to Ireland. 'Good, mild, uncontentious' was Charlotte's verdict, and for once she was wrong – on two counts. Good he was, but in matters of love, stubborn and pugnacious. Rejected, he replied to Mr Brontë with a letter of resignation. He immured himself in his room at the sexton's, refusing his meals, unwilling to speak to solicitous clergy (conspicuously glum, even, during a formal visit from the puzzled bishop*), and not ashamed to set Haworth buzzing about his state.

Nearly two years younger than Charlotte, Arthur Bell Nicholls was born in County Antrim, Ireland, on 6 January 1818. At the age of seven, he was adopted** by his uncle, Dr Alan Bell, headmaster of the Royal High School, Banagher. His uncle and aunt enjoyed an exceptionally happy marriage, and the boy became part of a warm-hearted, civilised family, living in Cuba House, a late seventeenth-century house of Palladian design on a small rise, painted white and furnished in parts rather barely. Arthur made a genealogy of the Bell family from the time of their settlement in Ireland at the Revolution in 1690. There is repeated reference to Sir Michael Bell, Colonel of Foot and Governor of Athlone, who came to Ireland with William III and was knighted at the Battle of the Boyne. (The professional middle-class origins of the Bells were superior socially to those of the peasant, Brunty, whose righteous outrage at his curate's proposal was the forced fruit of swift rise.) In 1844, Nicholls graduated in divinity with second-class honours from Trinity College, Dublin, and at the age of twenty-seven arrived in Haworth, in

* Dr Longley, Bishop of Ripon, who became Archbishop of Canterbury in 1862.
** ABN's parents were then still living. His mother died in 1830 and his father in 1849.

May 1845. He was a strong, handsomely bearded man with a long, straight nose and fine eyes. Amongst the books he brought with him there were no novels (though later he bought a volume of Cowper's poems); he read *Practical Sermons* by the Revd G. W. Woodhouse (second edition, 1841), *The Churchman's Companion* (1845), and *A Discourse on Church Government* by John Potter (seventh edition, 1845). He was licensed as curate to Mr Brontë on 5 June by the Vicar of Bradford, William Scorseby and, a little after a year, ordained as priest by Charles Thomas, Bishop of Ripon, on 30 September 1846. He proved conscientious and quietly concerned for the welfare of villagers. In church, as Charlotte observed, he had a good voice and read well, though she could not share his unbending attitude to Dissent. Later, Mrs Gaskell, as the wife of a Unitarian minister, called him 'bigoted', and Charlotte, too, feared that, after marriage, his High Church theology would forbid further contact. His rigidity might be seen as a sign of narrowness; it was certainly part of a stubborn character, with assertive opinions backed by temper.

The year after Mr Nicholls' arrival in Haworth, Ellen heard of his interest in Charlotte, then aged thirty. Six years later, when Mr Nicholls proposed, Charlotte remarked her surprise that quick Ellen ('*too* quick, I have sometimes thought') did not, at this later time, pick up the signs of Mr Nicholls' regard: his stifled silences, his threats to leave. Back in 1846, when Charlotte had denied Ellen's rumour, she had fortified her denial with a conviction of her unworthiness: to have it said that she, a slight, plain 'spinster', cared for the young curate, would have made her the laughing stock of the neighbourhood. This was no ordinary diffidence or shyness, but shame for her body dictated by current norms of acceptability. Her awareness of physical flaws – and pity from men like Smith and Thackeray – made her wince in public. During a visit to Mrs Gaskell in Manchester in April 1853, she confided her mortification over her looks as 'something almost repulsive' and spoke of her fear of loving as much as she could because she 'had never been able to inspire the kind of love she felt.' This fear was projected into a cancelled exchange in the manuscript of *Jane Eyre*. When Rochester admits to inducing jealousy in Jane through attentions to Miss Ingram, Jane says:

> '. . . to be candid in my turn – I was not only then but am still
> pricked in one point – compared with her, physically speaking,
> I am nothing.'
>   'Not much in the matter of bulk and weight – but you will
> do – at least I will graciously excuse deficiencies.'

Even the keenest of lovers is not expected to be very reassuring on this point. Charlotte believed that once strangers looked at her, they would avoid looking in her direction again. Mrs Gaskell said this was not true, but it does suggest that Charlotte saw herself as conspicuously ugly. In *Villette*, Charlotte projected this fear once more in the scene where Lucy and Paul Emanuel make their commitment known to each other:

> 'Ah! I am not pleasant to look at –?'
>   I could not help saying this; the words came unbidden: I
> never remember the time when I had not a haunting dread of
> what might be the degree of my outward deficiency . . . Was it
> weak to lay so much stress on an opinion about appearance? . . .
> I fear it was . . . I must own a great fear of displeasing . . .

There was this continuity between the resolute girl of twelve who told herself she could never marry and the young woman of twenty-six who caricatured herself as squat and ugly in a sketch sent to Ellen from Brussels, in which a lone, disfigured Charlotte waves across the Channel to a rounded, womanly Ellen with a man (possibly her current admirer, Mr Vincent) at her side, and the continuity remains with the thirty-six-year-old woman who was pained when her father could not see her in the light of a wife. In the winter of 1852–3, when Mr Brontë humiliated Mr Nicholls for presuming to think of himself as

Charlotte's husband, he did not realise how far he provoked his daughter's sympathies for a slighted fellow-creature – for she knew, too well, what it was like to sustain a passion yet appear unfit in the eyes of the world. Her blood boiled at the injustice of the epithets ('unmanly driveller') her father applied to Mr Nicholls. Mr Brontë declared his wish 'that every woman may avoid him forever unless she should be determined on her own misery.' It is impossible to know how far a detached sympathy for Mr Nicholls was deepened by her surprising discovery that this ordinary, decent man loved her desperately, but I think this would weigh with a woman who perceived herself unlovable. She must feel cautious gratitude, even if she thought him unsuitable; and this is what Charlotte expressed repeatedly during her engagement in 1854.

Charlotte's denial of Ellen's suspicions in 1846 had been fortified not only by this harsh self-image but also, perhaps, by Emily who had treated Mr Nicholls with uncompromising contempt. Emily had no time for the unimaginative, and would dive past him without a word. From the early 1840s, she retained a hold on Charlotte who had transferred her strongest bond from Branwell to this 'genius' of a sister. After Emily's death, Charlotte was wholly occupied in nursing Anne, and after that, threw herself into writing, encouraged by her growing friendship with her publisher. During the fluctuations of that indeterminate tie, the breakdown, and the writing of *Villette*, Mr Nicholls would have remained at the periphery of Charlotte's consciousness. She was aware of his constancy as he walked the Parsonage dogs or admired her portrait. She must have shared jokes with him, for when she was recuperating at Filey, on the Yorkshire coast, at the beginning of June 1852, she sent Mr Nicholls a comic message:

> On Sunday afternoon I went to a church which I should like
> Mr Nicholls to see . . . At one end there is a little gallery for the
> singers, and when these personages stood up to perform, they

all turned their backs upon the congregation, and the congregation turned *their* backs on the pulpit and parson. The effect of
this manoeuvre was so ludicrous, I could hardly help laughing;
had Mr Nicholls been there he certainly would have laughed
out.

This represents virtually the only light note in the course of
her prolonged depression. She continued to be aware of Mr
Nicholls' regard, but did not give him any serious attention until
he demanded it by his dramatic offer, followed by starvation tac-
tics, shaking voicelessness in church when Charlotte, on her
return from visits to Mrs Gaskell and Ellen, attempted to take
communion on 15 May (his emotion was so patent, that congre-
gants' sobs came to her ears), and a farewell scene on 26 May
when Charlotte discovered him weeping furiously at her garden
door – with an anguish worthy of *Wuthering Heights*. He did not
arrest her until he revealed emotion on the Brontë scale. And if
he lacked the Brontë mind, he had a fierceness of his own in the
form of tenacity. Long before she made up her mind to care for
him, Charlotte observed to Ellen that he was a man of very few
attachments, but these ran strongly a narrow, underground
course.

During the printing of *Villette*, in mid-January 1853, when
Charlotte had stayed with the Smiths, she had noted the way a
'really fearful' load of work was telling early on the appearance
of her publisher. His complexion, his face, the very lines of his
features had altered. But she found his mind and manners better
than ever. In contrast, James Taylor's temper had suffered from
the Indian climate. Charlotte heard at Cornhill that he had
become difficult to live with.

Following her return to Haworth, George Smith sent her a
portrait of Thackeray, which she hung in the dining-room beside
the Duke of Wellington and her own portrait by Richmond –
earlier gifts from Smith. She wrote to him on 26 February: 'I

wonder if the giver of these gifts will ever see them on the walls where they now hang; it pleases me to fancy that some day he may.'

The following spring, as reviews came in, Charlotte was in steady contact with Cornhill. Amongst the many approving reviews, it was the critique of one 'Mr Fraser' which mattered, she told Smith: 'I am bound to admit, however, that this gentleman confined his approving remarks to the two first volumes, tacitly condemning the third by the severity of a prolonged silence.' Mr Fraser, she imagined, belonged with those readers who chose the milder doom for Paul Emanuel, drowning, in preference to the worse fate of matrimony with 'that – person – that – that – individual – "Lucy Snowe"'. Another quickening in her correspondence with George Smith came with the immediate success of *Villette* as they took the pulse of public response. She had an unexpectedly 'generous' review from George Henry Lewes, though it was not, in her opinion, deep. There was much talk of the open ending of *Villette*, an eagerness to know the fate of Lucy Snowe, which focused, for women readers, on the question of a husband: would Paul Emanuel return? Currer Bell was pressed for a conclusive answer by readers like Lady Harriet St Clair (wife of the German ambassador, Count Münster). Charlotte's reply to Lady Harriet was 'so worded as to leave the matter pretty much where it was.' It was reported that one woman, who had undertaken not to marry unless she found the equivalent of Mr Knightley,* had now put this ideal aside in favour of Professor Emanuel. Charlotte teased Cornhill, recalling George Smith's dismay: 'You see how much the ladies think of this little man, whom you none of you like.'

The shift of Lucy's interest from one man to another, even though Graham proved untenable, did evoke criticism from those who saw confirmation of Currer Bell's coarseness. 'I don't make my *good* women ready to fall in love with two men at

---

* Hero of Jane Austen's *Emma* (1815).

once', Thackeray wrote to Mrs Carmichael Smyth on 28 March 1853. 'That's a plaguy book that *Villette*', he continued on 4 April to Mrs Procter. 'How clever it is! and how I don't like the heroine . . .' The subject he thought 'vulgar'; the author, he predicted to Lucy Baxter, would 'wither away into old maidenhood with no chance to fulfil the burning desire.' Matthew Arnold also attacked the fire: 'It is one of the most utterly disagreeable books I have ever read – and having seen [Charlotte Brontë] makes it more so. She is so entirely – what Margaret Fuller [the New England feminist] was partially – a fire without aliment . . .' What really hurt Charlotte was the unexpected betrayal by a woman she considered her friend. She was devastated when Harriet Martineau attacked her, first in a letter and then in the *Daily News*, for the shift from man to man and for an obsession with love which (Miss Martineau argued) did not reflect the nature of most women: '. . . There is an absence of introspection, an unconsciousness, a repose in women's lives of which we find no admission in this book.' (The agenda, here, was to join the public 'interests' of feminists like Martineau with the domestic 'interests' of mild women so as to ward off the passionate and less clearly defined phenomenon emerging in *Villette*.)

Charlotte marked with red ink the offending passage in the letter, which at first struck her 'dumb'. She then wrote:

My dear Miss Martineau,

. . . I protest against this passage; and were I brought up before the bar of all the critics in England to such a charge I should respond, 'Not guilty.'

I know what *love* is as I understand it; and if man or woman should be ashamed of feeling such love, then there is nothing right, noble, faithful, truthful, unselfish in this earth, as I comprehend rectitude, nobleness, fidelity, truth, and disinterestedness.

Yours sincerely,
C.B.
To differ from you gives me keen pain.

This was the only instance when Charlotte ended a friendship. She confided to George Smith that language did not convey the same meaning to Harriet Martineau as to herself. She had come to the conclusion that to meet Miss Martineau would be 'most perilous and inadvisable . . .' It was not adverse opinion that upset Charlotte so much as a sense of betrayal, for their association had begun when Miss Martineau had reassured Charlotte that she had found no evidence of coarseness in *Jane Eyre*. The hurt from this review was heightened by the attention it (and other adverse reviews) received from Charlotte's circle. Friends sent little notes of condolence when the *Guardian*'s critic declined the honour of an acquaintance with Jane and Lucy as females who did not realise his idea of ladyhood. In a letter to Cornhill, on 29 March, she looked there for an ally:

> Favourable reviews may pass very quietly without a whisper of comment, but those of a contrary character are pretty sure to be read, discussed and passed rapidly from hand to hand . . . For my own part I can only record this significant fact. I am indebted to my publishers for all I know of the favourable notices of 'Villette'. The hostile notices have been the care of my friends. When I resolve this consideration it makes me smile. My friends are very good – very. I thank some of them for the pains they have taken to enlighten me.

It is surprising that Charlotte rather enjoyed the heated response of the *Christian Remembrancer*. Calling *Jane Eyre* a 'dangerous book', Anne Mozley granted that the author of *Villette* had gained in propriety 'since she first presented herself to the world – soured, coarse and grumbling', but she agreed with Harriet Martineau that a wrong model of womanhood prevailed:

We want a woman at our hearth; and [Currer Bell's] imper-
sonations are without the feminine element, infringers of all
modest restraints, despisers of bashful fears, self-reliant, contemptuous of prescriptive decorum; their own unaided reason,
their individual opinion of right and wrong, discreet or impru-
dent, sole guides of conduct and rules of manners – the whole
hedge of immemorial scruple and habit broken down and
trampled upon.

This review accords with the fuming of Elizabeth Rigby (now
Lady Eastlake) in the *Quarterly Review* in 1848, which had greatly
upset Charlotte. She had called these two journals the 'heavy
Goliahs of the periodical press'. Now, secure in strengths of her
own, it amused her to study the blustering Philistine (whom
she took to be a man). In a letter to William Smith Williams, she
pictured her opponent as a High-Church ecclesiastic, hating
Currer Bell's latitudinarianism, yet feeling, in the very heat of
resistance, the compulsion of the Reader:

. . . He snarls, but still he reads. The book gets hold of him he
curls his lip, he shows his teeth, he would fain anathematize;
excommunicate the author; but he reads on, yes – and as he
reads – he is forced both to *feel* and to *like* some portion of what
is driven into his hostile iron nature. Nor can he . . . altogether
hide the involuntary partiality; he does his best; he still speaks
big and harsh, trying to inflict pain, striking at hazard, guessing
at weak points, but hoping always to hit home. And that
author reads *him* with composure, and lays down the review
content and thankful – feeling that when an enemy is so influenced – he has not written in vain.

This is a bravura performance: Currer Bell in vigorous form,
enjoying the battle in which she asserts all the composure of a
David with a supreme power behind her. Apart from the hostility of Miss Martineau, Charlotte enjoyed the encounter with

The portrait of M. Heger at the age of fifty-nine best shows the man Charlotte described in letters and fiction more than twenty years before.

Charlotte thought herself 'something almost repulsive'. In this self-caricature of 1843, a lone, squat Charlotte waves across the Channel to Ellen with a suitor at her side.

Charlotte sent M. Heger this drawing of two trees leanings towards each other (August 1845).

In this *carte de visite* photograph (*c.*1854), Charlotte does not appear plain; she looks sensible, as Harriet Martineau observed.

George Smith as an urbane young publisher, at about the time of his friendship with Charlotte.

The actress Rachel, by William Etty. Her public displays of rampant passion gripped and shocked Charlotte, who recreated her as Vashti in *Villette*.

Left: Mary said, 'I can never think without gloomy anger of Charlotte's sacrifices to the selfish old man'. Mr Brontë as an old man, with his alert, hard stare.

Below: The footpath between Haworth and Oxenhope where Charlotte met Mr Nicholls in January 1854, when Mr Brontë still resisted their marriage.

The Revd Arthur Bell Nicholls. This photograph of *c.*1861 shows his more lovable aspect, not evident in the harder look of an earlier photograph. He gained weight soon after his happy marriage to Charlotte.

Charlotte built her own longing for letters into the loneliness of Lucy Snowe in *Villette*. Edmund Dulac's illustration of this heroine with a letter in her hand.

her Reader, as he or she took shape in response to her work. A letter to a reader, Lucy Holland (possibly Mrs Gaskell's aunt), owns that 'the secretly and deeply felt wish to be something more than a self-seeker' meant more to her 'than all the eulogiums on intellect that ever men uttered . . . This hope sustained me while I wrote – that while many of the prosperous or very young might turn distastefully from the rather sad page – some – tested by what you will term "the pitiless trials of life" – might hear in it no harsh and unsympathetic voice.'

In May 1853, when she tried out fragments for a new story, she was never more concerned with those 'pitiless trials of life' as she turned from the hidden trials of a lone woman to a more Dickensian subject: the obvious trials of an unprotected child. In the case of a child-victim, the bond between author and Reader is instant and strong. As Currer Bell read the reviews and letters, her Reader drew close in the first half of 1853. It was a time of buoyancy and recovery in which the responses of the Reader were more compelling to Currer Bell than the 'flaysome' look which Arthur Bell Nicholls directed at the back of Charlotte Brontë as she vanished upstairs – as Martha Brown, the Parsonage servant (and daughter of Mr Nicholls' landlord), reported to her mistress with loyal outrage.

After he handed his resignation to Mr Brontë, Mr Nicholls asked to withdraw it. Mr Brontë said he might do so on condition he would promise never to approach Charlotte again. Since Mr Nicholls could not promise, he duly left Haworth in May 1853 for a curacy at Kirk-Smeaton, also in Yorkshire, near Pontefract. It was when he came to the Parsonage to say goodbye, and Charlotte did not appear, that she found him howling at the gate. Again, he begged her to give him hope. She could not, and though she pitied him 'inexpressibly', his departure was a relief. As far as Charlotte was concerned, the episode was over, and she turned to plans for her new fiction, 'The Story of Willie Ellin'.

Its subject was not really new: it was an attempt to revive the fiction she had shared with Branwell. Its main interest is that the bond with Branwell should have continued to vibrate, even now, thirteen years and three successes after her 'Farewell to Angria'. Again and again, in the juvenilia, in *The Professor*, and now in the spring of 1853, she returned to the old topic of a clash between two brothers. Clearly, the non-acceptance of *The Professor* still rankled. She did not submit it yet again to Smith, but resorted once more to recasting its materials: a loyalty, we might say, to her imaginative past, or was it a certain stubbornness? She never lost faith in *The Professor*. The domineering persecution of William by the industrialist, Edward Crimsworth, in *The Professor*, looks back to Edward and William Percy in the juvenile stories of 1833–4, and was now revived once more in the physical brutality of the industrialist, Edward, to his child half-brother, William Ellin. This social theme of cruelty was promoted by the Condition-of-England question which exercised many of the foremost minds of the day: Disraeli in his awareness of 'two nations' – the rich and the poor, Carlyle in *Chartism* (1839), Friedrich Engels in *The Condition of the Working Class in England in 1844 and 1845*, and Henry Mayhew whose influential articles on *London Labour and the London Poor* were collected in 1851–2. There is no evidence that Charlotte read these works apart from *Chartism*, but they were part of the conscience of the age and part of what was happening about her in the industrial north, prompting her sympathetic view of unrest in *Shirley* and, in 'Willie Ellin', her sympathy for an orphan boy, unprotected by law from sadistic lashings. A year later, Dickens was serialising his factory novel, *Hard Times*, and Mrs Gaskell, *North and South*. 'Willie Ellin' was closer to the macabre Dickens than to the industrial realism of Mrs Gaskell: like Dickens, Charlotte Brontë sets out grotesque details of abuse – there is no physical nightmare in Dickens more sinister and violent than the flogging administered by Edward Ellin in all the oblivion of blind power – but there is also, in both novelists, a more diagnostic search for twisted states of mind that underpin the social system. Edward Ellin is locked into habits of punitive dominance in a way that recalls Mr Brocklehurst and Mr Murdstone, and looks forward to the teacher, Gradgrind, entrenched mentally behind the wall of his forehead, or the industrial upstart, Bounderby, entrenched behind his favourite cliché that what workers really want is to eat off golden spoons.

This kind of novel may already have been in Charlotte's mind during her last visit to London from 5 January to 2 February 1853 when she astonished Mrs Smith by preferring to spend her time visiting the Foundling Hospital and the prisons, Newgate and Pentonville. At Newgate, she fixed her attention on a girl with an expression of the deepest misery, who had killed her illegitimate child. George Smith recalled how 'Miss Brontë walked up to her, took her hand, and began to talk to her. She was, of course, quickly interrupted by the prison warder with the formula, "visitors are not allowed to speak to the prisoners".'

'The Story of Willie Ellin' consists of five fragments, which try out different voices: that of the old family housekeeper, Mrs Widdup, a type of Nelly Dean (the servant-narrator in *Wuthering Heights*); that of the victim, Willie, terrified, pleading, resigned; and, rather wonderfully, that of a disembodied, timeless spirit in the vicinity of Ellin Hall – a spirit of place, not people. This last was not a voice easy to sustain, but it provides a clue to the venture: after the intensely autobiographical *Villette*, with its associated depression, there may have been some relief in detachment. Willie's visible torments, pitiful as they are, were conveniently distant from the inward trials of silenced passion. This was a turn outwards, away from herself, towards the public world of power and advantage, brute and victim. It must be said that in these preliminary fragments the issue is all; the characters are as thin as in the melodramas of Angria. Although there is, of course, a huge difference between the purple prose of the juvenilia and the professionalism of Charlotte Brontë's writing in 1853, she had, in fact, relapsed into rudimentary emotions: tyranny, fear, and – at the end of the last fragment – the sweet comfort that comes to Willie, after his lashing, in the shape of a beautiful girl of seventeen, a cardboard Angel in the House.

One fragment suggests the lines of the plot: the cruel half-brother will lose Ellin Hall, but when he dies (prematurely), Willie will come into his own, recover his ancestral home, and return there one dark night, unannounced, through the gothic gloom of his solitary and tormented past. So dark is his heart that he would like his brother's deeds cancelled from memory.

Charlotte appears to have dropped 'Willie Ellin' after the interruption of an illness in June. She would have expected, as in the past, to make false starts and begin afresh. In the new novel which she began in November, William Ellin reappears in a different aspect: a cool bystander, with the qualities of an amateur detective, as a mystery unfolds at a girls' school. In 'Emma', Matilda Fitzgibbon, decked out like a doll with her flowing sash, quilted dress, and leghorn hat, appears at first a most desirable show-pupil to Miss Fetherhed who is impressed also with her father's carriage, his country-gentleman address, and the lavish manner of his assent to all possible extras for his daughter. Matilda, whose manner is distant and inanimate, is petted determinedly by Miss Fetherhed, but estranged by this from schoolmates. Her distance is reinforced by some inward estrangement easily mistaken for proud airs. Then, at Christmas, when the term draws to a close, Mr Fitzgibbon does not reply to a query about the holidays. It is now revealed that his address was bogus. Mr Ellin, investigating, confirms this and also the fact that his grand name is untraceable. Who, then, is the girl?

This is sure Charlotte Brontë territory: we are, again, at the frontier of a new region. Its indigenous creature is no longer an unprotected and physically maltreated boy but an unprotected and mentally tormented girl. For the furbelows of 'Matilda Fitzgibbon' have always been at odds with her paleness. Long before Miss Fetherhed suspects a mystery, she cannot like the stiff child and has to pet her 'on principle'. It is Mr Ellin who discerns the misery in the child's face, a secret life which is confirmed when she sleepwalks, all white in her nightdress with her hands stretched out; and confirmed again, when she is discovered one night, frozen on the landing, her eyes half-closed in a 'fit'. It proves hard to wake her. When Miss Fetherhed, in the last scene, confronts her with the question 'Who are you?', the girl blanches even more. All that comes from her are sounds of pure distress: a 'half-interjection' and a cry as she falls. Mr Ellin 'gathered from the floor what had fallen upon it.' In the last paragraphs, cut in the manuscript, he comes forward with new authority to warn Miss Fetherhed that a mystery of nature must take precedence over the mystery of social identity: 'That kind of nature is very different from yours – It is not possible for you to like it – but let it alone –'.

'What' is the crucial word in the whole piece. 'What' is centre stage, on the floor. What is she in the depths of her nature? This is the real question, the true mystery, which of course cannot be answered in a girls' school concerned only with that question, 'Who are you?', which required a social answer. For Miss Fetherhed, 'who' is simple: a girl is who her father is – and if her father does not exist, her own identity, her very existence is called into question. It is no wonder this girl appears pale, inanimate, frozen and, eventually, 'palsied'. Jolted with a peremptory query, she cannot speak.

Although 'Emma', like 'Willie Ellin', is drawn from old themes of the 1830s, particularly the fashionable school and rogue father in 'Ashworth', Charlotte Brontë is at the furthest remove from her juvenilia in her critique of her old idol, the languishing fashion-plate who had enchanted her protracted adolescence. In 'Emma', fragmentary as it is, Charlotte Brontë was clearly posing a challenge to the feminine facade – that 'eminently artificial thing'. The girl exists more as emblem than character – like Willie Ellin, an emblem for the age. In this last work, it seems that Charlotte Brontë was moving into a new and more ambitious phase of her career which would bring out the figurative meaning in the most powerless member of society: the abandoned girl. In 'Emma' there is the possibility of an art which both appropriates and erodes allegory in order to define an alternative exemplar. This is the art of *Clarissa*, *Mansfield Park*, and *The Scarlet Letter*. Allegory, for Charlotte Brontë, derived from her childhood absorption in *Pilgrim's Progress*, and from her conception of her own life as a pilgrimage with burdens to be borne. That latent allegory was redefined through the flaws, trials, and triumphs of Jane Eyre; and now, with the unknown girl in 'Emma', the erosion of allegory is more marked. She presents a visual image that conveys an automatic meaning (petted doll) which must be exploded and reconceived through the empirical methods of the novel, until we, as readers, penetrate a true image of the age. Ellin, as investigator, directs our attention. Without him and without the reciprocal effort of the reader, the true girl cannot emerge except under cover of night, in a weird 'fit', an obstacle on a dark stair. Authenticity struggles with accustomed artifice, freezing her 'blue'. Authenticity and artifice had confronted each other, visibly, in the opera-box of 'Henry Hastings', in the school dormitory of 'Ashworth', and in Mrs Reed's drawing-room; in 'Emma' they converge within one small girl: a pale face versus massed ringlets, an inner life versus an image. If Charlotte Brontë had lived to complete this work, the unidentified girl may have become an emblem of her sex, more than a decade before Mill set out his theory of an artifice so sealed that it would be virtually impossible to uncover women's nature.

It was habitual for women to think of the self as 'girl' or 'woman' or that Victorian category of 'lady' which Charlotte could never forget. 'Emma' challenges the given modes. It repeats the challenge presented by the increasing enigma of Lucy Snowe when she is asked 'Who are you?' Both the promise of a 'rising character' and the nocturnal outbreak of the unidentified girl direct our attention to the inner life. Charlotte Brontë demonstrates through 'Matilda' a different order of being from the contemporary model of angelic repose. Here, a rigidly constructed façade – an upright back marching to and fro in the playground, with hands in a muff, and ringlets cascading about the face – is set against mental turmoil whose only outward index is the pale face set with eyes in dark orbit. Victorian medicine assumed that a correct female mind was the healthy extension of correct appearance, both rigidly controlled, but here we are shown an extreme antithesis between mind and body. The disturbance of the child's mind tells of a divided existence: a self concealed and inadmissible in the shadow of a constructed facade.

Two people find 'Matilda' an object of interest. The first is the narrator, an intelligent widow of about forty, with whom, it seems, the girl will eventually find some haven. The other is Mr Ellin in his watching, knowing aspect. It is he, the stranger, who can read the girl's face. This adult version of Ellin (who is said to appear older than he is) turns out to be continuous with Willie Ellin, the child, in so far as he owns – to people's surprise – to having once been a 'worker'. Like 'Matilda' he has no visible connections, but is accepted by society as a man of independence and means. By virtue of this status, he exerts authority over Miss Fetherhed as he steps forward to defend the girl. I have wondered why Charlotte Brontë cancelled this dramatic scene at the end of the fragment: possibly, it is because Ellin carries the girl to her bed.

Ellin could be more central than he appears in the opening of the novel. To the discerning in the neighbourhood, he is an enigma whose antecedents are unknown, who is 'changeable', and who, as worker, must have had a dual history on both sides of the two nations. His mysteries have their parallels in the unidentified girl, and they would, in time, make a match.

At the time Charlotte was finishing *Villette*, she said to George Smith: 'I cannot write books handling the topics of the day; it is no use trying'. She implied apologetically, that she could not be ranged with Mrs Gaskell, Charles Kingsley, and Disraeli, but her self-deprecations, like her gestures of meekness and pathos, cannot be taken at face value. It is true that her so-called industrial novel, *Shirley*, was her weakest and that 'Willie Ellin's' attempt to take on the issue of physical abuse was weak on character, but in all her more ambitious works, and all the more strongly in 'Emma', she took up one of the foremost topics of the day, the Woman Question. Most compelling in her treatment of this question is her power to look beyond the immediate economic and political issues, towards the more long-term internal issues of education, emotions, and emergence in the largest sense of what women at full strength might yet contribute to civilisation. Nowhere in her work are these issues more sharply set out than in the suggestive opening of 'Emma'.

At the beginning of the summer of 1853 two ongoing events initiated that obscure passage from which, a year later, the ambitious Currer Bell emerged as compliant Mrs Nicholls.

Mr Nicholls followed his departure from Haworth with persistent letters. At first, Charlotte did not reply – but Mr Nicholls refused to forget her. Letters, it must be remembered, had a peculiar hold on Charlotte: she could wait for letters as other people crave sustenance. Though Mr Nicholls could not have known this, his distance from Haworth would have helped his cause, for Charlotte would have been more likely to respond to letters than to physical presence. With James Taylor, the physical impact of his cold will had turned her veins to ice. Then, when he retreated, she had welcomed his letters once more. Arthur Bell Nicholls was a different sort of character, with less intellect and more feeling. It seems likely his hot, stubborn temper amused Charlotte, in the same way Rochester's temper amused Jane – troublesome no doubt, but rather a challenge to a woman who can tease it away with unruffled wit. Mr Nicholls' letters would not have shown the intense knowing of Monsieur nor the playful spark of George Smith, but they would have been vehement. He presented the spectacle of unrequited emotion that mirrored her own. Charlotte could sympathise with, even admire, such a furore of feeling, such reckless exposure to ridicule – conjoined as it was with strict principle. It may even have presented a favourable contrast with Graham Bretton who had no 'tyrant-passion' to encumber his way. In her youth, Charlotte had shared, then resisted, anarchic feeling; in 1853 she rediscovered it in – of all people – the highly proper Revd Nicholls. Here was a model clergyman who broke through the facades of politeness; and his unsuppressed, unflagging letters did not repel her as did iron masculinity and hard stares. Was it not also a relief from that ladylike denial of vehemence – all those meek statements that God sends us burdens to bear?

During the summer of 1853, when Charlotte was still resisting Mr Nicholls, she may at the same time have entertained her first thought of marriage. To follow an elusive change, it helps to mark the dates of letters. On 9 July 1853, writing to Mrs Gaskell as an author who was also a married woman with family obligations, Charlotte mulled over a question that would have been vital to her if she were thinking, even remotely, of marriage. What I am venturing to suppose, on the basis of uncommon underlining, is that it was not a wholly idle question:

> A thought comes to me. Do you . . . find it easy, when you sit down to write, to isolate yourself from all those ties, and their sweet associations, so as to be quite *your own woman* . . . ? Don't answer the question; it is not intended to be answered.

What clearly disturbed her was this question of solitude: marriage was the obvious solution to the loneliness of the woman, but would it put an end to the privacy of the writer? How, she wondered, did Mrs Gaskell, with a husband, four daughters, and parish duties, protect herself from the constant tug of encircling opinion so that no fond cloud came between her and that 'severe Truth' as she knew it in her 'own secret and clear-seeing soul?' As Mrs Gaskell saw it, a work of art was a shelter from the 'daily

Lilliputian arrows of piddling cares', but she did not underplay the difficulty of deciding 'where and when to make one set of duties subserve and give place to another.' Later, George Smith captures her multiple roles in a charming valentine in which he pictures Mrs Gaskell as a robust milkmaid shouldering the pails while, behind her ample skirts, she slips her publisher (bearded in 1864 and bowed down at her heels with a pleading expression) her latest manuscript. The flirtatious, deeply affectionate relationship he developed with Mrs Gaskell puts his letters to Charlotte in perspective: her limited knowledge of sophisticated men led her to overinterpret, somewhat, Smith's habitual warmth to his women authors.

At what point Charlotte began to correspond with Mr Nicholls is not known. But one transforming event can be inferred from Charlotte's subsequent comments: it is that Mr Nicholls switched from sullen anger towards Mr Brontë to disarming words of consideration – in fact, a handsome offer to care for Mr Brontë for the rest of his life. Charlotte knew Mr Nicholls well enough to trust his promise: 'This will not be mere *talk* with him', she thought, 'he is no talker – no dealer in professions'. It is likely that this offer may have been Mr Nicholls' entrée to her heart as she corresponded with him during the second half of 1853. Pity, alone, would not have changed her intentions: during the first six months of 1853, she often expressed pity for Mr Nicholls, but remained obdurate. Possibly, it was from the time of this subsidiary offer that Charlotte began to look on Mr Nicholls as her destiny – a man Providence had sent to care for Papa. This, she told herself (and later others), was the best she could do for her father. And Mr Nicholls was, after all, a man who had loved her 'for many years' in her home character and cared nothing for her celebrity. Years before, when he had heard a rumour in Keighley that Charlotte was Currer Bell, he had come to her, 'cold & disapproving', to ask if this were true.

In corresponding with Mr Nicholls without her father's

consent or knowledge, even at the age of thirty-seven, Charlotte was contravening the rules of conduct which protected daughters from their follies. She herself was unhappy about this deception, but for some months dared not tell her father. When she did, it was 'very hard and rough work'. Back in April, just before Mr Nicholls departed from Haworth, when he and Mr Brontë were still not speaking to each other, Charlotte had felt a degree of doubt about Mr Nicholls which, as she put it, 'will not suffer me to take one step in opposition to papa's will, blended as that will is with the most bitter and unreasonable prejudices.' A month later, she told Ellen that Papa remained 'implacable on the matter' and she dared not mention Mr Nicholls' name. 'Compassion or relenting is no more to be looked for than sap from firewood.'

It has become customary to rescue Mr Brontë from the aspersions of Mrs Gaskell. The current view is that Mr Brontë had his harmless eccentricities, to be expected in the father of such original children. But this overlooks the prime evidence of Mrs Gaskell's response when she met Mr Brontë during her visit to the Parsonage in September 1853: she was intimidated by this tall, fearless, fine-looking man with his head of bristles. She marked his stern eye on Charlotte; heard him speak 'at' her. Though he treated his guest with old-fashioned politeness, he glared over his spectacles at his daughter who had not repudiated an offer of marriage quite as promptly and thoroughly as he wished. He taunted the two women for refusing to be lionised by a passing stranger: they were, he said, 'proud minxes'. And Mrs Gaskell was not the only discerning woman who was uneasy with Mr Brontë; Mary and Ellen, who had known him in earlier days, spoke of him (between themselves) as a tyrant. 'I can never think without gloomy anger of Charlotte's sacrifices to the selfish old man', Mary confided to Ellen in 1856. 'Villainous old Mr Brontë', said Ellen when asked to recall him in 1876. Of course, he was not a villain. He must have feared for his only surviving child, and wished to protect her from the dangers of childbirth. It was

Charlotte who detected a more discreditable motive which she relayed to her friends.

For the first time in her life, Charlotte took an oppositional stand to her father, based on her growing sense that his motive for rejecting Mr Nicholls had been nothing but '*ambition*'. Wealth was a motive she despised. In a level tone, she called her father 'unjust'. This rational tone was to govern all her subsequent actions until some weeks after her return from honeymoon – after which her tone changed, again, to one of fondness for her husband.

The other event in this obscure period was that George Smith became engaged. A letter from Charlotte, on 12 June 1853, confessed to 'fever' with a severe pain in her head, recurring daily, and for a time resisting any remedy. She told Smith that 'it quite incapacitated me from occupation.' This is exactly what Mrs Smith would have feared: her son's involvement with an older woman in poor health.

George Smith met his future wife at a ball at Clapham Common in April 1853. It was characteristic of the decisiveness on which he prided himself that he made up his mind at first sight. He did not tell Charlotte, but with her almost preternatural powers of apprehension, she sensed some disturbance in him which she ascribed to overwork. It seems plausible that prolonged worry about the firm was not unconnected with his engagement in November to Elizabeth Blakeway, the daughter of a wine merchant in Bedford Street, London, and granddaughter of Edward Blakeway of Broseley Hall in Shropshire. When Mrs Gaskell met her in 1856, she saw a 'pretty Paulina'. In other words, Charlotte had been prophetic in *Villette*, after all. She had been accurate in a faintly, oh so faintly ironic letter to George Smith which had assured him that such a wife as Paulina would make Dr John's happiness: 'Lucy must not marry Dr John; he is far too youthful, handsome, bright-spirited, and sweet-tempered; he is a "curled darling" of Nature and Fortune, and must draw a prize in life's lottery. His wife must be young,

rich, pretty; he must be made very happy indeed.' George, like
Dr John, might have partnered a genius who wished to make
him greater than he was, but he was too responsible to his family,
and perhaps too proper to partner any other than a conventional Victorian wife. Smith's two volumes of 'Recollections'
make no mention of her as a person in her own right; a strict
public decorum leaves her faceless and characterless, beyond
Smith's assurances of his domestic happiness. Like Paulina Home,
Elizabeth Blakeway was well-connected and presumably also
well-to-do since George's slaving (said Mrs Smith at the time of
their engagement) was now somewhat relieved. Elizabeth concerned herself with the firm's interests to the extent that her
husband left her the charge of the *Dictionary of National Biography* in
his will.

Between July and November 1853, Charlotte heard strangely
little from Cornhill. In this period she was replying to letters
from Mr Nicholls, but she remained concerned about George
Smith. In mid-November, she made plans to visit London on
some unnamed 'business', but resolved to find lodgings rather
than stay with the Smiths. Then, on 21 November, she wrote to
Mrs Smith. After not hearing much, Charlotte had recently
received a note from George Smith in which she sensed 'a good
deal of uneasiness and disturbance of mind.' She had wondered
if this had to do with mourning for a relative.

'What ails him?' she asked Mrs Smith directly. 'Do you feel
uneasy about him, or do you think he will soon be better? Is he
going to take any important step in life – as some of his expressions would seem to imply – is it one likely to conduce to his
happiness and welfare?'

The draft of Mrs Smith's reply for some reason survived in the
files of Smith, Elder – did George look it over? It was an attempt
to convey her son's engagement in the most simpering, circum-
locutory language his mother could command, using the
elaborate forms of politeness to distance her (and her own) from
the letter's recipient.

If Mrs Smith's letter was anything like its draft, Charlotte's response is explicable. On 24 November, with a portmanteau already packed, Charlotte cancelled her visit to London. Ten days after she began 'Emma', on 6 December, she wrote to William Smith Williams, intimating that, through no wish of her own, her ties with the firm must fade, and might as well end there and then. This is curious in view of the promise of 'Emma' which would surely have sustained her future with Smith, Elder, and Co., but as Charlotte had told George Smith in the course of *Villette*, her productivity depended on his willingness to grant not his hand in marriage but a little bit of his finger. Given the intensity of Charlotte's attachment, her quickness to react, George Smith's prolonged silence in the run-up to his engagement may have seemed some definite sign that she had lost her hold on him and that his marriage would end their tie. She wrote to Mr Williams:

> Do not trouble yourself to select or send any more books. These courtesies must cease some day, and I would rather give them up than wear them out.
>
> > Believe me, yours sincerely,
> > C. Brontë.

The frozen tone implies that Charlotte was more emotionally involved than she pretended. Four days later, she penned a curt formal congratulation to George Smith. It was as though his silent evasion and his mother's fingertip nicety had locked Charlotte in a dead language she did not otherwise use: correct, mechanical words. It was also at this time that she abandoned the flowing narrative of her new novel.

Instead, she now contemplated the lone prospect of the single woman who was not phlegmatic but had 'received from nature feelings of the very finest edge. Such feelings when they are locked up – sometimes damage the mind and temper.'

Soon after, Charlotte relented towards Mr Nicholls. The

sequence of events does look as if this move took place on the rebound. She retracted her refusal of his offer without, as yet, any commitment. In January 1854, he came to stay for ten days with Mr Grant at Oxenhope (the same whom Charlotte had caricatured as the presuming curate, 'Mr Donne' in *Shirley*), and was permitted to take the footpath to Haworth so that she might know him better. She urged her father's consent to Mr Nicholls' visits.

'Father, I am not a young girl, nor a young woman, even – I never was pretty. I now am ugly. At your death I will have £300 besides the little I have earned myself – do you think there are many men who would serve seven years for me?'

But could you bring yourself to marry a curate, Mr Brontë demanded.

Charlotte, who shared his pride, held her position with relentless realism: 'Yes, I must marry a curate if I marry at all; not merely a curate but *your* curate; not merely *your* curate but he must live in the house with you, for I cannot leave you.'

Mr Brontë stood up and said solemnly, 'Never. I will never have another man in this house,' and with that, walked out of the room.

For a week he did not speak to his daughter. She had not yet made up her mind about Mr Nicholls and was torn between the pressure of that decision and her worry over her father's continued resistance. Eventually, Tabby asked Mr Brontë: 'Do you wish to kill your daughter?' She stated her view bluntly that it was all Mr Nicholls' fault for not having 'more brass'.

Mr Brontë did then receive Mr Nicholls – with bitter hostility – while Mr Nicholls behaved, from now on, with admirable forbearance. Where Charlotte met a man on trial, Ellen saw 'temptation'. Charlotte's affections, Ellen thought, were not under control. In February and early March, Ellen felt some neglect, and there was a rift for the only time in their long friendship. During this time dates again speak louder than words. On 11 February 1854, George Smith married Elizabeth

Blakeway. In March 1854, Charlotte became engaged to Arthur Bell Nicholls – in letters from the end of March to the beginning of April, she announced it to Ellen as a *fait accompli*. She announced it also to George Smith, but in a deliberately indirect way (in return for his own indirectness?) with a business letter asking that any money due to her should be transferred 'to another name' (as required upon marriage). Smith, in turn, wrote to congratulate her – again, a formal letter, as though the play of 'Mr and Miss Fraser' had never been. When Mrs Gaskell met George Smith two years later, he was by then the father of a small daughter. She thought he would have been handsome if he had not grown rather stout.

In the dark, many-cornered passage through the winter of 1853–4, when Charlotte's normally forthright letters to Ellen refer neither to Mr Smith nor to Mr Nicholls, she must have changed in some way that distanced her even from Ellen. To Ellen, Mr Nicholls was too 'obtuse to be mated with a being like Charlotte' who had always, until now, disparaged him.

Ellen complained of 'inconsistency' to Mary.

'You talk wonderful nonsense', Mary retorted. 'How wd she be inconsistent with herself in marrying? Because she considers her own pleasure? If this is so new for her to do, it is high time she began to make it more common. It is an outrageous exaction to expect her to give up her choice in a matter so important, and I think her to blame in having been hitherto so yielding that her friends can think of making such an impudent demand.' But neither Ellen with her grim talk of 'enduring to the end' nor Mary's rebellious 'pleasure' was central to Charlotte's debate.

Charlotte's explanation of her love for Ellen might serve to explain her eventual bond with Mr Nicholls. These were rooted, slow-growing affections which were not intellectual. Charlotte could admire those who were good rather than gifted. If Ellen spoke of literature, Charlotte would stop her ears, she told Mr Williams, 'but she is good – she is true – she is faithful and I love her.'

At this stage of decision, Charlotte was weighing the claims of 'the natural affections' against the claims of artistic aspiration. On 3 February, she told a poet, Sydney Dobell, that the true genius was not the ruthless man who made 'a Moloch' of the intellect to which he offered up a sacrifice of the natural affections. Her rationale is that the truly great artist is an 'instrument'. This fits Charlotte's growing view that she was in the hands of Providence who was bringing Arthur Bell Nicholls into her life.

Was Charlotte's decision gradual – rooted in a growing acknowledgement of the impossibility of further domestic loneliness; or did this problem strike with sudden urgency as she perceived the end of her special friendship with George Smith? To pause further in this indeterminate passage between bald facts: we might ask what that friendship still held for Charlotte near the end of 1853, and there is a simple answer: words. It was the stirring exchange of words that she had wanted from M. Heger, not adultery; it was this, again, she still wanted from George Smith, not marriage. With words, Charlotte was in her element; letters, it might be said, were as much her medium as fiction. And though this might seem strange, a quirk of her genius, to want words so badly that withdrawal caused her to break down, time may prove her less strange than she appears. When Virginia Woolf spoke of the imagination of the novelist, she saw it rush to 'the dark places where the largest fish slumber' and then come to a stop with a jolt, for she had 'thought of something, something about the body, about the passions which was unfitting for her as a woman to say . . . The consciousness of what men will say of a woman who speaks the truth about her passions had roused her from her artist's state of unconsciousness. She could write no more.'

As an artist, Charlotte Brontë had released some truth about the passions through Frances Henri, Jane Eyre, and Lucy Snowe – and in doing so had provoked instant hostility from

men like Thackeray, Arnold, and Lewes. Contrary to this automatic reaction, Constantin Heger had seemed to invite
response, but then drew back when it made its own demands.
He liked to feel the play of that feeling under his baton but
could not tolerate it when Charlotte took the baton from him
through urgent letters. With George Smith, she translated the
play of feeling into the play of wit and vivacity. There was a
measure of unconventional liberty, but this time she was more
careful never to take the baton into her own hands. And yet,
there were covert needs – for an imaginary 'room' of her own in
his publishing house or for the tip of a finger – which he could
not meet. Arthur Bell Nicholls was the only man to offer this
meeting. I imagine that the sheer abundance of his long devotion, and perhaps even the non-cerebral simplicity of it –
released Charlotte from her lifelong fear of displeasing. For the
first time, it was her correspondent, not herself, who waited for
letters.

She left six letters unanswered before she wrote to beg Mr
Nicholls to calm his mind and forget her. Mr Nicholls promptly
replied that her letter had been such a help that he must have
her help again. Though he probably destroyed his letters and
Charlotte's replies, his public defence of Charlotte after her
death shows that he was no fool: he could put an argument
together. As he continued to write to Charlotte in the second
half of 1853, it is likely that she found relief in expressiveness to a
man who longed for her response. Words, then, vehement
words, played a crucial part in Charlotte's change. And playing
its part, too, was the unseen self. Where Monsieur had recognised her gift, and where George Smith and James Taylor had
valued her public aspect as celebrity, Arthur Bell Nicholls had
found it in him to love her home character. Though he was not
intellectually congenial as other men to whom she was drawn,
and though his Puseyite dogmatism put her off, he was the only
person who might free her from the growing fear she had owned
to Mary: the chill of Miss Snowe and Matilda; the almost

inescapable artifice of women's casing. He might free her, in short, from invisibility.

Engagement and marriage are fixed positions: what do women think and feel as they pass through rituals of public assent to an unequal order not of their making? Though Charlotte did find, in the end, more contentment than she had dared hope, at the same time her intransigent honesty allows us to glimpse through the veil, to follow doubt upon doubt, loss of time, space, and private agency, and earnest questioning of marriage in its effects on women.

The main change demanded by marriage until the last decades of the twentieth century was that women should surrender their work. When Frances Henri consents to marry the professor, this is an issue. Her wish to continue teaching is so unconventional that she has to make a special case; and it is clear that the professor is a rare man to encourage her vocation and that, even so, work may coexist with marriage only through a transformation Frances effects each evening as her thinking, active self switches into the compliant repose of the Victorian wife.

Charlotte had thought this all out in 1846, but now had to put it into practice. How would she mediate between the long-established habits of the professional writer and her new role as a wife? Hence her hesitant question to Mrs Gaskell, as a possible model, the summer before. Would Arthur (as she now called him) back her continued efforts or would he block them?

To George Smith, she wrote: 'My expectations . . . are very subdued – very different, I dare say, to what *yours* were before you married . . . In the course of the year that is gone, Cornhill and London have receded a long way from me; the links and communication have waxed very frail and few . . . All things considered, I don't wish it otherwise.' It is as though her career had been dependent on the personal tie with her publisher, something which he may have understood when he plied her with letters and invitations to London, and contemplated a journey to Haworth when she stopped writing in January 1852. His marriage propelled hers which, in turn, put an end to her writing, all of which she seems to have foreseen at the time of Mrs Smith's intimation of his engagement.

To Mrs Gaskell, she said: 'I cannot deny that I had a battle to fight with myself; I am not sure that I have even yet conquered certain inward combatants . . . I could almost cry sometimes that in this important action in my life I cannot better satisfy papa's perhaps natural pride.'

To Ellen, she confided her perplexity, fears, and need to check her regrets that Arthur could not share her thoughts. Nearly everything Charlotte said during the three months of her engagement, from April to June 1854, suggests continued doubt, measured against Arthur's undoubted goodness and future benefit to her father.

In May, she went on the last of her three visits to Mrs Gaskell's home in Plymouth Grove, Manchester. There, in her bedroom, in the company of women, she aired more freely her doubts about marriage, at first alone with a family friend of the Gaskells, the future translator of German hymns*, Miss Catherine Winkworth, then in a threesome, with Mrs Gaskell tossing comments as she moved in and out on domestic errands.

'Katie,' said Charlotte, 'it has cost me a good deal to come to this.'

'You will have to care for his things, instead of caring for yours, is that it?'

'Yes, I can see that beforehand.'

Miss Winkworth, who was only twenty-six, tried to comfort her: 'But you have been together so long already that you

---

* Her translation of *Lyra Germanica*, a companion volume to her sister Susanna Winkworth's translation of *Theologia Germanica*, was published a year later, in August 1855, with great success.

know what his things are, very well. He is very devoted to his duties, is he not? – and you can and would like to help him in those?'

Charlotte reassured her that she was used to such duties, and that it pleased her that the parish rejoiced at the return of her husband-to-be. But those duties, she went on, 'are not everything, and I cannot conceal from myself that he is *not* intellectual; there are many places into which he could not follow me intellectually.'

Miss Winkworth put the case for constant affection and practicality over brilliant gifts. Charlotte owned the validity of this position. 'Still', she said honestly, as Mrs Gaskell entered, 'still, such a character would be far less amusing and interesting than a more impulsive and fickle one; it might be dull!'

'Yes, indeed,' said Mrs Gaskell.

Miss Winkworth appeared not to yield. Home, she said, was not a place for storms and excitement; it should be the one untroubled region in one's lot. Besides, she added thoughtfully, a faithful partner would have the advantage that a wife's imagination would then be freed to entertain dreams of an alternative – 'which would be a relief sometimes.'

'Oh, Katie, if *I* had ever said such a wicked thing,' cried Mrs Gaskell.

'Oh Katie,' Charlotte joined, 'I never thought to hear such a speech from *you*!'

'You don't agree with it?'

'Oh, there's truth in it,' granted Charlotte, 'so much that I don't think *I* could ever have been so candid.' Was she thinking of her knowledge of '*love*', that emphatic word she had hurled at the oblivion of Miss Martineau, but a word she never used in relation to Mr Nicholls? 'There is danger,' she told the two women: the mental licence invited by a safe marriage 'might be led on to go too far.'

Her apprehension of marriage is most palpable in a letter on 12 June, less than three weeks before the wedding. Arthur had insisted on coming, again, when she had expected to have time to herself. It was thoroughly provoking.

'I wrote immediately that he positively should not stay the whole week, and expostulated seriously[.] I am afraid of trying Papa's patience – besides – I wish he would have kept away till July', she muttered to Ellen. 'I wish you were here.'

With Ellen, there was no threat to a writer's life; with Arthur, she was losing her last shreds of privacy. His visits showed no awareness of the needs of the intellect. She foresaw that part of herself – her 'rising' self – could not enter this marriage. And yet he did welcome her vivacity, humour, her great forehead, shining eyes, and vehemence. This rather stern, rigid man was strongly affectionate. I imagine that, brought up by an affectionate aunt, he was more demonstrative than any of the Brontës, brought up by Aunt Branwell and distanced by their father. On another occasion, when she had tried to keep him at Kirk-Smeaton, he had claimed to be dying. Alarmed, she said he might come. She had seen enough of death to know at once, on his arrival, that he was perfectly well – in fact, he lived on into the next century. In the late May of 1854 he was only pining. She marvelled at masculine weakness.

'When people are really going to die – they don't come a distance of some fifty miles to tell you so', was her aside to Ellen.

They were married on a dim morning, before breakfast, on Thursday, 29 June. Charlotte, who, it was said, looked 'like a snowdrop' in white embroidered muslin and a white bonnet trimmed with green leaves, was given away by Miss Wooler. At the last moment, Mr Brontë declined to attend the wedding. The only other guests were the faithful Ellen, the Revd Mr Sowden of Hebden Bridge who married the pair, and Tabby and Martha. The wedding night was spent at a comfortable inn at Conway in Wales: before retiring, Charlotte wrote a brief note to Ellen, mindful of her father's callous remark to Ellen that marriage would change their friendship. (For once, Charlotte had turned on Papa with a flash of indignation.) Her note to Ellen at this time was one of her most thoughtful acts, aware as she must have been that Ellen would feel bereft. She signed it with her new name: C. B. Nicholls.

After a few days at Bangor on the coast of north Wales, from 30 June to 3 July, the following six weeks were spent in Ireland, with the Bell family at Banagher and then touring Killarney, Glengariff, Tarbert, Tralee, and Cork. On arrival at Dublin, they were met by a cousin Joseph Bell who was a student at Trinity College, his brother, Alan, and Arthur's favourite cousin, Mary Anne Bell, a pretty young woman of twenty-four with dark eyes and hair and a limp, the result of a riding accident. Charlotte was pleased with her gentle, welcoming manners, with Arthur's aunt who nursed her skilfully through a cold, and with the educated air of the Bell men. Cuba House looked like a gentleman's country seat, the rooms lofty and spacious, the drawing-room and dining-room handsomely furnished – though the passages were bare and their own bedroom, on the ground floor, would have been rather gloomy were it not for a turf fire burning in the wide old chimney. Arthur's fine background, with its 'English' order and repose, came as something of a surprise to his bride, and it impressed her that he had been too much the gentleman to boast of it. How delightful it was to hear Arthur's praises on all sides and to be told by some of the family servants of her good fortune to have got 'one of the best gentlemen in the country' – a far cry indeed from the disappointment to her father's 'natural pride' and the mean position of a curate in Yorkshire who earned only £100 a year. 'My dear husband . . . appears in a new light in his own country', she wrote. Her letters declare that he took most tender care of her, yet had the understanding to leave her alone with the wild sea of the west. She began to be sure she had made 'what seems to me a right choice.'

After a few months of marriage, she told Ellen that her own time had vanished: 'It is almost inexplicable to me that I seem so often hurried now, but the fact is, whenever Arthur is in, I must have occupations in which he can share, or which will not at least divert my attention from him.' If he had a bias towards a particular course (that is, if he wished her to cancel a visit to Ellen on the pretext that she had a cold) 'I make no stir, but just adopt it.' This was not the plaint of a frustrated writer; she spoke with tolerance, even humour, and much affection for her demanding husband. It is extraordinary, in view of her uncontrollable need to write from 'The Young Men' at the age of eleven to 'Emma' at the age of thirty-seven, that she could relinquish without a murmur what had been the prime activity of her life. Yet she did so, in the end, without the slightest undertone of restiveness. A simple answer was assumed by certain dignitaries of Charlotte's time: give a woman a man, and she will stop making unnatural efforts of intellect. Mrs Gaskell saw the marriage as an answer to 'tears' — God wipes away the tears, she said. In 1857, she wreathes marriage in a Victorian image of sweet repose: 'Henceforward the sacred doors of home are closed upon her married life . . . We thought of the slight astringencies of her character, and how they would turn to full ripe sweetness in that calm sunshine of domestic peace.' In 1860, Ellen drafts a similar sentimentalised image of a married Charlotte, directed at George Smith. This drift of overblown cliché was part of a growing battle for possession of Charlotte's memory: '. . . Would that Charlotte's literary friends could have seen her as I saw her . . . A halo of happiness seemed to surround her — a holy calm pervaded her . . . circumstances had as it were no power to ruffle her holy peace'.

Of course, we shall never know exactly how Charlotte managed her extraordinary adaptation to marriage, except for one statement to the effect that it was *not* wholly a simple matter. When the day-to-day reality of marriage emerged on their return to the Parsonage in August 1854, it became apparent that Arthur assumed she would sink her existence in his.

'I think many false ideas are propagated perhaps unintentionally, I think those married women who indiscriminately urge their acquaintance to marry – much to blame . . .', she wrote gravely to Ellen. 'Indeed – indeed Nell – it is a solemn and strange and perilous thing for a woman to become a wife. Man's lot is far – far different.'

These are not rebellious words; but they do measure soberly the sheer extent of the change which marriage demanded. It might be argued that Charlotte had only nine months of marriage and, had she lived, she might have returned to her work. But children would have taken even more of her time – whatever time Arthur did not absorb. He never conceived of domestic arrangements which would have left her some freedom. It never occurred to him that she might wish for sustained time alone, and in this he was not in the least unusual. Charlotte soon found that 'the married woman can call but a very small portion of each day her own'. When she told Ellen of the way marriage drew you away from yourself, she was talking of an institution she had no power to alter. It was one of those instances to which she had referred in one of her letters to Mrs Gaskell about the position of women: evils deep-rooted in the social order 'which no efforts of ours can touch'. Given this situation, she had the maturity to make the best of it. A long time since, she had crossed the divide of privacy and loneliness, and, from the time of Smith's marriage, knew she could walk that path no farther.

The success or failure of a marriage turns, of course, on intimacy. This does not necessarily have to be full sexual intimacy – there are obviously many other forms of intimacy that can make a marriage (like that of Harold Nicolson and Vita Sackville-West) succeed. But everything in Charlotte Brontë's writings tells us that such alternatives would not have satisfied her. Jane Eyre unites completely with her husband as bone of his bone and flesh of his flesh. The really desirable man, M. Paul, insists on the existence of 'passion': it is a word that prim English 'Miss Snowe' must hear and acknowledge. Fire surrounds Rochester; pungent smoke lingers in the wake of Paul Emanuel. By day, a woman's body was constricted by the kind of lacing that forced her to sit upright – in such clothes she could not relax. At the Pensionnat Heger, it was noted with disgust that Emily's dress hung against her body – what was seen as absurdly limp was Emily's refusal of the unnatural constructions into which all other women placed their bodies. Currer Bell made the point more than once that love, for the women in her novels, turned on unusual freedom to move as they wished. With Paul Emanuel, Lucy was not *asphyxiée*: she yawned if she felt like it, and relaxed her limbs. Brontë women long to be natural, but fear to be thought unwomanly if they abandon decorum. Frances, eight years into her successful marriage to the professor, is still very, very careful not to impose an unlooked-for caress – and when, on one occasion, she does this, her husband is amazed by the sudden flash of a nature he has never seen. Jane understands that Rochester will like her more for her game of evasion during their engagement. She is not temperamentally restrained, but it does have its value for her in the short space between declaration and marriage, part of a code that defers the act of possession (which is how Rochester sees their coming union). In fact, Rochester jokes about the independence Jane allows herself – those liberties, he teases, will soon end. Possession will close off that space in which Jane can play out feelings and expressions of her own. In the event, Rochester's blindness, in their first years of marriage, allows Jane to sustain her space and liberties as part of their exceptional union.

In the course of her thirties, Charlotte Brontë had speculated a great deal about marriage from a woman's point of view, and in terms so honest that reviewers and even advanced friends like Harriet Martineau and Elizabeth Gaskell found her unseemly. Mrs Gaskell speaks of her touching 'pitch' and argues that she was but for a moment 'defiled' because the tragedies of her life 'purified' her. It is a peculiar argument, based as it is on a distorted model of ladyhood, a model Dickens satirised in 1856–7: Little Dorrit, in training to become a lady, is told by Mrs General that ladies do not see unpleasant things;

nor do they utter words that would stretch the lips beyond the rosebud proprieties of 'Papa, potatoes, poultry, prunes and prism, prunes and prism'. In that same year, Mrs Gaskell was pleading with readers to forgive the unfeminine liberties of Charlotte Brontë living as she did amongst Yorkshiremen who spoke more freely to women than was customary in polite society. Also, she pleaded – and this was her own cause as much as her friend's – Charlotte Brontë had wanted to show life as it really was. Such a plea, of course, never had to be made on behalf of Dickens.

If Charlotte thought so candidly about marriage in her novels, it is unlikely that she did not give the matter her most searching attention during the long period when she gradually attached her feelings to Mr Nicholls. Given his conventionality, she would have had to recognise how impossibly far her thoughts lay beyond the realities of a Victorian marriage. Her husband would take control, and work would have to go. She saw that clearly. (A letter from Mr Nicholls to a newspaper shows how strictly he detested publicity in women. Except when he felt called upon to defend Charlotte's honour in the columns of the *Halifax Guardian*, and his pleasure in Thackeray's praise of her in the *Cornhill Magazine*, he was on guard to protect Charlotte from any notice beyond what was due to her as his wife.) And yet the happiness that came to her in this marriage – a level of happiness she had not dared to expect – suggests that this strict man was also demonstrative in a way that was vital to Charlotte.

Mrs Gaskell, as a Victorian, was obliged to 'close the door' on marriage, as Charlotte did, permitting only this glimpse in September 1854 when she wrote of her husband to Miss Wooler: 'As to his continued affection and kind attentions – it does not become me to say much of them but as yet they neither change nor diminish.' It contented her to hear him declare his happiness in brief, plain phrases. Her own attachment was growing stronger each day, she told Miss Wooler in November: 'My life is different from what it used to be. May God make me thankful for it!'

Not only did Charlotte give herself to Arthur's concerns — his school, his times for walks, his afternoon visiting of poor parishioners — she also allowed him to monitor her letters to Ellen. Now, as she wrote as always to her oldest friend, Arthur was looking over her shoulder, deploring her freedom of expression. Letters were dangerous, he told her. She could laugh at this as, understandably, Ellen could not. He said he would rule out any further correspondence unless Ellen agreed, in writing, to burn all Charlotte's letters. Humour him, Charlotte begged her three times. Ellen devised a dodgy reply which satisfied Mr Nicholls but, privately, left her options open. In the event, she destroyed only a few of the letters (and it is to the great bulk which remained that we owe almost all direct details of the writer's unchecked opinion).

Mr Nicholls deplored the element of licence in Charlotte's letters. His motives were rather mixed: as he saw it, he was now and forever Charlotte's protector. But he was also Ellen's rival for intimacy, and ultimately her rival for possession of Charlotte and Charlotte's past — a battle they were to fight for the rest of the century.

Objectively, Arthur had no reason to fear the letters. Charlotte had rid herself of the dangerous batches before her marriage. I won't say that she destroyed them, because M. Heger believed she would not have done so. It would have been in character to bury them, as Lucy buries the precious relics of a relationship which could not be. Oral tradition in Haworth has it that at the time of Charlotte's marriage, she planted the two Corsican pines which now stand tall in the garden of the Parsonage, and I have wondered if she could have buried her past there. Alternatively, there was the convenient stretch of the moors: to leave the voice of a great love immanent in the timeless moors would have been a further bond with the author of *Wuthering Heights*.

Whatever her action, Charlotte had closed the door with loyalty and decorum; and the present morsels of gossip were harmless. She vanishes – almost – into the role of wife whose sentences begin 'Arthur . . . Arthur . . . Arthur . . .' Arthur flourishes, she repeats, and had gained weight. Arthur had been called a *'consistent Christian and a kind gentleman'* at a tea and supper they had given in the schoolroom on their return from Ireland, which five hundred children, teachers, bell-ringers, choir-singers, and other villagers had attended. It had touched her deeply, for was not goodness superior to fame? She was proud, too, when Sir James Kay-Shuttleworth offered Arthur the living of Padiham, attached to Gawthorpe Hall in Lancashire – unaware that she was the real prize for that most persistent of lion-hunters. Of course, Arthur had refused on account of his promise to Papa. Arthur was in a rather refractory mood about some Dissenters. Arthur had wished Ellen were well settled in life. Ellen must know that if Charlotte heard anything to the disparagement of single women, she would explode 'like a bomb-shell'. Arthur was now waiting to begin his walk, so she must scrawl hurriedly. Arthur always had a task for her, and she hoped that she was not sorry to help him.

One evening in November, as they sat in the dining-room, she remarked to Arthur: 'If you had not been with me I must have been writing now'. On an impulse, she ran upstairs, fetched 'Emma', and read it aloud. When she had finished, all Arthur could find to say was that critics would accuse her of repetition, since the setting was again a school. But pretentious Chalfont Lodge is not in the least like Lowood, except for the fact that both schools shape girls to an artificial design. It was an unaccountably thick response – unaccountable, given the fact that Mr Nicholls did have the wit to appreciate *Shirley*. Did he expect what both Ellen and Mrs Gaskell expected when, eventually, they came to read 'Emma', and did not find? They looked for the quieting effect of marriage – a sentimental repose. Mrs Gaskell, who had hoped to find less asperity, had the sense to see the strength of 'Emma', but Mr Nicholls, she told George Smith, had 'always *groaned literally*' when Charlotte talked of its continuance. He, on the contrary, denied he had ever discouraged his wife's writing and, in a literal sense, this is probably true. How did Mrs Gaskell know that he groaned – she had no contact with Charlotte after her marriage. When Mr Nicholls edited 'Emma', a few years later, he proved remarkably free of prudery in restoring a final scene which Charlotte herself had cancelled. The suggestiveness of this scene, where Ellin carries the girl to bed, was typical of what the Victorians found 'coarse' in Charlotte Brontë. I think he meant no harm by his initial response, but was simply unimaginative in the usual way of even quite able people who cannot see a book's potential in its draft.

Cheerfully, she explained to him the nature of a draft: 'I always begin two or three times before I can please myself.' It was an unplanned test with a clear outcome: Arthur could not take the place of her sisters. If he did not resist her writing, neither did he encourage it. The manuscript was put aside.

For a few months she was remarkably well, less prone to headaches and indigestion. Then, in December, Tabby fell ill with diarrhoea. Food seemed to pass through her immediately, and Charlotte wrote to Mr Ingham, the surgeon, for medicine. The next month Charlotte began to complain of sickness. Though vomiting was thought by Charlotte herself to be the common sickness at the start of pregnancy, it is more likely that the increasing severity of her sickness was due to the contagion from Tabby – some killer like typhoid, deriving from the polluted drinking water which killed so many Haworth inhabitants at this time. The Babbage Report on Haworth in 1850 notes that the annual mortality was 25.4 in a thousand, while that of a neighbouring village was only 17.6. The average age of death in Haworth, twenty-five, corresponded with that in some of the worst areas of London. There was still no sewerage and the exposed cesspools as well as the piled-up privies and other uncollected animal refuse were recognised dangers to public health.

The water supply was reported to be 'deleterious'. It flowed through what Mrs Gaskell called the 'pestiferous' graveyard adjoining the Parsonage.

For several weeks Charlotte's stomach could not absorb anything, including liquids; then she rallied in the last two or three weeks and begged for food. But, by then, her body had been depleted for too long by ceaseless vomiting, day and night – this seems to have been more violent than the nausea of pregnancy which, however constant, does not usually produce blood. It has been suggested that Charlotte was not pregnant but was suffering from Addison's disease. (This suggestion was designed to rescue her from an absurd notion that sustained and severe bouts of morning sickness are a neurotic sign that a woman rejects the foetus.) Since Addison's disease includes some of the same troubles as early pregnancy – anorexia, nausea, and loss of weight – the suggestion is not implausible, but the facts are too few to be sure. I am inclined to accept Charlotte's belief that she was pregnant, but agree that pregnancy was not the immediate cause of death. In all the theories surrounding Charlotte Brontë's death so far, everyone seems to have overlooked the obvious fact that there was an increasingly serious illness in the Parsonage when her first symptoms appeared: a mortal infection of the digestive tract.

Tabby died in February 1855; Charlotte, at the end of March. Both were ill, then, approximately the same length of time. Because of Tabby's age (eighty-four) and Charlotte's pregnancy, the two illnesses in the house have not been connected, but it is unlikely for anyone to die from the nausea of pregnancy unless there is some other ill. Dr MacTurk, the most able physician in Bradford, who examined Charlotte at the end of January, saw no danger. Two weeks later, at the time Tabby died, Mr Nicholls noted his wife's 'frequent fever' and uncertainty as to its cause. It has been assumed that Charlotte had tuberculosis, brought out by a cold: this was the conclusion of the death certificate. But she herself was convinced that the blood came from her stomach, not her lungs, due to excessive straining. Her husband said that she died of 'exhaustion', which may have been dehydration. He nursed her himself, and she expressed her gratitude in faint pencil notes to her Brussels schoolmate, Laetitia Wheelwright, to Amelia Taylor, and of course to Ellen. All these notes confirm her final bond with him:

'No kinder, better husband than mine, it seems to me, can there be in the world . . .'

'I am not going to talk about my sufferings, it would be useless and painful – I want to give you an assurance . . . that I find my husband the tenderest nurse, the kindest support – the best earthly comfort that any woman had . . .'

'As to my husband – my heart is knit to him –'.

SURVIVING

Charlotte was the only Brontë to die with human love on her lips. For Emily, death was the final bound to union with the divine. For Branwell, there was contrition. Anne died with piety and consideration for others. Though gentle in manner, a strong moral sense had made it possible to endure the cold world of the governess. *Agnes Grey*, which tells the hard truths of such employment, is a triumph of the inward spirit over deadening conditions. Her two novels, particularly her portrait of a resourceful woman who manages to leave her degenerate husband in *The Tenant of Wildfell Hall*, will live always in their own right. One reviewer said that no woman could have shown such 'familiarity with the sayings and doings of the worst type of fast men', while Kingsley said that no real wife would have had the heart to write down so horrible a record. Acton Bell must have had heady moments, as she exposed the ordeals of abused wife or shunned governess, but there was too little life for her beyond the scope of that watchful mind. Her death poem, at the early age of twenty-eight, is unbearably bleak.

Charlotte, as survivor, witnessed six curtailed lives. The effect on an ordinary person would have been a debilitating grief, but Charlotte Brontë was not ordinary. Repeatedly, she found new forms of imaginative life within plots of existence which would have deadened others: the effaced governess, the useless 'spinster', the dutiful wife and daughter. She had the determination of a pilgrim. Hopelessness was not her mode; when hope failed in one prospect, she turned to another. During her marriage, she was in better health than she had been for years, and it is likely that her death was due to a chance infection rather than to the long-term consumption of her sisters. After their deaths, she stated firmly that she had no constitutional illness of that kind, and she took care to nurse a cold the instant it appeared. What she had no control over was the drainage system in Haworth. Hers was not the sad, romantic death of lingering illness; it was the sharp sickness brought on by unsanitary conditions. Although she made a will on the day of Tabby's death, 17 February, she did not (unlike her sisters) expect to die. When her husband prayed for her, she said: 'I am not going to die, am I? God will not separate us, we have been so happy.'

Happiness was the achievement of her last year – not work. Through a cautiously deliberated choice in the early months of 1854, she transformed her life, choosing life over art. When Yeats debated 'Perfection of the life, or of the work', it was not, for him, a real dilemma; the debate itself was the material of art. For him, as for others, art had an absolute priority – whatever they said. Tolstoy, Hardy, and Eliot sacrificed their lives in terms of human happiness and lived what Yeats called the 'intended' life of the immortals. Charlotte's choice, in this context, was unusual: at the pinnacle of her career, when she had started what might have become her greatest novel, she had the daring to remake herself. Although, for an ordinary woman, marriage would seem a predictable choice, for her it was not. Her letters to Ellen, particularly those to do with the increasing mindlessness of Amelia Taylor, show her doubts about the way marriage narrowed women to a domestic enclosure.

Doubt accompanied Charlotte all the way into marriage. It was, if anything, at its strongest and most articulate during the last weeks of her engagement when she talked in the Manchester bedroom with Mrs Gaskell and Katie Winkworth. Yet, from another point of view, to choose Mr Nicholls was a continuation of her 'Farewell to Angria' – an even more drastic farewell to an enclosed existence in the imagination. In youth, she had discarded dreams of high life in order to confront the 'spinster' reality, the worker reality, and the industrial reality. Now she would test married reality – not fiction's dessert course of cakes and ices. Her denial of that was evident, already, in *Villette*. Approaching an actual marriage, Charlotte Brontë was as far as possible from the purple sunset of Angrian romance. She was sober, unexcited, deliberate. She had witnessed what Victorian marriage did to wives – wiping out independent character – and with full consciousness, she allowed herself to vanish in this way.

Her last words as Currer Bell were telling. To the poet, Sydney Dobell, she said in February 1854 that genius must be 'patient' and experience the claims of natural affections. To Ellen, she said that women must beware what wifehood will do to their natures. As she vanishes, she still holds in balance the antinomies of her venture: her commitment to duty; her commitment to independence. The drama of her life, as of her art, takes place there, at that point of ferment, at the intersection of opposing modes: on the one hand, a frail and shrinking lady; on the other, the pilgrim resilience. Art is not born of ideologies, but at their interface. In this sense, the character Charlotte Brontë distilled in her work continued in her life – the searching spirit not the hard outline – as she fades from sight between fixed positions.

That final debate of life or work defines Charlotte Brontë: the rare case of a genius who resigned art in favour of life. In caring quite so much for life, she forecasts writers like George Eliot and Sylvia Plath who would risk much in order to live as other women. Their advantage was to experience the facts of shadowed lives, to join the roar from the other side of silence, and like Charlotte Brontë, to raise voices which could speak to 'Reader' with intimate truth.

Charlotte's intangibility continued after her death. It remains to record her elusiveness as she slips between the positions of those who knew her in one way or another, who claimed her memory, and controlled her works.

In her sickbed, watched over by Arthur Bell Nicholls, Charlotte made a will which left everything to him. It is with this document that the battles for possession began. To Arthur, she was his wife; to Ellen and Mr Brontë she was also Currer Bell whom the world must continue to know. At Ellen's suggestion, Mr Brontë invited Mrs Gaskell, in June 1855, to write a life. Mr Nicholls thought this 'little short of desecration', but could not thwart Mr Brontë. In July, when Mrs Gaskell (accompanied by interested Katie Winkworth) came to see the Brontë papers, Mr Nicholls brought out about a dozen letters, mainly to Emily, written between 1839 and 1843. In other words, he expected Mrs Gaskell to do the biography on this minuscule basis, without knowledge of the huge quantity of juvenilia, or any sight of the manuscripts of *The Professor* and 'Emma'. (A year later, Sir James Kay-Shuttleworth who, by virtue of his social status, had some sway with Mr Nicholls, borrowed these manuscripts for Mrs Gaskell by the simple expedient of demanding them with customary crassness.)

Without Charlotte's transforming presence, some actors fell into postures; their words died on the page. Charlotte had infused into her image of Miss Wooler something of her own Fortitude; 'How hard to some people of the world it would seem to live your life – how utterly impossible to live it with a serene spirit and an unsoured disposition! It seems wonderful to me . . .' This schoolmistress, whom Charlotte had seen as a model for single women, responded to Mrs Gaskell's *Life* as the rather small-minded person she probably always was, obedient to the opinions of her betters, especially those of the clergy. She had thought *Jane Eyre* a bad book because she had heard it maligned. Now, in 1857, when the *Life* was attacked by supporters of The Clergy Daughters' School, Miss Wooler bleated the opinion of a local curate: Mrs Gaskell had been worldly-wise in furnishing gossip.

Mrs Gaskell insisted that Charlotte's letters to Miss Wooler were the best of all the batches, and she did so because they fit the virtuous image both Mrs Gaskell and Charlotte wished to promote – successfully, as it turned out, for this opinion was sustained well into the next century. To Miss Wooler, Charlotte is at her most proper and respectful, as befitted her relation to a schoolmistress who had little to teach her but had been affectionate in those far-off evenings at Roe Head when Miss Wooler had paced the schoolroom arm-in-arm with her pupils, a steady friend over the years, and a source of relief on that morning in June 1854 when she had taken the parental part in giving the bride away.

Mrs Gaskell's second-favourite letters were those to refined, grey William Smith Williams, another less-intimate batch. Again, Mrs Gaskell was selecting for the propriety which would blot out the unladylike image of Currer Bell.

Mr Brontë enjoyed the reverberations of fame, a visit from the Duke of Devonshire, and letters from all over the world with requests for samples of Charlotte's handwriting. In November 1860, Mrs Gaskell and her daughter, Meta, found him with abundant white hair, sitting up in bed, fresh and clean, cutting Charlotte's letters into strips of one line to send to admirers. He continued to pronounce his orotund platitudes, and when Mrs Gaskell pressed him for information, dressed 'up facts in such clouds of vague writing' that she found it no use to apply to him. He was clear, though, that Mrs Gaskell was to obliterate the fact that he was unaware of his daughter's work till some time after the publication of *Jane Eyre*. Yet he was big enough to overlook Mrs Gaskell's exaggeration of his eccentricities, in view of the triumph of Charlotte's biography. Together, he and Mr Nicholls selected a few of Emily's poems and one of Charlotte's, about an 'inward light' that longs for 'holier fire', for the *Cornhill Magazine*. Mr Brontë's faculties remained unimpaired until his death in his eighty-fifth year. In accordance with his promise to Charlotte, Mr Nicholls stayed with him to the end.

Mr Nicholls' guardianship was intensified by his position as a latecomer in Charlotte's life. He knew little, if anything, of its inward events. She knew better than to bother him with her passion for Monsieur or her teasing familiarities with George Smith. Still, Arthur remained anxious over the freedom of her epistolary style, not only her candour but what the Victorians called 'strong expressions', which may seem innocuous but appeared, then, unladylike. Though she joked about the tight-lipped brevity of the man of affairs, Arthur would not budge.

She had told Ellen that she had destroyed her correspondence before their marriage. But, as Ellen found, she had not done this thoroughly, for a month after Charlotte's death, Mr Nicholls found letters from James Taylor. Unable to conceal his upset, he approached Ellen for clarification. He was aware that Ellen knew things he did not. He feared revelations – to himself, I imagine, as well as posterity. He was therefore angry when Mrs Gaskell published extracts from three hundred and fifty of Charlotte's letters to Ellen: his understanding had been that Mrs Gaskell would be lent some letters in order, only, to form an impression of her subject's 'mode of thought'. A letter from Mr Nicholls to George Smith on 3 December 1856 refused to author-ise Mrs Gaskell to publish a line of his wife's correspondence. On 6 December, Mrs Gaskell is writing to thank George Smith 'for the permission from Mr Nicholls'. The only way to account for this discrepancy is that George Smith took it upon himself to set Mrs Gaskell's conscience at rest while he dealt with Mr Nicholls in a forceful way. On 11 December, Mrs Gaskell quotes George Smith's mention of a 'fierce correspondence' with Mr Nicholls.

Unfairly, Mr Nicholls blamed Ellen who returned the resent-ment. It occurred to her that Mr Nicholls' 'ignorant nursing' might have played a part in Charlotte's death, 'when better aid was proposed.' She wrote to Sir Wemyss Reid: 'but for his *selfish-ness & want* of *perception* I believe Charlotte would have been alive now.' And, however querulous by this time, she did have a point. It was a sign of Mr Nicholls' possessiveness that he had not allowed Ellen to come (though Ellen's experienced nursing had restored Charlotte during her illness in December 1851–January 1852), nor had he summoned Mrs Gaskell who hinted that if he had, she would have persuaded Charlotte to terminate the pregnancy, to save her life.

Ellen also resented the will which gave Mr Nicholls sole control over Charlotte's papers. She deplored his 'most selfish appropriation of every thing to himself.' All her life she kept the lock of Charlotte's hair which Martha Brown had cut for Ellen on the day of her friend's death (to this day it retains its warm mid-brown colour) and in the decades following Charlotte's death, Ellen tried to establish the importance of the letters, first by way of Mrs Gaskell's *Life*. From the early 1860s, Ellen tried repeatedly to publish a separate edition of Charlotte's letters, the great bulk of which remained after she destroyed a batch in 1855 as soon as a life was under way. From her point of view, she had acted responsibly, and with consideration for her friend's husband, but she could not get past Mr Nicholls' ban.

She was foiled in her approach to Smith, Elder, and Co. in 1869: George Smith encouraged Ellen to set down memories interspersed with Charlotte's letters, but warned her that Mr Nicholls held the copyright. Ellen did write three pieces, one on her first impressions of Charlotte at Roe Head in 1831, one on her first visit to the Parsonage in 1833, and a final one on the Brontës as young women in the late 1830s, their polite but inept behaviour as hostesses at an annual party for teachers in the Sunday School, their lack of dress sense, their nightly walks in the dining-room, and their miserable inadequacy as governesses. Ellen had already provided an account of the last days of Anne's life for Mrs Gaskell's biography. These are all marvellous records – empathic, astute, detailed, well-written – but if she were to press on with this memoir, Ellen needed a man to act for her. When Smith declined to intervene on her behalf with Mr Nicholls, Ellen dropped this effort. She was foiled in another approach to Scribner in 1870 (with a view to an American edition). In 1876 she infuriated Mr Nicholls by allowing Sir Wemyss Reid to make use of a few letters in a monograph on Charlotte Brontë (for which Ellen received a third of the profits). Between 1889 and 1895 Horsfall Turner of Bradford printed some three hundred and seventy letters, to accompany a volume of Brontëana. Just before publication, Mr Nicholls got wind of this, and ordered the edition destroyed. It was duly burnt, except for ten or twelve copies.

It may have been part of his battle with Ellen, a reaction to her claims and plans, that on 31 March 1895 Mr Nicholls allowed a plausible scholar, Clement Shorter, to carry away the greatest haul of Brontë manuscripts. Shorter's cohort, Thomas Wise, was a scholar-scoundrel. The two wheedled letters from Mr Nicholls and Ellen on the understanding that the letters would be given to the South Kensington Museum as a gift to the nation, but once the letters were in their hands, they denied any such promise. Carelessly, Wise divided the manuscripts and sold them to the highest bidders around the world. Some of the booklets were taken apart, and the Angrian saga, the Roe Head fragments, 'Henry Hastings', 'Ashworth', and the drafts and fair copies of the Brontës' poems, were scattered far and wide. But the roots of this story lay, far back, on that day in the dining-room which had been the sisters' room for writing, then Charlotte's room, and was no longer her own – that day in October 1854 when Arthur bent over his wife's shoulder, afraid of the indiscretion of words which spoke of a long shadow-life which Ellen had shared and from which he had been excluded, and saw in his wife's letters a rival he must '*burn*' so that no one in Yorkshire, no one in England, no one in the oncoming posterity that lay ahead for his own dear wife, no one must see. He lived the rest of his life, another fifty years, waiting to meet her in the next world.

Who owned Charlotte's memory? As Mr Brontë cut up her letters for souvenirs and Ellen tried to preserve her literary remains, Mr Nicholls' guiding idea was to block almost everything. When Ellen arrived at the Parsonage within hours of her friend's death, Mr Nicholls said to her: 'Any letters you may have of Charlotte's you will not show to others'. In 1895, when Ellen tried to find out what had become of her letters to Charlotte, Mr Nicholls offered his opinion that Charlotte had burned them as soon as read. Most likely, he burnt them himself; if Charlotte really did so, it could only have been at her husband's insistence. In the Nineties, the age of the New Woman, he continued to deplore Mary Taylor's letters (many never came to light) and said – inexplicably – that Charlotte's letters to her father (unfailingly attached and considerate) were still not for publication. He seems to have been unable to distinguish Ellen's claims from those of mercenary dealers, the cultishness of souvenir-hunters (whom, understandably, he loathed) from the warm interest of Haworth locals. When a new stone for Charlotte was laid in the church, he saw to it that the old one was broken into a myriad pieces and buried at least four feet deep in the earth. He was angry when the sexton, Mr Greenwood, wished to honour his last baby with the name of 'Brontë'. He refused to baptise the child. At length, little Brontë Greenwood was smuggled to Mr Brontë, in bed at the Parsonage, who gleefully performed the deed.

So, after Charlotte's death, Mr Nicholls was not popular in the village of Haworth. Nor was it forgotten that he had refused to bury Michael Heaton of the long line of Heatons who had lived for centuries at the hall on the edge of the moor. When Mr Brontë died in the summer of 1861, Mr Nicholls was not offered the living. In November 1861 he returned to Ireland, taking his wife's dresses, her drawings, her portrait by Richmond which he had been the first to see, and a heap of Brontë manuscripts. On 25 August 1864 he married his cousin, Mary Anne Bell, the gentle young woman who had met Charlotte and Arthur when they had arrived in Dublin ten years before. Mary induced him to marry her by inviting his opinion on another offer. After their wedding, Mr Nicholls took her to the same Welsh inn where he had spent his first days with Charlotte. It could be a sign he had been happy there or merely a sign of regular habits. He became a farmer in Banagher, attending local markets and idolised in his home at Hill House. The new Mrs Nicholls allowed him to hang Richmond's portrait of Charlotte in the living-room. So he lived on and on and into the next century, in that remote, unvisited place, in a home filled with Brontë memorabilia, while a package and box of increasingly valuable Brontë papers gathered dust at the bottom of a cupboard. He never examined the 'little books', but he cut out Emily's head from a painting of the family and discarded the others. It was not till after his death that Mrs Nicholls set eyes on Branwell's now-famous painting of the three sisters.

Ellen lived till 1897, when she would have been eighty, courted from time to time by Brontë scholars, but warped by uselessness. What seems to have happened to Ellen is what Charlotte had feared for herself: that bitter winter that could befall women of small means to whom no useful activity lay open. It was in view of this possibility that Charlotte had admired the steady enterprise of Miss Wooler in running her school and the good works of the 'spinsters' in *Shirley*. Ellen was less placid than Charlotte had imagined, for Ellen, like Mary Taylor, had some restless intelligence which could not be satisfied with running stalls at church bazaars. A model woman would have been content with her lot, but it is not difficult to sympathise with the spurts of irritability that break out along the flow of Ellen's letters: irritability at Nicholls for his sweeping appropriation of Charlotte alive and dead; irritability at Mrs Gaskell for her failure to acknowledge Ellen as her prime source; and irritability for the fact that though the *Life* was a commercial as well as critical success, Ellen – whose letters had been the bedrock of the *Life* and who now could not afford to stay at Brookroyd when her mother died – got nothing at all. Ellen came to see this as an oversight by George Smith who had wished Mrs Gaskell to swell the *Life* to two volumes, whose firm had the profits, and who could be 'tight-fisted' (as he and Charlotte used to joke) – not with authors who knew how to ask for handsome sums, but with a single lady of modest manners like Charlotte herself.

Ellen, declining into genteel poverty, would not have asked for payment, but on 20 February 1869 she did ask for a donation of books for her church stall. George Smith refused courteously. Ellen repeated the request: this time, he refused curtly – Miss Nussey's was one of too many charities which beset busy men with their hands on the ropes. Only connect, one wants to say. A notion that his firm had exploited Miss Nussey would never have occurred to a man like George Smith because she appeared in the light of a woman of no importance. By this time Smith was the pre-eminent English publisher of the age, settled into that image of the bearded, cheery commander of a sound ship whom Leslie Stephen encountered when he arrived in London from Cambridge in the late 1860s.

Three years after Smith's refusals, he asked Ellen to identify the precise locales of places in Charlotte Brontë's books for the illustrated edition.

'I should esteem it a favour', Smith wrote on 30 March 1872. 'The interest you have always felt in Charlotte Brontë and her sisters, will, I hope, induce you to excuse my thus troubling you.'

This mannered politeness plays on Ellen's devotion to her friend, though, in fact, he was requiring her to do an unpaid job for his firm. On 28 May 1872 there was a letter of thanks for her 'valuable information' – thanks was all she was to get, apart from one free copy. Smith's manner to Ellen was controlling and, in one case, impatiently blunt when he told her that some poems she had submitted were not up to the mark. George Smith was one of many intelligent men, like Thomas Huxley and Leslie Stephen, who visited George Eliot but did not take their wives, for though she was recognised as the greatest English novelist in the 1860s and 1870s, proprieties had to be preserved. As Smith explains the matter: 'Our daughters were growing up; we were living in Hampstead, the favourite abode of Mrs Grundy [prudery]. George Eliot was more or less a public character: her actual position [living permanently with Lewes] was perfectly well known, and unpleasant social results may have followed if young girls had been known as her visitors.' It became a marital joke when Elizabeth Smith questioned her husband's frequent visits to another woman to whom she was not introduced. Then, one night at the opera, Mrs Smith saw George Eliot. Contemplating the writer's tired, broad, melancholy face, she assured her husband brightly that he was free to see that woman every day of the week.

Not only did George Smith retain his conventional attitude to beauty and respectability, he remained tight-fisted with those who could least afford it. In 1880, as an act of benevolence, he built a sanitary block to house forty families in George Yard in the heart of Whitechapel; at the same time, he was determined to prove that charity of this sort could pay. He thought it 'odd to note the dread and hate the poor cherish for the workhouse' when he was told of the frantic pleas of a tenant, a widow too old to earn. The widow trusted Mr Smith to protect her; Smith's agent replied that he was a man of 'iron'. Unlike the 'iron' of James Taylor, his will was encased in the softest of gloves: with patient reasonableness and unfailing courtesy, he persuaded the widow to accept eviction: to the workhouse, indeed, she must go. Another instance of 'benevolence', as he liked to call it, was to turn out a family for the peace of other tenants who complained that the wife's screams when her husband beat her were a continual disturbance. Smith described his handling of the situation with humorous complacency:

> I tried to explain to him [the husband] that I was far too liberal-minded to object to a man beating his wife as much as he wished. What I did object to was that his wife insisted on screaming, and disturbing the other lodgers when he beat her. I doubt if my explanation was entirely satisfactory to the husband but he had to seek other quarters where he could thrash his wife to his heart's content . . .

He was no different, really, from other paternalistic Victorians of his prospering class; decisive, buoyant, affectionate as he was, he could on occasion fall below the princeliness Charlotte Brontë once hoped of him, and below the compassionate morality she practised and preached. (Once, when Charlotte sent a sovereign to a poor man who broke his leg, Papa said that women were often impulsive in deeds of charity. She replied: 'In deeds of charity men reason much and do little; women reason little and do much, and I will act the woman still.') At the age of seventy, in 1894, George Smith was graced by an honorary degree from Oxford for producing the *Dictionary of National Biography* – the proudest moment for a boy who had been expelled from school at the age of fourteen. He died in 1901, a millionaire with a mansion on Park Lane.

In these scenes, there is no residue of the living Charlotte Brontë – she became an object for competing interests. Harriet Martineau saw her 'a shadow again – vanishing from our view'. She might have vanished completely, existing solely in the shadow of her works, were it not for three other people whose characters, as Charlotte had known them, continued, and whose words and memories did not fade.

Mary Taylor was not one to change. A person who spoke the truth, she saw the necessity to watch her words. Her reminiscences for Mrs Gaskell end when she realises she is crossing the frontier of unpublishable opinion. *Sotto voce*, she marks Charlotte's sacrifice to 'tyranny' in the form of that 'selfish old man', a daughter's sacrifice too common to strike people as it ought. Mary shared with Charlotte a Yorkshire forthrightness: with Mary, it was ideological. She wished women had the nerve to '*grumble hard*'. She had no sense of the pleasures of the imagination, so that her pity of 'poor Charlotte' seems close to Mrs Gaskell's – for opposite reasons: Mrs Gaskell pitied Charlotte for a becoming, ladylike weakness; Mary pitied her as a feminist pities a victim. There was truth to both views, but each had its reductive agenda. Charlotte was indeed a lady in the Victorian sense, but she was also strong in spirit and expression; she did indeed pander to her father, but she did also love him and live by ideals of duty and selflessness which she scorned to discard and which she practised in defiance of what she felt to be the shallow-hearted politics of Harriet Taylor Mill.

Mary did not prosper in New Zealand following her cousin's death in 1852. Back in 1846, Charlotte had predicted that Mary would 'remain in New Zealand as long as she can there find serious work to do – but no longer –'. This is exactly what happened. Mary developed no attachment to the country, and had no opinion of its inhabitants. To be starved for books sounds an odd reason to return to England, but books, above all, were what Mary craved. Increasingly, she preferred to lie on the sofa with a good book to the company of 'narrow minded and ignorant' mamas. Though she was too sensible not to recognise that her acquaintance in Wellington was not inferior to what she would have elsewhere and though she made new friends, she could not believe in them. In the end, she grew impatient with the remoteness of a nineteenth-century colony where news from home took months to arrive. In 1860 she returned to Gomersal, and with her own earnings, built a house, High Royd, where she lived to 1893.

'Pag', as Mary signed letters to Charlotte, seems in one way to vanish together with the strong, subversive aspect of the living Charlotte. She refused to talk to Brontë enthusiasts. As the recipient of Charlotte's confidence about Monsieur (in response, perhaps, to her own honesty about her unreciprocated attraction to Branwell), she destroyed Charlotte's letters – all but one about the first visit to George Smith's office in the summer of 1848. Mr Nicholls, never having seen Mary and knowing nothing of mutual confidence, baulked simply at the tone of a woman who wished to set the world to right on many points, and it seems likely that he burnt almost all 'Pag's' letters to Charlotte. In this gap, we must pause, again, to 'hear' lost voices: their honesty about women's lives. 'Pag', or Mary, belongs with those who continued the living idea of Charlotte Brontë; those of her words which do come down to us are burning – not flames of eloquence but hard, gritty lumps of coal. She came to regret the loss of Charlotte's letters, but lived out whatever they had reflected of their shared mind. Both had deplored the compulsory inactivity which depleted women. The idea survives in Mary Taylor's novel, *Miss Miles, or A Tale of Yorkshire Life Sixty Years Ago*, begun in New Zealand in the 1850s when (she had told Charlotte proudly) it was full of 'disputing' and 'original views of life'. It was finally published in her seventies, in 1890. Here, Dora, aged twenty-five, describes a life much like that of Caroline Helstone in *Shirley*: 'I sit by myself till I know myself on the verge of idiocy. I know too, what I have so long dreaded, that this is an ordinary fate. Women die off so sometimes. The first step is, of course, that they sink out of sight – no one knows what becomes of them.'

Mary thought it would be impossible for Mrs Gaskell to tell the truth, but found that she had. Where others' memories went on in silence, Mrs Gaskell opened hers to the public. Her record is, as Mr Brontë concurred, 'full of truth and life': the rare conjunction of a moving and eloquent storyteller with a great subject of whom she had first-hand knowledge. We hear Charlotte speak, and we see her physically through these representative eyes: with ill-set features, shrinking before contemporary notions of feminine beauty, a modest presence at The Briery at Windermere in August 1850, a slight figure in mourning, saying little of her losses, but speaking a good deal of sense in a hesitant, sweet voice. More important, we hear from Charlotte's own lips of certain autobiographical sources for her fiction. At the Parsonage in September 1853, while Mr Brontë smoked his clay pipe in his study, and Mrs Gaskell sat with Charlotte before the fire in the dining-room, she heard the story of Maria's death 'just like that of Helen Burns' and of Emily's character as a model for Shirley. It was directly from Charlotte that Mrs Gaskell had the idea of Emily as 'a remnant of the Titans, great-granddaughters of the giants who used to inhabit the earth.'

Mrs Gaskell undertook a brave task in writing a biography

when most of the participants were very much alive. 'No quail-ing', Mr Brontë urged. She told the truth about Carus Wilson, and blamed Mrs Robinson for her sport with Branwell, and attacked Lady Eastlake for her vicious dismissal of Currer Bell as one unfit for the society of her sex. Mrs Robinson (widowed, and now cavorting about London as Lady Scott) threatened legal action, and the friends of Carus Wilson raised a furore of protest. So, Mrs Gaskell came to regret the biography in the years imme-diately following its publication. Yet, in fact, she did achieve what she had hoped in securing her friend's reputation. Charles Kingsley reflects the effect of the *Life* on adverse opinion of Currer Bell. He wrote eagerly to Mrs Gaskell to declare his con-version: '"Shirley" disgusted me at the opening, and I gave up the writer and her books with a notion that she was a person who liked coarseness. How I misjudged her!' He now regarded her as 'one who is a whole heaven above me.' Mrs Gaskell had given a picture 'of a valiant woman made perfect by sufferings.'

Mrs Gaskell tells a coherent story, as Dr Johnson does in his *Lives of the Poets* or T. S. Eliot in his biographical booklet on George Herbert. All convey a lasting imaginative truth based on a selec-tion of facts. Mrs Gaskell's selection went back to the sad account Charlotte gave of her life, in her period of greatest mourning in the second half of 1850 – that period of 'dark & durable regrets' which follow the first phase of mourning when death appears a mercy. What Elizabeth Gaskell heard that day at Windermere in the summer of 1850, and again on her visit to the Parsonage in September 1853, and what she relays for posterity, is a tragedy of deathbeds and gravestones. Her view was coloured by the fact that their friendship was active during Charlotte's bleakest years from 1850 till her marriage in 1854: 'one felt how lonely and out of the world she must be, poor creature.' She persisted in this view despite the counter-truth which Charlotte revealed to her of the 'liberty' of solitude, a view she took also with the editor of *The Christian Remembrancer*: seclusion, she argued, was 'more congenial' than social circles.

The version of her life that Charlotte gave Mrs Gaskell was touched not only by her grief and loneliness in a particular phase, but by acute feelers which would have picked up Mrs Gaskell's initial doubts as to her delicacy. She was always perfectly ladylike with Mrs Gaskell, as with the Kay-Shuttleworths who brought them together. When talk at The Briery turned to the notion that certain authoresses had overstepped a line which men felt to be proper, Charlotte said earnestly: 'I trust God will take from me whatever power of invention or expression I may have, before He lets me become blind to the sense of what is fitting or unfitting to be said!' Mrs Gaskell's letters on meeting Charlotte suggest that she collaborated in the biographical impression Mrs Gaskell at once formed, but the Charlotte who stayed with the Kay-Shuttleworths was Charlotte at her most repressed and socially uncomfortable. The fact that she confided in Elizabeth Gaskell in the interstices of their stay seemed revelatory – but she was confiding only the respectable image of restrained mourning in place of the equally respectable image of trembling timidity which she offered to London society (an image which Thackeray underlined sentimentally after her death in his 'Last Sketch': 'The trembling little hand was to write no more.' How does this fit with the boldly opening hand that revealed the disturbance of 'Emma'?). Charlotte showed people only that part of herself they would wish to see. It was not necessarily deceptive; it is simply a fact that different associates call out different aspects of our natures in response to their own tastes and beliefs.

In this way, Charlotte muted the satiric edge she expressed freely with her sisters and old friends, and allowed Mrs Gaskell no sign whatever of her verbal abandon with Monsieur nor her sparring with Smith. Smith himself concealed their tie. Despite much pressure from Mrs Gaskell, he would not allow her to see the bulk of Charlotte's letters to him. They 'contain matter of too purely personal a nature', he told her. When Mrs Gaskell sat before the fire at the Parsonage in September 1853, she owned to

Charlotte that she did not like Lucy Snowe. And what did Charlotte think? Although she appeared to tell Mrs Gaskell so much at this time (including the courtship of Mr Nicholls), Mrs Gaskell's dislike of 'that – person – that . . . "Lucy Snowe"' would have sealed off any mention of passion. And, indeed, this restraint fits Mrs Gaskell's need to insist on the lady's refined separation from the darker revelations of her heroines. As Mrs Gaskell put it to George Smith, she wished people to 'honour her as a woman, separate from her character as authoress.' So it was that, while Mrs Gaskell opened up some of the autobiographical sources of Charlotte's fiction, she closed off others. The manuscript of the *Life* shows how Mrs Gaskell edited letters on the page as she revised, editing Charlotte's character, so as to miss out what was free-spoken and natural, her humour and tartness. When Mrs Gaskell detected a satiric edge, it appeared to her mildly undesirable – an indication that Charlotte was deprived of the comforts of marriage and had not yet attained that serenity that was the ideal of Victorian wifehood.

What Mrs Gaskell wished to exclude was any hint of a nature that was other than perfectly proper. She told George Smith that she particularly wanted to include Charlotte's pleasure in his mother's chaperonage when she met men of letters 'which is a piece of womanliness (as opposed to the common ideas of her being a "strong-minded emancipated" woman) which I should like to bring out'. Although Mrs Gaskell met M. Heger and read the letters in his keeping, she argued, on the basis of Charlotte's rejection of the Revd Mr Nussey and Mr Taylor, that, unlike her heroines, Charlotte herself was not 'easily susceptible' of 'the passion of love'. 'Easily' ensures that this assertion is strictly true, yet it is also misleading in a biography where the passion for M. Heger is omitted. This is not a criticism of the *Life*: any hint of passion would have been disastrous at that time. (Ellen tried to cover up Charlotte's passion for M. Heger with a bogus statement that the reason she suffered so much in Brussels and after was because Mr Brontë, together with his curate, Malone, 'fell

into habits of intemperance' in Charlotte's absence. With growing anger towards Mr Brontë, Ellen pictured a noble daughter
reclaiming her father.) Mrs Gaskell also played down Charlotte's
independent vehemence and exposés of religious hypocrisy. She
was concerned about the publication of *The Professor* (edited by Mr
Nicholls), following on the heels of the *Life*, in June 1857: she had
found it 'disfigured by more coarseness, – & profanity in quoting
texts of Scripture disagreeably than in any of her other works'.
Mr Nicholls, she thought, had not expunged enough of those
phrases which would detract from the image of Charlotte Brontë
which she had drawn.

'But oh! I wish Mr Nicholls wd have altered more!' she wrote
to George Smith. 'For I would not, if I could help it, have another
syllable that could be called coarse to be associated with her
name.'

Though there were limits, then, to Mrs Gaskell's view, it was
accurate within these limits, and in so far as it presented itself as
a woman's record of a woman, with its emphasis on private life,
domesticity, obscurity, rather than public achievement, it has
been called even 'subversive'. As Mrs Oliphant said, it was new in
its plea for 'every woman dropped out of sight'. In these terms,
Mrs Gaskell gives a live picture of the way Charlotte appeared to
many sympathisers of her time: modest, refined, scrupulous,
dutiful, and quietly suffering.

The most living memory comes appropriately from M. Heger,
as his voice rises from the busy obscurity of a teacher's life on 7
September 1863. In that year, Ellen Nussey wrote to ask if he
would consider translating five hundred of Charlotte's letters
into French with a view to publication. His voice comes forward
to make an eloquent plea for complete silence. And he is very
persuasive because he felt nothing of the possessive fear of Mr
Nicholls, only a sensitive awareness of what letters had meant to
Charlotte. His views were based, obviously, on the expressiveness
of the letters Charlotte wrote to him in French, still in his
possession and shown in confidence to Mrs Gaskell on the

understanding that she would not reveal them. M. Heger, whose wife had misinterpreted Charlotte's letters and refused to see Mrs Gaskell, realised that only the recipient himself could hear the subtle nuance of her language – untranslatable in his view:

> *Quant à la traduction en français quelque soit le mérite du traducteur, il me parait que, de toutes les oeuvres littéraires, ce sont les lettres qui perdent le plus à être traduites. Dans la correspondance intime, l'àpropos, la liberté de l'allure, l'allusion voilée, les demi-mots, même les charmantes negligences d'une forme toute spontanée donnent, aux moindres choses, une grâce, un charme* intraduis- ibles. [As for the translation into French, whatever may be the merit of the translator, it seems to me that of all literary work it is *letters* which lose most by being translated. In intimate cor- respondence, the associations, the freedom of expression, the veiled allusion, the half-hints, even the charming carelessness of their entire spontaneity, give the smallest things an *untrans- latable* grace and charm.]

He was convinced that intimacies of this kind, '*où rien ne déguise le mouvement intime de sa pensée*' ['where nothing disguises the inner- most movement of her thought'], should not be published, much less translated: what was said '*à voix baissée, à l'oreille de mon cœur*' ['whispered at the ear of my heart']. In these terms, Heger expressed his inability ('*mon impuissance*') to do as Ellen desired: it would be like attempting to paint the flight or to notate the song of a bird.

These words suggest his capacity to know her as she wished to be known through the flight of words. It was this epistolary act in the course of her life that brought her closest to the imagina- tive acts of art. Monsieur's response shows how readily he grasped this, and there cannot have been any statement after Charlotte's death which would have pleased her more. His live words leap from the page. In the retrospect of a century and a half, the sojourn in Brussels does not appear another episode in the Brontë tragedy, but amazing luck that of the relatively few people Charlotte met in her sequestered and short lifetime, she happened on this man who could release the voice held within her. It was a fusion of passion and creativity which should not be seen in solely sexual terms. What was so rare was not that Charlotte should have responded to Monsieur in the way she did, but that Monsieur should have existed at all: a man who prepared the way for the experiments in teachers' love which she devised in fiction. 'I know what *love* is', she protested to Harriet Martineau, and she believed with the utmost conviction that what she had experienced must be repressed neither by the caution of prudery nor by the agenda of practical feminism. What she had shared with her '*maître*', the reach of words, was central to her hidden life as she explored a forbidden path, opening up the question of passion.

An unforgettable love for her teacher, a craving for letters, and burning words, were part of the writer's passion, not 'something flighty and skin deep' (as Charlotte put it to Ellen), but the 'genuine fire'. It is easy to see this life as a series of losses – the loss of Maria, the loss in Branwell of her writing-partner, the withdrawal of Monsieur, the deaths of Emily and Anne, the fading of her exuberant friendship with George Smith – yet loss does not explain the central fact of Charlotte Brontë's existence: her capacity to use her experience as the material of art. Unrequited love might have crushed another; she transmuted it into the natural but inadmissible desire of Frances for the professor, Jane for Rochester, Caroline for Robert Moore, Lucy for Graham Bretton. The intimacy and candour of these stories draw out readers' reflections, and come to carry the burden of readers' lives. This reciprocity, different perhaps for every generation, is vital to the writer's survival.

The 1890s and the first decade of the twentieth century saw the last of those who had known Charlotte in person. In 1908, the son-in-law of George Smith heard from the son of the artist, George Richmond, something his father had remarked.

Was it that Charlotte had luminous eyes and carried herself a little awkwardly? By now, memories were rather vague, while Brontë legend – the doomed family in Romantic solitude – grew and flourished, drawing thousands (in high summer, it could be two thousand a day) to remote Haworth (dotted with Jane Eyre Souvenir Shoppes), the most visited literary shrine in England next to the far more accessible Stratford-upon-Avon. For Haworth remains hard to reach. On a dark, rainy Monday in February there were changes of trains and long waits on northern platforms. There is still no easy transport between Keighley and Haworth. (The Brontës used to walk the four miles in all weathers.) The taximan grumbled at the tourists and the lure of Brontë legend: do you believe that, he wanted to know.

In fact, the Parsonage Museum is careful to abjure legend and 'purple heather' so as to place the family in the industrial context of West Yorkshire. And it's worth coming any distance to see the paisley muslin dress worn by Charlotte in the early 1850s (prettier than the sombre clothing of her heroines), her paint box on the table in the dining room, and the narrow room where Emily had her visions. The Parsonage also has a superb collection of manuscripts and books. It is through these, of course, that Charlotte Brontë survives: in the Roe Head fragments, scrawled on scraps, the hot words still scald the page. Her bond with her closest intimate, whom she called 'Reader', vibrates more strongly than ever as women come forward in public life. Stale labels – Romantic or feminist rebel or spirit of the moors or dutiful daughter – fade before the subtle promise of her positions. Our view changes, as the Victorians recede behind the horizon of a century and more.

The strange passion of Charlotte Brontë disturbed her contemporaries. They called her unladylike because they could not define it. In 1852, the year *Villette* was completed, Florence Nightingale noted the fact that ladies were told they had no passions. She observed that the 'accumulation of nervous energy' made them feel every night when they went to bed 'as if they were going mad' and obliged them 'to lie long in bed in the morning to let it evaporate and keep it down'. Charlotte Brontë addressed this buried life, from her first outbursts at Roe Head to the strange 'fit' of the showpiece schoolgirl in her last fragment. This seethed, unseen, beneath the crust of the 'eminently artificial thing'. The bold step was publication: the unstoppable vehemence which exploded into the open when Jane declares – voices – her love for Rochester.

Voicing was what was at issue for author and character, speaking as complement to burning: the 'I' that comes forward with such pressing truthfulness in *Jane Eyre* and the 'I' forced inexorably to the surface, from its frozen shelter, in *Villette*. Across the Atlantic, Emily Dickinson, reading everything the Brontës published, voiced an 'I' of her own in terse revelations, speaking beyond her lifetime to future readers who would know how to hear her: 'I held my life with both my hands / To see if it was there –', she wrote. 'My Life had stood – a Loaded Gun –'.

When Henry James summed up the nineteenth century's history of decent reticence, he omitted Charlotte Brontë from the line-up of hallowed names:

> Miss Austen and Sir Walter Scott, Dickens and Thackeray, Hawthorne and George Eliot, have all represented young people in love with each other; but no one of them has . . . described anything that can be called a passion – put it into motion before us and shown us its various paces . . . Miss Austen, Walter Scott and Dickens will appear to have omitted the erotic sentiment altogether, and George Eliot will seem to have treated it with singular austerity. Strangely loveless, seen in this light, are those large, comprehensive fictions 'Middlemarch' and 'Daniel Deronda.' They seem to foreign readers, probably, like vast, cold, commodious, respectable rooms, . . . across whose acres of sober-hued carpet one looks in vain for a fireplace or a fire.

In *Jane Eyre*, fire is not *wanting*. Passion, *Villette* insists, does exist and must be defined in terms which retrieve it from voyeuristic invitation in the name of art. The painting of 'Cleopatra' (derived from '*Une Almée*' [a dancing girl] by Defiefve which Charlotte had seen in Brussels) belongs in the tradition of secular art which views women's bodies as acres of inviting flesh. In a picture of a marriage market, painted by Edward Long in 1875, voyeurism again played its part in one of the great crowd-pleasers of the Victorian age.* The fact that parts of *Jane Eyre* continued to be seen as improper reading for girls in the 1880s, where Long's covert pornography was welcomed as perfectly proper, suggests the degree of confusion over the question of passion.

'The Babylonian Marriage Market' took its subject from George C. Swayne's *The History of Herodotus* (1870) which described the custom of the Babylonians who would auction off young women in an order judged on their appearance. The artist shows twelve women, ranged in order from pretty to ugly, awaiting their auction at an eastern market. Only the title's reassurance that the buyers intend marriage, not prostitution, lends a veneer of respectability. The pornographic prompt was an obvious part of this painting's success, however much art critics went on about the 'great technical triumph' of the women's jewels. (The notices in the journals of 1875 were, without exception, ecstatic.) Each woman is presented on a platform and unveiled in turn for inspection: the women in the foreground, awaiting their show, pander to fantasy by mindless compliance. The best are shown as quietly self-satisfied; the worst are talkers – talk as disturbance. None has character in the sense of Jane Eyre or Lucy Snowe: these are not women to be known as Rochester and Paul Emanuel know women.

The market scene repeats itself in Virginia Woolf's account of

---

* Commissioned by an MP at a vast price, it was sold at Christie's in 1882 for £6,615 (a saleroom record at that time) to Mr Holloway. The painting is now in the collection of the Royal Holloway and Bedford New College, Egham, Surrey.

the parade of women at society balls in Edwardian London, which she and her sister, Vanessa, were compelled to attend. She notes the unknowability of society women in their compliant artifice: 'The dinner bell, striking eight, calls them into existence.' She herself would creep behind a curtain to escape the shame of selection or non-selection (for almost no one asked her to dance), and behind the curtain, she would read Tennyson.

This kind of invisibility is continuous with the 'new region' opened up in the journal, letters, and fiction of Charlotte Brontë: space as potency that lurks in shadow, that walks – of necessity – concealed, that finds utterance behind the veil of 'Currer Bell'. Jane staring at the horizon from the roof of Thornfield, Lucy musing in the forbidden alley, open a new topography of the mind, a counterspace to the linearity of action. Within a few years of Charlotte's death, Emily Dickinson was creating a more revolutionary counterspace in poems which literally pushed words apart, as 'Existence' itself broke through the bars of routine. At night, Dickinson, like the Brontës, took possession of this space of her own. Something of this region is revealed in *Giselle*, a ballet of the 1840s. In the second act, a prince who has toyed fatally with a peasant girl, ventures into a dark wood, beyond his habitat. There he discovers the Willis, buried women whose passions have been denied. Theirs is a shadowy, nocturnal life that fades by day, insubstantial – and yet invincible. By day, Giselle had been no more to the prince than a subject at his disposal. By night, Giselle is empowered to dance the prince to death, yet she remains emotionally partnered, sustaining an unprecedented existence between two modes. She refuses the daily mode of casual surrender; and refuses, too, the dehumanised coldness of the Willis' vengeful power. For the Willis demonstrate the terrible obverse of passion, which was Charlotte Brontë's long fear: the freezing effect of wilful purity, the chilling ideology of automatised lives.

As Giselle must exist between the inauthentic daylight world of exploited passion and the hidden moonlit world of destructive anger, between movements of maddened abandon and those in regimented lines of a sterile decorum, so Jane Eyre finds some ground of her own *between* the opposite tyrannies of reckless licence and frigid constriction. These polarities derived most immediately from *Wuthering Heights*, and may represent, at the deepest level, the imaginative affinity that drew Charlotte to her sister, Emily, whose heroine, Catherine Earnshaw, exists between two impossible men and between two houses: the anarchic Heights and the tame Grange with its lifeless order. Catherine exists only in her restless moving *between* these abodes of men, with no institutionalised habitation of her own. Men reproach her for not fitting the given modes: Heathcliff condemns her betrayal of their wild affinity; Edgar, her husband, regrets her waywardness, unlike proper wives. In different ways, the ghost-lives of Giselle, the buried nun, and Catherine demonstrate the impossible choices that faced women, denying them full-bodied existence.

It is Lucy Snowe's salvation to find a place between the sterile emptiness of the school and 'the great deep' of mental break-down, when she comes to rest in 'a cave in the sea'. This is a private room at the Brettons, white and green. Here, in this 'submarine home', she finds a new form of existence, between shore and high water, between the artifice of daily safety and destructive nightmare. Lucy thinks the glass in her room 'might have mirrored a mermaid' – a more sensible mermaid than Hans Anderson's who oscillates pathetically between the deeps and the shore's social order, between a below-sea identity with her strange fishtail and the contrived leggy image she must assume if she is to satisfy her need for sexual love, between incommunicable love – her tongue cut out – and eventual dissolution in the foam of the sea. The cave makes it possible for Lucy to survive, quiet on the surface where the public gaze falls, yet holding within reach 'a portion of my existence' which illness had opened as the 'new region'.

Charlotte Brontë draws her reader into this uncharted

region, analagous to the imaginative region she and her sisters had shared when they had paced the darkness after the rest of the household had retired, the same space Charlotte went on pacing night after night in her sisters' ghostly footsteps – as Mrs Gaskell realised when she heard those steps as she lay in bed during her visit to the Parsonage. The reader is drawn into this refuge of freedom and free speech, a counter to society, with its own laws and modes of being. It is curious how strongly this counter-space is present in the most realist of nineteenth-century worlds like *Villette*, 'Mr Gilfil's Love-Story', *The Mill on the Floss*, *Middlemarch*, and *The Portrait of a Lady* where women try so hard to do right by the social laws they have internalised. It is as though it is precisely when women feel society's claims most forcefully that some undefined, shadowy life detaches itself from their outward life and comes, as it were, into being. In this counter-drama there is being without, as yet, form. When Charlotte Brontë speaks of a 'rising' character, the present participle is not an accident. We first glimpse this character in Elizabeth Hastings through the eyes of her brother, recalling the fact that Charlotte's identity as a writer emerged, at first, through her tie with her brother. Henry Hastings observes his sister from a window as she moves in and out of darkness: 'A figure came towards the window and paced back again and was almost lost in the shadow . . .' Again and yet again, Charlotte Brontë invites us to peer into shadow: to see Miss Hall by the flickering candle in the empty dormitory; to see Jane Eyre in the dimmest corner of Mr Rochester's drawing-room; to see Lucy Snowe as she recedes down the forbidden alley to meet the ghost of her buried self; to see in 'Emma' the sleepwalking girl who is unable to say who she is.

As readers, we share, too, the expanse offered by the tension of delay. Charlotte Brontë explored passion from an alternative point of view, not as conquest or possession, but as unfolding of a character whose mystery is sustained by delay. Beyond the limits of staling roles there extends an immense expanse of shade: passion as authenticity, logic, moral acumen, and verbal sway.

In the last chapter of _Villette_, the letters between lovers are a locus of expanded passion. And then, when the body of the lover seems lost, Lucy turns away: 'There is enough said . . .', a final gesture of privacy ensuring the continuation of this love in the reader's imagination. There is, in this open end, a moving together of author and character into an unseen space behind the text which links them with the reader. This allows desire to circulate in the spaces between people and in their absence. Charlotte Brontë is at the height of her genius when she suggests that passion may find alternative expression in the act of writing which preserves desire forever live, waiting – somewhere – to be fulfilled.

Outwardly, Charlotte Brontë preserved her cover as model Victorian. Entering Thackeray's soirée in London, in gravity, in silence; at The Briery with the Kay-Shuttleworths and Mrs Gaskell, saying that God should take away her gift if she ever knowingly infringed what was proper: wherever Charlotte surfaced in public, she appeared tame and quiet. But with her sisters and the friends of her youth, she was fiery, truth-telling, articulate. A space for this 'home' character was crucial to her writing, as to Anne's. For Emily, it was simply not an issue. She exemplified in its purest form Dr Johnson's dictum that 'the province of poetry is to describe Nature and Passion, which are always the same.' For her, the norms of public conduct were impossible to feign. She never left the Parsonage after 1842, the year in Brussels when she had locked Charlotte to her side. She shunned the world with fierce contempt on her path to 'infinity'. It was harder for Charlotte and Anne who opened some intercourse with the world. The only possible terms on which they could do so was not to surrender whatever they voiced as they paced, each night, around the table. This was hidden even from Papa who had no notion of the dreams, ambitions, and scorn stirring across the narrow hallway.

What was decisive in such lives did not lie, primarily, in external event; it was secreted in turns of mind like Charlotte's refusal of the idea that for her soul to be saved some of our most human attributes must be denied: the tenacity of passion, the need for words, the unfolding of character. At some unknown point, she conceived a new life for the spirit which could encompass nature: natural desire; natural expressiveness. Nothing was so 'dark' for her as the unnatural manner of Emily's death, a re-enactment of Maria's. Where Maria had submitted in holy resignation to what was done to her as a child, Emily as a vigorous, tall adult had seemed to draw death upon herself, driving her body to its end. During this brief passage, she had refused to communicate on the subject with her sister who, again, had to watch in helpless silence. Against this model, Charlotte devised another which did not oppose body to spirit. Life beat strongly in her small form so that she, the 'puniest' of Papa's children, was at length sole survivor. Though a life-denying faith may have seemed, at times, the only consolation in the face of lives which were cruel and short, the survival of Lucy Snowe was Charlotte's mature answer to her dead sisters: nature not sublimity; nature disciplined and infused with a dauntless spirit.

Her visible aspect disarmed her contemporaries with the manners of her time: the little mittens, the brown silk ribbon in place of the fashionable coronet of plaits, the self-effacing, courteous replies. The very intactness of her privacy allowed her to reply so obediently to Southey's ruling that literature should not be the business of a woman's life. In her time, she could not permit herself to lift the veil – even for a moment, even to Mrs Gaskell. She told Mrs Gaskell that Southey had been 'kind and admirable; a little stringent but it did me good.' Was it good to face the facts of the social system with bleak endurance? Or was she, after all, a respectable Victorian, accepting her place in society with all the humility of an Esther Summerson or a Little Dorrit whose first concern was care for a father or guardian? Once, when Branwell set fire to his room, Anne's first thought was that Papa must not be disturbed. Quietly, she called Emily who was strong enough to carry their stupefied brother. Life at the Parsonage turned on the convenience of Mr Brontë, and Charlotte, who played the leading and longest part in this enterprise, did believe in it. Altruism had an absolute religious sanction. It was not only duty; it was born of filial piety and genuine care for Papa's health and privacy. This self-command was an achievement of a high order: she had to integrate her gift with the generosity to think of others. In this sense, Charlotte Brontë remains a speaker for the soul as well as for women. It could be said that she conferred a soul on the Cause which was then coming into being. This declared soul and her struggles to preserve it against the distortions of excess – rage, passion, obedience – shapes the riveting figure of Jane Eyre: a pilgrim along the difficult path between venture and selflessness. In bringing these together, Charlotte Brontë formed her rising character.

This was a woman who walked invisible. Her life was shaped by ties with those to whom she revealed her nature, her sisters and friends; and shaped, too, by men who could not sustain her emergence. The distress caused by Constantin Heger and George Smith was not because they could not know her, but because of their promise: they invited her to a tantalising partial emergence, and then withdrew when she voiced notes alien to their sense of fitness. Only in novels did she emerge fully; there, alone, did she call up men adventurous enough to give assent to the woman to be.

What such a woman was to be remained in the making, as her energy and passion surged forward, inexorably, through Charlotte Brontë's works. What is the nature of women? This is the overwhelming question she left behind, and any answer remains, as yet, uncertain – to some a shadow of obscurity, to others a shadow of promise. Pause, and pause again: how are women's lives to be defined? That question echoes beyond her time, and beyond ours.

CHRONOLOGY

1816

Born in April in Thornton, near Bradford, West Yorkshire, the third daughter of the Revd Patrick Brontë from Ireland (aged 39) and his wife, Maria Branwell, from Cornwall (aged 33).

1817

Only brother, Patrick Branwell, born in Thornton.

1818

Third sister, Emily Jane, born in Thornton.

1820

Fourth sister, Anne, born in January in Thornton. Mrs Brontë unwell. In April, the Brontë family moved to the moorland parish of Haworth, West Yorkshire.

1821

Aunt Branwell arrived from Cornwall to nurse her sister. Mrs Brontë died of cancer in September.

1824

In July, the eldest Brontë girls, Maria (aged 10) and Elizabeth (aged 9) entered the grim Clergy Daughters' School in Cowan Bridge, on the road to the Lake District, through Lancashire. In August, Charlotte (aged 8) entered the school, followed in November by Emily (aged 6) – the youngest child in the school.

1825

In February, Maria sent home from school, with neglected TB; died on 6 May. In May, Elizabeth sent home, also with neglected TB; died in June. On 1 June, Mr Brontë removed Charlotte and Emily from the school.

1826

Mr Brontë's return from Leeds with twelve toy soldiers for Branwell which sparked the children's imaginative play.

1831

In January, Charlotte (aged 14) entered Roe Head School, run by Miss Wooler. Silver medal for ladylike manners. Met Ellen Nussey and Mary Taylor.

1832

Charlotte left school at the end of the summer 'half'.

1832–5

Charlotte taught her sisters at home. The Angrian saga, co-authored by Branwell, flourished.

c.1833

Branwell aspired to be an artist. Painted the so-called 'gun group' portrait of himself with his sisters. It appears that Mr Nicholls thought it was a poor likeness, and destroyed it, retaining only the profile of Emily.

c.1834

Branwell painted the famous 'pillar' portrait of his three sisters (aged 18, 16, and 14).

1835–8

Charlotte's intense misery as a teacher at Roe Head School. Private outbursts in the 'Roe Head Journal', the source of her mature vehemence.

1837

Ambiguous correspondence with Poet Laureate, Robert Southey: private sarcasm covered by the smooth verbal glide of submission. Tries out the slave-to-duty image with great success.

1838–9

Parted from Branwell, Charlotte began to go her own way with the invention of new heroine: volcanic interior life of an apparently subdued governess.

1839

In March, refused first suitor, Ellen's dull brother. From May–July, misery and suppressed anger as governess for the Sidgwicks of Stonegappe, near Skipton, Yorkshire. In August, refused her second suitor, the Revd David Bryce, believing an Irish curate was beneath her.

1840

Despite 'Farewell to Angria', continued to use shallow high-life material in 'Ashworth'. Sent 'novel' to Hartley Coleridge who was justly critical.

1841

Early in the year, still trying to revise 'Ashworth'. March–December, governess for the 'low' Whites of Upperwood. Refuses Miss Wooler's offer of a school of her own because of longing for study abroad.

1842

Went with Emily to the Pensionnat Heger in Brussels. First heady recognition of her gift as a writer from her demanding teacher, M. Heger. Aunt's death. Return to Haworth.

1843

Charlotte returned alone to teach and study further at the Pensionnat Heger. Love for M. Heger who withdrew. Desperate loneliness and depression, but put poems in order.

1844–5

Apparent stagnation in Haworth, but exercising verbal abandon through passionate letters in French to M. Heger. Obsessive waits for the post. Estrangement from Emily who was absorbed in 'Gondal Poems'. Anger with Branwell for repeated failure and imbroglios with low life of Yorkshire.

1845

Mary Taylor left to start a business in New Zealand. Branwell dismissed in disgrace from tutor's post at Thorp Green. Anne, too, returned to the Parsonage after over four years as governess at Thorp Green, bringing two-thirds of *Agnes Grey*. Charlotte discovered Emily's poems and devised a plan for joint publication. The three sisters resumed creative sharing. Invention of pseudonyms.

1846

Publication of *Poems* by Currer, Ellis and Acton Bell. Charlotte completed *The Professor* (rejected six times) and began *Jane Eyre*, in August-September, while nursing her father after an eye operation in Manchester.

1847

George Smith of Smith, Elder accepted *Jane Eyre*, and published it within a few weeks, in October, with instant success. Charlotte unable to enjoy this because Emily Brontë's *Wuthering Heights*, published in December, was maligned for its savagery.

1848

Anne Brontë's *The Tenant of Wildfell Hall*. To squash rumour that the Bell brothers were one person, Charlotte and Anne revealed their identities to George Smith in his office at 65 Cornhill in London. While in London, the two sisters insisted on further cover as 'the Misses Brown'.

In September, Branwell suddenly died. Immediately, Emily sickened with TB. Died in December (aged 30). Anne became ill.

1849

Charlotte nursed Anne. Together with Ellen, Charlotte took Anne for last look at the sea at Scarborough. There, in May, Anne died (aged 29). Charlotte survived through burst of writing; completed *Shirley*. Triumphant post-publication visit to George Smith in London. Met her literary hero, Thackeray.

1850

Friendship with Harriet Martineau. In June, second stay with George Smith's family in Bayswater, London. Wrecked Thackeray's party in her honour. Blissful few days in Scotland with George Smith. Uneasy stay with literary lion-hunter, Sir James Kay-Shuttleworth, at Briery Close, Windermere, but there met Mrs Gaskell. Immediate friendship between two novelists. Edited posthumous edition of sisters' works, with 'Biographical Notice', which began Brontë legend.

1851

George Smith proposed Rhine journey to Charlotte. Beginning *Villette*. In April, turned away third suitor, James Taylor, literary manager of Smith, Elder, who soon left to found branch in India. In May-June, third hopeful then distressful stay with George Smith and family. George Smith and Charlotte disguised themselves as 'Mr and Miss Fraser' on jaunt to Richmond. Intensive correspondence with Smith on Charlotte's return to the north. As correspondence waned in the autumn, Charlotte went into decline, breakdown, and physical illness associated, again, with waits for the post. Refused repeated invitations to visit the Smiths.

1852

In January, George Smith contemplated mid-winter journey to Haworth. After four-month break, resumed *Villette*, incorporating recent viscissitudes of friendship with Smith, contrasted with memories of M. Heger. In November, George Smith shocked by third volume which dismisses the hero based on him in favour of Belgian teacher. Underpaid Charlotte for this novel. In December, Charlotte refused Mr Nicholls.

1853

Last visit to London to see *Villette* through the press. Smith seemed older but even more charming. Charlotte's visits to London prisons, madhouse, and hospitals. Renewed fictional attention to abused and abandoned children in 'The Story of Willie Ellin' and unfinished novel, 'Emma'. George Smith engaged in November; Charlotte relented to Nicholls.

1854

In February, Smith married; in March, Charlotte became engaged to Nicholls. March-June, continued doubts about marriage, especially in confidence to Mrs Gaskell during last visit to her home at Plymouth Grove, Manchester. June marriage (aged 38), given away by Miss Wooler since, at last moment, Mr Brontë refused. Faithful friend, Ellen, attended. Wedding tour in Ireland. Increasingly happy and well. Nicholls unencouraging about 'Emma' and wished to burn correspondence with Ellen.

1855

Parsonage servant, Tabby, had digestive-tract infection, possibly typhoid which killed an exceptionally high number of Haworth inhabitants in the mid-nineteenth century. Charlotte possibly infected by Tabby; also pregnant. On 17 February, Tabby died after six-week illness; on 31 March, Charlotte died after a six-week fever: vomiting blood from the stomach and unable to eat. Last letters expressed gratitude to husband. Her will left everything to him.

1857

Mrs Gaskell's profoundly sympathetic, classic biography retrieved her friend's reputation for 'coarseness' (by which Victorians meant vehemence and passion). Followed blueprint for Brontë legend set out in Charlotte's 'Biographical Notice' (1850) on her sisters. Smith, Elder finally published *The Professor*, after their three rejections in Charlotte's lifetime (making nine rejections in all).

1861

Mr Brontë died. Arthur Bell Nicholls returned to Ireland, taking Brontë manuscripts and memorabilia which he retained until 1895.

ABBREVIATIONS

Some archives and works are abbreviated throughout the Source Notes, as listed below. Otherwise, a full reference is given for the first citation of a work or source; thereafter it is given in a short form.

AB	Anne Brontë
ABN	Arthur Bell Nicholls, Curate of Haworth, eventually husband of CB
Berg	Berg Collection, New York Public Library
BL	British Library
Bon	Bonnell Collection, Brontë Parsonage Museum
BPM	Brontë Parsonage Museum
Brotherton	Brotherton Collection, University of Leeds
BST	*Brontë Society Transactions*
CB	Charlotte Brontë
CBEW	*An Edition of the Early Writings of Charlotte Brontë*, i–ii, ed. Christine Alexander (Oxford: Blackwell, 1987–1991)
CBL	*The Letters of Charlotte Brontë with a selection of letters by family and friends*, i–iii, ed. Margaret Smith (Oxford: Clarendon Press, 1995–2004)
CBP	*The Poems of Charlotte Brontë*, ed. T. J. Winnifrith (Oxford: Blackwell, 1984)
CH	M. Constantin Heger, CB's teacher in Brussels
EB	Emily Jane Brontë
EG	Elizabeth Gaskell, a fellow-writer and biographer of CB

EGL	*The Letters of Mrs Gaskell*, ed. J. A. V. Chapple and Arthur Pollard (Manchester University Press, 1966)
EN	Ellen Nussey, CB's lifelong friend and correspondent
Essays	Charlotte and Emily Brontë, *The Belgian Essays*, transl. and ed. Sue Lonoff (New Haven: Yale University Press, 1996)
GHL	George Henry Lewes, critic; later, partner of George Eliot
GS	George Smith, CB's publisher
GSR	George Smith, 'Recollections of a Long and Busy Life', two vols, The National Library of Scotland, MSS 23191–2
HM	Harriet Martineau, a fellow-writer
JE	*Jane Eyre: An Autobiography*, ed. Margaret Smith (1847; repr. Clarendon Press, 1974). Also in World's Classics paperback (without appendices)
JT	James Taylor, manager at Smith, Elder, and Co.; admirer of CB
LFC	*The Brontës: Their Lives, Friendships and Correspondence*, i–iv, ed. Thomas J. Wise and J. Alexander Symington (Oxford: Blackwell, 1933, repr. 1980). This has inaccuracies and omissions, but for many readers (Virginia Woolf for one) provided a highly readable arrangement of primary documents brought together conveniently in one collection.
Life	Mrs Gaskell, *The Life of Charlotte Brontë*, intro. Winifred Gérin (1857; repr. London: Dent/Everyman, 1971). This is the first, unexpurgated edition, but without the additions to the third edition.
MT	Mary Taylor, CB's close friend and correspondent
PBB	Patrick Branwell Brontë
PB	The Revd Patrick Brontë
PML	Pierpont Morgan Library, New York
RHJ	The Roe Head Journal, a collection of fragments

	(1835–8) in BPM and PML, printed at the end of *Tales of Angria*, ed. Heather Glen (London: Penguin Classics, 2006)
S-G	The Seton-Gordon Collection, BPM and John Murray archives
Sh	*Shirley*, ed. Herbert Rosengarten and Margaret Smith (1849; repr. Oxford: Clarendon Press, 1979). Also in World's Classics paperback (without appendices)
V	*Villette*, ed. Herbert Rosengarten and Margaret Smith (1853; repr. Oxford: Clarendon Press, 1984). Also in World's Classics paperback (without appendices)
WMT	William Makepeace Thackeray
WSW	William Smith Williams, reader at Smith, Elder, and CB's first supporter.

SOURCE NOTES

EPIGRAPH

vii '*I wanted to speak . . .*': BPM. Bon. 98. RHJ, 455.

CHAPTER ONE: THE UNSEEN SPACE

7 '*A private governess . . .*': From Stonegappe, Yorkshire (8 June 1839), *CBL*, i, 191.

'*. . . looked on vacancy*': *Agnes Grey*, ed. Hilda Marsden and Robert Inglesfield (1847; repr. Oxford: Clarendon edition of the Brontës, 1988), ch. 13.

the rising character: Winifred Gérin, *Charlotte Brontë: The Evolution of Genius* (Oxford University Press, 1967; repr. 1971) said rightly that with CB fulfilment was more than a literary achievement; it was the creation of character (Introduction, xv).

'*externals*': 'Biographical Notice of Ellis and Acton Bell' (19 Sept. 1850) to posthumous edition of Ellis [Emily] and Acton Bell [Anne Brontë], *Wuthering Heights and Agnes Grey, with A Selection from their Literary Remains*, (Smith, Elder, and Co., 1850), repr. in most current editions of the Brontës.

8 '*superior talent*': This dream is central to 'Captain Henry Hastings', the second last of five 'novelettes' which CB wrote in her early twenties. They are collected by Winifred Gérin, ed., *Five Novelettes* (London: Folio Press, 1971), 243.

'*I said . . .*': *CBL*, i, 191.

'*by whose wealthy . . . members . . .*': *JE*, iii, ch. 4.

'*Never a new idea . . .*': *Agnes Grey*, ch. 11.

9 *closed eyelids*: 'Roe Head Journal'. See ch. 3 for discussion of these writings.

expressive grey eyes: Observed by many, including Matthew Arnold (in letter 21 Dec. 1850), EG, and GS.

like one with early hip trouble: Impression of the artist, George Richmond (who drew CB in June 1850), recalled by his son, John, in a letter to Reginald Smith, son-in-law of GS (30 Dec. 1909). BPM. S-G 102.

teeth: CB to EN (29 Oct. or early Nov. 1847), *CBL*, i, 556.

10 '*never yet submitted . . .*': CB to Mary Dixon (who wished to draw CB in Brussels between 30 Jan. and June 1843). Berg. *CBL*, i, 313.

'*home*' *character*: CB's phrase 'natural home-character' is in letter to EN (12 Mar. 1839). BPM. Gr: E2. *CBL*, i, 187.

12 *PB's background*: See John Lock and Canon W. T. Dixon in *A Man of Sorrow: The Life, Letters and Times of the Rev. Patrick Brontë* (London: Nelson, 1965); Edward

Chitham, *The Brontës' Irish Background* (London: Macmillan, 1986); J. Horsfall
Turner, ed. *Brontëana: The Rev. Patrick Brontë's Collected Works* (Bingley: T. Harrison
and Sons, 1898) and Erskine Stuart's essay on Brontë nomenclature in *BST* 8:
43, 83. Some details from 'Currer Bell', *Belfast Mercury* (Apr. 1855). Juliet
Gardiner provides a fine summary of essential facts in *The World Within: The
Brontës at Haworth: A Life in Letters, Diaries and Writings* (London Collins & Brown,
1992), ch. 1.

13 *Two letters concerning PB*: Henry Martyn to associates of Wilberforce, requesting
financial assistance for PB. One letter is undated; the second dated Feb. 1804.
Bodleian Library, MSS. Wilberforce d. 14.

choosing 'Brontë': *Sh*, iii, ch. 3.

15 *'scarcely striking'*: 'Prefatory Note to "Selections from Poems by Ellis Bell"' (Smith,
Elder, 1850), repr. as Appendix to *Wuthering Heights* (Oxford University Press,
World's Classics, 1981), 369.

nature as on the body of a mother: JE, iii, ch. 2: 'I have no relative but the universal
mother, Nature: I will seek her breast and ask repose.'

16 *'Meeting of the Waters'*: EN's reminiscences of her first visit to the Parsonage,
summer 1833, *LFC*, i, 112–13.

'our Land of Silence': CB to EG (30 Sept. 1854). Manchester University Library.

Mungo Park's and Major Denham's expeditions: Gérin's introduction to *Five Novelettes*, 8.
The expeditions of Mungo Park (1771–1806) would have reached the Brontës
through *Blackwood's Magazine*. It has been suggested that they also read Park's
Travels in the Interior of Africa (1799) in the library of Ponden Hall, across the
moor.

Grammar of General Geography: The Brontës' copy is in BPM. Noted in Gérin, *Anne
Brontë* (London: Thomas Nelson, 1959), 51.

'the vast sweep of the Arctic Zone': *JE*, i, ch. 1.

'pictured thoughts . . .': See CB's 'Lines on Bewick' (dated 27 Nov. 1832), *CBP*, 139.

18 *prone to say 'very little . . .'*: PB to EG (24 July 1855). John Rylands University Library,
Manchester.

19 *a loaded pistol*: EG to a friend (Sept. 1853), *LFC*, iv. 91.

Modern Domestic Medicine: By Thomas John Graham (1826). PB's copy, heavily
annotated, in BPM. Bon 38.

PB's letters to Mary Burder: *LFC*, i, 60–68.

speaking from behind a mask: *Life*, 36. The lack of independence in the daughters'
replies (with the exception of EB) was first noted by Katherine Frank, *Emily
Brontë: A Chainless Soul* (London: Hamish Hamilton; NY: Viking Penguin, 1990),
44–5.

21 *'slave'*: 'Plead for Me', *The Complete Poems*, ed. Janet Gezari (Harmondsworth:
Penguin, 1992), 22–3. Chosen by EB herself to be published in *Poems* (1846).

23 *it suggested . . .*: Gérin, *CB*, 10.

variant of Prunty: History of the family name discussed in Chitham, *The Brontës' Irish
Background*. Any firm fact seems hard to determine.

24 *She dislikes . . .*: CB's version of the Cowan Bridge disaster in *JE*, i, chs. 5 to 9.

25 *'The Advantages of Poverty in Religious Concerns'*: *LFC*, i, 24–7.

26 *When she considered 'them'*: I am indebted to Allegra Huston of Weidenfeld & Nicolson for this point.

27 *'the pain . . . from hunger . . .'*: EG to Catherine Winkworth (25 Aug. 1850), *EGL*, 75: 125, and *LFC*, iii, 143.

    'During many years she had walked with God . . .': *LFC*, i, 59.

    'Last Lines': *The Brontës: Selected Poems*, ed. Juliet R. V. Barker (London: Dent, 1985; repr. 1993), 99.

    'Misery': The second half of this poem was completed 2 Mar. 1836. *The Poems of Patrick Branwell Brontë*, ed. Tom Winnifrith (Oxford: Blackwell, 1983), 23–33. The *Works of Patrick Branwell Brontë*, ed. Victor Neufeldt, ii, 492.

    'That hour . . .': Quoted in PBB's letter (Dec. 1835) to the editor of *Blackwood's Magazine* in Mrs Oliphant, *Annals of a Publishing House: William Blackwood and His Sons*, ii (Edinburgh: Blackwood, 1897), 177–9.

28 *'the rigid & lengthened corpse'*: Part of the 'Roe Head Journal', BPM. Bon 98/6. RHJ, 464.

    'she described Maria . . .: EN's 'Reminiscences of Charlotte Brontë', *Scribner's Monthly*, ii (May 1871), 18–31. These were originally written to accompany a volume of CB's letters to EN. In the end, only a few letters were published in *Hours at Home* (1870), and the 'Reminiscences' followed separately. *LFC*, i, 92–100.

    Miss Andrews . . . jerked Maria from the bed: A school-fellow described the scene to EG who related it in *Life*, 45.

    Charlotte's dream: MT's Reminiscences for EG (18 Jan. 1856), printed in *Life*. Given in full in Joan Stevens, *Mary Taylor, Friend of Charlotte Brontë: Letters from New Zealand and elsewhere* (Oxford University Press and Auckland University Press, 1972), Appendix B. The scholarly scrupulousness of transcriptions of MT material makes this compilation always preferable to *LFC*.

29 *'must be tenacious of life'*: *JE*, i, ch. 13.

30 *'You have lived the life of a nun . . .'*: *JE*, i, ch. 13.

    Anne Brontë on education: *The Tenant of Wildfell Hall*, ed. Herbert Rosengarten (1848; repr. Clarendon, 1992), ch 3.

31 *CB letter to Miss Wooler* (30 Jan. 1846), *CBL*, i, 448.

    Miss Beale on the school: Elizabeth Raikes, *Dorothea Beale of Cheltenham* (1908), quoted by Gillian Avery, *The Best Type of Girl: A History of Girls' Independent Schools* (London: André Deutsch, 1991), 50.

    'coarseness': *Life*, 375: 'I do not deny for myself the existence of coarseness here and there in her works, otherwise so entirely noble. I only ask those who read them to consider her life . . .' The same view is expressed by HM in the *Daily News* (Apr. 1855): 'the coarseness which, to a certain degree, pervades the works of all the sisters, and the repulsiveness which makes the tales by Emily and Ann[e] really horrible to people who have not iron nerves.' See also review by Elizabeth Rigby, 'Vanity Fair and JaneEyre', *QuarterlyReview*, lxxxiv (Dec. 1848), 153–85: 'a great coarseness of taste'. Inga-Stina Ewbank explores the connotations of 'coarse' in *Their Proper Sphere: A Study of the Brontë Sisters as Early Victorian Female Novelists* (London: Edward Arnold, 1966), 46.

    'life of desolation': EG to Tottie Fox ('Tuesday' [27] Aug. 1850) *EGL* 79: 129–31, and *LFC*, iii, 147. 'Poor Miss Brontë', Emily Winkworth wrote to her sister, Catherine

Winkworth, after reading EG's letter describing CB's cruel life as one which had taken every spark of merriment out of her and left her, surely, tainted with the consumption which had killed her sisters (30 Aug. 1850), *LFC*, iii, 151.

32 *EG's tendency to dramatise her reports:* Jenny Uglow, *Elizabeth Gaskell: A Habit of Stories* (London: Faber, 1993), 242–3.

33 *religious bias of PB and Aunt Branwell:* See Tom Winnifrith, *The Brontës and Their Background: Romance and Reality* (London: Macmillan, 1973), 36–8, and Rebecca Fraser, *Charlotte Brontë* (London: Methuen, 1988), 46.

Aunt Branwell's influence on Anne: Gérin, *Anne Brontë*, 101.

'*the pattern*', '*There is no other way . . .*': Thomas à Kempis, *The Imitation of Christ*, abridged by John Wesley (1803). See title page and ch. 12. BPM.

CHAPTER TWO: FALSE IDOLS, TRUE FRIENDS

35 '*the nature of women*': J. S. Mill, *The Subjection of Women* (1862, revised 1869), repr. in John Stuart Mill and Harriet Taylor Mill, *Essays on Sex Equality*, ed. Alice S. Rossi (University of Chicago Press, 1970), ch. 1, 148.

confinement and '*stagnation*': *JE*, i, ch. 12.

36 *no other educated family:* CB to WSW (3 July 1849), *CBL*, ii, 227.

the Brontës were masked at school: Life, 47.

Tabby blowing the fire: CB to EB from Brussels (1 Oct. 1843), *LFC*, ii, 305.

37 *a box of twelve soldiers:* PB brought this from Leeds, after a conference there, on 5 June 1826.

'*We then chose . . .*': *CBEW*, i (1826–32), 6.

38 '*Bed plays . . .*': 'The History of the Year', *CBEW*, i, 5.

Kanhoji Angria: CBEW, ii, part 1 (1833–4), xx.

39 *EB and AB dissatisfied: CBEW*, ii, part 2 (1834–5), xiii.

nowhere in the juvenilia: The Early Writings of Charlotte Brontë (Oxford: Blackwell, 1983), 226–7.

40 '*wandering outlaw . . .*', '*What am I . . .*': Byron, *Childe Harold's Pilgrimage*, canto III.

41 '*Corner Dishes: A Day Abroad*': *CBEW*, ii, part 2, 108–10.

'*My Angria and the Angrians*': Ibid., 245–50.

43 '*Visit to Young Soult*': Ch. 4 in 'Visits in Verreopolis' (later, Verdopolis), begun 11 Dec. 1830. *CBEW*, i, 309–12.

'*my feelings . . .*': Ibid., 311.

'*The Poetaster: A Drama*': Ibid., 180–96. Based on Ben Jonson's *The Poetaster, or His Arraignment* (1601) in which Jonson attacks the poetry of Thomas Dekker and John Marston. As Jonson identifies with Horace at the top of the hierarchy of poets, so CB identifies with the respected Glass Town writers, Captain Tree and Lord Charles Wellesley (details from Christine Alexander). Vol. i, dated 3 July 1830, is in Harvard College Library: Lowell I (2). Vol. ii, dated 8 July 1830, is in the PML: Bonnell Collection. Both volumes are handsewn booklets of sixteen pages.

44 *most of her juvenilia is boring:* Christine Alexander speaks of 'a fascination that borders on the tedious', *CBEW*, ii, part 2, Introduction, xvii.

the *Angrian saga and CB's mature work*: In *The Early Writings of CB*, 244, Christine
  Alexander acknowledges that 'it would be wrong to exaggerate the importance of the juvenilia to the later work.' She says again, 246, that Angria 'had
  stunted her development as a writer of realistic fiction'.

  Illustration of Marian Hume: BPM.

45 *The Complaint*: PB's copy in BPM: 526.

  '*All my days* . . .': From 'Long My Anxious Ear Hath Listened' (12 Oct. 1830). Not
  in *CBP*. With story 'Albion and Marina', printed privately by Clement Shorter
  in *Latest Gleanings* (London, Jan. 1918). Copy in Berg.

  '*blighted lily*': 'A Peep into a Picture Book', *CBEW*, ii, part 2, 90.

  '*creeping plant*': 'Passing Events' (dated 29 Apr. 1836), Gérin, ed., *Five Novelettes*, 72.

46 '. . . *I've nothing else to exist for* . . .': 'Passing Events', ibid., 44.

  '*patient Grizzles*', '*I recollect* . . .': Draft of letter from CB to Hartley Coleridge
  (Dec. 1840) on wrapper in which he returned her early version of 'Ashworth',
  an incomplete novel. Transcribed by Melodie Monahan, *Studies in Philology*,
  lxxx, 4 (Fall 1983), 124. *CBL*, i, 237.

  '*black day*', '*foolish love-stories*': CB to Hartley Coleridge (10 Dec. 1840), in Coleridge
  Collection, University of Texas, quoted by Monahan, ibid., 129.

47 *nip a child 'in the bud*': 'Thoughts Suggested to the Superintendent and Ladies'
  (1824), cited by Rebecca Fraser, *CB*, 38.

48 *Tall, cylindrical chimneys*: I draw on CB's description in *The Professor*, ed. Margaret
  Smith and Herbert Rosengarten (written in 1846, published 1857, repr. Oxford:
  Clarendon Press, 1987, and World's Classics, 1991), ch. 2.

  '*visiting' families*: I owe this information to Audrey W. Hall, a descendant of one
  such West Yorkshire family.

  CB's appearance and EN's recollections of CB at school: EN's 'Reminiscences of CB'.

49 '*out of our range*': MT, Reminiscences for EG (1856), Stevens, *MT*, Appendix B.

50 '*Her idea of self-improvement* . . .': MT to EG (mid-1857), Stevens, ibid., Appendix B.
  This was a second letter to EG, incorporated in 3rd ed. of *Life*.

  '*I should long ago* . . . *Frenchified fool*': CB to EN (26 Sept. 1836), *CBL*, i, 152.

  '*I had imbibed* . . .': *JE*, i, ch. 10.

51 *drink and opium*: Christine Alexander, in her Introduction to *The Early Writings of
  CB*, 161, 173, 284, suggests 1837–8 as the time the partnership dissolved when
  CB's own maturing moral awareness exposed PBB's limitations. After this
  date, too (Fraser notes, *CB*), EB and AB no longer participated, even in a marginal capacity, in Angria.

52 *EN's appearance*: from CB's drawing of EN as a girl. BPM.

53 '*suited*': CB to WSW (27 May 1849), *LFC*, ii, 333.

  '*an uneasy vacuum* . . .': CB to Amelia Ringrose (24 Dec. 1847), *LFC*, ii, 67.

  '*nonentity*', '*outsiders*': EN to Sir T. Wemyss Reid (9 July 1880). Berg.

  lost EB: I owe this idea to Juliet Gardiner. In conversation, July 1992.

  '*like twins*': EN, on her first visit to the Parsonage in 1833, *CBL*, i, Appendix: 598.

54 *EB tall, long-armed*: EN told EG, *Life*, 81.

  PB's weird stories: EN to Sir T. Wemyss Reid (24 Nov. 1876). Berg.

55 '*Polly, you did me good*': MT's Reminiscences, Stevens, *MT*.

CB's exchanges with MT: Ibid.

56 '*Yorkshire has such families* . . .': *Sh*, i, ch. 9.

   sagacity, '*thoroughly English*': Mr Yorke in *Sh*, i, ch. 4.

   '*too pretty to live*', etc.: EN's reminiscences of MT, *LFC*, ii, 231–2.

57 '*When it was moonlight*': Ibid.

   MT and Rose Yorke: See *Sh*, i, ch. 9.

   '*First this hemisphere* . . .': *Sh*, ii, ch. 12.

   Miss Miles: (1890; repr. Oxford University Press, 1990), 347, 362–3.

58 '*nearly as mad as myself*': CB to EN (26 Sept. 1836), *LFC*, i, 146.

   '*one tall lady* would *nurse me*': EN's 'Reminiscences of CB', *CBL*, i, Appendix.

59 *Brontë faces*: EN's holograph ms. relating to the Brontës. Berg. Copy also in the King's School, Canterbury. *CBL*, i, Appendix.

   CB and MT corresponded about politics: CB notes this in letter to EN when she sends, at EN's request, a Mary-type letter. MT subsequently destroyed nearly all CB's letters.

CHAPTER THREE: EGYPT AND THE PROMISED LAND

60 '*At 19* . . .': CB in conversation with EG, reported in letter from EG to Catherine Winkworth (25 Aug. 1850), *LFC*, iii, 143, or *EGL*, 75: 125.

   '*I am sad* . . .': CB to EN (2 July 1835), *CBL*, i, 140.

   '*this delusive* . . . *world*': PB to Mrs Franks in Huddersfield (6 July 1835), *LFC*, i, 130.

61 '*dolts*': 'Roe Head Journal'. In *The Early Writings of CB*, Alexander dates six fragmentary autobiographical pieces as written between 1836–7: 'Well here I am at Roe Head' (4 Feb. 1836); 'Now as I have a little bit of time' (5 Feb. 1836); 'All this day I have been in a dream' (11 Aug.–14 Oct. 1836); 'I'm just going to write because I cannot help it' (c.Oct. 1836); 'My Compliments to the weather' (c.Mar. 1837); 'About a week since I got a letter from Branwell' (c.Oct. 1837). It is not impossible that other fragments of CB's writings belong with the 'Roe Head' group.

   '*that happy home circle* . . .': *Life*, 107.

   starved: See Frank, *Emily Brontë: A Chainless Soul*, 98–9.

   '*Liberty*': CB, 'Prefatory Note to "Selections from Poems by Ellis Bell", posthumous edition of Ellis and Acton Bell, 369.

62 *Dorothea*: Dorothea Casaubon (née Brooke) in *Middlemarch* (1871–2).

   Maggie Tulliver: Heroine of George Eliot's *The Mill on the Floss* (1860).

63 '*quite gone*': *CBEW*, ii, part 2, 379–85. This is a prose coda to the well-known poem, 'We wove a web in childhood', a six-page, untitled ms. in the Huntingdon Library, California. It is dated 19 Dec. 1835, i.e. written after CB's return to Haworth for the Christmas vacation.

   '*I now assume my own thoughts* . . .': From a fragment of 'Roe Head Journal' (dated 'Friday afternoon, Feb. 4, 1836'), beginning 'Well here I am at Roe Head'. Transcribed from the MS. PML, 2696. RHJ, 447.

64 '*Must I* . . .': BPM. Bon 98/8. Dated 'Friday August 11th'. RHJ, 452.

   '*I shall be called discontented*': *JE*, i, ch. 12.

'*shrivelled*': *Life*, 107.

65 *MT's views on women's occupations*: MT to EN (9 Feb. 1849). Berg. Stevens, *MT*, 80.

Mary Wollstonecraft: Thoughts on the Education of Daughters in *The Works of Mary Wollstonecraft*, iv, ed. Janet Todd and Marilyn Butler (London: Pickering, 1989), 25.

The First Duty of Women: (London: Emily Faithfull, 1870).

'*How do they make a business of [influence]?*': Ibid., 14.

'*a creature who likes self-sacrifice*': Ibid., 74.

66 '. . . *I am in prison*': *Miss Miles*, 305.

'*longingly at the horizon*': Ibid., 291.

67 '*If you knew my thoughts . . .*': CB to EN (10 May 1836), *CBL*, i, 144.

I am just going to write . . . : BPM. Bon 98/7. RHJ, 456.

68 *Look into thought . . .* : BPM. Bon 98/7. Transcribed from ms., with some differences from the printed version in *CBP*, 211, entitled 'Diving' and dated May 1837. RHJ.

a breeze: 'Well here I am at Roe Head', PML (MA 2696). RHJ, 447.

All this day . . .: Dated 'Friday August 11th'. BPM. Bon 98/8. RHJ, 452–3.

69 '*Miss Wooler came in with a plate of butter . . .*': (Dated 'Friday afternoon, Feb. 4, 1836'). Quashia and Miss Wooler appear in Roe Head fragment, PML (MA 2696). RHJ, 449–50.

70 '*a continual waking Nightmare*': Fragment of letter, CB to Miss Wooler (Nov. Dec.? 1846), *CBL*, i, 505.

'. . . *I wanted to speak . . .*': BPM. Bon 98/9. RHJ, 455.

71 '*the vasty deep*', etc.: BPM. Bon 98/6. RHJ, 457.

72 *probably composed in May 1837*: The fragment is on the same page as a rather uninspired poem dated 12 May 1837. BPM. Bon 98/5. RHJ, 462.

'*Remembrance yields . . .*': BPM. Bon 98/6. RHJ, 459.

73 '*coming not in gusts . . .*': BPM. Bon 98/7. RHJ, 456.

Mrs Franks and Amelia Walker: See the astute account of the episode in Gérin, *Anne Brontë*, 95–6.

74 *fear that she might appear mad*: See postscript to letter to EN (10 May 1836), *CBL*, i, 144: 'Don't think me mad . . .'

75 '*I am a very coarse . . . wretch*': To EN (1836), *CBL*, i, 153.

'*polluted*': To EN (1836), *LFC*, i, 140.

'*I abhor myself . . .*': To EN (1836), *CBL*, i, 154.

mending Miss Lister's clothes: To EN (14 Dec. 1836?), *CBL*, i, 157.

76 '*Well of Life . . .*': To EN (10 May 1836), *CBL*, i, 144.

'*corrupt . . . cold to the spirit . . .*': To EN, *CBL*, i, 156.

'*guilty of all*': PB, 'On Conversion' in *The Pastoral Visitor* (Feb-Oct, 1815), BPM. Bon 262.

Southey's reply: *CBL*, i, 165–8.

'*public tribute*': Quoted by Norma Clarke, *Ambitious Heights: Writing, Friendship, Love: The Jewsbury Sisters, Felicia Hemans, and Jane Carlyle* (London: Routledge, 1990), 61.

77 '*humor*': EB's and AB's manuscript diary paper (26 June 1837). BPM.

forms glancing into the firelight: *Life*, 97.

Their walk was a march, etc.: EN, holograph ms. relating to the Brontës. Berg.

'*Evening Solace*': *CBP*, 58. Published 1846.

Night and Day: In Virginia Woolf's second novel, published by Duckworth in 1919, Katharine Hilbery does mathematics alone in her room at night. By day she devotes herself to family and other social duties.

'"*the singular property . . .*"': To EN (11 Sept. 1833), *CBL*, i, 124.

'*flighty*': Robert Southey to Caroline Bowles, *LFC*, i, 156.

78 *Southey's first letter*: *CBL*, i, 165–8.

CB's reply: *CBL*, i, 168–9.

done her good: In conversation with EG, *Life*, 103.

79 '*In vain I try . . .*': From "Tis not the air I wished to play'. BPM. Bon 98/5. This is the second part of 'The Teacher's Monologue', *CBP*, 53–4. Published 1846.

'*toil*': See also 'Life will be gone' (n.d.). BPM. Bon 98/3.

80 *Miss Wooler's sleepless nights*: CB to EN (4 Jan. 1838), *CBL*, i, 174.

81 '*Am I to spend . . .*': BPM. Bon 98/8. Dated 'Friday August 11th'. RHJ, 452.

Anne in need of care: CB to EN (4 Jan. 1838), *CBL*, i, 173–4.

'*. . . slavery*': CB to EN (2 Oct. 1838), *CBL*, i, 182.

'*Parting*': *CBP*, 62. One of the poems CB copied out in Brussels in 1843. It was set to music and published in 1853.

'*roused and soothed me*': (9 June 1838), *CBL*, i, 178.

'*one of the most rousing pleasures . . .*': CB to EN (15 Apr. 1839), *CBL*, i, 190, after a repeat visit of the Taylors to Haworth.

82 '*those first feelings . . .*': 'Often rebuked, yet always back returning', Gezari, ed., *The Complete Poems*, 198 (in section of Poems of Doubtful Authorship) and 220 (in section of poems edited by CB in 1850, entitled 'Stanzas'). CB is known to have substantially revised most of the poems she printed in 1850, and since no manuscript of this poem survives, its authorship has been disputed. But it does seem to me to have the vigour of EB rather than the droopy pathos of much of CB's far inferior poetry.

'*half savage . . .*': *Wuthering Heights*, i, ch. 12.

'*So wild was her longing . . .*': 'Captain Henry Hastings', Gérin, ed., *Five Novelettes*.

83 *Miss West*: Two-page unpublished prose fragment, 'But it is not in Society that the real character is revealed' (c.late 1838). BPM. Bon 113/6–7. Extracts quoted by Christine Alexander, *The Early Writings of CB*, 184–7, and by Fraser, *CB*, 118–19. Alexander, 246, recognises the importance of 'emotional commitment', glimpsed in the juvenilia only in the 'Roe Head Journal' and passages relating to Miss West and Elizabeth Hastings.

84 *poem on the preceding page*: Immediately precedes the prose fragment on Miss West: 'O never, never leave again'. BPM. Bon 113/3–6. *CBP*, 327–8, 226 ('The voice of Lowood'). Editors have published this as two separate poems, but the manuscript suggests they were possibly part of the same poem.

85 '*Captain Henry Hastings*': The second last of *Five Novelettes*. Gérin notes the autobiographical aspects and states (173) that Elizabeth Hastings' similarity to CB is 'a first step towards those prototypes of herself, Jane Eyre and Lucy Snowe.' (I do not agree with Gérin that 'Mina Laury', one of the earlier novellas, is especially distinguished. It is much on a par with earlier Angrian tales.)

Alexander, in *The Early Writings of CB*, 186, observes rightly that in Elizabeth Hastings CB searched the depths of her own character, and adds, 217, '. . . her experience also heralded a new type of heroine.'

86 *PBB's letter to Wordsworth*: (19 Jan. 1837), *LFC*, i, 151–2.

88 *Lady Rosamund Wellesley*: Christine Alexander notes her grave (in *The Early Writings of CB*, 186), and that Zamorna had lured her from her family and then abandoned her.

89 *eccentric, etc.*: CB to Revd Henry Nussey (5 Mar. 1839), *CBL*, i, 185.

  'habit to study . . .': Ibid. Quoted by Gérin, *CB*, 128.

  Henry Nussey's diary: BL. Egerton MS 3268A.

  'land of Egypt . . . Bondage': CB to EN (1 July 1841), *CBL*, i, 258. CB also uses the phrase 'term of bondage' to EN (30 June 1839), *CBL*, i, 194.

90 *when Mr Sidgwick strolled with his children*: CB to EB (8 June 1839), *CBL*, i, 191.

  background of Mrs Sidgwick: I owe these details to the research of Audrey W. Hall who has shared her work most generously.

91 *clergy and status*: Leonore Davidoff and Catherine Hall, *Family Fortunes: Men and women of the English middle class, 1780–1850* (London: Hutchinson, 1987), show the clergy becoming professionalised in this period.

  PB's cold shoulder to Branwell relations: EN to Sir T. Wemyss Reid (20 Nov. 1877). Berg. It must be noted that EN became openly hostile to PB after CB's death, but no one outside the Parsonage would have been more informed about its issues and secrets. It is for this reason that, later, ABN, after his marriage to CB, became anxious about her letters to EN.

92 *'Vain attempt!'*: EN, holograph ms. relating to the Brontës. Berg.

  neither was it elevated: Winnifrith, *The Brontës and Their Background*, 148.

  William Sidgwick and the exploitation of children: Reported by Gérin, *CB* 146, quoting 'The State of Children Employed in Manufacture' (1816).

93 *first time employer spoke to her for five minutes*: CB to EN (30 June 1839), *CBL*, i, 194.

  'wretched touchiness': To EN (26 Sept. 1836), *CBL*, i, 152.

94 *the 'rust and cramp'*: *The Professor*, ch. 4.

  'a tabooed woman', etc.: *Sh*, ii, ch. 10. CB quotes the words of Elizabeth Rigby, *Quarterly Review* (Dec. 1848). Miss Rigby owns that the situation is a 'cruel' one, but insists that it is necessary for the decorum and reserve of English life, and that a governess should not murmur against the place appointed for her according to God's scheme.

80 *'tyrannised over' governess*: CB writing later about her bitter experience to WSW who had consulted her on behalf of his daughter (12 May 1848), *CBL*, ii, 65.

  Mary Ingham: Barbara Whitehead, *Charlotte Brontë and her 'dearest Nell': The story of a friendship* (West Yorkshire: Smith Settle, 1993), 84.

  'I hate and abhor . . .': Quoted in *Life*, 122.

  'coup de grâce': Margaret Smith, 'The Letters of CB'.

96 *answered advertisements in vain*: To EN. BPM. MSS 44–5.

  'minds and hearts . . .': To EN (3 Mar. 1841), quoted in *Life*, 135.

  'a new servitude': *JE*, i, ch. 10.

'*are condemned to a stiller doom* . . .': *JE*, i, ch. 12.

AB's drawing: 'Woman gazing out to sea' (dated 13 Nov. 1839, a month before her dismissal). BPM.

'. . . *Ça ira*': CB to EN (June 1840), *CBL*, i, 222.

97 *EN on the Brontës as governesses*: Holograph ms. relating to the Brontës. Berg.

'. . . *estrangement from their real characters* . . .': Ibid.

98 *Eliza Branwell Williams*: To EN (14 Aug. 1840). BPM. Bon 166. *CBL*, i, 225.

99 *the dark side of respectability*: In conversation with EG, *Life*, 114.

Jane Fairfax: *Emma*, ch. 20.

'*Mary alone* . . .': BPM. Gr E:3.

'*a desperate plunge*': MT to EN (19 Feb. 1849). Berg. Stevens, *MT*, 80.

MT to EN from Wellington: (9 Feb. 1849 and 4–8 Jan. 1857). Berg.

101 '*the cleverest woman*': 'Caroline Vernon', the last of *Five Novelettes*, ed. Gérin, 309.

'. . . *We must change* . . .': *Miscellaneous and Unpublished Writings of C and PBB*, 404, or *The Juvenilia of Jane Austen and Charlotte Brontë*, ed. Francis Beer (Harmondsworth: Penguin, 1986), 366–7.

102 *known as 'Ashworth'*: This is a separated manuscript, sold off in fragments. The manuscript's editor, Melodie Monahan, suggests that it may have been Thomas J. Wise (a scholar-scoundrel – see ch. 10 below) who separated the sheets of 'Ashworth' in order to effect two sales rather than one. She thinks it possible that more parts of 'Ashworth' exist, as yet unlocated. One fragment ('Mr Ashworth and Son') (n.d.), is in the Harry Elkins Memorial Collection, Widener Library, Harvard University. Four other fragments (n.d.) are in the Henry H. Bonnell Collection, PML (MS MA2696). All these fragments are on the same paper. Melodie Monahan has made a plausible reconstruction of this text in '*ASHWORTH*: An Unfinished Novel by Charlotte Brontë', *Studies in Philology*, lxxx, 4 (Fall 1983). See pp. 54–9, 65, for the interesting parts.

Phoebe Ashworth: Details from Audrey Hall, in conversation, 3 Aug. 1993.

104 '*novel*': CB to Hartley Coleridge. For draft and final letter, see Monahan, op. cit., Appendix II, 124, 129. The draft on the inside of the wrapper is in the Bonnell Collection, PML. The letter of 10 Dec. is in the Coleridge Collection, Humanities Research Center, University of Texas.

dating of 'Ashworth' and letters to Hartley Coleridge: See Melodie Monahan, '*ASHWORTH*'.

105 *not yet discarded Angria*: In *The Early Writings of CB*, 244, Christine Alexander notes that 'Ashworth' merely confirmed the fears expressed in CB's 'Farewell to Angria' and indicated the need for new material.

106 '*Emma*': See ch. 9 below.

'*Well I can believe* . . .', etc.: CB to EN (4 May 1841), *CBL*, i, 252.

107 *soothing thought*: *V*, i, ch. 10.

'*rude familiarity*': To EN (3 Mar. 1841), *CBL*, i, 246.

'*cold frigid–apathetic exterior*': To EN (7 Aug. 1841), *CBL*, i, 266. Quoted with 'rigid' for 'frigid' in *Life*, 139–40.

'. . . *ideas and feelings* . . .': to EN (7 Aug. 1841), *CBL*, i, 266.

'*clever, wicked*' *French volumes*: To EN (20 Aug. 1840), *CBL*, i, 226.

'*My home is humble* . . .': To Revd Henry Nussey (9 May 1841), *CBL*, i, 255.

108 '*such a vehement impatience* . . .': To EN (7 Aug. 1841), *CBL*, i, 266.

'*obscure and dreary place*': To EN (2 Nov. 1841), *CBL*, i, 272.

'*promised land*': To EN (9? Dec. 1841), *CBL*, i, 274.

109 *in the position of her father*: To Elizabeth Branwell (29 Sept. 1841), *CBL*, i, 269.

'*poetical*' *adolescence*: To Revd Henry Nussey (11 Jan. 1841), *CBL*, i, 245.

CHAPTER FOUR: LOVE'S LANGUAGE

111 *flat fields*: See *The Professor*, ch. 7.

school's setting: *Life*, 148.

112 '*a little black ugly being*', '*delirious Hyena*': To EN (May 1842), *CBL*, i, 284.

'*fishing-rod*': 'William Wallace and other Essays in Prose and Verse'. BL. Ashley 160.

devoirs: BL, BPM, Berg, Princeton, and Brotherton have several holograph *devoirs*. *Life* prints two in full with CH's corrections. See *Essays*.

'*sacrifice*': CH's words of '*conseil*', (4 May 1842) at the end of CB's '*Le Nid*' (30 Apr. 1842) Berg. Transl. by Lawrence Jay Dessner, *BST* 16:83, 213–18. *Essays*, 42–3.

'*his olive hand* . . .': *V*, iii, ch. 29. The numerous parallels between biographical and fictional views of CH suggest that CB drew an exact portrait of her teacher in *V*.

'*From others of the studious band* . . .': From poem, 'I gave, at first, Attention close'. BPM. Bon 118. The original draft is in an exercise book used in Brussels in 1843. Another version of the poem is in Berg. See *The Professor*, ch. 23. See also Edward Chitham and Tom Winnifrith, *Brontë Facts and Brontë Problems* (London: Macmillan, 1983), 1–13; and *CBP*, 235–9 ('Master and Pupil').

'. . . *parcequ'il y a dans certaines natures* . . .': '*Portrait de Pierre l'Hermite*' (31 July 1842). See *Life*, 154–7.

113 '*étudiez la forme* . . .': CH's '*Observations*' at the end of CB's *devoir*, '*La Chute des Feuilles*' (30 Mar. 1843), *BST*, 12: 65, 376–83. *Essays*, 249.

'*The task* . . .': 'Master and Pupil', *CBP*, 235.

One draft: I quote from the version in Berg. See Rochester's song to Jane Eyre, *CBP*, 72, and 'At first I did attention give', *CBP*, 337.

'*his mind* . . . *my library*': *V*, iii, ch. 33.

114 *lacked the calm of force*, etc: *V*, ii, ch. 20.

'*a vessel for an outpouring*': *V*, iii, ch. 28.

'*veritable dramas*': Janet Harper, 'Charlotte Brontë's Heger Family and their School', *Blackwood's Magazine*, cxcl (Apr. 1912), 461–9.

115 *CH's evening classes*: See Fraser, *CB*, 162, for a full and astute description of the Hegers.

CH's method with the Brontës: CH explained this to EG, *Life*, 154.

CB on Pierre l'Hermite: EG prints the entire *devoir* (dated 31 July 1842), *Life*, 154–7. There is an earlier version, '*Portrait Pierre L'Ermite*', dated 23 June [1842], BL. Ashley MS. 2444. *Essays*, 118–31.

CH's view of EB: Told to EG, *Life*, 151.

116 *CH and Joan of Arc*: Ibid., 157.

'*Elle était nourrie de la Bible.*': Ibid., 157.

CH's letter to English pupil: Letter to Meta Mossman (21 Nov. 1887). Edith M. Weir, 'The Heger Family: New Brontë Material Comes to Light. Letters from Constantin and Zoë Heger to former pupils and from Louise Heger', *BST*, 11: 59, 249–61. Quoted by Gérin, *CB*, 262–3.

117 *Frederika Macdonald*: To Dr Nicoll (26 Feb. 1894). Brotherton. She had been a pupil at the Pensionnat Heger, saw CB's letters, and obtained three of her *devoirs*.

CB gave CH a few Angrian writings: Enid L. Duthie, *The Foreign Vision of Charlotte Brontë* (London: Macmillan, 1975), 40. These booklets were bound and sold in a Brussels bookshop decades later. Now in BL.

booklets: BL. Add MS 34, 255. The various possibilities were discussed with Siamon Gordon.

118 *belief in the interior basis of art*: '*Je crois que toute poésie réelle n'est que l'empreinte fidèle de quelque chose qui se passe, ou qui s'est passé dans l'âme du poète . . .*'. Essay on Millevoye's '*La Chute des Feuilles*' (30 Mar. 1843), *BST* 6:34, 236–46, and *BST* 12: 65, 376–83. *Essays*, 244–5.

'*To write . . .*': Ibid.

'*Genius without study . . .*': CH's '*Observations*' at the end of CB's *devoir* '*La Chute des Feuilles*' (30 Mar. 1843), *BST*, 12: 65, 382. *Essays*, 248.

Genius must be rash: CB's introduction to '*La Mort de Napoléon*' (31 May 1843), *BST*, 12: 64, 274. *Essays*, 270–1, 282.

'*learnt to read . . .*', 'The strong pulse . . .': 'Master and Pupil', *CBP*, 237–8. The poem appears as 'When sickness stayed awhile my course', *The Professor*, ch. 23.

119 '*black Swan*': To PBB (1 May 1843), *LFC*, i, 297.

'*respectful avowal . . .*': Mme Heger to K— who had been at the Pensionnat in 1860; Mme recalled this in a letter of 1884. Edith M. Weir, 'The Heger Family'.

120 '*contempt is charity's brother*': *BST*, 12: 64, 276.

unamiable: To EN (May 1842) *LFC*, i, 260.

Mme Heger's background: Gérin, *CB*, 192.

'*such occupation . . .*': *The Professor*, ch. 18.

'*celebrity . . .*': Ibid., 139.

121 *Louise de Bassompierre*: Gérin, *CB*, 208. Fraser, *CB*, 171.

122 '*We are completely isolated . . .*': CB to EN (May 1842), *LFC*, i, 260.

CH's view of EB's domination: Told to EG, *Life*, 151.

the question of class: See Winnifrith, *The Brontës and Their Background*, 148–53.

Sunday afternoons with Mrs Jenkins: Mrs Jenkins gave these details to EG, *Life*, 147.

'*hard*', '*heavy*', etc: CB's views of Belgian girls are summed up in *The Professor*, ch. 12.

124 '. . . *we have some thoughts . . .*': *Agnes Grey*, ch. 13.

125 '*friend*': *V*, ii, ch. 27.

126 '*I — love — you*': recalled by Janet Harper in Weir, 'The Heger family'.

'*universal bienveillance*': CB to EB (29 May 1843), *CBL*, i, 320.

Das Neue Testament: The copy, printed in London in 1834, is in BPM 36.

'*I lead . . .*': CB to PBB (1 May 1843), *CBL*, i, 317.

'. . . *Robinson Crusoe-like condition* . . .': CB to EB (29 May 1843), *CBL*, i, 320.

'*thinking meantime my own thoughts* . . .': *V*, i, ch. 13.

127 *CB's 'confession'*: (2 Sept. 1843), *CBL*, i, 329.

MT's 'service': MT to EG (18 Jan. 1856). Stevens, *MT*, Appendix B.

128 '*the language of an artist*' *and CH's response*: Duthie, *The Foreign Vision of CB*, 43–5.

'*Athènes Sauvée par la Poësie*': *BST*, 12: 62, 90–96. *Essays*, 334–51.

129 *escaping from the classroom*: From an unfinished letter in French, '*Ma chère Jane* . . .'
(possibly, an autobiographical *devoir*) to an imaginary correspondent. BPM.
Undated, see Duthie, *The Foreign Vision of CB*, 56. It is similar to a homesick
plaint CB scrawled into her *General Atlas of Modern Geography* on 14 Oct., after
her first attempt to give notice.

'*pronounced with vehemence*', '*exciting to passion*': CB to EN (13 Oct. 1843), *CBL*, i, 334.

130 *urgent letter*: '*Lettre d'un pauvre Peintre à un grand Seigneur*' (17 Oct. 1843), ed. Sue Lonoff,
'The Struggles of a Poor and Unknown Artist: A *Devoir* by Charlotte Brontë',
BST, 18: 95, 373–82 (1985). *Essays*, 358–67.

132 '*I suffered much* . . .': To EN? (23 Jan. 1844), *LFC*, ii, 3.

old poems: It is known that she copied out 'Parting' and 'Life' in Brussels.

133 '—*encore une fois adieu* . . .': I quote here and below from the original letters to CH
in BL. The letter of 24 July 1844 is Add MS 38,732A. *CBL*, i, 357.

cared as much for language: Suggested by Ellen Moers, *Literary Women* (London: The
Women's Press, 1963; repr. 1978), 161.

scenes of bilingualism and translation: Noted by Penny Boumelha, *Charlotte Brontë*
(Hemel Hempstead: Harvester, 1990), 10, who points out that both Frances
Henri and Shirley learn to compose in the language of their lovers.
Boumelha sees this in the context of the dependence of nineteenth-century
women on men who are prepared to confer on them a creative language.

'*she took the word*', '. . . *excitement in . . . making his language her own*': *Sh*, iii, ch. 4.

134 '*je dépéris*': To CH (18 Nov. 1845). BL. Add MS 38, 732C. *CBL*, i, 345.

135 *Mme Heger intervened*: Louise Heger, her daughter, told Frederika Macdonald
who reported to Dr Nicoll (26 Feb. 1894). Brotherton.

'*Williams Shackspire*': *V*, iii, ch. 28.

'*quand je prononce les mots français* . . .': (24 July 1844). BL. Add MS 38, 723A. *CBL*, i, 355.

'*courtly love*': An interesting suggestion by Fraser, *CB*, 220.

136 *letter of 24 October 1844*: BL. Add MS 38, 732B. *CBL*, i, 369.

'*On souffre* . . .': BL. Add MS 38, 732D. *CBL*, i, 378.

a pulse perhaps foreign to English: That pulse was present in English in the mid-
eighteenth century in the passionate voice of Clarissa Harlowe, and it is not
surprising that CB mentions Richardson as her mentor in 1840 (see ch. 3).
Kathleen Tillotson, in *Novels of the Eighteen-Forties* (Oxford University Press,
1954; repr. 1962), suggests that the 1840s were relatively free of the Victorian
prudery registered in the Podsnappery of the 1850s, but this is refuted by
Winnifrith in a careful examination of the reviews of the Brontës which
show gross and hostile prudery in the late 1840s. See *The Brontës and Their
Background*, chapters on Prudery and Reviewers.

Sara Dudley Edwards: In conversation with the author, March 1991.

'*I looked at my love . . .*': *JE*, ii, ch. 11.

'*mon maître de littérature . . .*': BL. Add MS 38, 732A. *CBL*, i, 356.

137 *no connotation of self-abasement*: Mina Laury does call Zamorna 'Master' in the worshipful language of romance but, by this stage for CB, worship had changed into something more intelligent.

138 *as Diderot*: Sara Dudley Edwards.

'*la carrière des lettres . . .*': (24 July 1844). BL. Add MS 38, 723A. *CBL*, i, 356.

'*exaltée*': (8 Jan. 1845). BL. Add MS 38, 732D. *CBL*, i, 378.

139 '*Si mon maître . . .*': Ibid.

'*narrow cell*': 'Frances', *CBP*, 24.

'*esclave à un regret . . .*': (18 Nov. 1845). BL. Add MS 38, 732C. *CBL*, i, 434.

'*sounded like music . . .*': Ibid.

140 *According to . . . Louise . . .* : Noted by Frederika Macdonald, (26 Feb. 1894). Brotherton.

'*Farewell . . .*': (18 Nov. 1845) BL. Add MS 38, 732C. *CBL*, i, 435.

to protect CB from misunderstanding: CH's reciprocal feeling for the indefinable in CB's letters is marvellously expressed in a letter to EN in 1863, quoted and discussed in ch. 10. He says here that her spontaneous subtlety and intimacy make her letters liable to misunderstanding.

'*He saw my heart's woe*': *CBP*, 244–5.

uncontrolled resentment in CB's letters to CH: Noted by Duthie, *The Foreign Vision of CB*, who notes, too, that resentment is not one of the passions CB recreated in fiction.

141 '*Devoid of charm*': 'Reason', *CBP*, 243.

'*Reason*': *CBP*, 244.

142 *unlock desire from sexuality*: See Boumelha, *CB*, 19.

CB felt buried in Haworth: MT to EG (18 Jan. 1856). Stevens, *MT*, Appendix B.

143 *MT's 'plunge'*: MT to EN (19 Feb. 1849). Berg. Stevens, *MT*, 80.

'*one day resembles another . . .*': (24 Mar. 1845), *LFC*, ii, 28.

'*MT finds herself free . . .*': To EN (2 Apr. 1845), *LFC*, ii, 30.

'*quand le corps est paresseux . . .*': To CH (24 July 1844). BL. Add MS 38, 732A. *CBL*, i, 356.

144 '*savez-vous . . .*': Ibid.

exercise book: BPM. Bon 118 (1–8). Fraser, *CB*, 192, suggests that already in Brussels CB used this German workbook for plans and rough drafts. I think this unlikely because CB was so neat in her exercises that for her to scribble suggests she was using up paper after the workbook had served its formal purpose.

'*Her veil is spread . . .*': BPM. Bon 118. *CBP*, 239–40.

145 *In the light of Miss Wooler . . .* : See letter to Miss Wooler (30 Jan. 1846), quoted in *Life*, 203.

'*A lover masculine . . .*': *Sh*, i, ch. 7.

made offers to eligible men: MT reported this to EG (mid-1857). Stevens, *MT*, Appendix B.

146 '*Frances*': *CBP*, 22–30. First published in *Poems* (1846).

soon after July 1845: This was soon after AB's return to Haworth in June. She mentions CB's Paris plan in her diary paper at the end of July.

147 *'Lucia'*: Brussels exercise book, BPM. Bon 118 (7). This is no more than the opening page of a novel which was obviously soon abandoned.

   Lucia in The Professor: *The Professor*, ch. 25.

148 *'a touch of phlegm'*: To EN (13 June 1845), *CBL*, i, 398.

149 *Preface to* The Professor: Written later, after the publication of *Sh* (1849), with a view to publishing *The Professor*. (It was turned down once again by Smith, Elder, and Co.)

   'toujours un peu entêté . . .': Ibid., ch. 24 *The Professor*, ch. 23.

150 *'. . . I should like . . .'*: Ibid.

151 *'I knew . . .'*: Ibid., ch. 25.

152 *Crimsworth sees the fire*: Ibid., ch. 19.

   '. . . in intimate conversation . . .': Ibid. ch. 24. Boumelha, *CB*, 21, is good on Crimsworth's limitations.

   '. . . marriage must be slavery . . .': *The Professor*, ch. 25.

   'a real feeling . . .': *The Half Sisters*, ii, ch. 12.

153 *ending*: I disagree with Gérin's opinion, *CB*, 316, that the last parts of this novel are 'particularly uninteresting'.

CHAPTER FIVE: A PUBLIC VOICE

154 *'I will prove to you . . .'*: HM relates this anecdote in her obituary for CB, *Daily News* (Apr. 1855), repr. in *The Brontës: The Critical Heritage*, ed. Miriam Allott (London: Routledge, 1974), 301–5.

   'So hopeless is the world without . . .': 'To Imagination' (3 Sept. 1844). Published in *Poems* (1846). *The Poems of Emily Brontë*, ed. Roper and Chitham, 25.

   EB's 'Gondal Poems': The MS is in BL. See Gezari, ed., *The Complete Poems*.

155 *'formerly we used to show each other . . .'*: CB, 'Biographical Notice'.

   'some poetry': AB, diary-paper (31 July 1845), *CBL*, i, 409–11.

   'I must hurry . . .': EB, diary-paper (30 July 1845), *CBL*, i, 407–9.

156 *'A distant relation . . .'*: *CBL*, i, 228.

   'but too natural . . .': To WSW (4 Jan. 1848), *CBL*, ii, 3.

   PBB's account of his relation to Mrs Robinson: Letter to Francis Grundy (Oct. 1845), *LFC*, ii, 64–5.

157 *'ceaseless art'*: 'Frances', written *c*.1843, first published in *Poems* (1846). *CBP*, 24.

   'the final bound': 'Julian M. and A.G. Rochelle', Gezari, ed., *The Complete Poems*, 177–81. Dated 9 October 1845, it is in the 'Gondal Poems' notebook, and Janet Gezari notes the suggestion that EB was copying this very poem into her notebook when CB first came upon it. Parts of the poem were published in *Poems* (1846).

   'the mirror . . .': CB to WSW (21 Dec. 1847), *CBL*, i, 580.

158 *'escaped'*: Diary-paper, (31 July 1845), *CBL*, i, 409–11.

   completed two-thirds: Ibid.

159 *'all' her love*: PBB to J.B. Leyland (*c*.June or July 1846), *LFC*, ii, 99.

   sin 'a species of insanity': To WSW (4 Jan. 1848), *LFC*, ii, 173.

'*I shall be 31*': BPM. Bon 191. *LFC*, ii, 30.

fair copy of JE: BL. Add MS 43474–6. Part of the George Smith Memorial Bequest. First page is dated 'March 16th 1847'. This is a neat ms. in contrast with that of V.

160 *collected earlier poems*: Juliet Barker, Notes to *The Brontës: Selected Poems*, 106.

Caroline Helstone: *Sh*, i, ch. 7.

'*sternly rated . . .*': CB's first recollections are in a letter to WSW (Sept. 1848), *CBL*, ii, 119.

161 '*unlike the poetry . . .*': CB, 'Biographical Notice'.

'*crude and rhapsodical*': CB to WSW (Sept. 1848), *CBL*, ii, 119.

EB's unworldly will: CB, 'Biographical Notice'.

162 *AB's reserve*: Ibid.

'*I have lain . . .*': PBB to Francis Grundy, op. cit.

'*Averse to personal publicity . . .*': CB, 'Biographical Notice'.

163 '*respectable young man*': To Mrs Rand (26 May 1845), *CBL*, i, 393.

'*A cold, far-away sort of civility . . .*': To EN (10 July 1846), BPM. Gr E: 10. *CBL*, i, 483.

'*Currer Bell will avow . . .*': CB to EG (17 Nov. 1849?). *CBL*, ii, 288.

'*sister*': *A Room of One's Own* (London: Hogarth; NY: Harcourt, 1929), 74.

164 '*Is the time coming . . .*': (27 Mar. 1919) *The Diary of Virginia Woolf*, ed. Anne Olivier Bell (London: Hogarth; NY: Harcourt, 1977), i, 259.

Mary Wollstonecraft: See Claire Tomalin, *The Life and Death of Mary Wollstonecraft* (London: Weidenfeld & Nicolson, 1974; repr. New American Library, 1976), 225–6, and William St Clair, *The Godwins and the Shelleys* (London: Faber, 1989), ch. 14.

official biography of Sylvia Plath: Lyndall Gordon, 'The Burden of a Life', *Poetry Review*, lxxix (Winter 1989–90), 60–62.

'*coarseness*', '*. . . forfeited the society of her sex*': '*Vanity Fair* and *Jane Eyre*', *Quarterly Review*, lxxxiv (Dec. 1848), 153–85. See ch. 1 above.

166 *Henry Colburn*: Gérin, *CB*, 327.

source for JE: *Life*, 91.

Ann Radcliffe: CB mentions *The Italian* (1797) in *Sh*. Her most famous novel, a bestseller of the 1790s, is *The Mysteries of Udolpho* (1794).

167 '*utter privation of light*', '*perfect quiet*': To EN (31 Aug. 1846), *CBL*, i, 496.

'*in her element . . .*': To EN (13 Sept. 1846). BPM. Bon 189. *CBL*, i, 497.

'*She sits on a wooden stool . . .*': To EN (29 Sept. 1846), *CBL*, i, 500.

168 *a blender of character*: EN to Clement Shorter (20 Oct. 1895): 'Charlotte was a *blender* of character putting two in one.' Brotherton.

EB and AB as sources for the Rivers sisters: JE, iii, ch. 2. See Gérin, *CB*, 303.

'*real enough . . .*': To WSW (28 Oct. 1847), *CBL*, i, 553.

170 '*lust*', '*vice*', *and* '*despair*': JE, iii, ch. 1.

'*Who in the world . . .*': Ibid.

'*— mentally, I still possessed my soul . . .*': Ibid.

'*All self-sacrifice is good . . .*': To Charles Bray (11 June 1848), *The George Eliot Letters* ed. G. S. Haight (Oxford University Press; New Haven: Yale, 1954), i, 268.

172 '*. . . Nature herself . . .*': CB to WSW (Sept. 1848), *CBL*, ii, 118.

'*An unusual . . . character . . .*': *JE*, iii, ch. 1.

close to Heger's style: See CH's letter to an English pupil quoted above, ch. 4.

'*You entered . . .*': *JE*, iii, ch. 1.

'*. . . no transitory blossom . . .*': Ibid.

'*I am not an angel . . .*': Ibid, ii, ch. 9.

173 '"*Sir,*" *I interrupted . . .*': Ibid, iii, ch. 1.

EB reclaimed the souls: I owe this to Sally Howgate, from an outstanding essay on *WH* which she wrote as a student at Ruskin College, Oxford.

EB saw the impossibility of spiritual wholeness . . . : Ibid.

174 '*It is moorish . . .*': CB, 'Editor's Preface to the New Edition of *WH*' (Smith, Elder, and Co., 1850). Appendix to World's Classics ed. of *WH*, 366.

Heaton history: M. A. Butterfield, *The Heatons of Ponden Hall* (Stanbury, 1976); Edward Chitham, *A Life of Emily Brontë* (Oxford: Blackwell, 1987), 67; Gérin, *A Life of Patrick Branwell Brontë* (London: Nelson, 1961), 43; *Brother in the Shadow*, research by Mary Butterfield, ed. R. J. Duckett (Bradford Information Service, 1988), 70, 139–45. The last quotes from Mrs Percival Hayman, 'The Heatons and the Brontës', typescript (March 1982). Main source is William Shackleton's typescript, 'Four hundred years of a West Yorkshire Moorland Family' (1921) and other papers in the Heaton Records, Keighley Reference Library.

176 *a loneliness Byron at times felt . . .* : Zoë Teale, optional thesis on EB, Oxford Finals, 1990.

'*From my youth . . .* : Byron, *Manfred*, Act ii, scene 2, line 50 ff.

he 'sees' her through blindness: I am indebted to Marni Feld for this point.

177 '*The action of the tale . . .*': Contemporary review in the *Atlas*, quoted in Clarendon ed. of *JE*, Appendix V, 631.

'*It is an autobiography . . .*': *Fraser's Magazine* (Dec. 1847) 686–95, repr. *The Brontës: The Critical Heritage*, 84; also Clarendon ed. of *JE*, Appendix V, 630.

178 '*. . . in time, I think . . .*': *JE*, i, ch. 14. See also Rochester's image of Jane as a caged bird who, if freed, would soar 'cloud-high'.

the hidden alien: I have appropriated phrasing from Julia Kristeva, 'Women's Time', in *The Feminist Reader: Essays in Gender and the Politics of Literary Criticism*, ed. Catherine Belsey and Jane Moore (London: Macmillan, 1989), 214.

'*as critical as Croker*': From a review of *Sh*, *Fraser's Magazine* (Dec. 1849), 692, repr. *The Brontës: The Critical Heritage*, 152. Cited by Kathleen Tillotson, *Novels of the Eighteen-Forties*, 19–20. Croker was a venomous critic, particularly of Keats, during the Romantic period.

'*it is soul speaking to soul . . .*': *Fraser's Magazine*, op. cit.

179 '*I have not been petrified . . .*': *JE*, ii, ch. 8.

180 '*We talk . . .*': *JE*, iii, ch. 12.

Bertha as a warning to Jane: For the mad wife as alter-ego of Jane, see Sandra M. Gilbert and Susan Gubar, *The Madwoman in the Attic* (New Haven and London: Yale University Press, 1979), 348: '. . . Jane first hears . . . mad Bertha, Rochester's secret wife and in a sense her own secret self.'

'*. . . if he was subjugated . . .*': BL. Add MS 43475, ii, 466.

181 '*but now – I thought.*': Ibid., 501.

182 'I have as much soul . . .': JE, ii, ch. 8.

184 'I had given in allegiance to duty . . .': JE, i, ch. 10.
   in her 'natural element': Ibid.

185 Richardsonian aspect: Tillotson, Novels of the Eighteen-Forties, 149.
   'Mr Rochester was not to me what he had been . . .': JE, ii, ch. 11.

186 'There are no good men . . .': MT to CB (June-24 July 1848). Stevens, MT, 74.
   'Rochester airs': Reported in a newspaper. CB enclosed this unnamed article,
      published while she was in London in June 1850, in letter to EN (15 July 1850),
      CBL, ii, 425.
   'suggestive': CB to WSW (22 Jan. 1848). BPM. Bon 196. CBL, ii, 17. Miss Kavanagh's
      review was in the Morning Herald.

187 WMT to WSW: (23 Oct. 1847), LFC, ii, 149.
   Lockhart on JE: LFC, ii, 169.
   Anne Mozley: The Brontës: The Critical Heritage, 202–8.
   'I am afraid . . .': EGL, 1982a: 860.
   Mrs Oliphant: Blackwood's Magazine (May 1855), repr. in The Brontës: The Critical Heritage,
      312–13.

188 'a woman was more likely to transmit such an infection . . .': Richard Davenport-Hines,
      'Necessary Precautions', Nature (21 February 1991), 661. I am indebted to Siamon
      Gordon for these facts.
   'if "Jane Eyre" be the production of a woman . . .': Quoted by CB to WSW (16 Aug. 1849),
      LFC, iii, 11.
   'emasculation': I first heard this view in classes at Columbia University in the late
      sixties. It derived from Richard Chase, 'The Brontës, or Myth Domesticated'
      in Forms of Modern Fiction: Essays Collected in Honor of Joseph Warren Beach, ed. William
      Van O'Connor (University of Minneapolis, 1948), 102–19, repr. Norton Critical
      Edition of JE (1971), 467: 'Rochester's injuries are, I should think, a symbolic
      castration.'
   'You are very different . . .': MT to CB (June-24 July 1848). Berg. Stevens, MT, 74.

CHAPTER SIX: TO WALK INVISIBLE

190 'It is a woman's writing . . .': WMT to WSW (23 Oct. 1847), LFC, ii, 149.
   comment of a local clergyman: CB to WSW (4 Jan. 1848), CBL, ii, 3–4.
   Miss Evans' history: Gérin, CB, Additional Notes, 592.
   'Papa, I've been writing a book.': CB recalled this scene and subsequent details in con-
      versation with EG while both were guests at the Kay-Shuttleworths,
      reported by EG to Catherine Winkworth (25 Aug. 1850), LFC, iii, 144. PB's
      words of surprise are often said to be 'better than likely' (as reported in the
      Life, 1857), but here EG reports CB's slightly different version immediately
      after she heard it.

191 It had been a dream . . .: 'Henry Hastings', Gérin, ed., Five Novelettes.

192 'It would take a great deal to crush me': To WSW (4 Jan. 1848), CBL, ii, 3.
   not a place for ladies: The opinion of Mrs Smith, mother of GS.
   'with colossal phlegm . . .': CB recalled this in The Professor, ch. 7.

London seen from St Paul's: CB recalled this in *V*, i, ch. 6.

193 *AB 'had been called on to contemplate . . .'*: CB 'Biographical Notice' (1850).

194 *'in queer inward excitement'*: To MT (4 Sept. 1848). This is the only letter from CB to MT which survives. The version in *LFC* is grossly inaccurate. Stevens, *MT*, Appendix E. *CBL*, ii, 111–15.

background of WSW: Gérin, *CB*, 362.

'the happiest . . .': GSR, i, ch. 6.

198 *GS's strength*: GSR, i, ch. 5.

sweetness in a plumed bonnet: See CB's tease of GS (BPM. S-G 31), quoted almost in full below, ch. 7.

GS's impression of CB: 'Charlotte Brontë', *Cornhill Magazine* (Dec. 1900), 783–4, repr. *George Smith: A Memoir With Some Pages of Autobiography* (London, 1902). The latter was printed for private circulation after GS's death. Copy in BPM (Henry James's copy). Additional details from GSR.

199 *'clownish'*: CB to MT (4 Sept. 1848), Stevens, *MT*, Appendix E. *CBL*, ii, 111–15.

200 *'Babylon' or 'Nineveh'*: CB to EN, congratulating EN on being unspoiled by a visit to London (19 June 1834), *CBL*, i, 128.

'wholesome contempt': 'Caroline Vernon', Gérin, ed., *Five Novelettes*, 320.

'At such times . . .': (31 July 1848), *CBL*, ii, 95.

'upside down': To EN (Jan. 1847), *CBL*, i, 511.

All coteries . . .: To WSW (26 Apr. 1848). BL. Add MS 39763. *CBL*, ii, 55.

'Ellis . . . would soon turn aside . . .': CB to WSW (15 Feb. 1848), *CBL*, ii, 28.

'the proper study . . .': Alexander Pope, 'An Essay on Criticism' (1711).

201 *'a passport . . .'*: MT to Mrs Gaskell (18 June 1856), *LFC*, i, 276.

'the love passages . . .': WMT to WSW (28 Oct. 1847). Berg. *LFC*, ii, 150.

explained his situation: In note to CB enclosed in letter to WSW, *Letters and Private Papers of William Makepeace Thackeray*, ed. Gordon N. Ray (Oxford University Press and Harvard University Press, 1945), ii, 340–41.

202 *'quiet'*: CB's view of WMT is given in two letters to WSW (28 Oct. 1847 and 29 Mar. 1848), *CBL*, i, 553; ii, 45.

'melodrama': CB to GHL (6 Nov. 1847). BL. Add MS 39763. *CBL*, i, 559. (GHL's letters to CB have disappeared and were probably destroyed.)

'John Henry': Appendix D of Clarendon ed. of *Sh*, 805–35. It consists of two chapters and the beginning of a third.

'. . . unromantic as Monday morning': *Sh*, i, ch. 1.

203 *PBB made no reply to CB*: CB to EN (3 Mar. 1846), *LFC*, ii, 83–4.

'The Wanderer from the Fold': This was the title given by CB in 1850, well after PBB's death, to a poem by EB 'E.W. to A.G.A.' dated 11 Mar. 1844 when PBB was still a tutor at Thorp Green. What is interesting here is CB's view of EB's relation to PBB, which she reads into a Gondal poem. 'On a life perverted' was CB's pencilled heading on the ms. Gezari, ed., *The Complete Poems*, 157–8. See Juliet Barker's note in *The Brontës: Selected Poems*, 127.

CB's physical likeness to PBB: Noted by PBB's friend, George Searle Phillips, *LFC*, ii, 257.

wide foreheads: CB called PBB's forehead 'noble' when she looked at him as he lay dead. CB to WSW (6 Oct. 1848), *CBL*, ii, 124.

'*the inadequacy . . .*': To WSW (6 Oct. 1848), Ibid.

'"*condition of women" question*': (12 May 1848), *CBL*, ii, 66.

'*Has the world . . .*': MT to CB after reading *JE* (24 July 1848), *CBL*, ii, 87.

'*very slender*': CB to GHL (12 Jan. 1848). BL. Add MS 39763. *CBL*, ii, 9.

'*Almost all that we require . . . she has*' etc.: Quoted by Rosemary Ashton, *G. H. Lewes: A Life* (Oxford: Clarendon Press, 1991), 67.

204 '*second only . . .*': GHL, review of *Sh*, *Edinburgh Review* (Jan. 1850), 153–73, repr. *The Brontës: The Critical Heritage*, 162.

imagination '*speaks rapidly . . . in our ear . . .*': CB to GHL (6 Nov. 1847). BL. Add MS 39763. *CBL*, i, 559.

'*mild eyes*', '*to finish more . . .*': To GHL (12 Jan. 1848). BL. Add MS 39763. *CBL*, ii, 10. (CB quotes his words back to him.)

205 *the Passions unknown to Miss Austen*: To WSW (12 April 1850), *CBL*, ii, 383.

'*Miss Austen's clear common sense . . .*': *CBL*, ii, 14.

'*full of the writer's self*': To GHL (17 Oct. 1850). BL. *CBL*, ii, 485.

resistance to Jane Austen: CB to GHL (12 Jan. 1848). BL. Add MS 39763. *CBL*, ii, 10.

'*disclosed the secret . . .*': 'Memoirs of a Novelist' (1909), *The Complete Shorter Fiction of Virginia Woolf*, ed. Susan Dick (1985; rev. NY: Harcourt, 1989), 75.

206 '*the divine gift*': CB to GHL (18 Jan. 1848). BL. Add MS 39763. *LFC* ii, 180–1.

Ranthorpe not a success: CB to GHL (12 June 1848). *CBL*, ii, 10; also 45.

'*You have a sound, clear judgement . . .*': The following rebuttals of GHL are taken from two letters to WSW in late April–early May 1848, *CBL*, ii, 54–55, 57–59.

'*I submit to your anger . . .*': (18 Jan. 1848), *CBL*, ii, 14.

207 *GHL savaged her*: Review of *Sh*, op. cit., 163.

GHL excused: Margaret Smith, 'The Letters of CB'.

Luddites . . . : See Gardiner, *The World Within*, 133.

208 '*Misery generates hate*': *Sh*, i, ch. 2.

'*Hollow's Mill*': See CB to WSW (21 Aug. 1849), *CBL*, ii, 237.

'*Details . . .*': CB to WSW (28 Jan. 1848). Berg. *CBL*, ii, 23.

'*This world's laws never came near us . . .*': *Sh*. iii, ch. 1.

209 *a blend*: EN to Clement Shorter (20 Oct. 1895). Ellen Nussey Papers, Brotherton.

210 *curates 'photographed from the life*': CB to WSW (c.10 Feb. 1849), *CBL*, ii, 181. Sources for the curates supplied by Herbert Rosengarten in Explanatory Notes to *Sh*, 648.

ABN thought mad: CB to EN (28 Jan. 1850), *CBL*, ii, 337.

212 '*Poor Anne . . .*': CB to EN (13 Dec. 1846), *CBL*, i, 507.

'*It is with difficulty . . .*': CB to EN (7 Oct. 1847), *CBL*, i, 547.

finished fair copy of Sh, i: Dated 'September 1848' at the end of first volume.

Grundy's visit to PBB: *LFC*, ii, 258.

Domestic Medicine: BPM. Bon 38.

213 *PBB's deathbed cry*: Gardiner, *The World Within*, 130.

'*. . . the wreck of talent . . .*': To WSW (2 Oct. 1848), *CBL*, ii, 122.

'*My poor father . . .*': Ibid.

214 '*. . . I have never seen her parallel . . .*': CB, 'Biographical Notice'.

'*poisoning doctor*': CB to EN (10 Dec. 1848), *CBL*, ii, 152.

'. . . *relentless conflict* . . .': CB to WSW (25 Dec. 1848), *CBL*, ii, 159.

'*Weary, weary* . . .': 'On the Death of Emily Jane Brontë', *CBP*, 241.

'*torn from us* . . .': CB to WSW (25 Dec. 1848), *CBL*, ii, 159

seventeen inches across: Gardiner, *The World Within*, 129.

215 *Papa's dread of sickrooms*: CB told EG, EG to Catherine Winkworth (25 Aug. 1850), *LFC*, iii, 144.

narrow plank: CB to WSW (15 Jan. 1849), *CBL*, ii, 168.

'*My literary character* . . .': Ibid.

'*Worse than useless*': CB to WSW (16 Apr. 1849), *CBL*, ii, 203.

'*nights of sleeplessness* . . .': CB to WSW (5 Apr. 1849), *CBL*, ii, 196.

York Minster and the evening of 27 May: EN gave EG a description of AB's last days for *Life*. *LFC*, ii, 336.

'*Take courage* . . .': Ibid.

'*A year ago* . . .': To WSW (13 June 1849), *CBL*, ii, 220.

216 '*If men could see us as we really are* . . .': *Sh*, ii, ch. 9.

217 *contend with Omnipotence, etc*: *Sh.*, ii, ch. 7.

Woman God, etc.: *Sh*, iii, ch. 4 ('The First Blue-Stocking'). Shirley writes this parable as a French *devoir*. CB translated it into English at her publishers' request. As with her letters to CH, it may have been liberating for her to express her most hidden thoughts in a foreign language.

'*God-given strength*': *Sh*, iii, ch. 4.

218 '*a genii-life*': *Sh*, ii, ch. III ('Two Lives').

Truth is better than Art: CB to WSW (5 Apr. 1849), *CBL*, ii, 197.

'*When shall we be free?* . . .': *The Years* (London: Hogarth; NY: Harcourt, 1936), 1917 section, 320.

219 *Shirley chained in marriage and CB's control of EB*: I owe this point to Lucasta Miller, in conversation, May–June 1993.

'*burns away our strength*': *Sh*, ii, ch. 3.

'*screened* . . .': *Sh*, ii, ch. 2.

220 '*seemed walled up in him* . . .': *Sh*, iii, ch. 3.

Shirley sings: *Sh*, iii, ch. 8.

Rose: *Sh*, ii, ch. 12.

'*How we work!* . . .': MT to EN (11 Mar. 1851). Berg. Stevens, *MT*, 104. Transcribed from the original.

A Vindication of the Rights of Woman: (Repr. NY: Norton, 1967), 223.

221 '. . . *This great necessity* . . .': MT to CB (Apr. 1850). BPM. Stevens, *MT*, 94.

'*Probably* . . .': MT to EN (11 Mar. 1851). Berg. Stevens, *MT*, 104.

'*What a little lump of perfection* . . .': MT to CB (13 Aug. 1850). Berg. *LFC*, iii, 135.

the position of the governess: See Appendix C (ed. Margaret Smith) to Clarendon ed. of *Sh*: 'A Word to the "Quarterly"'. This was CB's intended preface to *Sh*, dwelling on the untenable position of the English governess as confirmed by offensive quotations from Elizabeth Rigby's adverse review of *JE* for the *Quarterly*. Miss Rigby makes implied claims to superiority through her sole concern for the requirements of the upper classes.

222 '*old maid*': *Sh*, i, ch. 10 ('Old Maids').

'*Not always . . .*': *Sh*, iii, ch. 2.

223 '*Can spirits . . . communicate . . .*': *Sh*, iii, ch 1.

'*Faith whispers . . .*': To WSW (19 Nov. 1849). *CBL*, ii, 291.

'*the weakest, puniest . . .*': To WSW (4 June 1849), *CBL*, ii, 216.

'*I am happy . . .*': *Sh*, iii, ch. 14 ('The Winding-Up').

224 '*triumphed in his own character.*' To EN (28 Jan. 1850), *LFC*, iii, 71.

'*we watch him . . .*': *Sh*, ii, ch. 1.

225 '*groan a little*': ABN groaned when he read the opening of *Sh* from which the following quotes are taken. CB to EG (26 Apr. 1854), John Rylands University Library, Manchester.

'*give your soul . . .*': *Sh*, iii, ch. 3.

226 '*a truculent spirit*' etc.: *Sh*, i, ch. 4.

Ellis and Acton met reviews in silence: CB to WSW (22 Nov. 1848), *LFC*, ii, 287. This was at the time EB was dying and AB sickening.

'*hard derision*', '*merciless contempt*': *Sh*, i, ch. 4.

'*a boundless waste . . .*': *Sh*, ii, ch. 1.

227 '*Because Ellis's poems are short . . .*': CB to WSW (16 Nov. 1848), *CBL*, ii, 140. CB writes after reading an adverse review in the *Spectator* of Smith, Elder's recent reprint of the Bells' *Poems*.

'*. . . a certain harshness . . .*': CB to WSW (2 Nov. 1848), *CBL*, ii, 133.

*glorious wind, Tempest's roaring, and '*A principle of life . . .*'*: Poem 123: 'Aye, there it is!', dated 6 July 1841, Gezari ed., *The Complete Poems*, 131.

manuscript of Sh: George Smith Memorial Bequest, BL. Add MS 43477–9.

228 '*. . . work is my best companion . . .*': CB to WSW (26 July 1849), *CBL*, ii, 232.

'*The loss of what we possess . . .*': CB to WSW (21 Sept. 1849), *CBL*, ii, 260–1.

'*I have given . . .*': To EN (3 May 1848), *CBL*, ii, 62,

229 '*Shake hands.*': CB to PB (5 Dec. 1849), *CBL*, ii, 301.

WMT careless of reticence: GSR, i, ch. 10.

'*New to the London world . . .*': 'The Last Sketch', accompanying his Introduction to 'Emma', *Cornhill*, i (1860).

230 *Anne Thackeray recalled . . .*: 'Chapters From Some Memories' (1894), quoted in Gérin, *Anne Thackeray Ritchie: A Biography* (OUP, 1981), 49–51. Anne was thirteen at the time. *CBL*, ii, Appendix, 754–6.

'*not unamiable*': CB confides her perceptions of WMT's character to GS, on receiving from him a present of Thackeray's portrait (26 Feb. 1853), *CBL*, iii, 128.

dinner with seven critics: CB to Laetitia Wheelwright (17 Dec. 1849) and CB to WSW (19 Dec. 1849), *CBL*, ii, 309, 313.

231 '*the art of impressing ladies . . .*': To EN (31 July 1845). BPM. Gr E: 7. *CBL*, i, 412.

'*while their minds . . .*': To EN (26 Aug. 1846), *CBL*, i, 494.

232 '*. . . If her husband has a strong will . . .*': To EN (29 June 1847), *CBL*, i, 532.

WMT scorned pretence: GSR, i, ch. 10.

Miss Procter and the Sidgwicks: with thanks to Audrey W. Hall.

*Thackeray called her '*Currer Bell*'*: Charles and Frances Brookfield, *Mrs Brookfield and her Circle*, ii (London: Pitman and Sons, 1905), 305.

GS recalled: *GS: A Memoir*, 98.

233 *WMT escaped from his party*: Gérin, *Anne Thackeray Ritchie*: 49–51.

CHAPTER SEVEN: THE LIMITS OF FRIENDSHIP

234 *sisters' constitutions eroded by school*: CB in conversation with EG, reported by EG to
      Catherine Winkworth (25 Aug. 1850), *LFC*, iii, 143.

      'puniest': See ch. 6. To WSW (4 June 1849), op. cit.

      'I saw myself . . .': *V*, i, ch. 4.

      Hope and 'Fortitude': To GS (22 Sept. 1851), *CBL*, ii, 700.

234 *Florence Nightingale*: See *Cassandra*, written in 1852, drastically revised and printed
      privately 1859, Appendix to Ray Strachey, *The Cause: A Short History of the Women's
      Movement in Great Britain* (1928; repr. London: Virago, 1979), 395–418.

      'There are parts of "Mary Barton" . . .': CB to EG (26 Sept. 1850), *CBL*, ii, 476.

236 *'I have not accumulated . . .'*: HM, obituary for CB, *Daily News* (Apr. 1855).

      'who utterly mistake . . .': To EN (12 Apr. 1850), *CBL*, ii, 384.

      'The Enfranchisement of Women': In *Westminster Review* (1851), thought by some to be by
      J. S. Mill and discussed in CB's letter to EG (20 Sept. 1851), *CBL*, ii, 695–6. The
      essay repr. in Rossi, ed., *Essays on Sex Equality*.

      'that slow monotonous incessant walk . . .': EG to a friend (Sept. 1853), *LFC*, iv, 93.

      could not invite JT: CB to WSW (24 Aug. 1849), *CBL*, ii, 239–40.

      '. . . but one precious thing . . .': To Laetitia Wheelwright (12 Jan. 1851), *CBL*, ii, 552.

237 *letter on* The Soul *to JT*: (c. 19 Dec. 1849), *CBL*, ii, 314.

238 *'a perfect subduing . . .'*: CB to EN (9 Apr. 1851), *CBL*, ii, 600.

      of the Helstone order: To EN (5? Dec. 1849), *CBL*, ii, 299.

      tests JT on Dr Arnold: To JT (6 Nov. 1850), *CBL*, ii, 495–6.

      poked his determined nose: To EN (5? Dec. 1849), *CBL*, ii, 299.

239 *'prop'*: To EN (19 Dec. 1849), *CBL*, ii, 311.

      tall, well-knit: As recalled by Sydney Lee (second editor of the *Dictionary of National
      Biography*, founded by GS), in *GS: A Memoir*.

      chivalrous 'to the backbone': As recalled by Leslie Stephen (first editor of the *Dictionary
      of National Biography*), ibid.

      'quick and clear': Ibid., 96.

      'cherished one': To EN (19 Dec. 1849), *CBL*, ii, 311.

      CB and HM: *CBL*, ii 304; EG to Ann Shaen (?20 Dec. 1849), *EGL*, 60:96; and HM,
      Autobiography, ii, (1877; repr. London: Virago, 1983), 323–8.

240 *beautiful hair*: HM, obituary for CB, *Daily News* (Apr. 1855).

      'no bump of secretiveness at all': MT to EN (19 Apr.–10 May 1856). Berg. Stevens, *MT*, 126.

      'Quakerlike waiting on the spirit': CB to GS (n.d.), *LFC*, iii, 292.

241 *stubborn character*: CB to Miss Wooler (27 Jan. 1853), *CBL*, iii, 111.

      absence of 'feeble egotism': HM, obituary for CB, *Daily News* (Apr. 1855).

      habit of self-control: Ibid.

      'our cause': CB to Mrs Smith (9 Jan. 1850), *CBL*, ii, 327.

      Mrs Smith: Details from GSR, i, ch. 1.

242 *mother's expressions used 'verbatim'*: *GS: A Memoir*, 103.

'exactly *like Mrs Bretton*': EG to EN (9 July 1856), *LFC*, iv, 201.

CB on Macready and on Elizabeth Barrett Browning: To Miss Wooler (14 Feb. 1850), *CBL*, ii, 344.

243 *bonnets*: CB to GS. BPM. S-G. 31. *CBL*, ii, 318.

245 *'deficient neither in spirit nor sense'*: To EN (14 Sept. 1850), *CBL*, ii, 469.

'*curled darlings'*: See CB to GS (3 Nov. 1852), *CBL*, iii, 78. Gérin notes the similarity of Willie Weightman and GS in their handsome pampered aspect, *CB*, 169. From *Othello*, I. ii, 68.

246 *Without much imagination . . .* : Sydney Lee in *GS: A Memoir*.

Leslie Stephen: Ibid.

'*scarely gave him a chance.*': Catherine Winkworth to Emily Shaen (23 Mar. 1853), *LFC*, iv, 53.

247 *first fragment of* V: BPM. Bon 124-1, 124-2, 125-2, 125-3. See Clarendon ed. of *V*, Appendix I, 753–64.

249 *Mrs Smith never downcast*: GSR, i, ch 1.

GS suggested Cornhill: CB to GS (11 Mar. 1851), *CBL*, ii, 582.

to the House of Commons: GS's reminiscences about CB in *GS: A Memoir*.

250 *'The giant . . .'*: Copy of letter to EN in John Murray archive. *CBL*, ii, 414.

251 *'naughty' books*: *GS: A Memoir*.

GHL's coarse remarks: GSR, i, ch. 13.

CB and the Duke of Wellington: GSR, i, ch. 7.

CB's eyes: John Richmond, son of George Richmond, to R[eginald] Smith, son-in-law of GS (30 Dec. 1909), recalling his father's words about CB. BPM. S-G. 102. This drawing was eventually left to the National Portrait Gallery by ABN.

it did require a certain degree of closeness: I owe this observation to Allegra Huston of Weidenfeld & Nicolson.

252 *so like AB*: Richmond told this to GS, GSR, i, ch. 7. It is often misreported that CB likened her looks to those of EB.

plainness: GHL, for instance, spoke of CB as 'a little plain . . . old maid.' Reported by J. W. Cross, *George Eliot's Life* (Edinburgh: Blackwood, 1885), i, 307.

silk or wool: I am grateful to Audrey W. Hall for details of clothing in this period.

she and GS understood each other: To EN (21 June 1850), *CBL*, ii, 419.

253 '*as happy . . .*', etc.: To WSW (20 July 1850), *CBL*, ii, 427.

'*a certain faculty for reading men*': GSR, i, ch. 5.

'*adroit*' *advice*: EG quotes GS's adjective back to him (June 1855), agreeing it is the perfect word for CB's advice. *EGL*, 349.

'*Conceive a dell . . .*': *V*, ii, ch. 23, Fraser, *CB*, 377, makes the apt connection between the Edinburgh holiday and this passage in *V*.

'*a lyric . . .*', '*mine own romantic town*': To WSW (20 July 1850), *CBL*, ii, 428. The latter is a quotation from Scott's *Marmion*.

'*received some overtures*': CB to EN (15 July 1850), *CBL*, ii, 425.

254 *a wish for an introduction to a publisher*: EG to GS (5 Apr. 1860), *EGL*, 462: 611.

'*Sir James was warning me . . .*': CB to GS (late Aug. 1850), *CBL*, ii, 454.

'*she-artist*': CB to Miss Wooler (27 Sept. 1850), *CBL*, ii, 477.

255 *CB 'altogether plain' and told EG the story of her life*: EG to Catherine Winkworth (25 Aug. 1850) and to Tottie Fox (Aug. 1850), *LFC*, iii, 140–47.

256 *talked without hurry, etc.*: Comments by EG's friend, Susanna Winkworth, quoted in A. B. Hopkins, *Elizabeth Gaskell: Her Life and Work* (London, John Lehmann, 1952), 312.

    colourful stories: A full and excellent portrait of EG is to be found in Uglow, *Elizabeth Gaskell*, 237ff.

    the full scope: In 1967, Gérin made astute suggestions about the place of GS in CB's life. Twenty years later, the scope of this correspondence was shown by Rebecca Fraser, the first biographer to use S-G Papers.

    'tougher': Uglow, *Elizabeth Gaskell*, 266.

    EG's rumour: EG to Catherine Winkworth (25 Aug. 1850), *CBL*, ii, 446–9.

257 *'Poor Miss Brontë'*: Emily Winkworth to Catherine Winkworth (30 Aug. 1850), *LFC*, iii, 151.

    asked EG not to pity: BPM. BS 71.7. (17 Nov. 1849). *CBL*, ii, 288. In 'Charlotte Brontë and Currer Bell', Rebecca Fraser notes the excessive pity of EG, *Brontë/Gaskell Societies Joint Conference Papers*, 1990.

    'indiscriminate visiting . . .': CB to Miss Wooler (27 Sept. 1850), *CBL*, ii, 477.

    allusion to marriage: To EN (14 Sept. 1850), *CBL*, ii, 468.

258 *'bad days . . .'*: To HM (Oct.? 1850), *CBL*, ii, 481.

    'soft pathos': To WSW (c. 19 Nov. 1850), *CBL*, ii, 513.

    CB on In Memoriam: To EG (27 Aug. 1850), *CBL*, ii, 457.

    'disastrous experience teaches . . .': CB on George Sand to GHL (17 Oct. 1850). BL. Add. Ms 39763.

259 *interpreted her sisters to the world*: Juliet Gardiner's well-phrased statement in her Introduction to *The World Within*, 11.

    'Men and women . . .': CB, 'Biographical Notice'. *CBL*, ii, Appendix.

    anti-Catholicism: CB to GHL (23 Nov. 1850), *CBL*, ii, 517.

    fear of her own susceptibility: An idea of EG's cancelled in the MS. of the *Life* (MS f. 241): 'The strong feeling against the Roman Catholic religion was considered as hatred against the Roman Catholics, and yet I imagine that part of its vehemence arose from the fact that she was aware of her own susceptibilities'. Cited by Angus Easson, *BST* 16: 84, 282.

260 *'the lofty Matt'*: GSR, i, ch. 15.

    'past thirty and plain': To Miss Wightman (21 Dec. 1850), *Letters of Matthew Arnold 1848–88*, i, ed. George W. E. Russell (Macmillan, 1895), 15.

    CB on Arnold: To JT (15 Jan. 1851), *CBL*, ii, 554.

    'hunger, rebellion, and rage': To Mrs Forster (14 April 1853), Russell, ed., *Letters of Matthew Arnold*, i, 34, repr. *The Brontës: The Critical Heritage*, 201.

261 *Dickens and Ellen Ternan*: See Phyllis Rose, *Parallel Lives: Five Victorian Marriages* (1984; repr. Harmondsworth: Penguin, 1985), 143–92, and Claire Tomalin, *The Invisible Woman: Ellen Ternan and Charles Dickens* (Harmondsworth: Viking, 1990).

    'fever': To EN (20 Jan. 1851), *CBL*, ii, 557.

    the 'undercurrent' exchange: CB to EN (20 Jan. 1851), ibid.

262 *Both women needed 'wisdom'*: *CBL*, ii, 558.

'*Venus*' *and* '*Jupiter*', *etc.*: CB to EN (30 Jan. 1851), *CBL*, ii, 567.

'*as a doting parent towards an idiot child*': CB to GS (5 Feb. 1851), *CBL*, ii, 572.

263 '*Don't be alarmed.*': CB to GS (11 Mar. 1851), *CBL*, ii, 582.

a poem on the Highlands: CB to GS (5 Aug. 1850), *CBL*, ii, 437.

letter a better form of '*utterance*': BL. Add MS 43481 b. 12, p. 283. CB has corrected 'letter' to 'written language' in *V*, ii, ch. 21.

264 '*You happen not quite to know yourself*': CB to GS (7 Jan. 1851), *CBL*, ii, 546.

'. . . *young distinguished, and handsome* . . .'*V*, i, ch. 7.

'*glanced from face to face* . . .': *V*, i, ch. 10.

265 *mystery, concealment*: I have drawn on a superb article by Stuart Hampshire, 'What the Jameses Knew', *New York Review of Books* (10 Oct. 1991).

266 *looked at her in his keen way*: To EN (5 Apr. 1851), *CBL*, ii, 600.

'*ran ice*': To EN (9 Apr. 1851), Ibid.

267 '*a great wish* . . .': (17 Apr. 1851), *CBL*, ii, 604.

not made of granite: To GS (19 Apr. 1851), *CBL*, ii, 606–7.

268 '*no ailment*': CB to GS (19 Apr. 1851) ibid. See also CB to Mrs Smith (7 Apr. 1851), *CBL*, ii, 604.

'*temporary*': To EN (22 May 1851). BPM. Bon 236. *CBL*, ii, 621.

'*I dare not* . . .': CB to EN (12 Apr. 1851). BPM. Bon 325 *CBL*, ii, 602.

269 *EB's esteem of EN*: CB to EN (27 Nov. 1848), *CBL*, ii, 146. This letter was written while EB was dying.

'*John Taylor is a noodle*': To EN (10 May 1851), *CBL*, ii, 612.

GS changed: To EN (2 June 1851), *CBL*, ii, 628.

270 '*white stone*', '*very happy*': Ibid.

'. . . *strangely suggestive to hear the French language* . . .': Ibid.

271 '*more than ordinarily tender* . . .': GSR, i, ch. 1.

GS and Sir James Stephen: GS: *A Memoir*, 102.

'*Generally* . . .': Ibid.

sick and weak: To EN (11 June 1851), *CBL*, ii, 625–6.

272 '*add to solitude*': Ibid.

'*Babylon*': To PB (14 June 1851), *CBL*, ii, 636.

WMT calling CB '*Jane Eyre*', *etc.*: Recalled by GS, *GS: A Memoir*, and GSR.

'*There's a fire* . . .': To Mary Holmes (25 Feb. 1852) Ray, ed., *Letters and Private Papers of WMT*, iii, 12.

273 '*her soul was in it*': (11 June 1851), Brotherton. *CBL*, ii, 634.

'*a wonderful sight* . . .': To EN (24 June 1851), *CBL*, ii, 648.

'*Lucia*': At the end of *The Professor*. See ch. 4 above.

publicity was degrading: To WSW (19 Dec. 1849), *CBL*, ii, 312.

'*There is something divine* . . .': To WSW (1 May 1848), *CBL*, ii, 59.

274 '*shadow*': CB to GS (8 July 1851), *CBL*, ii, 663.

resolving to moderate her attachment: See CB to WSW (21 July 1851), *CBL*, ii, 667–8.

intending to extend her abstinence: To GS (8 July 1851), *CBL*, ii, 663.

avoid the misanthropy: CB to WSW (21 July 1851), *CBL*, ii, 667.

'*a glad emotion* . . .': *V*, ii, ch. 21.

'*he had written in benignant mood*': *V*, ii, ch. 22.

275 '*I wanted a portrait* . . .': CB to GS (2 July 1851), *CBL*, ii, 656.
   made a copy: Ibid.
   to use the intellectual promise: To GS (8 July 1851), *CBL*, ii, 663.
   austere hand: To GS (4 Aug. 1851), *CBL*, ii, 675.
   '*with grace* . . .': To GS (9 Aug. 1851), *CBL*, ii, 680.
276 '*a touch of Mephistopheles* . . .': To GS (n.d.), *CBL*, ii, 684.
   '*of which* [we] *should partake* . . .': CB to GS (1 July 1851), *CBL*, ii, 655.
   message reappears in V: *V*, iii, ch. 38.
   correspondence coincided with the progress of V: Gérin, *CB*, 495.
   '*since you say* . . .': CB to GS (8 July 1851), *CBL*, ii, 663.
277 *three or four half-tender lines*: *V*, ii, ch. 23.
   correspondence reached its peak: CB to GS (15 Sept. 1851), *CBL*, ii, 690–1.
278 '*very happy*', etc.: CB to GS (22 Sept. 1851), *CBL*, ii, 699.
279 '*painful mental worry* . . .': CB to EN (6–7? Nov. 1851). *CBL*, ii, 711.
   the Lady of Shalott: In Tennyson's famous poem (1832, revised 1842), *The Poems of Tennyson*, ed. Christopher Ricks (London: Longmans, 1969; NY: Norton, 1972).
   a solid morsel: This draws on Lucy's response when she receives an unexpected letter from Graham Bretton in *V*, ii, ch. 21 ('Reaction').
   GS and Mrs Humphry Ward: Letter (8 Aug. 1898), quoted by Gérin, *CB* 436.
   Virginia Woolf's memory of GS: To Lady Cecil (25 July 1932), *The Letters of Virginia Woolf*, v, ed. Nigel Nicolson, assisted by Joanne Trautmann (London: Hogarth; NY: Harcourt, 1979), 80. VW owned that this happened 'a million years ago' and the memory was unreliable.
280 '*freak of taste*': Gérin, ed., *Five Novelettes*, 241.
   Captain Wybrow: 'Mr Gilfil's Love-Story', *Scenes of Clerical Life* (1857; repr. Harmondsworth: Penguin, 1989), ed. David Lodge, 164. George Eliot told her publisher, Blackwood, that in *Scenes of Clerical Life*, she had attempted things she might never be able to do again.
281 '. . . *a low nervous fever* . . .': CB to GS (n.d.), BPM. S-G.92. *CBL*, ii, 731.
282 '*my mind has suffered somewhat too much* . . .': *V*, i, ch. 15.
   '*I passed such a winter* . . .': To WSW (18 July 1852), *CBL*, iii, 59.
   '*Some long stormy days and nights* . . .': To Laetitia Wheelwright (12 Apr. 1852), *Life*, 474.
283 *For four months* . . . : CB to Miss Wooler (12 Mar. 1852), Allbut Bequest, Fitzwilliam Museum, Cambridge. *CBL*, iii, 28–9.
   Thackeray 'unjust to women . . .': To GS, (14 Feb. 1852), *CBL*, iii, 18.
   '*twaddling*' of *Esther Summerson*: To GS, (11 Mar. 1852), *CBL*, iii, 27.
   '*insane* . . .': *V*, ii, ch. 21.
   '*I suppose animals kept in cages* . . .': *V*, ii, ch 24.
284 '*privation, penury* . . .': *V*, ii, ch. 21.
285 *That goodly river*: *V*, ii, ch. 26.
286 *a buried* '*passage of feeling*': *V*, iii, ch. 31.
   '*Good night* . . .': *V*, iii, ch. 31.
   manuscript: Smith Bequest, BL: CB's fair copy Add. MSS 43480–2.
   excised: Ibid. Margaret Smith notes, in her Textual Introduction to *V* (xxx), that of forty such excisions more than twenty are to do with Graham Bretton.

most heavily revised passages: Details from Margaret Smith, *V*, xxxii.

287 *with some haste*: Ibid.

    26 October: The date is mentioned in a letter to WSW that accompanied the ms. Bodleian Library MS. Eng. letters e. 30. *CBL*, iii, 72.

    '. . . *blue and silver turban* . . .': *V*, ii, ch. 20.

    '. . . *opinion of Dr John* . . .': *V*, ii, ch. 18.

288 'His *friendship* . . .': *V*, iii, ch. 35.

    would not permit WSW to read: CB to EN (9 Dec. 1852), *CBL*, iii, 91.

    '*I am afraid* . . .': CB to GS. BPM. S-G.77. *CBL*, iii, 87.

    cheque: CB to Miss Wooler (7 Dec. 1852), *CBL*, iii, 89.

    '*to see what was the matter* . . .': CB to GS (6 Dec. 1852), *CBL*, iii, 88.

    '*It is not pleasant* . . .': Ibid.

    She also asked . . . : Reported by CB to EN (9 Dec. 1852), *CBL*, iii, 91.

289 *communications to Ellen*: Ibid.

CHAPTER EIGHT: BURIED FIRE

290 '*heretic narrative*': *V*, i, ch. 15.

    I wish . . . : (1 Nov. 1849), *CBL*, ii, 275.

291 *CB's retort to GHL*: (Jan. 1850), *CBL*, ii, 330. GHL attacked *Sh* in the *Edinburgh Review*, repr. in *The Brontës: The Critical Heritage*, 162.

    '. . . *the sheltering shadow of an incognito*': To GS (30 Oct. 1852), *CBL*, iii, 74.

    '*My wish* . . .': To WSW (26 Oct. 1852), Bodleian Library MS. Eng. letters e. 30. *CBL*, iii, 72.

292 *George Eliot on V*: To Mrs Bray (15 Feb.; 5 and 12 Mar. 1853), Haight, ed., *The George Eliot Letters*, ii, 87, 91, 92.

294 '*acute and insensate*' '. . . *Though I Knew*': *V*, i, ch. 8.

    '*As to the name of the heroine* . . .': To WSW (6 Nov. 1852), *CBL*, iii, 80.

295 '. . . *rising character* . . .': *V*, ii, ch. 27.

    Harriet Taylor Mill: 'The Enfranchisement of Women'. See ch. 7 and note above.

    Florence Nightingale: *Cassandra*.

    '. . . *going on, and still to be*': 'Wages' (1868), *The Poems of Tennyson*, ed. Christopher Ricks, 1205.

296 '*new region*': *V*, ii, ch. 17.

    slumbers idle: *V*, i, ch. 4.

    '*Two hot, close rooms* . . .': *V*, i, ch. 4.

    staid manner: *V*, i, ch. 5.

    '*my inner self* . . .': *V*, i, ch. 6.

297 *Giselle*: Heroine of the ballet *Giselle*.

    Odette: Heroine of the ballet *Swan Lake*.

    '*no more to be parted with* . . .': *V*, i, ch. 12.

    '. . . *the quick of my nature.*': *V*, i, ch. 12.

    '*base habit of cowardice.*': *V*, i, ch. 8.

298 *was the portal of a vault* . . . : *V*, i, ch. 12.

'*the whole night . . .*': *V*, iii, ch. 31.

'*gown of mist*', 'shadow': Ms. of *V*, i, 217. BL. Add MS 43480. The manuscript alterations are noted by Margaret Smith, *V*, xxxiii.

'*I know you!*': *V*, i, ch. 15.

299 '*a chainless soul . . .*': 'The Old Stoic', *Poems* (1846); Gezari, ed., *The Complete Poems*, 31.

'*Take courage, Charlotte*': EN's record of the last days of AB's life for EG, *CBL*, ii, Appendix: 739–41.

'*prison*': *V*, ii, ch. 16.

the unwritten plot of desire: Boumelha elaborates on this brilliantly, *CB*, 16–20. Interestingly, T. S. Eliot, in a little-known piece on Virginia Woolf, observes what is '*left out*' in her work: 'And this something is deliberately *left out*, by what could be called a moral effort of the will. And being left out, this something is, in a melancholy sense, present.' ('T. S. Eliot "places" Virginia Woolf for French Readers', in *Virginia Woolf: The Critical Heritage*, ed. Robin Majumdar and Allen McLaurin (London: Routledge, 1975), 192.

300 '*an inhospitable bar . . .*': *V*, i, ch. 15.

'*the writer's individual nature . . .*': *V*, ii, ch. 21.

flaunt its untold story: Boumelha, *CB*, op. cit.

Cleopatra: *V*, ii, ch. 19. Derived from '*Une Almée*' by Defiefve which CB had seen in Brussels. Discussed further below, ch. 10.

'*La vie d'une femme*': *V*, ch. 19. Triptych identified by Gérin, *CB*, 210, who notes the interesting fact that one critic, Eugène Landoy, responded to the flat formal manner of the painting with the advice that the artist might study the great painters' 'treatment of shadows'.

Vashti: *V*, ii, ch. 23.

301 *CB's reading of Heathcliff as demon*: CB's Preface to the 1850 edition of *WH*. *CBL*, ii, Appendix: 748–51.

'*he judged her as a woman . . .*': *V*, ii, ch. 23.

Miss Wooler was not proud: See CB's reply to Miss Wooler (14 Feb. 1850), *CBL*, ii, 343, and comments to EN (16 Feb. 1850), *CBL*, ii, 347.

302 '*The mood of one hour . . .*': *V*, ii, ch. 22.

'*His "quiet Lucy Snowe" . . .*': *V*, ii, ch. 27.

letters of uncensored self-expression: Boumelha, *CB*, op. cit.

no plot to follow: Ibid.

303 '*dreads and vindictively detests*': *V*, iii, ch. 31.

'*What do you start for? . . .*' *V*, iii, ch. 29.

not 'asphyxiée': Ibid.

'*to be passed by as a shadow*': *V*, iii, ch. 28.

304 '*I am ignorant . . .*': *V*, iii, ch. 30.

the most active thing in the novel: Boumelha, *CB*, op. cit.

305 *Virginia Woolf on 'illness'*: Virginia Woolf, 'On Being Ill' (1930), *Collected Essays*, iv, ed. Leonard Woolf (London: Hogarth; NY: Harcourt, 1967), 193–203.

T. S. Eliot's illness and The Waste Land: See Lyndall Gordon, *T. S. Eliot: An Imperfect Life* (NY: Norton 2000), ch. 5.

'*it is a commonplace . . .*': Facsimile edition of *The Waste Land Manuscript*, ed. Valerie Eliot
   (London: Faber and Faber; NY: Harcourt, 1971), 129.

'*back woods of America . . .*': To EG (1 June 1853), *CBL*, iii, 172.

306 '*severe Truth*': CB to EG (9 July 1853), *CBL*, iii, 182.

'*He came . . .*': *V*, iii, ch. 36.

'*clear-eyed endurance*': George Eliot to Mme Bodichon (26 Dec. 1860), J. W. Cross,
   George Eliot's Life, ii, 283.

Evangelicalism which banished cynicism: A. O. J. Cockshut, *Truth to Life: The Art of
   Biography in the Nineteenth Century* (London: Collins, 1974), 71.

307 *rehearses, alone in the attic*: *V*, i, ch. 14.

'*tongue once got free*', etc.: *V*, i, ch. 14.

308 *depression is a form of buried utterance*: See Julia Kristeva on depression as a form of discourse to be learnt in *Black Sun: Depression and Melancholia* (1987; transl. Leon S.
   Roudiez, Columbia University Press, 1989).

ms. of V: BL. Add MS 43480 b.11 (vol. i); Add MS 43481 b.12 (vol. ii); Add MS 43482
   (vol. iii). Part of the George Smith Memorial bequest.

'*grief*': MS, ii, 501.

309 *Graham's emotional limitations*: MS, i, where the child, Paulina, understands that
   Graham does not have it in his nature to care for her as she cares for him.

'*struggles with the natural character*': MS, ii, 298. The truncated version comes at the
   beginning of 'La Terrasse'.

'*madness*': MS, iii, 730, and MS, ii 460.

'*Speak of it!*': MS, ii, 460.

'*No need to dwell on the result.*': MS, ii, 349.

'*dimness & depression*': MS, ii, 504.

'*shadow*': See above, the ms. description of Lucy's dress at the school fête. In vol.
   ii of the MS, 347, the thought of her return to solitude comes over Lucy like
   a shadow.

310 '*Put your grief . . .*': *V*, ii, ch. 18.

No novel was ever written so close to unfolding event: Gérin, *CB*, 494, was aware that *V* was
   exploring the present as well as the past of its author: '– a present so unpredictable that it left the author continually in suspense as to the issue.'

'*stamped it . . .*': *V*, iii, ch. 30.

the last great devoir: Gérin, *CB*, 509.

the longest love-letter: I owe this observation to Siamon Gordon.

311 *lusus naturae*: *V*, iii, ch. 30.

reconciliation: MS, iii, 598–9. The long cut comes in the chapter called 'M. Paul'.

too volatile: MS, iii, 566.

'*for a show . . .*': *V*, iii, ch. 30.

much-revised passage: Noted by Margaret Smith in her Textual Introduction to *V*.

Southey's letters: This point was made by Jane Miller in her persuasive view of *V* in
   Women Writing About Men (London: Virago, 1986), 100.

eight excised pages: Noted by Margaret Smith in her Textual Introduction to *V*. CB
   cut (with scissors) part of the original folio 609 to the upper part of folio 617.
   Margaret Smith makes a different suggestion: the cut leaves could have been

recopied into the chapter on Lucy's examination. There is no proof for either suggestion.

secret of her creativity: I draw, again, on Jane Miller, *Women Writing About Men*, 100.

'*my mind filling like a rising well . . .*': V, iii, ch. 35.

312 '*La Justice Humaine*': BST, 12: 62, 89–90. *Essays*, 204–15.

'*did not suit*': V, iii, ch. 35.

'*. . . I could talk . . .*': V, iii, ch. 36.

'*wordless language*': V, iii, ch. 41.

'*In such inadequate language . . .*': V, iii, ch. 41.

313 *Ginevra* '*. . . suffer[ed] as little . . .*': V, iii, ch. 40.

CB thought Paulina an artistic failure: To GS (6 Dec. 1852), *CBL*, iii, 88.

CHAPTER NINE: MARRIAGE

315 '*Providence*': CB to EN (11 Apr. 1854); CB to Miss Wooler (12 Apr. 1854); CB to GS (25 Apr. 1854), *CBL*, iii, 240, 242, 250.

not unaware of his regard: To EN (15 Dec. 1852), *CBL*, iii, 93.

'*like lightning*': Ibid.

316 '*The Story of Willie Ellin*': BST (1936), 3–22.

'*Emma*': Transcribed by Herbert Rosengarten in Appendix to *The Professor*, 249–69. Ms. in the Taylor Collection, Princeton. Twenty pages, dated 27 Nov. 1853, in pencil which indicates, with CB, a first draft. It is heavily corrected. '*Emma*' was first published, inaccurately, in GS's new *Cornhill Magazine* (Apr. 1860) with an introduction by Thackeray.

'*uncongenial*': To EN (18 Dec. 1852), *CBL*, iii, 95.

'*dear boy*': To EN (26 Dec. 1854), *CBL*, iii, 312.

'*entirely passive*': To EN (6 Apr. 1853), *CBL*, iii, 149.

'*pain*': To EN (15 Dec. 1852), *CBL*, iii, 93.

'*like whipcord*': Ibid.

'*cruel*': To EN (18 Dec. 1852), *CBL*, iii, 94.

'*know something of him*': Ibid.

Virginia Woolf opened up the area of daughters' fear: *Three Guineas* (1938; repr. Harmondsworth: Penguin, 1977), 148–55.

317 '*a stern, harsh, selfish woman*': CB to EN (4 Mar. 1852), *LFC*, iv, 319.

'*again and again . . .*': Ibid.

'*slight astringency*': *Life*, 395.

'*if so, I had a mind to the encounter . . .*': V, ii, ch. 26.

318 '*Good, mild, uncontentious*': To EN (27 July 1851), *CBL*, ii, 671.

319 *ABN's books*: BPM.

'*bigoted*': EG to John Forster (23 Apr. 1854), *LFC*, iv, 117.

CB feared: Catherine Winkworth, the German translator (daughter of a Manchester silk manufacturer, part of the Gaskell circle), to Emma Shaen (8 May 1854), *LFC*, iv, 123.

'*too quick . . .*': To EN (15 Dec. 1852), *CBL*, iii, 92.

'*something almost repulsive*': EG to John Forster, *EGL*, 155: 230.

320 *cancelled exchange*: BL. MS. of *JE*, ii, 446.

  '*Ah! I am not pleasant to look at*' etc.: *V*, iii, ch. 41.

  CB's self-caricature: Pen and ink sketch in letter to EN (6 Mar. 1843). See illustration.

321 '*that every woman may avoid him . . .*': PB to CB while CB was in London (Dec. 1852–
    Jan. 1853). CB sent it to EG. *BST*, 63: 3, 199 (1953).

  Emily's contempt: EN to Clement Shorter (Apr. 1895), Ellen Nussey Papers,
    Brotherton.

  transferred her strongest bond to EB: EG notes that CB's love was 'poured out' on EB,
    Life, 107.

  On Sunday afternoon . . .: CB to PB (2 June 1852), *CBL*, iii, 50.

322 *few attachments*: CB to EN (2 Jan. 1853), *CBL*, iii, 101.

  '*really fearful*': CB to EN (11 Jan. 1853), *CBL*, iii, 102–3.

  Thackeray's portrait: CB to GS, *CBL*, iii, 128.

323 '*I am bound to admit . . .*': CB to GS (16 Feb. 1853), *CBL*, iii, 124.

  '*that – person . . .*': CB to GS (26 Mar. 1853), *CBL*, iii, 142.

  review from GHL: CB to WSW (8 Apr. 1853). *CBL*, iii, 151.

  Lady Harriet St Clair: CB to WSW (23 Mar. 1853), *CBL*, iii, 138–9.

  a woman who had undertaken not to marry . . . : Ibid.

  CB teased Cornhill . . . : Ibid.

324 *WMT's attacks on V*: (March and April 1853) Ray, ed., *Letters and Private Papers of
    WMT*; repr. *The Brontës: The Critical Heritage*, 197–8.

  Arnold's attacks on V: To Clough (21 Mar. 1853), *The Letters of Matthew Arnold to Arthur
    Hugh Clough*, ed. Howard Foster Lowry (Oxford University Press, 1932), 132.

  HM attacked in a letter: HM to CB (*c*.Jan. 1853) *LFC*, iv, 41.

  attack in Daily News: see *Life* 373–6 and *LFC*, iv, 43–4.

  '*dumb*' etc: CB to HM, *CBL*, iii, 118.

325 *language and HM*: CB to GS (16 Mar. 1853), *LFC*, iv, 55.

  '*most perilous . . .*': CB to Miss Wooler (13 Apr. 1853), *CBL*, iii, 154.

  Favourable reviews . . . : CB to GS (29 Mar. 1853). BPM. BS.87. *CBL*, iii, 146.

326 *We want a woman at our hearth . . .* : Repr. *The Brontës: The Critical Heritage*, 207.

  '*heavy Goliahs . . .*': To WSW (1? Mar. 1849), BPM. Bon 208. *CBL*, ii, 185.

  '*. . . He snarls . . .*': To WSW (8 Apr. 1853). BPM. Gr:F2. *CBL*, iii, 152.

327 *EG's aunt*: I am indebted to Jenny Uglow for this information.

  '*the secretly and deeply felt wish . . .*': CB to Lucy Holland (28 May 1853). BPM. BS.89.2.
    CBL, iii, 171.

  '*flaysome*' *look*: CB to EN (4 Mar. 1853), *CBL*, iii, 129.

  '*inexpressibly*': To EN (6 Apr. 1853), *CBL*, iii, 149.

329 *CB at Newgate and Pentonville*: GS: *A Memoir*, 91.

  Nelly Dean: The housekeeper-narrator in *Wuthering Heights*.

330 *Miss Fetherhed*: In the course of the draft, CB uses also the names: 'Miss
    Featherhead', 'Fetherstone', and finally 'Miss Wilcox'. I have retained
    'Fetherhed' to underline the allegorical character.

333 *CB cancelled this dramatic scene*: Despite this, the *Cornhill Magazine* published the
    final scene (Apr. 1860).

  '*I cannot write books . . .*': CB to GS (30 Oct. 1852), *CBL*, iii, 75.

335 '*tyrant-passion*': *V*, ii, ch. 27.

'*A thought . . .*': CB to EG (9 July 1853), *CBL*,, iii, 182.

As EG saw it . . . : *EGL*, 68: 106.

336 *GS's valentine to EG*: Bodleian Library, Oxford. Printed by Jenny Uglow, *Elizabeth Gaskell*, illustration no. 18, following p. 338.

'*This will not be mere talk . . .*': CB to EN (15 Apr. 1854), *CBL*, iii, 244. I am assuming, here, that CB had this thought for quite some time before she communicated it, for it was very much part of her decision in ABN's favour.

'*for many years*': CB to GS (25 Apr. 1854), *CBL*, iii, 250.

'*cold & disapproving*': CB told EG, EG to John Forster (23 Apr. 1854), *CBL*, iii, 248.

337 '*very hard and rough work*': CB to EN (1 Apr. 1854), *CBL*, iii, 239.

'*will not suffer me . . .*': To EN (6 Apr. 1853), *CBL*, iii, 149.

'*Compassion or relenting . . .*': CB to EN (16 May 1853), *CBL*, iii, 166.

heard PB speak '*at*' *CB*: EG to a friend (Sept. 1853), *LFC*, iv, 91.

'*proud minxes*': Ibid., 89.

tyrant: MT to EN (19 Apr. to 19 May 1856). Berg. Stevens, *MT*, 126. The word MT uses is 'tyranny'.

'*I can never think . . .*': Ibid.

'*Villainous old Mr Brontë*': EN to Sir T. Wemyss Reid (3 Nov. 1876), in which she recalls MT calling PB 'that wicked old man'. Berg.

338 '*ambition*': To EN (15 Apr. 1854), *CBL*, iii, 244.

'*unjust*': To EG (18 Apr. 1854), *CBL*, iii, 247.

'*fever*': CB to GS. BPM. S-G.83. *CBL*, iii, 174.

'*Lucy must not marry Dr John*': To GS (3 Nov. 1852), *CBL*, iii, 77–8.

339 (*said Mrs Smith . . .*): In holograph draft of a letter to CB, conveying GS's engagement. BPM. S-G.87. *CBL*, iii, 210.

GS left wife in charge of DNB: In letter to Sir Sydney Lee (29 Oct. 1901), Elizabeth Smith says she was 'entrusted with the care of the *DNB*'. Bodleian Library MS. Eng. misc. d. 180.

CB to Mrs Smith: BPM. S-G.86. *CBL*, iii, 209.

340 *CB to WSW*: *CBL*, iii, 212.

curt formal congratulation: (10 Dec. 1853). BPM. S-G.88. *CBL*, iii, 213.

lone: CB to Miss Wooler (12 Dec. 1853), *CBL*, iii, 213. She praises Miss Wooler for her unsoured temper.

341 '*Father . . .*': CB recounted this exchange to EG, on a visit to Plymouth Grove later that spring, which EG related to John Forster, *EGL*, 195: 289.

342 '*to another name*': CB to GS (18 Apr. 1854). *CBL*, iii, 245.

distanced from EN: EN's view of CB's 'temptation' and a brief rift between the two friends is referred to in a holograph letter from Mary Hewitt to EN (21 Feb. 1854), Brotherton. On 24 Apr. 1854 another letter from Mary Hewitt refers to a 'reconcilement', *LFC*, iv, 118.

'*obtuse . . .*': EN to Sir T. Wemyss Reid (3 Nov. 1876), Berg. Though this is a view EN expressed twenty years after CB's death, a negative view could have been derived from CB herself before she changed towards ABN. This would explain the charge of 'inconsistency' below.

EN's complaint and MT's retort: MT to EN (24 Feb.-3 Mar. 1854). BL. Ashley. Stevens, *MT*, 120.

'*but she is good . . .*': To WSW (3 Jan. 1850), *CBL*, ii, 323.

343 *told Sydney Dobell*: *CBL*, iii, 225.

'*the dark places . . .*': 'Professions for Women', *Collected Essays* (London: Hogarth, 1972), ii, 287–8. This was a paper read to the Women's Service League in 1932. A fascinating draft is printed in *The Pargiters*.

344 *public defence of CB*: ABN contributed cogent arguments in defence of CB's truth-telling in *JE* during the Cowan Bridge controversy that followed the publication of the *Life*.

345 '*My expectations . . .*': (25 Apr. 1854), *CBL*, iii, 250.

346 '*I cannot deny . . .*': (18 Apr. 1854), *CBL*, iii, 246–7.

aired more freely her doubts about marriage: Catherine Winkworth to Emma Shaen (8 May 1854), *Memorials of Two Sisters: Susanna and Catherine Winkworth*, ed. Margaret J. Shaen (London: Longmans, 1908), 112–15. *CBL*, iii, 256–8.

348 '*I wrote immediately . . .*': CB to EN (12 June 1854). BPM. Gr: E28. *CBL*, iii,268.

ABN claimed to be dying: CB to EN (27 May 1854), *CBL*, iii, 265.

dim morning: CB to Miss Wooler (22 Aug. 1854), *CBL*, iii, 286.

'*like a snowdrop*': *Life*, 395. EG heard this expression from Haworth villagers.

turned on Papa: EN to Sir T. Wemyss Reid (3 Nov. 1876). Berg. EN notes this happened on her last visit alone to the Parsonage, i.e. the last before the wedding visit. Although she is querulous about PB's attempt to alienate CB from her 'faithful friend', she seems to remember accurately: 'She turned upon him with rage as we breakfasted when he made some kind of hypocritical remark to me on the vicissitudes of life'.

349 *wedding tour*: Deft summary in *Life*, 395.

'*It is almost inexplicable to me . . .*': CB to EN (7 Dec. 1854), *LFC*, iv, 164–5.

350 '*Henceforward . . .*': *Life*, 519.

'*. . . Would that Charlotte's literary friends . . .*': EN, sketch of a letter to GS, dated Mar. 28th [c.1860], from Woodhouse, Leeds, in which EN mentions that the *Cornhill* had recently published some literary remains of CB. Berg. The letter sent is in Murray archive.

'*I think many false ideas . . .*': (9 Aug. 1854), *CBL*, iii, 283–4.

351 '*the married woman . . .*': CB to EN (7 Sept. 1854), *CBL*, iii, 288.

'*which no efforts of ours can touch*': CB to EG (27 Aug. 1850), *CBL*, ii, 457. CB comments on John Parker's article on 'Women's Mission', *Westminster Review* (Jan. 1850): '. . . There are . . . evils . . . of which we cannot complain – of which it is advisable not too often to think.'

flesh of his flesh: *JE*, iii, ch. 12.

352 *freedom to move limbs*: See *JE* (where Jane has 'not been petrified' with Rochester) and *V* (where Lucy 'did not sit "asphyxiée"' – see above, ch. 8).

touching 'pitch': *Life*, 375.

353 '*Papa*', *etc.*: *Little Dorrit*, Book II, ch. 5.

letter from ABN: To *Halifax Guardian* (30 June 1857), repr. *LFC*, iv, 306, reproving a defender of The Clergy Daughters' School, Mrs Sarah Baldwin, for 'being a stranger to that delicacy of feeling which causes a lady to shrink from having her name paraded before the public.' Interestingly, ABN's main opponent, the son of Carus Wilson, cannot resist a snide comment about having no wish to defend Mrs Baldwin, which suggests that he concurs with ABN in the matter of women putting themselves forward in the public eye.

'As to his continued affection . . .': CB to Miss Wooler (19 Sept. 1854), *CBL*, iii, 291.

growing stronger: (15 Nov. 1854), *CBL*, iii, 301. See also CB to EN (26 Dec. 1854).

354 *in character to bury letters:* I came to this conclusion independently, and was pleased to find that Gérin had the same idea, *CB*, Appendix A, 573.

355 *'like a bomb-shell':* To EN (20 Oct. 1854), *CBL*, iii, 295.

'If you had not been with me . . .': ABN to GS (11 Oct. 1859), Appendix, *The Professor*, 250.

read 'Emma' to ABN: ABN recounted this scene in a letter to GS (11 Oct. 1859), ibid.

sentimental repose: EG to EN (9 July 1856), *LFC*, iv, 202: 'Her happy state of mind during her married life would probably have given a different character of greater hope and serenity to the fragment.'

356 *'always* groaned literally': EG to GS, Appendix, *The Professor*, 250.

CB wrote to Mr Ingham: BPM. BS.98. *CBL*, iii, 314.

357 *'pestiferous':* Letter to friend from Haworth (Sept. 1853), *LFC*, iv, 88.

Addison's disease suggested: By Gerson Weiss of the New Jersey Medical School, as reported by Nigel Hawkes in the *Herald Tribune* (31 March 1992). The condition is caused by the failure of the adrenal glands, at the upper end of the kidneys, to secrete several hormones which are important in maintaining the body's balance of water and salts. Since biochemical tests did not exist in CB's life-time, such a diagnosis could not have been ascertained.

'frequent fever': ABN to EN (14 Feb. 1855), *CBL*, iii, 324–5.

358 *'exhaustion':* ABN to EN (31 Mar. 1855), breaking the news of CB's death during the night, *CBL*, iii, 330.

'No kinder . . .': CB to Laetitia Wheelwright (15 Feb. 1855), *CBL*, iii, 325.

'I am not going to talk . . .': CB to EN (21 Feb. 1855), *CBL*, iii, 326.

'As to my husband . . .': CB to Amelia Taylor (Feb. 1855), *CBL*, iii, 327.

CHAPTER TEN: SURVIVING

359 *'familiarity . . .':* Quoted in Winnifrith, *The Brontës and Their Background*, 119.

Kingsley: Review (Apr. 1849), *Fraser's Magazine*, repr. *The Brontës: The Critical Heritage*, 271.

360 *'I am not going to die . . .':* Life, 400.

'Perfection of the life . . .': 'The Choice', *Collected Poems of W. B. Yeats* (London: Macmillan, 1958), 278.

'intended': 'A General Introduction for my Work' (1937), *Selected Criticism*, ed. A. Norman Jeffares (London: Macmillan, 1964), 255.

361 *dessert course:* Forty years later, Henry James would refuse happy endings in 'The Art of Fiction' (1884) in Henry James, *Essays on Literature, American Writers, English Writers* (NY: Library of America, 1984), 44–65.

the roar: George Eliot, *Middlemarch*, ch. 20.

362 *'little short of desecration'*: ABN to GS (1 Dec. 1856). Murray archive.

   'How hard . . .': CB to Miss Wooler (12 Dec. 1853), *CBL*, iii, 213.

   EG worldly-wise: To EN, *LFC*, iv, 228.

363 *sustained EG's view*: Gérin, *CB*, takes the same view as EG in citing the letters to Miss Wooler as the best.

   PB dressed 'up facts . . .': EG to GS, *EGL*, 322: 424.

   'inward light': From 'When thou sleepest' (1837), when CB was a teacher at Roe Head, *CBP*, 207–8. Copied by ABN and sent to GS on 4 Apr. 1861. Published in *Cornhill* (Aug. 1861), just after PB's death.

   PB unimpaired: ABN to GS (4 Apr. 1861 and 25 June 1861). Murray archive.

364 *CB destroyed correspondence*: EN to EG (July 1856), *LFC*, iv, 204, and EN to Clement Shorter (Apr. 1895), Brotherton.

   found letters from JT: EN to Clement Shorter (Apr. 1895), Brotherton.

   three hundred and fifty letters: Number given to EG, Uglow, *Elizabeth Gaskell*, 395.

   'mode of thought': ABN to EN (24 July 1855), Brotherton. *LFC*, iv, 191.

   ABN refused to authorise . . . : ABN to GS (3 Dec. 1856). Murray archive.

   EG's thanks for ABN's permission: EG to GS (6 Dec. 1856), *EGL*, 320: 422.

   'fierce correspondence': EG to GS (11 Dec. 1856), *EGL*, 322: 425.

   'ignorant nursing': EN to Clement Shorter (Apr. 1895), Brotherton.

   'but for his selfishness . . .': (3 Nov. 1876), Berg.

365 *'most selfish appropriation . . .'*: EN to GS (27 Feb. 1869), Brotherton. *LFC*, iv, 256.

   lock of CB's hair: EN kept it until 31 Jan. 1896. The lock was plaited in Oct. 1898. Now in BL. Egerton MS. 3268B.

   batch of letters: EN to Thomas Wise (18 Nov. 1892), Brotherton. In letter from EN to EG (26 July 1855), *LFC*, iv, 193, EN says: 'I have destroyed but a small portion of the correspondence.' Since this was her statement closest to the event, I assume it is more accurate than her later statement to Clement Shorter in Apr. 1895 (op. cit.) that she destroyed a 'large number'.

366 *Sir Wemyss Reid*: EN's holograph letters to him are in Berg.

   Thomas J. Wise: See Richard D. Altick on Wise's forgeries in *The Scholar Adventurers* (New York, 1950), 37–64, and see also 'T. J. Wise and the Brontës' in Winnifrith, *The Brontës and Their Background*, Appendix A, 195–201. One of Wise's ploys was to make false promises to ABN and EN that CB's letters would go to the South Kensington Museum. See above, ch. 3, Melodie Monahan's suggestion that it may have been Thomas Wise who separated the sheets of 'Ashworth' in order to effect two sales rather than one.

   'burn': CB to EN (20 Oct., 31 Oct., 7 Nov. 1854), *CBL*, iii, 295, 296. See also 298–9.

   almost everything: ABN did send GS transcripts of CB's and EB's poems for publication, as stated above.

367 *'. . . you will not show to others'*: EN to GS (19 Jan. 1869). Murray archive.

   EN tried to find out . . . : She first raised this with GS in the 1860s and obtained an answer, eventually, through Clement Shorter three decades later. ABN to Shorter (26 Apr. 1895), Brotherton.

   deplored MT's letters: ABN to Shorter (26 Apr. 1895), Brotherton.

   Nor was it forgotten that ABN refused to bury Michael Heaton: See ch. 5 above.

368 *never examined the 'little books'*: ABN to Shorter (18 June 1895), Brotherton.

369 *did ask for a donation*: EN Papers, Brotherton. Letters from EN to GS also in Murray archive.

   GS's letters to EN: EN Papers, Brotherton.

370 *GS, George Eliot, and the workhouse*: GSR, i, ch. 13, and ii, ch. 24. Details in Jennifer Glynn, *Prince of Publishers: A Biography of George Smith* (London: Allison & Busby, 1986).

   GS and wife abuse: GSR, ii, ch. 24.

371 *'In deeds of charity . . .'*: PB to EG (27 Aug. 1855), *LFC*, iv, 194–5.

   'a shadow again': HM, obituary for CB, *Daily News* (Apr. 1855).

   'tyranny': MT to EN (19 Apr. 1856), Berg. *LFC*, iv, 198–200.

   'grumble hard': Ibid.

372 *MT would 'remain in New Zealand as long as she can there find serious work to do . . .'*: CB to EN (13 Sept. 1846), from Manchester, while PB had operation. *CBL*, i, 497.

   'narrow minded . . .': MT to EN (4–8 Jan. 1857). Berg. Stevens, *MT*, 131.

373 *'disputing'*: MT to CB (Apr. 1852), *LFC*, iii, 329.

   'I sit by myself . . .': *Miss Miles*, 111. This telling passage has been quoted by Fraser, *CB*, 174–5.

   'full of truth . . .': PB to EG (2 Apr. 1857), Murray Archive. *LFC*, iv, 221.

374 *Kingsley*: (14 May 1857), *LFC*, iv, 222–3.

   adverse opinion of CB: A deft summary of hostile reviews is to be found in the chapters on prudery and reviewers in Winnifrith, *The Brontës and Their Background*.

   'dark & durable regrets': To EN (11 Oct. 1854), *CBL*, iii, 29.

   'one felt how lonely . . .': EG to Tottie Fox (20 Dec. 1852), *LFC*, iv, 31.

   'liberty': CB to EG (1 June 1853), *CBL*, iii, 172.

   letter to editor of The Christian Remembrancer: (18 July 1853), *CBL*, iii, 187.

375 *'I trust . . .'*: *Life*, 374.

   'The trembling little hand . . .': WMT, 'The Last Sketch', the first issue of *Cornhill Magazine* (Apr. 1860). ABN made a fair copy of 'Emma' for publication.

   CB's separation from heroines: Jane Miller, *Women Writing About Men*, 99.

   '. . . too purely personal': EG to EN (3 Nov. 1855), *EGL*, 271a: 874.

376 *'honour . . .'*: EG to GS, *EGL*, 347–8, quoted by Jenny Uglow, *Elizabeth Gaskell*, 391.

   autobiographical sources of CB's fiction: EG to a friend (Sept. 1853), *LFC*, iv, 90.

   miss: Jenny Uglow, *Elizabeth Gaskell*, 403. The ms. is in the John Rylands University Library, Manchester.

   '. . . a piece of womanliness . . .': EG to GS, *EGL*, 326: 430.

   CB not 'easily susceptible' to passion: *Life*, 337.

   EN's cover-up for CB's passion: An unaddressed note, presumably to EG while she was writing the *Life*. Murray archive.

377 *EG's concern about* The Professor: See Introduction by Herbert Rosengarten to *The Professor*.

   'disfigured . . .': EG to Emily Shaen (7 and 8 Sept. 1856), *EGL*, 410.

   'But oh! . . .': EG to GS (2 Oct. 1856), *EGL*, 417.

   'subversive': This finely judged perception is by Jenny Uglow, *Elizabeth Gaskell*, 391.

   'every woman dropped out of sight': Quoted ibid.

378 'Quant à la traduction en français . . .': CH to EN, *LFC*, iv, 247–51.

another episode in the Brontë tragedy: Gérin, *CB*, 313, talks of the Brussels episode as CB's 'unhappy adventure'.

'*something flighty . . .*': CB to EN (17 Aug. 1851), *CBL*, ii, 682.

son of George Richmond: John Richmond, see ch. 7.

380 '*accumulation of nervous energy*': *Cassandra*, 407–8.

381 '*eminently artificial thing*': J. S. Mill, see ch. 2, above.

Dickinson, reading everything the Brontës published: Her books are in the Houghton Library, Harvard University.

the 'I' in Dickinson poems: Her 'I' opening noted by Archibald MacLeish, cited in Cynthia Griffin Wolff, *Emily Dickinson* (Reading, Massachusetts: Addison-Wesley, 1988), 163 (in the section on the poet's voice).

'*Miss Austen . . .*': 'George Sand', *Galaxy* (July 1877), repr. Henry James, *Literary Criticism: French Writers, etc.* (NY: Library of America, 1984), 724.

382 '*Une Almée*': Identified by Gérin, *CB*, 209.

JE improper reading for girls in the 1880s: Kathleen Tillotson cites evidence in *Novels of the Eighteen-Forties*, 57: 'From many instances I choose one; Elizabeth Malleson (a lady of progressive views and a friend of George Eliot) read *Jane Eyre* aloud to her children some time in the eighties, "entirely omitting Rochester's mad wife, and so skilfully that we noticed nothing amiss with the plot!".'

383 *parade*: 'Thoughts Upon Social Success' (1903), *A Passionate Apprentice*, ed. Mitchell A. Leaska (London: Hogarth; NY: Harcourt, 1990), 167–9. Virginia Woolf was then Virginia Stephen.

'*Existence*': 'I tie my Hat . . .', c.1862, *The Complete Poems of Emily Dickinson*, 443, (London: Faber, 1970; repr. 1975), 212–13.

384 '*a cave in the sea*', etc.: *V*, ii, ch. 17.

'*a portion of my existence*': *V*, ii, ch. 17.

385 *tension of delay*: I owe this to Linda Brandon.

an immense expanse of shade: The phrase is from Michel Foucault on the rake and discourse in the 'classical age': *The Order of Things: An Archeology of the Human Sciences* (London: Tavistock Publications, 1970), 211.

386 '*There is enough said . . .*': *V*, iii, ch. 42 ('Finis').

final gesture of privacy: I owe this again to Linda Brandon.

unseen space behind the text: Ibid.

'*the province of poetry . . .*': *The History of Rasselas* (1759), ch. 10. (*Rasselas* is the book Helen Burns is reading in *Jane Eyre*.)

387 '*dark*': CB to EN (19 Dec. 1848), writing before EB died, on the very day of her death), *CBL*, ii, 154: 'Moments so dark as these I have never known.'

Southey 'kind and admirable . . .': In conversation with EG, see ch. 3 above.

ACKNOWLEDGEMENTS

Anyone writing on Charlotte Brontë is dependent on the treasures preserved at the Brontë Parsonage Museum. All quotations from manuscripts in its library are by courtesy of The Brontë Society. I should like to thank the Collections Manager Ann Dinsdale for her exceptional helpfulness. I have been dependent, too, on the accuracy of the Clarendon edition of the Brontës' novels, published in the 1970s and 1980s, and on the invaluable research of biographers and scholars, from Mrs Gaskell in 1857 to present experts including Rebecca Fraser, Sue Lonoff and Margaret Smith.

Audrey W. Hall advised on issues of class and on family papers of the Nusseys and the Sidgwicks. Robin E. Greenwood kindly shared his research on the local history of the Greenwoods.

I should also like to thank the following librarians for their assistance and permission to quote from papers in their possession: Dr Iain G. Brown, Assistant Keeper in the Department of Manuscripts, National Library of Scotland; Mr J. S. Cardwell, Reference Librarian at Keighley Reference Library, part of Bradford Libraries, West Yorkshire; P. G. Henderson, Walpole Librarian at The King's School, Canterbury; Francis O. Mattson, Curator of the Berg Collection in the New York Public Library, as well as Mr Crook and Mr Philip Milito; Christine Nelson, Assistant Curator of Autograph Manuscripts in the Pierpont Morgan Library, New York (who, helpfully, enlarged copies of their Roe Head fragments); Mr C. D. W. Sheppard, Sub-Librarian, and Mrs Farr in the Brotherton Collection of Leeds University Library; the librarians in the manuscript room of the British

Library; and the librarians in the Bodleian Library, Oxford. Reading papers at John Murray, London, was especially memorable for the beautiful room in Albemarle Street (where Scott and Byron met in 1811) and for the kindness of Mrs Virginia Murray. I am grateful for permission to quote from letters in the firm's archive.

Many ideas took shape in the course of tutorials at St Hilda's College, Oxford; two pupils who influenced me were Sara Dudley Edwards, with her clear, quick certainty, who helped to define the letters to M. Heger, and Linda Brandon, vivid, venturous, who continued our discussions about *Villette* in her letters from France. She died while I was writing this book, and it is dedicated to her.

In the last phase of revision, I benefited from the knowledge and persuasive opinions of Mark Bostridge, biographer of Vera Brittain and Florence Nightingale, and from discussions with Lucasta Miller, author of *The Brontë Myth*. Pamela Norris copy-edited with exceptional acumen and understanding – more like kinship – and there were helpful guidelines from editors Allegra Huston, Carmen Callil and Jenny Uglow.

A special thanks to publisher, Lennie Goodings, for her support, to Jenny Fry in publicity, and to Rowan Cope for editing this edition. Warm thanks also to agent Isobel Dixon.

After a talk on Charlotte Brontë at the 'Y' in New York, I was asked how long this biography took. It was hard to answer, for this book goes back to a life before my own – to my mother's affinity for the Brontës, their poetic language and their setting which she associated with her own childhood on the South African veld. At what was then the end of the railway line to Namaqualand, she was more remote from civilisation, an imaginative, bookish child. Since she died in 1999, I see all the more how much I owe to her reading and eloquence. The eloquence of novelist and critic Stevie Davies, her insights on Emily Brontë, and the grace of her language have provided a similar lift.

Finally, I must thank my husband, Siamon Gordon, for his interest in the merest draft, curiosity, questions, criticism and, not least, insistent encouragement.

SELECT BIBLIOGRAPHY

PRIMARY SOURCES

I have used the readily accessible World's Classics editions of the Brontës' novels, which are derived from the scholarly Clarendon edition of the Brontës. Where necessary I have turned to the Clarendon edition for its useful appendices and for more details about the manuscript of 'Emma'.

Charlotte Brontë was one of the greatest writers of letters in the English language, on a par with Jane Carlyle, Virginia Woolf, Olive Schreiner, Flannery O'Connor, and others (I mention the last two, in particular, because they were often isolated like Charlotte Brontë, distanced from friends, in their cases for reasons of health, and used letters similarly to explain themselves and their experience). I have argued, at the same time, that Charlotte Brontë's letters, as a genre, are closely linked, in an unusual way, with her writing of novels. The meticulous and well-annotated Clarendon edition of Charlotte Brontë's letters, in three volumes, replaced *The Brontës: Their Lives, Friendships and Correspondence*, i–iv, ed. Thomas J. Wise and J. Alexander Symington (Oxford: Blackwell, 1933, repr. 1980). The latter is a chronological and highly readable compilation of Brontë source materials and letters, but the edition is inaccurate in many places and incomplete. Since 1933 some 120 letters from Charlotte Brontë have been found; a few marvellous ones are in the Brontë Parsonage Museum, the best of which are quoted in this book. I have checked a number of the published letters in manuscript and give the source in the notes.

For full details of CB's manuscripts, see Christine Alexander,

A Bibliography of the Manuscripts of CB (Brontë Society in association with Meckler Publishing, Connecticut, 1982).

Arnold, Matthew, *The Letters of Matthew Arnold 1848–88*, ed. George W. E. Russell (London: Macmillan, 1895).

——, *The Letters of Matthew Arnold to Arthur Clough*, ed. Howard Foster Lowry (Oxford University Press, 1932).

Bewick, Thomas, *A History of British Birds*, i–ii (1797, 1804).

Brontës, *Tales of Angria*, ed. Heather Glen (London: Penguin Classics, 2006), including the later juvenilia: 'Mina Laury', 'Stancliffe's Hotel', 'The Duke of Zamorna', 'Henry Hastings', 'Caroline Vernon' and 'The Roe Head Journal Fragments'.

——, *The Art of the Brontës*, eds. Christine Alexander and Jane Sellars (Cambridge: Cambridge University Press, 1995).

——, *The Brontë Letters*, ed. Muriel Spark (London and Basingstoke: Macmillan, 1966). A novel-like selection, showing Spark's discernment of the creative lives of the sisters.

Brontës, *Selected Poems*, ed. Juliet R. V. Barker (London: Dent, 1985; repr. 1993). Useful notes.

Brontë, Anne, *The Poems of Anne Brontë*, ed. Edward Chitham (London: Macmillan, 1979).

——, Drawing of 'Woman gazing out to sea', BPM.

Brontë, Charlotte, 'Roe Head Journal' (Bon 98), BPM. Two additional fragments, 'Well here I am at Roe Head' and 'Now as I have a little bit of time' in the Pierpont Morgan Library, New York (MA 2696).

——, Juvenilia and letters to members of the Brontë family, Ellen Nussey, William Smith Williams, and George Smith (see S-G 31, 56, 83, 88, 92; BS 87), BPM. See also CB to Mrs Smith BPM. S-G 86. Copies of twelve of CB's most interesting letters to Ellen Nussey (e.g. about her call on Thackeray when for two hours she told him his faults) in John Murray archive, possibly done originally for Mrs Gaskell's *Life*.

——, Letters to M. Heger in BL (Add MS 38,732 A-D), as well as a number of *devoirs* and, as part of the Smith Bequest, fair copies of

Jane Eyre (Add MS 43474–6), *Shirley* (Add MS 43477–9), and *Villette* (Add MS 43480–2), the last with curious cuts and corrections. One particularly significant *devoir*, the last CB wrote for M. Heger, is in Berg; others in BPM and Brotherton.

——, The *devoirs* have been collected (with EB's) and translated as *The Belgian Essays*, ed. Sue Lonoff (New Haven: Yale University Press, 1996). *'La Justice Humaine'* provides a curious parallel with the defiant *devoir* written on that subject in *Villette*. The following are interesting for their advance in writing as well as for communications to M. Heger: *'Athènes Sauvée par la Poësie'*; *'La Mort de Napoléon'*; *'La Mort de Moïse'*; *'La Chute des Feuilles'*; and *'Lettre d'un pauvre Peintre à un grand Seigneur'*.

——, German notebook, used on return from Brussels (1844–5) as a writing notebook, in BPM.

——, Letters to Miss Wooler, part of Allbut Bequest, Fitzwilliam Museum, Cambridge.

——, Letters to Mrs Gaskell, Manchester University Library.

——, *The Letters of Charlotte Brontë*, ed. Margaret Smith, i–iii (Oxford: Clarendon Press, 1995–2004). All ms letters included.

——, letter from CB to WSW, on being a governess (22 Aug. 1850), transcribed by Polly Salter in 'Exciting Recent Acquisitions at the Brontë Parsonage Museum', *Brontë Studies* 32 (July 2007).

——, *Five Novelettes*, ed. Winifred Gérin (London: Folio Press, 1971).

——, 'Ashworth' (unfinished novel), transcribed by Melodie Monahan, *Studies in Philology*, lxxx, 4 (Fall 1983).

——, *The Poems of Charlotte Brontë*, ed. T. J. Winnifrith (Oxford: Blackwell, 1984).

——, 'I had the pleasure of knowing Mr Crimsworth very well', draft preface to *The Professor*. BPM Bonnell 109.

——, 'Emma', ms. in Taylor Collection, Princeton. Appendix to World's Classics edition of *The Professor*.

——, Letter to Mary Dixon (1843) in Brussels. Berg.

——, Letter to Mrs Gaskell (26 Apr. 1854), John Rylands University Library; letter to Mrs Gaskell (30 Sept. 1854), Manchester University Library.

——, Letter to Hartley Coleridge (May 1840?), Coleridge Collection, University of Texas.

——, Letter to William Smith Williams (26 Oct. 1852), Bodleian Library MS. Eng. letters e. 30.

——, Letter to Lucy Holland, BPM. BS 89.2.

——, Letter to Mrs Smith (mother of GS), BPM. S-G 86.

——, Letters to George Henry Lewes, BL. Add MS 39763.

——, Letter to Mr Ingham (surgeon) about Tabby's digestive illness (Dec. 1854), BPM. BS 98.

——, *An Edition of the Early Writings of Charlotte Brontë*, i–ii, ed. Christine Alexander (Oxford: Blackwell, 1987–1991).

——, *Miscellaneous and Unpublished Writings of Charlotte and P. B. Brontë*, ii, ed. James Wise and John Alexander Symington (Oxford: Blackwell, Shakespeare Head Press, 1938). This collection is inaccurate and has been grossly cobbled together, one of the many results of the editors' abuse of Brontë manuscripts.

——, *The Twelve Adventurers and Other Stories* (London: Hodder, 1925).

——, *The Juvenilia of Jane Austen and CB*, ed. Francis Beer (Harmondsworth: Penguin, 1986).

——, 'Long My Anxious Ear Hath Listened', *Latest Gleanings*, ed. Clement Shorter (London, 1918). Copy in Berg.

——, Miss West fragment, BPM. Bon. 113/6–7.

——, Booklets (juvenilia), given to M. Heger by CB, BL. Add MS 34, 255.

——, 'John Henry', the discarded first fragment of what became *Shirley*, Appendix D of Clarendon ed. of *Shirley*, 805–35.

——, Early fragments of what became *Villette*, BPM. Bon 124-1, 124-2, 125-2, 125-3. See Clarendon ed. of *Villette*, Appendix I, 753–64.

——, 'The Story of Willie Ellin', *BST* (1936), 3–22.

——, Lock of hair, BL. Egerton MS 3268B.

Brontë, Emily, *The Complete Poems*, ed. Janet Gezari (Harmondsworth: Penguin, 1992).

——, *The Poems of Emily Brontë*, ed. Derek Roper with Edward Chitham (Oxford: Oxford University Press, 1995).

Brontë, Maria (mother), 'The Advantages of Poverty in Religious Concerns' and letters to fiancé in *LFC*, i.

Brontë, Patrick, Eight letters to George Smith (1950–57), and three letters to Mrs Gaskell, John Murray archive. Another to Mrs Gaskell (24 July 1855), John Rylands University Library, Manchester. Letter to CB (Dec. 1852-Jan. 1853) which CB sent on to Mrs Gaskell in *BST* 63: 3, 199 (1953).

——, *Brontëana: The Rev. Patrick Brontë's Collected Works*, ed. J. Horsfall Turner (Bingley: T. Harrison & Sons, 1898).

——, *Two Sermons Preached in the Church of Haworth* [a sermon on 12 Sept. 1824 on an 'Earthquake and an Extraordinary Eruption of mud and water that had taken place ten days before in the moors', and a funeral sermon for Revd William Weightman, 2 Oct. 1842] (Haworth: R. Brown, 1885). Copy in Bodleian Library, Oxford.

——, 'On Conversion', *The Pastoral Visitor* (Feb.-Oct. 1815) BPM Bonnell 262.

Brontë, Patrick Branwell, *Poems*, ed. Tom Winnifrith (Oxford: Blackwell, 1983).

——, *Brother in the Shadow: Stories & Sketches by Branwell Brontë*, research and transcriptions Mary Butterfield, ed. R. J. Duckett (Bradford Libraries and Information Service, 1988).

——, *The Works of Patrick Branwell Brontë*, i–iii, ed. Victor A. Neufeldt (London: Routledge, 1997–99).

Byron, George Gordon, *The Complete Poetical Works*, ed. Jerome J. McGann (Oxford, 1980–1993).

Croxall, Samuel, *Aesop's Fables* (1825).

Eliot, George (Marian Evans), *The George Eliot Letters*, i. ed. G. S. Haight (Oxford University Press; New Haven: Yale, 1954).

——, 'Mr Gilfil's Love-Story', *Scenes of Clerical Life* (1857: repr. Harmondsworth: Penguin, 1985, ed. David Lodge).

Gaskell, Elizabeth, *The Letters of Mrs Gaskell*, ed. J. A. V. Chapple and Arthur Pollard (Manchester University Press, 1966).

——, *The Life of Charlotte Brontë*, intro. Winifred Gérin (1857; repr. London: Dent Everyman, 1971). This is the first, unexpurgated edition; its manuscript is in John Rylands University Library, Manchester.

———, *Mary Barton* (1848; repr. London: Dent Everyman, 1961).

———, *Ruth* (1853; repr. London: Dent/Everyman, 1967).

Goldsmith, Revd J., *Grammar of General Geography* (1823). Brontës' copy in BPM.

Graham, Thomas John, *Modern Domestic Medicine* (1826). Brontës' copy in BPM.

Grundy, Francis H., *Pictures of the Past* (London: Griffith & Farren), 1879).

Heaton Family Papers, Keighley Reference Library, West Yorkshire.

Huxley, Leonard, *The House of Smith Elder* (London, 1923). Privately printed. Copy in John Murray archive. See ch. 7 on CB and William Smith Williams.

à Kempis, Thomas, *The Imitation of Christ,* abridged by John Wesley (1803). CB's copy, inherited from her mother, in BPM.

Leyland, Francis A., *The Brontë Family with Special Reference to Patrick Branwell Brontë*, i–ii, (London: Hurst & Blackett, 1886).

Macdonald, Frederika (pupil at the Pensionnat Heger), letter to Dr Nicoll (26 Feb. 1894), Brotherton.

———, 'The Brontës at Brussels', in *Woman at Home* (July 1894), 279–91. Copy in Brontë Newspaper Cuttings Scrapbook, Keighley Reference Library.

Martineau, Harriet, *Deerbrook* (1839; repr. London: Virago, 1983).

———, *Autobiography*, i–ii (1877; repr. London: Virago, 1983).

Martyn, Henry, two letters to associates of Wilberforce about Patrick Brontë (c.Jan.-Feb. 1804), Bodleian Library. MSS. Wilberforce d. 14.

Mill, J. S. and Harriet Taylor, *Essays on Sex Equality*, ed. Alice S. Rossi (University of Chicago Press, 1970).

Morel, Sir Charles, *Tales of the Genii* (London, 1764).

Needhams and Taylors, Family Papers, BPM. Some social contexts in which the Brontës lived (with thanks for pointers to Audrey W. Hall).

Nicholls, Arthur Bell, Thirty-three letters to George Smith (21 Aug. 1856–25 June 1861 and one letter in 1896), John Murray archive.

Letters to Ellen Nussey and to C. K. Shorter, Brotherton. His books in BPM.

Nightingale, Florence, *Cassandra*, written 1852, privately printed in revised form 1859, repr. as Appendix to Ray Strachey, *The Cause: A Short History of the Women's Movement in Great Britain* (1928; repr. London: Virago, 1979), 395–418.

Nussey, Ellen, Four separate reminiscences in *LFC*: i, 92–100 (first impressions of CB at school, 1831); i, 112–13 (first visit to the Parsonage, 1833); ii, 231–2 (reminiscences of Mary Taylor); and ii, 333–6 (last days and death of Anne Brontë). *CBL*, Appendices to vols. i and ii.

——, Letters to Elizabeth Gaskell and twenty letters to George Smith (1857–89) as well as copies of two letters to her from GS, in John Murray archive.

——, Letters to Sir T. Wemyss Reid and additional holograph memories of the Brontës (not published in *LFC*), in Berg.

——, Letters to George Smith (1857–78), to A. B. Nicholls, to Clement Shorter, and to Thomas Wise, in the Ellen Nussey Papers, Brotherton.

——, *The Story of the Brontës: Their Home, Haunts, Friends and Work. Part Second — Charlotte's Letters* (Bingley: printed for J. Horsfall Turner, 1885–9). The suppressed edition.

——, MS diary (1849). BPM.

Nussey, Henry, Diary, BL. Egerton MS 3268A.

Oliphant, Mrs Margaret, *Annals of a Publishing House*, i–ii (Edinburgh: Blackwood, 1897).

Radcliffe, Ann, *The Italian* (1797; repr. Oxford: World's Classics, 1981).

Richmond, John, letter to Reginald Smith, with his father's recollection of CB, BPM. S-G 102.

Sand, George (Amandine Dupin, Baronne Dudevant), *Consuelo* (1842; transl. London, Parlour Library, 1847).

——, *Letters of a Traveller* in *The Works of George Sand*, vi, translated Eliza A. Ashurst, ed. Matilda M. Hays (London, 1847).

Scott, Sir Walter. CB would have read most of his writings, but tends to admiring generalities rather than mention of specific works.

Seton-Gordon Collection: Letters from CB to George Smith at BPM; Patrick Brontë and A. B. Nicholls to George Smith, John Murray archive.

Shaen, Margaret J., ed., *Memorials of Two Sisters: Susanna and Catherine Winkworth* (London: Longmans, 1908).

Smith, George Murray, 'Recollections of a Long and Busy Life', two vols, Smith Elder Archives, The National Library of Scotland MSS 23191–2. An edited version of his chapter on CB was printed in the *Cornhill Magazine* (Dec. 1900), repr. George Smith, *A Memoir With Some Pages of Autobiography* (London, 1902). The latter (including recollections by Leslie Stephen and Sydney Lee) was printed for private circulation after GS's death. Copies in BPM, John Murray archive, and Bodleian Library, Oxford.

——, letters to Ellen Nussey, Ellen Nussey Papers, Brotherton.

Smith, Elizabeth Murray (wife of GS), letter to Sydney Lee (29 Oct. 1901), Bodleian Library. MS Eng. misc. d. 180.

Taylor, Mary, some letters to CB and Ellen Nussey in Berg. Letter to CB (Apr. 1850), BPM.

——, *Mary Taylor, Friend of Charlotte Brontë: Letters from New Zealand and elsewhere*, ed. Joan Stevens (Oxford University Press and Auckland University Press, 1972). See especially Appendix B for MT's full reminiscences of CB. See Appendix E for the only surviving letter from CB to MT, her detailed, witty account of her first meeting with George Smith. The scrupulous transcriptions make this volume always preferable to *LFC*.

——, *The First Duty of Women* (London: Emily Faithfull, 1870). Articles collected from the *Victoria Magazine*, 1865–70.

——, *Miss Miles, or A Tale of Yorkshire Life Sixty Years Ago* (1890; repr. Oxford University Press, 1990).

Tennyson, Alfred, Lord, 'The Lady of Shalott' (1832, revised 1842) and 'Wages' (1868), *The Poems of Tennyson*, ed. Christopher Ricks (London: Longmans, 1969; NY: Norton, 1972).

Thackeray, W. M., *Letters and Private Papers*, ed. Gordon N. Ray (Oxford University Press and Harvard University Press, 1945).

——, 'The Last Sketch', *Cornhill Magazine* (Apr. 1860).

Wollstonecraft, Mary, *Works*, ed. Janet Todd and Marilyn Butler (London: Pickering, 1989).

SECONDARY SOURCES

Alexander, Christine, *The Early Writings of Charlotte Brontë* (Oxford: Blackwell, 1983).

——, and Smith, Margaret, eds., *The Oxford Companion to the Brontës* (Oxford: Oxford University Press, 2003).

——, 'Autobiography and juvenilia: the fractured self in Charlotte Brontë's early manuscripts', in Alexander, Christine, and McMaster, Juliet, eds., *The Child Writer from Austen to Woolf* (Cambridge: Cambridge University Press, 2005).

Allott, Miriam, ed., *The Brontës: The Critical Heritage* (London: Routledge, 1974).

Ashton, Rosemary, *G. H. Lewes: A Life* (Oxford: Clarendon Press, 1991).

Avery, Gillian, *The Best Type of Girl: A History of Girls' Independent Schools* (London: André Deutsch, 1991).

Barker, Juliet R. V., *The Brontës* (London: Weidenfeld & Nicolson, 1994).

Barnard, Robert and Louise, *A Brontë Encyclopaedia* (Oxford: Blackwell, 2007).

Boumelha, Penny, *Charlotte Brontë* (Hemel Hempstead: Harvester, 1990).

Brontë Society Transactions and *Brontë Studies: The Journal of the Brontë Society*.

Brookfield, Charles and Frances, *Mrs Brookfield and her Circle*, ii (London: Pitman and Sons, 1905).

Brookland, Victoria, exhibition of paintings, BPM.

Chitham, Edward, *The Brontës' Irish Background* (London: Macmillan, 1986).

—— and Winnifrith, Tom, *Brontë Facts and Brontë Problems* (London: Macmillan, 1983).

—— and Winnifrith, Tom, *Charlotte and Emily Brontë* (Macmillan, 1989).

——, *A Life of Anne Brontë* (Oxford: Blackwell 1991).

——, *A Life of Emily Brontë* (Oxford: Blackwell, 1987).

Clarke, Norma, *Ambitious Heights: Writing, Friendship, Love: The Jewsbury Sisters, Felicia Hemans, and Jane Carlyle* (London: Routledge, 1990).

Cockshut, A. O. J., *Truth to Life: The Art of Biography in the Nineteenth Century* (London: Collins, 1974).

Cross, J. W., *George Eliot's Life* (Edinburgh: Blackwood, 1885).

Crowe, Angela, *Miss Branwell's Companion* (Alethia Publications, 2007).

Davenport-Hines, Richard, 'Necessary Precautions', *Nature* (21 February 1991), 661.

Davidoff, Leonore and Hall, Catherine, *Family Fortunes: Men and women of the English middle class, 1780–1850* (London: Hutchinson, 1987).

Davies, Stevie, *Emily Brontë* (Hemel Hempstead, Hertfordshire: Harvester; NY: Simon and Schuster, 1988).

——, *Emily Brontë: The Artist as a Free Woman* (Manchester: Carcanet Press, 1983).

——, *Emily Brontë: Heretic* (London: The Women's Press, 1994).

——, *Emily Brontë* in *Writers and their Work* series (London: Northcote House / British Council, 1998).

——, *Four Dreamers and Emily* (London: Women's Press, 1996).

Dickinson, Emily, *The Complete Poems of Emily Dickinson* (London: Faber, 1970; repr. 1975).

Dinsdale, Ann, 'Haworth in the time of the Brontës' in *Reading the Brontës* (Haworth: The Brontë Society, 2000).

——, *The Brontë Connection* (Hendon, 2007). A visual record of places associated with the Brontës' lives.

——, and Warner, Simon, *The Brontës at Haworth* (London: Frances Lincoln, 2007).

Drabble, Margaret, 'The Writer as Recluse: the Theme of Solitude in the Works of the Brontës', *BST*, 16 (1974).

Duckett, Bob, ed., *The Brontë Novels: 150 Years of Literary Dominance* (Haworth: The Brontë Society, 1998).

Duthie, Enid L., *The Foreign Vision of Charlotte Brontë* (London: Macmillan, 1975).

Easson, Angus, 'Two Suppressed Opinions in Mrs Gaskell's *Life of Charlotte Brontë*', *BST*, 16: 84, 281–83 (1974).

Edgerley, C. Mabel, 'Ponden Hall and the Heatons,' *BST* 10: 55, 265–8 (1945).

Eichenberg, Fritz, illustrations to *Wuthering Heights* and *Jane Eyre*.

Eliot, T. S., 'T. S. Eliot "places" Virginia Woolf for French Readers', in *Virginia Woolf: The Critical Heritage*, ed. Robin Majumdar and Allen McLaurin (London, 1975), 192. Suggestive on what is deliberately '*left out*' in a certain kind of fiction.

Ewbank, Inga-Stina, *Their Proper Sphere: A Study of the Brontë Sisters as Early Victorian Female Novelists* (London: Edward Arnold, 1966).

Frank, Katherine, *Emily Brontë: A Chainless Soul* (London: Hamish Hamilton; NY: Viking Penguin, 1990).

Fraser, Rebecca, *Charlotte Brontë* (London: Methuen, 1988).

——, 'Charlotte Brontë and Currer Bell', *Conference Papers* (Brontë Society, 1990), 39–55.

Gardiner, Juliet, *The World Within: The Brontës at Haworth: A Life in Letters, Diaries, and Writings* (London: Collins & Brown, 1992).

Gérin, Winifred, *Charlotte Brontë: The Evolution of Genius* (Oxford University Press, 1967; repr. 1971).

——, *Anne Brontë* (London: Thomas Nelson, 1959).

——, *Anne Thackeray Ritchie: A Biography* (Oxford University Press, 1981).

Gilbert, Sandra M., and Gubar, Susan, *The Madwoman in the Attic* (New Haven and London: Yale University Press, 1979).

Glen, Heather, *Charlotte Brontë: The Imagination in History* (Oxford, Oxford University Press, 2002).

——, and Barker, Juliet, eds., *The Brontë Companion* (Cambridge: Cambridge University Press, 2002).

Glynn, Jennifer, *Prince of Publishers: A Biography of George Smith* (London: Allison & Busby, 1986).

Hampshire, Stuart, 'What the Jameses Knew', *New York Review of Books* (10 Oct. 1991).

Harper, Janet, 'Charlotte Brontë's Heger Family and their School', *Blackwood's Magazine*, cxcl (Apr. 1912), 461–69.

Hughes, R. E., '*Jane Eyre*: The Unbaptized Dionysos', *Nineteenth-Century Fiction*, xvii–xviii (June 1962–Mar. 1964), 347–64.

Hughes, Ted, 'Wuthering Heights' (poem) from *Birthday Letters* (London: Faber & Faber, 1998).

James, Henry, 'The Art of Fiction' (1884) in *Essays on Literature, American Writers, English Writers* (NY: Library of America, 1984), 44–65.

——, 'George Sand' (1877) repr. *Literary Criticism: French Writers, etc.* (NY: Library of America, 1984).

Johnson, Dr Samuel, *The History of Rasselas* (1759).

Knight, Charmian, 'Who's Afraid of the Brontë Sisters?' and 'Thornfield Hall Revisited' in *The Brontë Influence*, Knight and Stoneman, Patsy, eds., (Haworth: The Brontë Society, 2004).

——, and Spencer, Luke, with chapters by Ann Dinsdale and Rachel Terry, *Reading the Brontës* (Haworth/Leeds: The Brontë Society/Leeds University, 2000).

Kristeva, Julia, 'Women's Time', in *The Feminist Reader: Essays in Gender and the Politics of Literary Criticism*, ed. Catherine Belsey and Jane Moore (London: Macmillan, 1989).

Kucich, John, 'Passionate reserve and reserved passion in the works of Charlotte Brontë', *Journal of English Literary History* 52 (1985), 913–37.

Lane, Margaret, *The Brontë Story: A Reconsideration of Mrs. Gaskell's Life of Charlotte Brontë* (London: Heinemann, 1953).

Lee, Sydney, 'Memoir of George Smith', first published in Sept. 1901 in original ed. of supplement to the *Dictionary of National Biography*, now a preface, xxi–lix.

Lemon, Charles, *A Centenary History of the Brontë Society 1893-1993* (Haworth: The Brontë Society, 1993).

Lever, Sir Tresham, 'Charlotte Brontë and George Smith: an extract from the late Sir Tresham Lever's unpublished biography of George Smith', *BST*, 17: 87, 106–14 (1977).

Lock, John and Dixon, Canon W. T., *A Man of Sorrow: The Life, Letters and Times of the Rev. Patrick Brontë* (London: Nelson, 1965).

Malone, Catherine, 'Charlotte Brontë: Gothic Autobiographies', Doctoral thesis, Oxford (1993).

Miller, Jane, *Women Writing About Men* (London: Virago, 1986). Good on *Villette*.

Miller, Lucasta, *The Brontë Myth* (London: Jonathan Cape, 2001).

Moers, Ellen, *Literary Women* (London: The Women's Press, 1963 repr. 1978).

Picardie, Justine, *Daphne* (London: Bloomsbury, 2008).

Plath, Sylvia, 'Wuthering Heights' (poem) from *Collected Poems* (London: Faber & Faber, 1981).

Poovey, Mary, *Uneven Developments: The Ideological Work of Gender in Mid-Victorian England* (London: Virago, 1989).

Rego, Paula, drawings of Charlotte Brontë scenes.

Reid, Sir Wemyss T., *Charlotte Brontë* (London: Macmillan, 1877).

Rich, Adrienne, 'Jane Eyre: The Temptations of a Motherless Woman', *On Lies, Secrets, Silence: Selected Prose 1966–78* (NY: Norton, 1979; London: Virago, 1980), 89–106.

Rose, Phyllis, *Parallel Lives: Five Victorian Marriages* (1984; repr. Harmondsworth, Penguin, 1985).

Ruijssenaars, Eric, *Charlotte Brontë's Promised Land* (Haworth: The Brontë Society, 2001).

——, *The* Pensionnat *Revisited: More Light Shed on the Brussels of the Brontës* (Haworth: The Brontë Society, 2003).

Shackleton, William, 'Four Hundred Years of a West Moorland Family: A Brief Account of the Heatens of Ponden House.' (Aug. 1921) Typescript, Keighley Reference Library.

Showalter, Elaine, *The Female Malady* (London: Virago, 1985).

——, *A Literature of Their Own: British Women Novelists from Brontë to Lessing* (London: Virago, 1978; repr. 1997).

Smith, Margaret, 'The Letters of Charlotte Brontë: some new insights into her life and writing', *Conference Papers* (Brontë Society, 1990), 57–72.

——, 'New Light on Mr Nicholls', *BST* 19:3 (1987), 97–106.

Stephen, Leslie, 'Charlotte Brontë', *Cornhill Magazine* (Dec. 1877), repr. *Hours in a Library*, iii.

St Clair, William, *The Godwins and the Shelleys* (London: Faber, 1989).

Stoneman, Patsy, *Brontë Transformations: the Cultural Dissemination of* Jane Eyre *and* Wuthering Heights (Hemel Hempstead: Harvester/ Wheatsheaf, 1996).

——, *Jane Eyre on Stage, 1848–1898* (Aldershot: Ashgate, 2007).

Tillotson, Kathleen, *Novels of the Eighteen-Forties* (Oxford University Press, 1954).

Tomalin, Claire, *The Life and Death of Mary Wollstonecraft* (London: Weidenfeld & Nicolson, 1974; repr. New American Library, 1976).

——, *The Invisible Woman: Ellen Ternan and Charles Dickens* (Harmondsworth: Viking, 1990).

Uglow, Jenny, *Elizabeth Gaskell: a Habit of Stories* (London: Faber, 1993).

Vicinus, Martha, ed., *Suffer and Be Still: Women in the Victorian Age* (Bloomington: Indiana University Press, 1972).

Weir, Edith M., 'The Heger Family: New Brontë Material Comes to Light. Letters from Constantin and Zoë Heger to former pupils and from Louise Heger', *BST*, II: 59, 249–61.

Whitehead, Barbara, *Charlotte Brontë and her 'dearest Nell': The story of a friendship* (West Yorkshire: Smith Settle, 1993).

Whitehead, S. R., *The Brontës of Haworth: The Place and the People the Brontës Knew* (Haworth: Ashmount Press, 2006).

Winnifrith, Tom, *The Brontës and Their Background: Romance and Reality* (London: Macmillan, 1973).

——, *A New Life of Charlotte Brontë* (London: Macmillan, 1989).

Wood, Stephen, *Haworth* (Stroud: Tempus, 2005). Includes a good map.

Woolf, Virginia, *A Room of One's Own* (London: Hogarth, 1929; NY: Harcourt, 1929).

——, 'Thoughts Upon Social Success' (1903), *A Passionate Apprentice*, ed. Mitchell A. Leaska (London: Hogarth; NY: Harcourt, 1990).

——, *The Diary of Virginia Woolf*, i–v, ed. Anne Olivier Bell (London: Hogarth; NY: Harcourt, 1977–84).

——, 'Memoirs of a Novelist' (1909), *The Complete Shorter Fiction of Virginia Woolf*, ed. Susan Dick (1985; rev. NY: Harcourt, 1989).

——, *The Years* (London: Hogarth; NY: Harcourt, 1936).

——, 'On Being Ill' (1930), *Collected Essays*, iv, ed. Leonard Woolf (London: Hogarth; NY: Harcourt, 1967), 193–203.

——, 'Professions for Women' (1932), *Collected Essays*, ii, 287–88.

——, '"Jane Eyre" and "Wuthering Heights"', *The Common Reader* (London: Hogarth, 1925), 196–204.

——, *Three Guineas* (1938; repr. Harmondsworth: Penguin, 1977).

INDEX

Note: Illustrations, Chronology and Source Notes are not included in the index. n following a page reference indicates a footnote on that page.

Abbreviations used are: AB for Anne Brontë; ABN for Arthur Bell Nicholls; CB for Charlotte Brontë; EB for Emily Brontë; EG for Elizabeth Gaskell; EN for Ellen Nussey; GHL for George Henry Lewes; GS for George Murray Smith; Hth for Haworth, Yorkshire; *JE* for *Jane Eyre*; MT for Mary Taylor; NZ for New Zealand; PBB for (Patrick) Branwell Brontë; PB for the Revd Patrick Brontë; *Sh* for *Shirley*; *TP* for *The Professor*; *V* for *Villette*.

VIRGINIA WOOLF
A Writer's Life

Lyndall Gordon

Winner of the James Tait Black Memorial Prize

This prize-winning biography sees Virginia Woolf as she saw herself; the first book to set out the private life behind the well-known facts of her public career, *A Writer's Life* reveals an explorer of the 'infinite oddity of the human position'. Instead of the doom-and-death image often imposed on women of genius, here is the robust seeker for what was creative in our intimate lives, in women's nature, and in resistance to power. *A Writer's Life* brings out Woolf's ideas for biography itself: to fall on a life 'like a roll of heavy waters . . . laying bare the pebbles on the shore of the soul'.

'Sensitive and original'
Hermione Lee, *Times Literary Supplement*

'A masterpiece of the kind of intuitive biography in which
Virginia Woolf herself believed'
Times Higher Education Supplement

VINDICATION
A Life of Mary Wollstonecraft

Lyndall Gordon

Longlisted for the BBC Four Samuel Johnson Prize 2005

In this stunning biography of Mary Wollstonecraft, Lyndall Gordon explores the life of a woman often criticised by biographers, historians and feminists alike. Gordon challenges such views and reinterprets the genius of this extraordinary woman for the twenty-first century.

'This great biography is a biography of a time, a spirit, a way of thinking, that is brave, intelligent, radical, independent and, unless we are all soon for the dark, immortal'
Candia McWilliam, *Glasgow Herald*

'A biography that's as passionate and humane as its subject'
Kelly Grovier, *Observer*

virago

To buy any of our books and to find out more
about Virago Press and Virago Modern Classics,
our authors and titles, as well as events and
book club forum, visit our websites

www.virago.co.uk
www.littlebrown.co.uk

and follow us on Twitter

@ViragoBooks

To order any Virago titles p & p free in the UK,
please contact our mail order supplier on:

+ 44 (0)1832 737525

Customers not based in the UK should contact
the same number for appropriate postage
and packing costs.